European and Islamic Trade in the Early Ottoman State

The Merchants of Genoa and Turkey

International trade was of great importance for the Ottomans in the construction of their early empire. Kate Fleet's book examines the trade links that existed between European merchants and their Muslim counterparts from the beginnings of the Ottoman empire in 1300 to the fall of Constantinople in 1453. By using previously unexploited Latin and Turkish sources, and by focusing on the trading partnership between the Genoese and the Turks, she demonstrates how this interaction contributed to the economic development of the early Ottoman state and, indeed, to Ottoman territorial expansion. Where the previous literature has emphasised the military prowess of the early Ottoman state and its role as 'the infidel enemy', this book offers a rare insight into its economic aspirations and eventual integration into the economy of the Mediterranean basin. This is a readable, authoritative and innovative study which illuminates our understanding of an obscure period in early Ottoman history.

KATE FLEET is Curator of the Skilliter Centre for Ottoman Studies, Newnham College, Cambridge.

Cambridge Studies in Islamic Civilization

Titles in the series
STEFAN SPERL, *Mannerism in Arabic poetry: a structural analysis of selected texts, 3rd century AH/9th century AD–5th century AH/11th century AD*   0 521 354854
BEATRICE FORBES MANZ, *The rise and rule of Tamerlane*   0 521 345952 (hardback) 0 521 406145 (paperback)
PAUL E. WALKER, *Early philosophical Shiism: the Ismaili Neoplatonism of Abū Yaʿqūb al-Sijistānī*   0 521 441293
BOAZ SHOSHAN, *Popular culture in medieval Cairo*   0 521 43209X
STEPHEN FREDERIC DALE, *Indian merchants and Eurasian trade, 1600–1750*   0 521 454603
AMY SINGER, *Palestinian peasants and Ottoman officials: rural administration around sixteenth-century Jerusalem*   0 521 452384 (hardback) 0 521 476798 (paperback)
MICHAEL CHAMBERLAIN, *Knowledge and social practice in medieval Damascus, 1190–1350*   0 521 454069
TARIF KHALIDI, *Arabic historical thought in the classical period*   0 521 465540 (hardback) 0 521 58938X (paperback)
REUVEN AMITAI-PREISS, *Mongols and Mamluks: the Mamluk–Ilkhānid war, 1260–1281*   0 521 462266
LOUISE MARLOW, *Hierarchy and egalitarianism in Islamic thought*   0 521 564301
JANE HATHAWAY, *The politics of households in Ottoman Egypt: the rise of the Qazdağlis*   0 521 571103
THOMAS T. ALLSEN, *Commodity and exchange in the Mongol empire: a cultural history of Islamic textiles*   0 521 583012
DINA RIZK KHOURY, *State and provincial society in the Ottoman empire: Mosul, 1540–1834*   0 521 590604
THOMAS PHILIPP and ULRICH HAARMANN (eds.), *The Mamluks in Egyptian politics and society*   0 521 591155
PETER JACKSON, *The Delhi sultanate: a political and military history*   0 521 404770

European and Islamic Trade in the Early Ottoman State

The Merchants of Genoa and Turkey

KATE FLEET

CAMBRIDGE
UNIVERSITY PRESS

PUBLISHED BY THE PRESS SYNDICATE OF THE UNIVERSITY OF CAMBRIDGE
The Pitt Building, Trumpington Street, Cambridge CB2 1RP, United Kingdom

CAMBRIDGE UNIVERSITY PRESS
The Edinburgh Building, Cambridge CB2 2RU, UK   http://www.cup.cam.ac.uk
40 West 20th Street, New York, NY 10011–4211, USA   http://www.cup.org
10 Stamford Road, Oakleigh, Melbourne 3166, Australia

First published 1999

Printed in United Kingdom at the University Press, Cambridge

Typeset in 10/12pt Times   [CE]

A catalogue record for this book is available from the British Library

Library of Congress cataloguing in publication data

Fleet, Kate.
European and Islamic trade in the early Ottoman state: the merchants of Genoa and Turkey / Kate Fleet.
    p.   cm. – (Cambridge studies in Islamic civilization)
Includes bibliographical references (p.   ).
ISBN 0 521 64221 3 (hb)
1. Islamic countries – Commerce – Europe.   2. Europe – Commerce – Islamic countries.
3. Turkey – History – Ottoman Empire, 1288–1918.   I. Title.   II. Series.
HF3868.Z7E854   1999   382'.094017671–dc21   98–38430   CIP

ISBN 0 521 64221 3 hardback

Contents

Tables

Acknowledgements

I owe a deep debt of gratitude to Miss Julian Chrysostomides, who has guided my research with a meticulous rigour and constant support for which I shall always be grateful. Not only did she train me in palaeography and teach me the methods necessary for research, but she showed me what true scholarship should be.

I should like to thank Dr David Morgan and Dr Colin Imber, Dr Margaret Bainbridge, Dr Simonetta Calderini, Dr Delia Cortese, Dr Bülent Gökay, Dr Aslı Göksel, Dr Colin Heywood, Dr Uygur Kocabaşoğlu and Dr Catherine Otten. I am also most grateful to Marigold Acland, the editor, and Mary Starkey, the copy-editor, at Cambridge University Press.

I must also thank the staff of the Archivio di Stato di Genova, of the Società Ligure di Storia della Patria, Genoa, of the library of the School of Oriental and African Studies at the University of London, of the University Library, Cambridge, and of the library of the Faculty of Oriental Studies, Cambridge. I should also like to thank the Skilliter Centre for Ottoman Studies and the Principal, Fellows and Members of Newnham College, Cambridge.

Abbreviations

ASG	Archivio di Stato di Genova
ASLSP	*Atti della Società Ligure di Storia della Patria*
AST	Archivio di Stato di Torino
ASV	Archivio di Stato di Venezia
Belleten	Türk Tarih Kurumu, Belleten
BSOAS	*Bulletin of the School of Oriental and African Studies*
CFHB	Corpus Fontium Historiae Byzantinae
CSFS	Collana Storica di Fonti e Studi
CSHB	Corpus Scriptorum Historiae Byzantinae
EI2	*Encyclopaedia of Islam* (Leiden and Paris, 1960 sq.)
İA	*İslam Ansiklopedisi, İslam alemi Cosğrafya, Etnoğrafya ve Biyoğrafya Lugatı* (Istanbul, 1940 sq.)
JEEH	*Journal of European Economic History*
JESHO	*Journal of Economic and Social History of the Orient*
RIS	*Rerum Italicarum Scriptores*, ed. L. A. Muratori, vols. I–XXV (Milan, 1723–51)
ROL	*Revue de l'Orient Latin* (Paris, 1893–)
TOEM	*Tarih Osmani Encumeni Mecmuası*
WZKM	*Wiener Zeitschrift für die Kunde des Morgenlandes*
:	used in the references indicates a summary of a document
=	used in the references indicates a complete document

Introduction

Any economic history of the late Middle Ages is handicapped by the nature, and scarcity, of the sources. This problem is accentuated when dealing with Turchia[1] in the fourteenth and first half of the fifteenth centuries by the great dearth of Turkish sources for the period. The extant data do not deal in general with economic activity, concerning themselves more with the bloodthirsty activities of the various rulers. It may be too strong to say that without western sources there would be no economic history of Turchia in this period, but it does make the point that no worthwhile research into this area can be done without using western archives such as those of the city states of Genoa and Venice.

The history of western Anatolia in the fourteenth century has been described by Suraiya Faroqhi as a topic much used by research students for their theses because of the limited primary and secondary sources and the limited extension of the beyliks themselves. This lack of sources has, she says, acted as a challenge and 'scholars have squeezed the last drop of information out of a few inscriptions, chronicles and occasional references in early Ottoman or Venetian documents'.[2] In fact this does an injustice to the amount of material available.

The Genoese state archives are a rich and largely unmined source of material for this subject. The notary deeds, one of the most valuable sources for Turkish–Genoese trade, give information on commodities, prices, locations and, in the case of disputes, more general information on how these relations functioned. There are problems, however, in dealing with this material, the most important of which concerns the non-availability of analytical catalogues of the notary deeds. The catalogues for the notaries list one notary and one date while the *cartulare* (bound collections of deeds)

---

[1] The word Turchia is used with the meaning that it has in western sources, referring, initially, to Turkish-ruled Asia Minor, and, with Ottoman expansion, including also the easternmost area of Ottoman territory in Europe, roughly equivalent to that of the European section of the modern Turkish state. The term is useful as there is no modern equivalent.

[2] Suraiya Faroqhi, 'In Search of Ottoman History', in Halil Berktay and Suraiya Faroqhi (eds.), *New Approaches to State and Peasant in Ottoman History* (London, 1992), pp. 227–8.

themselves may contain deeds enacted by many different notaries at different dates and at different places of enactment, these remaining thus uncatalogued. It is not possible therefore to rely on the information in the catalogues when selecting which *cartulare* to consult for references to Turchia, and there is no alternative to wading through large quantities of irrelevant documents. The financial records and the accounts of the Comune in the Archivio di San Giorgio and the Antico Comune as well as the documents from the Archivio Segreto are also valuable, particularly for diplomatic and political relations.

Much western source material from the archives of Venice, Genoa and Florence has been published.[3] Venice, in particular, with the treaties between Venetian Crete and the beyliks of Menteşe and Aydın, the Senate's instructions to ambassadors, merchants' letters and notary deeds, provides invaluable information for this early period of Ottoman history. Other published sources of particular importance are merchant handbooks and accounts, giving information on commodities traded, ports used, prices, weights and measures. The manual of the Florentine merchant Francesco Balducci Pegolotti is of great importance for the earlier fourteenth century while the account book of Giacomo Badoer, who was active in Constantinople in the later 1430s, is particularly useful, giving details of all his commercial activities, including expenses incurred when buying commodities in Ottoman territories.

Other western sources that give some information useful for trade include accounts of travellers, for example those of the Aragonese ambassador, Ruy Gonzales de Clavijo, who travelled through Anatolia on his way to the court of Timur, and Bertrandon de la Broquière, who was in Ottoman territory in the 1430s.

Byzantine sources have only a limited value for the economic history of Turchia in this period, for while histories such as those of Pachymeres, Gregoras, Dukas, Kantakuzenos and Chalcocondyles discuss Turks, they tend to concentrate on what was of most significance for them, Turkish territorial expansion and gradual dominance of Byzantine politics, rather than on any commercial activity within the empire. In any case, medieval historians rarely touched on economic complexities.

Apart from western sources, there is some Arabic material, the works of ibn Battuta and al-'Umarī, and Ottoman sources. Ottoman material for the period before 1453, particularly for the fourteenth century, is very sparse, limited largely to a few chronological lists, the earliest of which dates from 1421, Ahmedi's *History of the Ottoman Kings*, probably from the 1390s, a few documents, the number of which increases slightly from the 1430s, and a small number of inscriptions and coins from the fourteenth century. Dating from the latter part of the fifteenth century there are chronicles

---

[3] See the bibliography for published sources.

dealing with the earlier period, those of Aşıkpaşazade, Oruç, the Anonymous Chronicles, and Enveri and Şukrullah. The works of Aşıkpaşazade, Oruç and the Anonymous Chronicles rely on the chronological lists and no longer extant chronicles from the fourteenth century. Aşıkpaşazade, born around 1400, incorporated into his *History of the House of Osman*, which goes to 1484, pieces from a history, now lost, written by Yahşi Fakih, as well as relying on his own memory. Neşri, writing slightly later, produced his history, using much of the work of Aşıkpaşazade.[4] None of the above histories is particularly helpful when dealing with trade. Apart from chronicles and chronological lists from the later fifteenth century, there are documents, such as *kanunname*s and *sicil*s from the reign of Mehmed II, which can be used, with caution, for comparative purposes and as indicators of what the position could have been in a slightly earlier period. It must, however, constantly be borne in mind that to rely entirely on material from a later period to elucidate an earlier one is open to danger.

Using predominantly western sources, this study investigates one aspect of Turkish economic life, that is, international trade between the Turks and the Genoese, in the period between the rise of the Turkish beyliks, among them the Ottomans, and the fall of Constantinople to the Ottoman sultan Mehmed II in 1453. International trade was of great importance from the very beginnings of the Ottoman empire, and the desire of Ottoman rulers to control international trade routes to a degree influenced their territorial expansion.[5] This book examines the commodities that made up Ottoman–Genoese trade and its importance, and considers whether the Genoese, with their capital and expertise, contributed in any way to the early development and success of the Ottoman state.[6]

---

[4] For Neşri's sources see V. L. Ménage, *Neshri's History of the Ottomans. The Sources and Development of the Text* (London, 1964), pp. 10–19.

[5] 'The Ottoman state, from its inception in the fourteenth century, sought to establish control over international trade routes. This consideration, in fact, largely determined the pattern of Ottoman territorial expansion', Huri İslamoğlu-İnan and Çağlar Keyder, 'Agenda for Ottoman History', in Huri İslamoğlu-İnan (ed.), *The Ottoman Empire and the World-Economy* (Cambridge, 1987), pp. 50–1.

[6] Persian merchants, for example, were important in state formation in southern India in the seventeenth century: Sanjay Subrahmanyam, 'Intra-Asia Elite Movements and Tax-Farmers' Careers in 17th century Southern India', paper read at the International Symposium on The State, Decentralisation and Tax-Farming, 1500–1850: The Ottoman Empire, Iran and India, Munich, 2–5 May 1990, referred to by Halil Berktay, 'Three Empires and the Societies they Governed: Iran, India and the Ottoman Empire', in Berktay and Faroqhi (eds.), *State and Peasant*, pp. 248, 249.

CHAPTER 1

Historical outline

At the beginning of the fourteenth century the world of the eastern Mediterranean was a counterpane of political powers with small states forming and large ones in decline. The Seljuks of Rum, dominant in Anatolia since the twelfth century, had been defeated at the battle of Kösedağ, north-west of Sivas, in 1243 by the Mongols, who then became the major power in the region. By 1300, however, Mongol power in Anatolia had declined. The Byzantine state was a mere remnant of its former glory, losing even its capital in 1204 to the fourth crusade. Although the emperor Michael VIII Palaeologos was able to regain the city in 1261 the empire's Asiatic possessions had by now been reduced to a small strip of land in western Anatolia. From this time the Byzantine rulers set out in a constant, but fruitless, search for help from the west in an attempt to guarantee their state's survival.

Off the coast of Anatolia, the patchwork of islands scattered through the Aegean was under Latin or Byzantine control. The Genoese were established in Chios, first under the control of the Zaccaria family from the early fourteenth century to 1329, and then, from 1346, under the Maona. The Genoese family of the Gattilusio controlled Lesbos (Mytilene) from 1354. The Genoese were also established in Phokaea (modern Foça), on the Anatolian coastline opposite Chios, initially under the Zaccaria family, from the late thirteenth century, and in Pera, on the European side of the Golden Horn opposite Constantinople, from 1267. Venice controlled Crete and Negroponte, and Venetian lords ruled in many of the islands including

This chapter is an historical outline of events, serving as a background to the discussion on trade. For more detailed histories, see in particular Franz Babinger, *Mehmed the Conqueror and his Time*, trans. Ralph Manheim, ed. with preface William C. Hickman, Bollingen Series 96) (Princeton, 1978); Michel Balard, *La Romanie génoise (XIIe–début du XVe siècle)*, *ASLSP*, n.s. v.18 (92), fasc. I; Bibliothèque des Ecoles Françaises d'Athènes et de Rome 235 (Genoa and Paris, 1978), vols. I–II;Claude Cahen, *Pre-Ottoman Turkey. A General Survey of the Material and Spiritual Culture and History c. 1071–1330* (London, 1968); Colin Imber, *The Ottoman Empire 1300–1481* (Istanbul, 1990); Halil İnalcık, *The Ottoman Empire. The Classical Age 1300–1600* (London, 1973); Elizabeth A. Zachariadou, *Trade and Crusade, Venetian Crete and the Emirates of Menteshe and Aydın* Library of the Hellenic Institute of Byzantine and Post-Byzantine Studies, 11 (Venice, 1983).

Naxos and Andros, which formed, together with other nearby islands, the duchy of Naxos, as well as on Mykonos, Karpathos and Santorini. The Hospitallers established themselves on Rhodes at the beginning of the fourteenth century and controlled the islands nearby, including Kos and Patmos. Like the Genoese, the Hospitallers too were later to establish themselves on the Anatolian coast, building a castle at Bodrum at the beginning of the fifteenth century. In 1344 combined Christian forces seized the harbour of İzmir, and the Latins remained there until its fall to Timur in 1402.

By 1300, the Turks had reached the Aegean coastline. Various petty states emerged. In the central area, based on Konya, was Karaman, the most important beylik in this period and one that was to continue as a thorn in the side of the Ottomans well into the fifteenth century. To the north-west, around Söğüt, was the small and, at this stage, insignificant, Ottoman beylik. Along the Aegean coast, from north to south, stretched Karası, Saruhan, Aydın, Menteşe and Teke. Inland from Teke was Hamid and east of Karası, based round Kütahya, was the beylik of Germiyan. The İsfendiyaroğulları controlled the Black Sea region round Kastamonu and Sinop.

The Ottoman beylik bordered on the remnants of Byzantine territory in Anatolia. Under its eponymous founder, Osman, the beylik expanded at Byzantine expense along the Sakarya river and westward towards the Sea of Marmara. It was under his son Orhan who succeeded him around 1324[1] that the Ottoman state developed considerably, the Byzantine cities of Bursa (Prusa), Ulubat (Lopadion), İznik (Nicaea) and İzmit (Nicomedia) all falling to the Ottomans between 1326 and 1337. The Byzantines were not the only ones to suffer from Ottoman advance for, sometime around the mid-1330s,[2] Orhan annexed the beylik of Karası. It was also under Orhan that the Ottomans gained their first foothold in Europe with the capture of Gelibolu (Gallipoli) in 1354.

This advance was maintained by Orhan's son Murad, who succeeded his father in 1362. In Anatolia, Murad annexed the beyliks of Germiyan and Hamid in the 1370s[3] and Teke in the 1380s,[4] and launched a successful attack on the beylik of Karaman. By the end of his reign Ottoman control in Anatolia stretched from the shores of the Bosphoros in the north to Antalya and the coastline of the Aegean in the south.

Gains in Anatolia were matched by those in Europe. Ottoman forces

---

[1] Imber, *Ottoman Empire*, p. 19.
[2] The conquest had to be after the visit of ibn Battuta in the early 1330s, as he met the independent ruler there. The earliest source to date it is the Chronological List of 1421, which places it 1348/9 (Imber, *Ottoman Empire*, pp. 21–2).
[3] Germiyan was taken probably soon after 1375. The Chronological List of 1421, the earliest source to date the event, places it in 1378/9 (Imber, *Ottoman Empire*, p. 27). Hamid fell shortly after the conquest of Germiyan (*ibid.*).
[4] Neşri dates it 1386, the Chronological List of 1421 to 1388 (Imber, *Ottoman Empire*, p. 28).

took Edirne (Adrianople), probably in 1369,[5] defeated the forces under the Serbian despots of Macedonia, Ugleša and Vlkašin in the battle of Çirmen on the Maritsa river in 1371 and, the way to Bulgaria and Macedonia now open before them, advanced into Bulgaria, taking Plovdiv (Philippopolis, Filibe) and Zagora and probably conquering much of Bulgaria. The Tsardom of Tarnovo seems also to have fallen under Ottoman suzerainty around this period while Ottoman attacks were launched into the kingdom of Bosnia and Serbia, Niş falling in 1385. Further south, Ottoman forces were active in Greece, taking Thessaloniki in 1387. Two years later Murad invaded Serbia. In the famous battle between the Ottomans and the Serbs on the plain of Kosovo both Murad and the Serbian prince Lazar were killed.

Serbia then descended into a period of internal feuding. The Ottoman state, however, appears to have been more stable for, although it is possible that there may have been a power struggle between Murad's son Bayezid and his brother in the period immediately after Murad's death, any such dispute was over by October 1389 when the Genoese *podestà* of Pera confirmed the peace treaty concluded between Genoa and Bayezid.[6]

Under Bayezid (1389–1402), the Ottoman state continued its expansion. In Anatolia, the beyliks of Menteşe and Aydın fell to the Ottomans in the winter of 1389/90 and Karaman once more came under attack. Accompanied by the Byzantine emperor Manuel II as his vassal, Bayezid campaigned against the İsfendiyaroğlu territory round Kastamonu and was probably successful in establishing control over northern Anatolia as far east as the Kızılırmak, which runs from the Black Sea, just west of Sinop, and passes just east of Ankara before turning east towards Sivas.

In Europe, Bayezid was locked into a power struggle over Serbia with King Sigismund of Hungary, a struggle in which Bayezid ultimately came out on top. Ottoman forces moved into Bulgaria and Wallachia. The menace of Ottoman advance forced both Sigismund and the Byzantine emperor Manuel, whose capital was now under Turkish siege and would remain so until 1402, to seek allies in the west. As a result a large crusading force was assembled, with troops from France, Germany and England, as well as those from Hungary. In 1396 this army met the Ottoman forces in battle at Nikopolis, on the Danube west of Ruse in modern Bulgaria, and was soundly defeated, thus effectively ending the era of Christian crusading to the east.

With the crushing of the crusaders, the position of Constantinople now looked very grave indeed and Manuel turned once more to the west for

---

[5] Imber, *Ottoman Empire*, p. 29.

[6] Imber, *Ottoman Empire*, p. 37; 1389.x.26 = ASG, Notario, Donato de Clavaro, c. 476, doc. 10; see appendix 5, doc. 2. Summary in M. Balard, Angeliki E. Laiou and C. Otten-Froux, *Les Italiens à Byzance et présentation de documents*, Série Byzantina Sorbonensia 6, Centre de Recherches d'Histoire et de Civilisation Byzantine (Paris, 1987), p. 33.

urgent help, which, apart from the arrival in the city of Marshal Boucicault, sent in 1399 by Charles VI of France, was not forthcoming. Bayezid moved on into Hungary and took Vidin. He was now master of the lands lying south of the Danube.

The Ottomans were also advancing in the region to the south, in Albania, Epiros and southern Greece, by means both of conquest and marriage. They were considerably helped in the Peloponnese by the presence of different warring Latin and Greek lords, among whom they could easily, allying with one against another, apply the principle of divide and rule. Ottoman advance was not merely on land, for Turkish ships increasingly conducted raids in the Aegean and harassed Latin navigation both there and through the straits.

Ottoman success in Europe was matched by continuing success in Anatolia. In 1397 Bayezid launched a campaign against Karaman as a result of which its ruler, Alaeddin, lost his life and the beylik lost its independence. To the north, Bayezid took Samsun from the İsfendiyaro-ğulları, and Amasya. To the east, Burhan al-Din, the ruler of Sivas, was killed, the Akkoyunlu clan defeated and Sivas taken. To the south Bayezid seized Malatya from the Mamluks. By the end of the century, Bayezid's control stretched from Sivas and Malatya in the east, across the central plateau and over the whole of western Anatolia. This control was, however, transient rather than solidly based and within two years the whole edifice was to be reduced to rubble by an enemy approaching from the east.

Timur, born in Transoxiana probably in the 1320s or 1330s,[7] swept at the head of his forces across Central Asia and, at the turn of the fifteenth century, into Anatolia. In 1402, at the battle of Ankara, Timur inflicted a shattering defeat on the Ottoman army and took Bayezid captive. Ottoman authority fractured into fratricidal fighting between Bayezid's sons, and the independent beyliks were re-established by Timur. Ottoman territory was now reduced to lands in northern Anatolia stretching from the Sea of Marmara to Bursa, Ankara and Sivas in the east and northwards to Amasya. After the defeat of their father, Bayezid's sons scattered. Süleyman fled to Europe, Mehmed to the region of Amasya, Tokat and Sivas, and Isa, apparently, to Bursa, while Musa appears to have been taken captive with his father. What happened to Mustafa is unclear.[8] There followed a period of internecine struggle among the sons of Bayezid from which Mehmed eventually emerged the victor.

It was during Mehmed I's reign (1413–21) that the Ottoman state was once more rebuilt. Mehmed was able both to overcome the internal revolts in Anatolia in 1416 under Şeyh Bedreddin and Börklüce Mustafa, and to

---

[7] For an account of Timur, see Beatrice Forbes Manz, *The Rise and Rule of Tamerlane* (Cambridge, 1989).
[8] He may perhaps have ruled Bursa for some period. See Imber, *Ottoman Empire*, p. 63 and n. 26.

extend his territories in Anatolia and in Europe. The beyliks of Aydın and Menteşe, revived by Timur, now lost their independence and passed under permanent Ottoman control. The İsfendiyaroğulları and Karaman too suffered defeats at the hands of the new Ottoman ruler while the Genoese lost their colony in Samsun to him in 1420. In Europe, Mehmed's forces advanced in Albania and reduced Wallachia to vassal status, raided Bosnia and attacked Negroponte. By 1421 therefore, when Mehmed died, the Ottoman state had re-emerged after the disaster of the battle of Ankara and the subsequent internecine fighting.

Although the position of the state was now far more stable than it had been ten years before, the early phase of the reign of Mehmed's son and successor, Murad II (1421–51), was by no means easy, for his initial task was to survive civil war. Challenged first by his uncle, Düzme Mustafa, and then by his brother Mustafa, Murad overcame both attempts to oust him from power. His initial task was to establish firm Ottoman control in the European section of the empire and in Anatolia where he campaigned against the perennial Ottoman enemy, Karaman, and secured Ottoman power in the north-east and west. In Europe, the position was complicated for the Ottomans by the presence of a successful commander, John Hunyadi, the *voyvoda* of Transylvania. Hunyadi defeated Ottoman forces both in 1441 and again in 1442.

Murad's main aim at this point was to secure peaceful relations with the surrounding powers. He had already made a treaty with the Byzantines in 1424, after his unsuccessful siege of Constantinople at the beginning of his reign. Now, after the Hungarian campaign of 1443, he concluded the treaty of Edirne with Serbia and Hungary in 1444 and an agreement with Karaman in the same year. It was at this point, having thus apparently stabilised relations with his neighbours, that Murad abdicated in favour of his son Mehmed.

Mehmed II's first reign was to be both brief and difficult. The treaty of Edirne did not prove to be very reliable for, in September, John Hunyadi and King Vladislav I of Hungary crossed the Danube against the Ottomans. Murad, who had returned from retirement to lead the campaign, commanded the Ottoman forces. The two armies met in battle near Varna. The Hungarian forces were defeated, Vladislav being killed and Hunyadi fleeing from the battlefield.

Murad's return to the political stage was temporary and after this Ottoman victory he once more withdrew, leaving Mehmed precariously in charge. Mehmed's reign, however, did not continue for long and was brought down two years later by a janissary revolt in Edirne. Murad's second reign now began with his recall to the throne and ended with his death in 1451. During this period Ottoman forces in Europe overcame John Hunyadi who, although defeated with the Hungarian forces at the battle of Varna in 1444, was not crushed until the second battle of Kosovo in 1448.

Another opponent of Ottoman rule in the Balkans was George Kastriote, who came to be known as Scanderbeg, a corruption of his Muslim name İskender Bey. Based in Albania, Scanderbeg was able to hold out against Murad by retreating out of reach after each encounter. Further to the south, Ottoman forces operated in the Peloponnese and against Venetian territories attacking Negroponte in the later 1440s, and the islands of Tinos and Mykonos in 1450.

Murad II's reign came to an end with his death in February 1451. Mehmed II (1451–81) ascended the throne once again and, two years later, captured the city of Constantinople and with it the Genoese settlement of Pera.

Genoa itself passed much of the 150 years between the beginning of the fourteenth century and the fall of Constantinople in a mess.[9] There was considerable political instability, civil war and foreign domination. From 1353 until 1356 the city was under Giovanni Visconti, in 1396 it fell to France, in 1409 to Teodoro di Monteferrati and several years later, in 1421, it was back under the domination of Milan, in the control of Filippo Maria Visconti. At other times, government was in the hands of the doge, whose hold on power could be flimsy. Between July and September 1393 there were five successive doges. At the same time, however, Genoa managed to be an extremely important commercial player in the Mediterranean and the Banco di San Giorgio was to be, by the early sixteenth century, a formidable financial power. Political instability at home left the Genoese colonies with a much freer hand than might otherwise have been the case in their dealings with the Turks.

Throughout this period Genoa's main rival in the Levant remained Venice, a state much more stable politically, and one with a much tighter control over its Levantine colonies. This rivalry resulted in various wars between Genoa and Venice, fought largely over control of the Black Sea and with largely inconclusive results for the balance of power between the two states in the eastern Mediterranean, the status quo remaining intact, with neither side being able to dominate the other. During the war of Curzola which took place between 1294 and 1299 the Venetians, in July 1296, set fire to the Genoese commercial settlement in Pera, attacked Caffa and devastated Phokaea, while the Genoese, enraged at the burning of Pera, murdered the Venetian *bailo* and Venetian merchants. From a Genoese standpoint, the result of this war, which was finally settled by the treaty of Milan, signed on 25 September 1299, was that Genoa remained dominant in the Black Sea, but had sustained considerable loss in Pera and Caffa.[10]

From 1351 to 1355 Genoa and Venice were once more at war, in the war

---

[9] For an account of the history of Genoa in this period see Steven A. Epstein, *Genoa and the Genoese 958–1528* (Chapel Hill and London, 1996).
[10] Balard, *Romanie génoise*, vol. I, pp. 58–61.

of the Straits, in which the two sides again disputed control of the Black Sea, and the outcome of which made no appreciable difference to the balance of power between them in the region.[11] This applies equally to the outcome of the war of Tenedos, or the war of Chioggia, which ended with the peace of Turin, signed in August 1381. Once again, neither Genoa nor Venice had succeeded in gaining the upper hand, and the status quo prevailed.[12]

From the early beginnings of the Ottoman state to the Ottoman conquest of Constantinople in 1453, the Ottomans and the Genoese maintained close relations. While the Genoese did on occasion take part in various anti-Turkish leagues organised by Latin powers, they were not as active in this regard as their main maritime rival Venice, refusing, for example, to join the crusade against İzmir in 1344.[13] Genoese behaviour was in part instrumental in ensuring that an anti-Turkish league between Genoa, Venice and Byzantium, urged by Pope Innocent VI in 1362–3 did not in fact get off the ground.[14] Even when Genoa was involved in anti-Turkish leagues, this does not always seem to have hampered contacts with the Turks, for Genoese sources show that there were frequent exchanges of embassies in the 1380s[15] while Genoa, in 1388, proposed an anti-Turkish league with Venice and a division of the Mediterranean into spheres of influence between them,[16] and, in the same year, the Genoese of Pera entered into treaty arrangements with the Hospitallers of Rhodes, the Maona of Chios and Francesco Gattilusio of Mytilene.[17] Frequent Turkish–Genoese contacts, however, continued, in the 1390s,[18] although in 1392 the Maona of Chios, the Gatillusi of Lesbos and the Hospitallers of Rhodes discussed joint action against the Turks,[19] and at the beginning of the fifteenth century,[20] and one may presume that this was true also for the much of the rest of the period but for which the sources have not survived.[21] As Professor Balard has said,

---

[11] See Balard, *Romanie génoise*, vol. I, pp. 78–83; and Michel Balard, 'A propos de la bataille du Bosphore. L'expédition génoise de Paganino Doria à Constantinople', *Travaux et Mémoires* 4 (1970), 431–69.

[12] Balard, *Romanie génoise*, vol. I, pp. 88–91.

[13] Zachariadou, *Trade and Crusade*, p. 45 (despite papal appeal).

[14] Balard, *Romanie génoise*, vol. I, p. 85.

[15] 1387.i.29 = ASG, Antico Comune 83, fo. 53; 1387.i.29 = *ibid.*, fo. 84; 1387.ii.27 = *ibid.*, fo. 54; 1388.vi.14 = *ibid.*, fo. 59; 1388.v.10 = *ibid.*, fos. 7–8; 1388.vi.25 = *ibid.*, fos. 66–67.

[16] Zachariadou, *Trade and Crusade*, p. 36; Balard, *Romanie génoise*, vol. I, p. 95.

[17] Zachariadou, *Trade and Crusade*, p. 74.

[18] There are many references in ASG: San Giorgio, Sala 34 590/1304; Antico Comune, 22; and Archivio Segreto, 498.

[19] Zachariadou, *Trade and Crusade*, p. 78.

[20] 1402.v.26 & 27 = ASG, San Giorgio, Sala 34 590/1306, fos. 97r–98r and 1402.v.11 = *ibid.*, fos.148r–152r and 1402.v.30 = *ibid.*, ffos101r–102r; 1413.i = ASG, Notaio, Giovanni Balbi, Sc. 46, filza 1, doc. 104.

[21] In this context it is a great pity that so few of the Massaria of Pera have survived. They are particularly useful in building up a picture of the exchange of embassies as they enter all related expenses.

for the Genoese 'il était plus important de maintenir contre les prétensions vénitiennes les comptoirs génois et le réseau commercial constitué en Orient que de participer à une alliance de la chrétienté contre les Turcs'.[22]

The Genoese certainly had close relations with the Turks, relations which began early on with Menteşe, for Genoa made an alliance with the beylik in 1311 for a joint attack on Rhodes and the surrounding islands,[23] and with Saruhan to whom the Genoese of New Phokaea were paying tribute in return for freedom to trade soon after the construction of the new city.[24] Treaties were made between the Genoese and Saruhan in, probably, the late 1340s,[25] and with Hızır of Aydın in 1351.[26] At the end of that year the Genoese requested provisions from Aydın for their fleet.[27] The treaty between the Genoese and the Ottoman ruler Murad I, enacted in 1387, is extant and, although no other Ottoman–Genoese treaty has apparently survived from the fourteenth century, the Genoese are known to have concluded treaties with the Ottomans in the winter of 1351–2[28] and in 1389.[29] They were also, together with the Byzantines, the Venetians and the Hospitallers, signatories to the treaty with Bayezid's son Süleyman in 1403.[30]

Genoese–Ottoman relations were based very firmly on mutual interest.

---

[22] Balard, *Romanie génoise*, vol. I, pp. 103–4.

[23] Zachariadou, *Trade and Crusade*, p. 108.

[24] Dukas, *Historia Byzantina*, ed. I. Bekker, CSHB (Bonn, 1843), pp. 162–3; Dukas, *Ducae Historia Turcobyzantina (1341–1462)*, ed. B. Grecu (Bucharest, 1958), p. 207, ll. 24–7; Dukas, *Decline and Fall of Byzantium to the Ottoman Turks*, ed. and trans. H. J. Magoulias (Detroit, 1975), p. 149. Tribute was also being paid to Saruhan in the 1330s: ibn Battuta, *Voyages d'ibn Batoutah*, ed. and trans. C. Defremery and B. R. Sanguinetti (Paris, 1854), vol. II, p. 314. Zachariadou, *Trade and Crusade*, p. 17 says, referring to ibn Battuta, that this tribute was probably new as it was unlikely that Saruhan could have extracted it when Zaccaria was established on Chios.

[25] 1364.x.8, ASG, Nota; Ignoti, XVIII. 14 refers to an agreement made between Saruhan and Leone Kalothetos, lord of Old Phokaea. See Kate Fleet, 'The treaty of 1387 between Murad I and the Genoese', *BSOAS* 56 (1993), 21–2.

[26] Zachariadou, *Trade and Crusade*, p. 58.

[27] A. Luttrell, 'Venice and the Knights Hospitallers of Rhodes in the Fourteenth Century', *Papers of the British School at Rome* 26/n.s. 5 (1958), 205.

[28] Concluded by Filippo Demerode and Bonifacio de Sauli, 1358.xi.20, ASG, San Giorgio, Manoscritti Membranacei IV, fo. 304r; = L. T. Belgrano, 'Documenti Riguardanti la Colonia Genovese di Pera', *ASLSP* 13 (1877–84), no. 21, p. 129. 1352.v.6 = *Liber Jurium, Reipublicae Genuensis*, ed. Ercole Ricotti, Monumenta Historiae Patriae 9 (Turin, 1857), vol. II, no. CCIII, p. 602, in the peace agreement between Genoa and the Byzantine emperor John VI, it was stipulated that the peace made by Pagano Doria with 'Orcanibei amirati' should remain firm and unaffected by this new agreement with Byzantium. Kantakuzenos, *Ioannes Kantakuzenos, Historiarum libri IV*, ed. L Schopen, CSHB (Bonn, 1828–32), vol. III, p. 288, ll. 8–19 and Gregoras, *Byzantina Historia*, ed. L. Schopen and I. Bekker, CSHB (Bonn, 1828–55), vol. III, p. 84, ll. 4–11, both speak of legates sent to Orhan to secure an agreement with him, though neither of them name these emissaries.

[29] 1389.x.26, ASG, Notario, 476, Donato de Clavaro, c. 476, doc. 10, see appendix 5 below, doc. 10.

[30] G. T. Dennis, 'The Byzantine–Turkish treaty of 1403', *Orientalia Christiana Periodica* 33 (1967), 72–88.

The Genoese were essentially pragmatic in their dealings with the Turks, something that was no doubt encouraged by the fact that Genoese Turkish policy was largely dictated by the Genoese on the spot in colonies such as Pera and Chios rather than directed from Genoa itself. Even during the siege of Constantinople, the Genoese of Pera managed to maintain their relations with the Turks while, simultaneously, siding with the defenders of the city, sending letters urgently requesting help to Genoa, ambassadors to the sultan in Edirne to renew treaty relations and express undying friendship, soldiers to Constantinople, oil for Turkish cannons to the sultan's camp and betraying Longo Giustiniano's scheme to set fire to the Turkish ships.[31] Relations were such that when Turkish cannon sank a ship belonging to Genoese merchants of Pera, loaded with merchandise and ready to leave for Italy, the Perotes complained. Explaining that they had not realised that the ship belonged to the Genoese of Pera, taking it rather as belonging to the enemy, the Turks assured them that, after the capture of the city, the merchants would be fully indemnified.[32] Once Constantinople had fallen, what the Genoese really wanted was to have Pera back and to continue trading as before, a situation for which they were quite prepared to pay tribute. Their overriding concern was to ensure freedom of movement and, in particular, access to and from the Black Sea.[33]

Relations between the Turks and the Genoese were thus highly developed with a constant exchange of embassies and conclusion of treaties and agreements of one sort or another. The main motivating force behind these relations was money, generated by an active and lucrative commerce.

[31] Dukas, *Historia Byzantina*, chap.38, p. 265, ll. 10–11, p. 267, ll. 8–11, p. 275, ll. 10–20, p. 277, ll. 13–14; Dukas, *Historia Turcobyzantina*, p. 329, ll. 25–6, p. 333, ll. 5–7, p. 343, l. 28 – p. 345, l. 4, p. 347, l. 13; Dukas *Decline and Fall*, pp. 211, 212, 217, 218.
[32] Dukas, *Historia Byzantina*, chap. 38, p. 278, l. 8 – p. 279, l. 8; Dukas *Historia Turcobyzantina*, p. 347, l. 29 – p. 349, l. 13; Dukas, *Decline and Fall*, p. 219.
[33] 1454.iii.11 = Belgrano, 'Documenti', no. 154, pp. 265–7.

CHAPTER 2

Money

The monetary aspect of the Turkish economy is an extremely complex issue and one much hampered by the nature of the sources.[1] While it is beyond the scope of this book to investigate this thoroughly, it is necessary to indicate the problems when dealing with currencies in the period and to look briefly at the methods of exchange used.

During this period certain currencies predominated in the eastern Mediterranean. Initially, the Byzantine gold coin, the *hyperpyron*, which was divided into 24 *karati*, was the major currency of the region. During the fourteenth century, however, it lost its predominance, becoming a money of account, and after the middle of the century the *hyperpyron* in circulation was silver.[2] The *hyperpyron* was replaced as the 'dollar' currency of the eastern Mediterranean by the *florin*. Struck first in 1252 in Florence, the *florin* largely dominated trade in western Europe but was then superseded by the Venetian *ducat*, a gold coin first minted in 1284 and which was so dominant in the fifteenth century that the term *ducat* became synonymous with gold coinage. The Genoese *genovino*, first struck, like the *florin*, in 1252, although of great importance in general in the Mediterranean, never became a dominant coinage in the Levant. The *hyperpyron–ducat (florin)* exchange rate was 2:1 for much of the fourteenth century, dropping after approximately 1389 to around 3:1.[3]

In Turchia, the major coin was the *akçe* (Greek *aspron*, Latin *asper*), a

---

[1] The importance of research into the monetary system is highlighted by A. S. Ehrenkreutz: 'To achieve meaningful progress in the field of medieval Near Eastern economic history one must take into account its monetary aspects' ('Monetary Aspects of Medieval Near Eastern Economic History', in M. A. Cook (ed.), *Studies in the Economic History of the Middle East from the Rise of Islam to the Present Day* (London, 1970), p. 37). In general, see Peter Spufford, *Money and its Use in Medieval Europe* (Cambridge, 1988); and Peter Spufford, *Handbook of Medieval Exchange*, Offices of the Royal Historical Society (London, 1986).

[2] T. Bertelé, 'L'iperpero bizantino dal 1261 al 1450', *Rivista Italiana di Numismatica e Scienze Affini*, series 5, 5/59 (1957), 81, 83; Spufford, *Money*, p. 286.

[3] Bertelé, 'Iperpero bizantino', 84.

silver coin struck also in Trabzon and Caffa.[4] The weight of the *akçe* and thus its value in relation to other currencies varied according to where it was minted. The various beyliks, such as Menteşe and Aydın, struck their own *akçe*[5] as did the Ottomans, whose coin came to predominate as they took over the main commercial centres, first Bursa, then Edirne and finally Constantinople. Under the Ottomans, the first coins struck with a date and place of minting were similar to coins of the Ilhans, whose style of coinage affected that of the Ottoman *akçe*.[6] Unfortunately, the lack of data makes it difficult to produce any precise idea of what the different *akçe* were worth at any specific point. From the accounts of Giacomo Badoer, a Venetian merchant active in Constantinople in the late 1430s, it is clear that in the Constantinople money markets of that period the Turkish *akçe–hyperpyron* rate of exchange fluctuated daily[7] but remained in the region of between approximately 10.5 and 11 *akçes* per *hyperpyron*. The exchange rate of *akçe*s of Samsun and a *hyperpyron* was, in the same period, around 19:1, while that of the *akçe* of Caffa was 20:1. On this basis, the rate of exchange between an Ottoman *akçe* and a Samsun *akçe* was 1:1.73. The *akçe–ducat* rate in the same period was around 33:1.[8]

Apart from a silver coinage, the Turkish rulers struck a gold *ducat* in imitation of that of Venice.[9] In the late 1430s there were in the region of 80 Ottoman *akçe*s to one Turkish *ducat* and one Turkish *ducat* to around 2.05 *hyperpyra*.[10] In Aydın, Turkish minting of imitation *ducats*[11] caused, in the assessment of the Senate, grave damage to Venetian interests, prompting Venice to send an ambassador to Theologos in 1368 to ensure that the emir

---

[4] For Turkish *akçe*s see İbrahim Artuk, 'Karesi-oğulları adına basılmış olan iki sikke', *İstanbul Üniversitesi Edebiyat Fakültesi Tarih Dergisi* 33 (1980/81), 283; İbrahim Artuk, 'Early Ottoman Coins of Orhan Ghazi as Confirmation of his Sovereignty', in Dickran K. Kouymjian (ed.), *Near Eastern Numismatics, Iconography, Epigraphy and History. Studies in Honor of George C. Miles* (Beirut, 1974), pp. 457–63; İbrahim Artuk, 'Murad'ın sikkelerine genel bir bakış 761–792 (1359–1389)', *Belleten* 184 (1982), 787–93; P. Wittek, *Menteşe Beyliği* (Ankara, 1986), pp. 155–9.

[5] al-'Umarī, 'Notice de l'ouvrage qui a pour titre Masalek alabsar fi memalek alamsar, Voyages des yeux dans les royaumes des différentes contrées (ms. arabe 583)', E. Quatremère in *Notices et Extraits des mss. de la Bibliothèque du Roi*, 13 (Paris, 1838), p. 335.

[6] Artuk, 'Early Ottoman coins', pp. 459, 461.

[7] The text gives no explanation for these small percentage fluctuations which were presumably the result of supply and demand on the money markets.

[8] See appendix 1 below.

[9] Saminiato de' Ricci refers to 'duchati d'Altoluogho' in his account book: Antonia Borlandi, *Il Manuale di Mercatura di Saminiato de'Ricci*, Università di Genova, Fonti e Studi 4 (Genoa, 1963), p. 110. The Turks also struck copper coins: see Artuk, 'Karesi-oğulları adına basılmış olan iki sikke', 284; Artuk, 'Murad'ın sikkelerine genel bir bakış', 789–90; Wittek, *Menteşe*, pp. 156, 157.

[10] See appendix 1 below.

[11] For imitation *ducats*, dating from *c.* 1350–60 and probably originating in the emirate of Aydın, see S. Bendall and C. Morrison, 'Un trésor de ducats d'imitation au nom d'Andrea Dandolo (1343–1354)', *Revue Numismatique*, series 6, 21 (1979) 184, 188.

ceased striking such coins.[12] This embassy was successful and the emir signed an agreement in which he agreed to destroy the mould for minting and to stop any striking in his territories of *ducat*s in the form of those of Venice.[13] Menteşe, too, minted imitation *ducat*s, persisting in this despite a clash with Venice.[14] Another western coin copied by the Turks was the *gigliato*, a silver coin of Charles II of Anjou, struck in Naples at the beginning of the fourteenth century.[15] Apart from imitation western coins there were also false *akçe*.[16]

One aspect of the European economy in the late medieval period was the bullion drain of silver from the west eastwards. Much silver did flow into the Mamluk empire, the main destination of European cash being Alexandria, a major emporium for luxury goods.[17] Silver bullion formed part of the cargo of ships sailing there from Venice.[18] Within Turchia too, cash played an important part in commercial exchange, and silver, and gold, were apparently in demand.

In fact, according to the Ottoman chroniclers Aşıkpaşazade, who completed his history in 1484, and Neşri, who, basing himself largely on Aşıkpaşazade, wrote towards the end of the fifteenth century, Anatolia suffered a shortage of gold and silver in the 1380s.[19] Dr Zhukov has

[12] 1368.iii,2 : F. Thiriet, *Régestes des délibérations du sénat de Venise concernant la Romanie* (Paris, 1958), vol. I, no. 451, pp. 115–16. The success of this mission, the other aims of which were the release of Venetian prisoners and the restitution of 2,000 *ducat*s taken from Niccolò Morosini, was seen as of such importance that should the ambassador be unable to secure the emir's co-operation, he was to order all Venetian merchants out of the emirate. See also 1369.x.12 : *ibid.*, no. 481, p. 122.

[13] 1370.x.1 = Thiriet, *Régestes*, vol. I, no. 481, pp. 160–1: 'delere cunium ducatorum, et precipere quod in terris suis vel aliqua ipsarum terrarum non stampentur amplius ducati ad formam ducatorum vestrorum'.

[14] 1370.x.1 = G. Thomas (ed.), *Diplomatarium Veneto–Levantinum* (Venice, 1890–99), vols. I–II: vol. II, no. 95, pp. 160–1.

[15] Wittek, *Menteşe*, p. 155; P. Lambros, 'Monnaie inédite de Sarukhan émir d'Ionie, frappée à Ephèse (1299–1346)', *Revue Numismatique* (n.s.) 14 (1869–70), 340; Bendall and Morrison, 'Trésor de ducats d'imitation', 186, n. 23; J. Karabacek, 'Gigliato des karischen Turkomanenfürsten Urchan-beg', *Numismatische Zeitschrift* 9 (1877), 200–15; J. Karabacek, 'Gigliato des jonischen Turkomanenfürsten Omar-beg', *Numismatische Zeitschrift* 2 (1870), 525–38.

[16] 1438.x.22 = Giacomo Badoer, *Il Libro dei Conti di Giacomo Badoer (Costantinopoli 1436–1440)*, ed. Umberto Dorini and Tommaso Bertelè, Il Nuovo Ramusio 3 Istituto Poligrafico dello Stato, Libreria dello Stato (1956), col. 230, p. 462, col. 249, p. 501, an entry for 17 false *asper*s.

[17] For bullion movements see Spufford, *Money*.

[18] Frescobaldi, *Visit to the Holy Places of Egypt, Sinai, Palestine and Syria in 1384 by Frescobaldi, Gucci and Sigoli*, trans. Fr. Theophilus Bellorini OFM and Fr. Eugene Hoade, OFM with preface and notes by Fr. Bellarmino Bagatti OFM (Jerusalem, 1948), p. 35. Frescobaldi travelled from Venice to Alexandria in 1384 on a ship part of whose cargo consisted of silver bullion.

[19] Aşıkpaşazade, *Die altosmanische Chronik des Ašıkpašazade*, ed. Fredrich Giese (Leipzig, 1929, repr. Osnabrück, 1972), p. 53, ll. 8–9; Aşıkpaşazade, *Tevarih-i al-i 'Osman*, ed. Ali (Istanbul, 1332), p. 56, l. 16; Neşri, *Ğihannüma die altosmanische Chronik des Mevlana Mehemmed Neschri*, ed. Franz Taeschner, vol. I. *Einleitung und Text des Cod. Menzel* (Leipzig, 1951), p. 55, l. 20; Neşri, *Ğihannüma die altosmanische Chronik des Mevlana*

explained this as being in part the result of the discontinuance of the transit trade in alum in Menteşe and Aydın after the Ottoman take-over of Kütahya in 1381, which thus deprived the emirs of hard currency.[20] Dr Zhukov further argues that the shortage of precious metals combined with the large volume of production was reflected in the low prices commented on by ibn Battuta. But ibn Battuta was referring to the 1330s, a period very different from the 1380s. Further, there was not a discontinuance of trade activity in this period and, in any case, the Ottomans would hardly have been affected by a discontinuance of the alum trade through Menteşe and Aydın, and indeed could only have benefited from their take-over of Kütahya.

Aşıkpaşazade and Neşri's remark is in fact hard to explain. The reign of Murad was one of increasing wealth both in terms of trade and of territorial expansion. That there was gold and silver available in this period is made clear by both these chroniclers when, having mentioned this shortage, they go on to a description of the presents brought by Evrenoz to the wedding of Bayezid to the daughter of the bey of Germiyan which included gold and silver trays filled with gold *florins*.[21]

In these accounts, the remark about the shortage comes in the section on the decision of the ruler of Germiyan to marry off his daughter to Murad's son Bayezid as a means of preserving his beylik. The section appears in the Giese edition of Aşıkpaşazade as follows: 'Murad Han'a geldi. İyi atlar peşkeş getirdi. Ol zamanda altın gümüş azdı. Denizli'de 'alemli ak bezler olurdı. Hil'at anı giydirirler. Sırtak tekele dikerlerdi. Alaşehir'in kızıl ivladısını sancak ederlerdi. Hil'at anı giydirlerdi.'[22] The Istanbul edition is almost the same except for referring to 'Alaşehir'in kızıl ifladısını', and 'ol zamanda altın, gümüş, kumaş az olurdı.'[23] The Neşri texts are very close to that of Aşıkpaşazade. The Menzel codex refers to 'ol zamanda Anatolı'da altın ve gümüş az olurdı', the Manisa codex to 'ol zamanda Anatolı'da altın gümüş az oldı', and the Istanbul publication to 'ol zamanda Anatolı'da altun gümüş az olurdı'.[24] Therefore the Aşıkpaşazade texts refer to 'altın gümüş', or to 'altın, gümüş, kumaş', while the Neşri texts have 'altın ve

Mehemmed Neschri, ed. Franz Taeschner, vol. II: *Text des Cod. Manisa 1373* (Leipzig, 1955), p. 84, l. 19; Neşri, *Kitab-ı Cihan-nüma*, ed. Faik Reşit Unat and Dr Mehmed A. Köymen (Ankara, 1949, 1957), vols. I–II: vol. I, p. 204.

[20] K. A. Zhukov, Эгейкие Эмираты XIV–XV BB (Moscow, 1988), p. 100. It seems too strong to refer, as Dr Zhukov does, to an almost complete paralysis of the alum trade in Aydın and Menteşe after the Ottomans took over the mines of Kütahya. His argument relies heavily on regarding Scorpiata as a new source of alum, which does not necessarily seem to have been the case. See chap. 7.

[21] Aşıkpaşazade, *Altosmanische Chronik* p. 53, ll. 3–6, *Tevarih-i al-i 'Osman*, p. 57, ll. 15–18; Neşri, *Menzel Cod.*, p. 56, ll. 11–13, *Manisa Cod.*, p. 55, ll. 16–19, *Kitab-ı Cihan-nüma*, p. 206, ll. 5–8.

[22] Aşıkpaşazade, *Altosmanische Chronik* p. 52, ll. 8–10: 'He [İshak Fakı] came to Murad Han Gazi. He brought good horses as a present. At that time gold and silver were in short supply. There were white marked cloths of Denizli. They dressed him in a robe of honour. They made a *sırtak tekele*.'

[23] Aşıkpaşazade, *Tevarih-i al-i 'Osman*, p. 56, ll. 15–19.

[24] Neşri, *Menzel Cod.*, p. 55, l. 20, *Manisa Cod.*, p. 84, l. 19, *Kitab-ı Cihan-nüma*, p. 204, ll. 4–5.

gümüş' or 'altın gümüş'. However, this reference here to gold and silver being scarce seems out of place. What would actually make more sense from the context is a reference to cloth. This would, however, necessitate cloth (كماش) being written as قومش. This would thus mean cloth of gold, so making sense both in the immediate context of the piece and in the historical context when such a shortage would be unexpected. That this is the correct interpretation is supported by the reading in the Codex Upsaliensis of Aşıkpaşazade where, in place of altın gümüş, there is altınlı kumaş.[25]

Western merchants adopted various methods of paying for their merchandise. One of these was cash, which the merchants took with them when they went into Turchia to trade.[26] Money was changed into Turkish *akçe*s in Constantinople where, in the 1430s, the bankers charged 1 per cent on the transaction.[27] Apart from *akçe*s, Turkish *ducat*s too were traded there.[28] Not only western merchants acted as bankers; Turks too handled currency, changing *asper*s and *hyperpyra*.[29]

That cash payment grew in importance as the Ottoman empire developed is indicated by the Ragusan government's concern in 1441 over the need to acquire silver, for the Turks required payment for everything in money.[30] This presumably represents a development in the economic strength of the empire under the early Ottoman rulers. Whereas, in the first part of the fourteenth century, the Turks, that is the rulers of the various beyliks in western Anatolia, and the Ottomans, were not in a position to insist on a method of payment, by the middle of the next century the Ottomans were strong enough to dictate economic terms. That the Ottomans would

[25] Aşıkpaşazade, *Altomanische Chronik*, p. 52, n. 7.

[26] 1437.xii.18 = Badoer, *Libro*, col. 44, p. 88, col. 152, p. 307, 1436.ii.15 = *ibid.*, col. 44, p. 88, col. 48, p. 97. Antonio da Negroponte took with him on his voyage to Samsun and Trabzon three Turkish *ducat*s and had with him in cash in Samsun 1,165 *asper*s of Samsun; 1438.iii.20 = *ibid.*, col. 197, p. 396, col. 186, p. 375 (*asper*s bought for trade in Tekirdağ (Rodosto) and Kırklareli (former Kırk Kilise, called XL Chiexie by Badoer), west of Edirne; 1437.iii.31 = *ibid.*, col. 125, p. 252, col. 186, p. 375 (*asper*s for trade in Gelibolu (Gallipoli)); 1436.xi.8 = *ibid.*, col. 33, p. 66, col. 18, p. 37, col. 16, p. 33 (19,000 Turkish *asper*s for trade in Bursa).

[27] 1438.x.21 = Badoer, *Libro*, col. 285, p. 572, an entry for 65 Venetian *ducat*s and 3,000 Turkish *asper*s sent to Constantinople from Edirne. One expense was for selling the *ducat*s: 'per provixion de vender i duchati e dar i denar a chanbio, meto in tuto [a] j per c'; 1437.vii.24 = *ibid.*, col. 92, p. 186, col. 88, p. 179, col. 77, p. 157, col. 47, p. 95; 1437.vii.26 = *ibid.*, col. 47, p. 94, col. 92, p. 187; 1437.xi.23 = *ibid.*, col. 121, p. 244, col. 47, p. 95, all entries concerning 5,100 Turkish *asper*s bought and sent to Bursa for purchasing pepper. The cost of buying *asper*s was 1 per cent: 'per acatar i diti asperi a una per c'.

[28] 1436.ii.13 = Badoer, *Libro*, col. 48, p. 96, col. 29, p. 59; 1436.ii.13 = *ibid.*, col. 48, p. 96, col. 3, p. 7.

[29] 1436.ix.7 = Badoer, *Libro*, col. 3, p. 6, col. 7, p. 15: 'per Saliet turcho per asp.2000 turchesci ch'el mese per mio nome in bancho'. A second entry two days later reads 'per el dito turcho ch'el mese in bancho fra asperi e perpari a mio chonto'.

[30] 1441.xii.15 : B. Krekić, *Dubrovnik (Raguse) et le Levant au Moyen-Age* (Paris–The Hague, 1961), no. 971, pp. 325–6.

increasingly find themselves in need of hard currency is understandable for, as the state developed, its needs could no longer be met solely by booty and the new administrative structures which grew up required payment in cash.

Cash was not, however, the only method used in commercial transactions and much exchange went on by means of bartering.[31] It seems reasonable to assume that bartering was used also by western merchants in Turchia for it would have been a highly practical way of trading, doing away with the necessity of carrying much cash or of converting other currencies into the various types of *aspers* used in Turchia.

Merchants were, however, by no means entirely restricted in their financial transactions to either bartering or cash, for there was also the letter of exchange. In the fourteenth century major economic developments were under way, particularly in the city states, developments which spread outwards linking much of western Europe.[32] Of these, one of the most important was the establishment of banking, which began first in Italy where Genoa led the field, other cities apparently being much slower to establish transfer banking.[33]

Before the development of the banking system, money changers had changed currency into pounds of unminted gold dust or cast ingots of silver, these being necessary for merchants paying for goods outside the area of the currency they held. This system was gradually transformed as money changers began in some large commercial centres, the most advanced of which in this respect was Genoa, to take deposits and then, on depositors' instructions, to transfer from one account to another. The next development was to transfer from one bank to another in the same city, and then to transfer from one account in a bank in one city to a bank in another city.[34] These bankers ran current accounts on which no interest was paid, and deposit accounts that did attract interest and in which money had to be

---

[31] Giacomo Badoer's account book gives many examples of bartering between merchants, e.g.. 1437.xi.18 = Badoer, *Libro*, col. 148, p. 298, Azi Baba, variously described as a Saracen ('sarain', 1437.xii.4 = *ibid.*, col. 148, p. 298) and a Moor ('moro', 1437.xi.17 = *ibid.*, c.1 48, p. 299) bartered cloth for pepper; 1438.ii.12 = *ibid.*, col. 251, p. 505; 1438.ix.18 = *ibid.*, col. 241, p. 484, col. 241, p. 485. E. Ashtor, 'Pagamento in contanti e baratto nel commercio italiano d'Otremare (secoli XIV–XVI)' in *Storia d'Italia Annali 6: Economia naturale, Economia monetaria* (Turin, 1983), pp. 363–6, says bartering was characteristic of trade in the Levant at the end of the fourteenth and beginning of the fifteenth centuries. See also E. Ashtor, 'Il commercio italiano col Levante e il suo impatto sull'economia tardomedioevale' in *Aspetti della Vita Economica Medioevale. Atti delle Convegno di Studi nel X Anniversario della Morte di Federigo Melis. Firenze–Pisa–Prato 10–14 marzo 1984*, Università degli Studi di Firenze: Istituto di Storia Economica (Florence, 1985), p. 47 where he refers to bartering of slaves and spices for cloth.

[32] For an account of the development of banking and the use of bills of exchange see Spufford, *Handbook*, pp. xxvi–l.

[33] Spufford, *Handbook*, p. xxxviii.

[34] Merchants could transfer from different banks in Genoa as early as the end of the twelfth century. By the early fourteenth century Florence was reputed to have as many as eighty banks (Spufford, *Handbook*, p. xxviii).

deposited for a certain length of time, so allowing its use by the banker, who was not then in danger of having the depositor withdraw his money for some time. This enabled bankers to invest in long-term trade ventures. Together with the banking system, there developed the use of the cheque.

The banking system developed more slowly outside Italy but was clearly functioning in much of western Europe in the early fourteenth century, although it remained throughout the fourteenth and fifteenth centuries restricted to certain commercial centres and its use was restricted to a small percentage of the population. Coin remained the major factor in economic exchange.

Apart from the development of a local banking system, there was a contemporaneous and analogous development of an international banking system which clearly had significant implications for the conduct of international trade. The development of the bill of exchange 'revolutionised' international trade in the thirteenth century and by the first half of the fourteenth century this system was commonly used between many cities of western Europe.[35] By combining local and international banking, a merchant was able to buy a bill of exchange by debiting one bank account in one country and crediting another in a different country.

Under the system of a bill of exchange a merchant in Genoa, for example, could remit money for goods in Avignon by paying the amount required in Genoa to a drawer or taker who drew up the bill which the merchant then sent to his fellow merchant in Avignon. There the other merchant presented the bill to the payer who acted as agent for the drawer of the bill in Genoa. Settlement of the bill had to be made within a fixed time, *usance*, the length of which varied according to custom. The charge for a bill of exchange varied, up to 5 per cent of the amount involved being commonly charged.

This system operated extensively in northern Italy, also functioning in commercial centres in southern Italy, France, Spain, England, the Netherlands and southern Germany. By the fifteenth century it was also possible to use bills of exchange in Prague, Krakow and Buda.

While it is true that as one moves east bills of exchange become less prolific, the system still operated and there were bills of exchange between Italy and Constantinople.[36] Letters of exchange were not always without

---

[35] Its early development can be seen in Genoa at the end of the twelfth century (Spufford, *Handbook*, p. xxxi).

[36] For example see 1438.xii.18 = Badoer, *Libro*, col. 241, p. 484, col. 234, p. 471; 1437.ix.18 = *ibid.*, col. 89, p. 180, col. 101, p. 205, 1437.ix.20 = *ibid.*, col. 89, p. 180, col. 29, p. 59 (from Venice); 1437.ix.16 = *ibid.*, col. 105, p. 212, col. 104, p. 211 (from Venice); 1437.ix.16 = *ibid.*, col. 105, p. 212, col. 104, p. 211 (from Venice); 1437.ix.16 = *ibid.*, col. 105, p. 212, col. 105, p. 213 (from Venice); 1437.ix.16 = *ibid.*, col. 105, p. 212, col. 89, p. 181 (from Venice); 1437.ix.16 = *ibid.*, col. 105, p. 212, col. 105, p. 213; 1437.ix.18 = *ibid.*, col. 105, p. 212, col. 101, p. 205 (from Venice); 1437.ix.26 = *ibid.*, col. 105, p. 212, col. 101, p. 205 (from Venice); 1437.ix.18 = *ibid.*, col. 90, p. 182, col. 105, p. 213 (to Venice); 1437.x.23 = *ibid.*, col. 129, p. 260, col. 105, p. 213 (to Venice); 1437.xi.13 = *ibid.*, col. 133, p. 268, col. 105, p. 213 (to

problems for sometimes the receivers refused to accept them.[37] As the bill of exchange was used extensively in transactions between merchants in Constantinople and city states such as Venice, it would seem unexpected if western merchants, accustomed to a system of letters of credit, did not adopt this system, at least on occasion, in their dealings with their own agents in cities in Turchia such as Bursa and Edirne. This, in fact, seems to have been the case. In 1437 Dimitri Argiti of Candia (Crete) travelled to Gelibolu taking with him 'un scrito' for 1,177 *aspers* which he delivered to Agustin di Franchi, a merchant trading there.[38] Dimitri Argiti also took 3,000 *aspers* to Gelibolu.[39] Although it is not stated that this was in the form of a letter of credit, it seems possible that in fact it was, for the wording of one of the two entries concerning the 1,177 *aspers* is simply 'per asp.1177 che Mandì' while that for the 3,000 *aspers* is 'per l'amontar de asp.3000 che i mandì'. In the same year a letter of credit was sent for 1,200 Turkish *aspers* to Bortolamio de Modena in Gelibolu[40] and Agustin di Franchi took 1,593 *aspers* to Gelibolu to settle with Aluvixe di Franchi a letter of exchange which Aluvixe had paid, in Giacomo Badoer's name, to the Jew Süleyman ('Sulaiman zudio').[41] In 1438 payment was to be made to Zuan Andrea and Jachomo de Chanpi for a letter of credit to Bortolamio di Franchi in Edirne.[42]

Venice); 1436.ix.18 = *ibid.*, col. 47, p. 94, col. 106, p. 215 (from Venice) 1438.x.8 = *ibid.*, col. 250, p. 502, col. 231, p. 465.

[37] 1439.iii.20 = Badoer, *Libro*, col. 266, p. 534, col. 320, p. 643, a letter of credit was not accepted in Venice; 1438.ii.3 = *ibid.*, col. 292, p. 586, col. 382, p. 767, an entry for 'una letera de chanbio' which Franzesco Trivixan did not wish to accept. 1408.viii.22 = ASG, Notaio, Giovanni Balbi, Sc. 46, filza 1, doc. 369, a 'littera pagamenti' was written concerning a certain number of *hyperpyra* given in Pera in exchange for 60 Turkish *ducats*, to be settled in Chios. When the letter was presented in Chios to the payer, he refused to accept it.

[38] 1437.iii.31 = Badoer, *Libro*, col. 125, p. 252, col. 204, p. 411: 'Dimitri Argiti de Chandia diè aver a dì 31 mazo per el viazo da Garipoli rechomandà a Agustin di Franchi, per un scrito de asp.1177 ch'el me fexe a dover chonsignar in Garipoli al dito Agustin, val a asp.11 el perparo'. Agustin di Franchi appears several times in the accounts for this year in connection with Gelibolu: 1437.x.9 = *ibid.*, col. 125, p. 252, col. 92, p. 187; 1437.iii.13 = *ibid.*, col. 55, p. 111; 1438.ix.18 = *ibid.*, col. 65, p. 131.

[39] 1438.iii.31 = Badoer, *Libro*, col. 125, p. 252, col. 186, p. 375.

[40] 1437.iv.30 = Badoer, *Libro*, col. 55, p. 110: 'per ser Charlo Chapel dal bancho per asp.1200 turchi ch'el dè per mio nome a ser Franzesco di Drapieri per una letera de chanbio che me mandò a pagar Bortolamio da Modena da Garipoli per altratanti asperi ch'el rezevè in Garipoi da Jeronimo da ... fator del dito ser Franzesco, val a asp.11 t.1 1/1 a perparo'.

[41] 1437.ix.2 = Badoer, *Libro*, col. 125, p. 252: 'per Charlo Chapelo dal bancho per l'amontar de asp.1593 ch'el sorascrito ser Agustin me mandò a pagar per una letera de chandio a miser Aluvixe di Franchi, val a asp.11, mancho t.51/1 a perpero', *ibid.*, col. 231, p. 465: 'per el viazo de Garipoli rechomandà a Agustin di Franchi, per l'amontar de asp.1593 che per mio nome el dè a miser Aluvixe di franchi per un chanbio da Garipoli val a asp. 11 mancho t. 5 a perparo, chome el tolse da Sulaiman zudio per mio nome.'

[42] 1438.xii.3 = Badoer, *Libro*, col. 233, p. 468: 'per ser Zuan Andrea e ser Jachomo da Chanpi, che fixi prometer al dito, hover al suo chomeso, per una letera che scrisi ai diti in Andrenopolli', *ibid.*, col. 234, p. 471: 'Ser Jachomo e Zuan Andrea da Chanpi diè aver a dì 3 dizenbre per ser Bortolamio di Franchi, per una promesa che i scrisi che i dovese far al dito ser Bortolamio, hover al suo chomeso'.

Various methods of payment were thus used by Genoese and other western merchants in their commercial transactions with the Turks. Apart from cash and bartering, credit and letters of exchange became increasingly important and by the 1460s credit had come to play an important role in the commerce of Bursa.[43]

[43] Halil İnalcık, 'Sources for fifteenth-century Turkish economic and social history', in Halil İnalcık, *The Middle East and the Balkans under the Ottoman Empire. Essays on Economy and Society*, Indiana University Turkish Studies and Turkish Ministry of Culture Joint Series, Volume 9 (Bloomington, 1993), p. 181.

CHAPTER 3

Commodities

From the early beginnings of the Ottoman state to the capture of Constantinople in 1453, Turchia was an area of intense commerce, one facet of
which was the trading activity of the western merchants, among whom the
Genoese and Venetians held a dominant position. The exchange of goods
consisted broadly of the export of raw materials from Turchia and the
import into the area of luxury items, although Turchia did produce and
export quality products of its own, such as worked cloth. At the same time,
Turchia acted as a transit market for eastern luxuries such as silks and
spices.

The Genoese were extremely active in the trade in Turchia, not merely
coming into the coastal ports from which the goods were exported, such as
Theologos and Balat (Palatia), but placing their own agents in such
commercial centres as Bursa, Edirne, Gelibolu and Samsun.[1]

The Turks, although appearing by name much less often in the sources,
were also active. At the end of the fourteenth century the İsfendiyar ruler
Süleyman Paşa was trading copper with the Genoese.[2] In the same period a
Turkish trader sold alum to a Genoese official in Chios.[3] At the beginning
of the next century, Hacı Mustafa traded copper in Chios[4] and Katib Paşa
sold cotton to Genoese merchants there.[5] In the 1430s Ahmed of Licomedia
(?Nicomedia, Izmit) bartered grapes for cloth,[6] Ramadan of Samsun, Ali

---

[1] For example Piero Palavexin in Bursa and Polo Moroson in Samsun, 1439.vii.8 = Badoer,
  Libro, col. 325, p. 652; 1437.xii.18 = *ibid.*, col. 44, p. 89.
[2] 1390.i.11 = ASG, Notario, Donato de Clavaro, c. 476, doc. 26. See appendix 5, document 3
  below.
[3] 1394.ii.18 = ASG, Notaio, Donato de Clavaro, Sc. 39, filza 1, doc. 97/240.
[4] 1404.xii.31 = ASG, Notaio, Gregorio Panissario, Sc. 37, filza 1, doc. 48; Paola Piana
  Toniolo, *Notai Genovesi in Oltremare. Atti Rogati a Chio da Gregorio Panissaro (1403–1405)*
  (Genoa, 1995), doc. 52, p. 105.
[5] 1414.iv.2 = ASG, Notai, Giovanni Balbi, Sc. 46, filza 1, doc. 286. See appendix 5, document
  11 below.
[6] 1436.i.14 = Badoer, *Libro*, col. 42, p. 84, col. 13, p. 27; 1436.i.14 = *ibid.*, col. 43, p. 86, col. 42,
  p. 85. There is a further entry concerning one *hyperpyron* to be paid to Ahmed, presumably in
  connection with the same transaction. 1436.i.19 = *ibid.* col. 42, p. 84, col. 16, p. 33.

Basa (Paşa), Chazi Rastan (Kadı), Choza Ise (Hoca Isa)[7] and Mustafa all sold wax.[8] In the same period a Turk called Saliet, Ismail and an unnamed Turk traded in crepe ('veli crespi') and Chazi Musi turcho (Kadı Musa) in muslin ('veli').[9]

As well as selling, Turks also bought commodities from westerners. In 1436 Jael, factor for Choza Muxalach (Hoca Mu'ala'), bought a large quantity of Florentine cloth, paying the very considerable sum of 1,625 hyperpyra 23 karati.[10] He purchased the cloth by bartering spices and incense.[11] The following year an unnamed Turk bought glassware ('bocha-leti').[12] Apart from trading, Turks earned money from western merchants in other ways. In 1437 a Turk called Jacsia (?Yahya) acted as a porter ('charatier') for hides bought in Edirne.[13]

Turchia was not merely a market to which western merchants came to sell their goods and ship their purchases home; they also bought western imports which they then traded elsewhere in the region, as was done, for example, in 1437 when goods bought in Samsun were taken to Trabzon and sold there.[14]

Certain commodities appear to have been dominant in Genoese–Turkish trade. Thus alum, cloth, grain and slaves in particular were commodities of major importance in the commerce between Turchia and the western states. Other items formed part of this commerce but have left fewer traces in the extant documentation. Among them was soap, a luxury commodity in the trade between the west Mediterranean and the Levant. Its manufacture dates back to Roman times when the process used in its production was

---

[7] The Ottoman term *hoca* in this period meant a merchant of importance, a patron, İnalcık, 'Sources', p. 183.

[8] 1437.vi.6 = Badoer, *Libro*, col. 71, p. 144, col. 36, p. 73 (Ramadan of Samsun); 1438.iv.31 = *ibid.*, col. 190, p. 382, col. 194, p. 391 (Ali Basa). In another entry concerning Ali Paşa and the sale of wax he appears on one page as Alì Basia and on the other as Choza (Koca) Alì: 1438.iv.31 = *ibid.*, col. 194, p. 390, col. 186, p. 375; 1438.xi.4 = *ibid.*, col. 200, p. 202, col. 200, p. 240, col. 231, p. 465 (Chazi Rastan); 1438.iv.26 = *ibid.*, col. 190, p. 382, col. 186, p. 375 (Choza Ise). The name is spelt 'Ise' in the first entry and 'Isse' in the second; 1438.iv.26 = *ibid.*, col. 190, p. 382, col. 186, p. 375 (Mustafa). The name is written with an accent, Mustafà, as is the name Alì. This presumably was a guide to how they were pronounced, with the stress falling on the final syllable, as it does in modern Turkish.

[9] 1436.ix.10 = Badoer, *Libro*, col. 7, p. 14, col. 8, p. 17; 1436.x.10 = *ibid.*, col. 22, p. 45; 1437.iii.24 = *ibid.*, col. 48, p. 96, col. 52, p. 105, (Saliet); 1437.viii.20 = *ibid.*, col. 88, p. 178, col. 68 (*bis*), p. 139 (Ismail); 1436.vii.8 = *ibid.*, col. 48, p. 96, col. 68 (*bis*), p. 139 (unnamed Turk); 1436.viii.20 = *ibid.*, col. 29, p. 58, col. 68 (*bis*), p. 139 (Chazi Musi turcho).

[10] 1436.x.25 = Badoer, *Libro*, col. 27, p. 54, col. 12, p. 25.

[11] 1436.x.10 = Badoer, *Libro*, col. 26, p. 52, col. 27, p. 55; 1436.xi.10 = *ibid.*, col. 13, p. 26, col. 26, p. 53.

[12] 1437.x.4 = Badoer, *Libro*, col. 88, p. 178, 'per veri case 4', col. 68, p. 137: 'per casa per el trato de una casa ne la qual iera bochaleti 500, venduda a un turcho perp.28'.

[13] 1437.iv.30 = Badoer, *Libro*, col. 56, p. 112, col. 36, p. 73: 'per agozo de pele 300, che pexò chant. 14, a asp. 5 per chanter'.

[14] 1437.xii.18 = Badoer, *Libro*, col. 152, p. 306, col. 152, p. 307.

described by Pliny the Elder.[15] In the fourteenth century, good soap for trade to the Levant had to be supple and made in small pieces while the boxes in which it came had to be so small that there were three to a *migliaro*.[16] Nearly 200 years later, Venetian soap was still preferred to that produced in Anatolia, which, being made of tallow (*sego*), was not good. For this reason Turkish women washed their cloths with Venetian soap.[17]

Soap was traded into the Levant[18] by western merchants who brought it from Venice, Ancona, Gaeta, Messina and Apulia, Cyprus and Rhodes to the markets of Constantinople and Pera,[19] of Chios,[20] Mytilene[21] and Lesser Armenia.[22] The Mamluks sought after it and it was sold in the markets of Alexandria.[23] In Anatolia, the Genoese were active in importing soap into Theologos,[24] from Naples,[25] Gaeta[26] and Chios,[27] and into Balat.[28] The Venetians too traded soap into Aydın[29] and it was sold in

---

[15] Pliny the Elder, *Natural History*, Loeb Classical Library (Cambridge, Mass., 1942), bk. 28, ch. 51, para. 191.

[16] 1345.v.26 = Pignol Zucchello, *Lettere di Mercanti a Pignol Zucchello (1336–1350)*, ed. Raimondo Morozzo della Rocca, Comitato per la Pubblicazione delle Fonti Relative alla Storia di Venezia, Fonti per la Storia di Venezia, Sez. IV, Archivi Privati (Venice, 1957), no. 15, p. 38: 'El savone che mandate sì fate che sieno di buona sorte e fate che le piache sieno sotigli e picciole e che le chasse sieno sì picciole che ne vada .III. per migliaro'.

[17] Bassano, *Costumi et i modi particolari della vita de'Turchi: ristampa fotomecanica dell'edizione originale – Roma, 1545*, ed. F. Babinger (Monaco di Baviera, 1963), p. 22.

[18] Soap was one of the items traded by the Venetian merchant Pignol Zucchello: 1345.v.15 = Zucchello, *Lettere*, no. 14, p. 34; 1344.iii.19 = *ibid.*, no. 8, p. 22; 1345.v.26 = *ibid.*, no. 15, pp. 37, 38; 1345.x.4 = *ibid.*, no. 16, p. 41 and 1345.x.5 = *ibid.*, no. 17, p. 42 (same soap); 1345.x.5 = *ibid.*, no. 18, p. 43; 1345.x.27 = *ibid.*, no. 19, p. 45.

[19] Francesco Balducci Pegolotti, *Fr Balducci Pegolotti, La Pratica della Mercature*, ed. A. Evans, The Medieval Academy of America 24 (Cambridge, Mass., 1936), p. 33; 1437.viii.23 = Badoer, *Libro*, col. 97, p. 196, col. 100, p. 203 (from Messina); 1437.viii.22 = *ibid.*, col. 96, p. 194, col. 97. p. 197 (also from Messina as the entry involves the same people as in the immediately preceding reference); 1437.ix.2 = *ibid.*, col. 119, p. 240, col. 97, p. 197 (from Gaeta); 1436.i.22 = *ibid.*, col. 43, p. 86, col. 16, p. 33, col. 17, p. 35 (from Ancona).

[20] 1349 (?) = Zucchello, *Lettere*, no. 67, p. 125 (Venetian soap).

[21] 1437 = Badoer, *Libro*, col. 96, p. 194, col. 97, p. 197 refers to a payment for soap, removed from a sack on a ship in Mytilene: 'a dì dito per saoni de raxon de ser Piero Michiel e Marin Barbo per l'amontar de peze 8 de saon ch'el me dise aver tolte de un sacho per far un prexente a Metelin, meto fose r 10, così d'avixo'.

[22] Pegolotti, *Pratica*, p. 59.

[23] Piloti, *L'Egypte au commencement du quinzième siècle d'après le traité d'Emmanuel Piloti de Crète (incipit 1420) avec une introduction et des notes par P-H Dopp* (Cairo, 1950), p. 20.

[24] 1377 = G. G. Musso, *Navigazione e commercio genovese con il Levante nei documenti dell'Archivio di Stato di Genova (secc. XIV–XV) con appendice documentaria a cura di Maria Silvia Jacopino* (Rome, 1975), pp. 169–70 (100 *kantars* of soap to Theologos).

[25] 1376.vi.22 = John Day, *Les Douanes de Gênes 1376–1377* (Paris, 1963), vols. I–II, vol. I, p. 271.

[26] 1377.iii.13 = ASG, Notai Ignoti, A, 7.1., doc. 99, published in Musso, *Navigazione*, pp. 232–3.

[27] 1394.ix.24 = ASG, Notaio, Donato de Clavaro, Sc. 39, filza 1, doc. 182; 1408.ii = Philip R. Argenti, *The Occupation of Chios by the Genoese and their Administration of the Island 1346–1566* (Cambridge, 1958), vols. I–III: vol. I, p. 422.

[28] Piloti, *L'Egypte*, p. 72.

[29] 1337.iii.9 = Zachariadou, *Trade and Crusade*, doc. 1337A, clause 7, p. 191; 1353.iv.7 = *ibid.*, doc. 1353A, clause 20, p. 214.

Antalya[30] and in Samsun where, in 1437, it fetched 205 *aspers* per *kantar*.[31] Calculating on an exchange rate of 19 *aspers* of Samsun per *hyperpyron*,[32] the soap sold in Samsun for 10.79 *hyperpyra* per *kantar*, comparable with what it would have fetched in Constantinople where in the same period soap from Ancona sold for 10 *hyperpyra* six *karati*,[33] that from Messina for 9.5 *hyperpyra* per *kantar*[34] and soap of unspecified origin at 10.5 *hyperpyra* per *kantar*.[35] Soap continued to be imported into the Ottoman empire into the sixteenth century.[36]

Soap was clearly a profitable item of trade, for in 1344 the merchant Francesco Bartolomei wrote from Chios to ask Pignol Zucchello in Venice to send him soap as he considered this commodity a good investment and one which, provided it was of good quality, he could do better with than any other.[37]

Being profitable, soap was, like any commodity, subject to plunder, as is attested by a surviving notarial document. In 1413 a settlement was organised between Vicencio Rubeo and Masimo Formica, arbitrators for Nani(?) de Paci, and Petro de Alticio, procurator for Lillio de Blaxio, part of which concerned forty-five cases of soap plundered by Petro de Laranda when on the ship of Johannes Alfirius(?) de Ancona, and forty boxes, also plundered by Petro, this time from Lillio's warehouse in Gelibolu.[38]

Soap was taxed on entry into the beylik of Aydın where, during the first part of the fourteenth century, the tax levied was either two gold *florins* per 23.5 *batman*[39] or per Cypriot *kantar*, if the soap was in a sack, or at the rate of one gold *florin* per *cassa*.[40] Aydın imposed a rate of two pieces of soap per *cassa* or two *stavrate*[41] in 1337[42] and 5 *çiliatos* (*gigliato*) per *cassa* in 1353.[43] Interestingly soap only appears as attracting a special customs rate in Aydın, no special rate being applied to it in the treaties between Venice and Menteşe or in extant documents from the reign of Mehmed II.

---

[30] Pegolotti, *Pratica*, pp. 57–8.
[31] 1437.xii.18 = Badoer, *Libro*, col. 44, p. 89.
[32] This rate is given by Badoer: 1437.xii.18 = Badoer, *Libro*, col. 44, p. 89. See also appendix 1 below for exchange ratios for Samsun *aspers* to *hyperpyron*.
[33] 1436.1.22 = Badoer, *Libro*, col. 43, p. 86.
[34] 1437.viii.23 = Badoer, *Libro*, col. 97, p. 196.
[35] 1437.viii.22 = Badoer, *Libro*, col. 96, p. 194.
[36] Bassano, *Costumi*, p. 22.
[37] 1344.iii.19 = Zucchello, *Lettere*, no. 8, p. 22.
[38] (?)1413.vi. = ASG, Notaio, Giovanni Balbi, Sc. 46, filza 1, doc. 69.
[39] According to Schilbach, the *batman* of Theologos differed in weight from that of Balat, the Theologos *batman* being equivalent to 9.993 kg, and the *batman* of Balat to 15.741 kg (Erich Schilbach, *Byzantinische Metrologie* (Munich, 1970), pp. 197–8). Zachariadou, however, suggests (*Trade and Crusade*, p. 152) that the weight was the same for both beyliks.
[40] Pegolotti, *Pratica*, p. 56. A *cassa* was a soap container used in the Black Sea region and Romania (Zachariadou, *Trade and Crusade*, p. 151).
[41] Professor Zachariadou has suggested that the *stavrate* was probably the *crocetto* of Pegolotti (*Trade and Crusade*, pp. 142–3).
[42] 1337.iii.9 = Zachariadou, *Trade and Crusade*, doc. 1337A, clause 7, p. 191.
[43] 1353.iv.7 = Zachariadou, *Trade and Crusade*, doc. 1353A, clause 20, p. 214.

Collection of the tax on soap was handled by tax farmers in the beyliks of Menteşe and Aydın. In the treaty of March 1337 between Menteşe and Crete a clause specified that if the emir of Aydın made peace with Venice but kept wine, alum and soap subject to *apalto*, then the emir of Menteşe, İbrahim, would make alum subject to *apalto* in Balat only.[44] The imposition of *apalto* on soap was, however, soon lifted for the Venetians.[45] It is presumably indicative of the importance of soap as an import that it was specifically mentioned in the treaties between Menteşe, Aydın and Crete, usually in conjunction with alum and wine.

Other luxury items were imported from the west into Turchia, including the aromatic gum, mastic, used for chewing and as a base for perfume,[46] which was produced only in Chios.[47] From there it was exported both to the west, being sold in Pisa in the early fourteenth century,[48] and to other parts of the eastern Mediterranean including Damascus and Alexandria.[49] Mastic sales in Turchia at the end of the fourteenth century were controlled by *apaltatores* of the Maona of Chios, a group of whom in 1394 bought for eight years control of the sales of 200 *kantars* annually in Turchia and Romania, for which they paid 25 gold *ducats* per *kantar*. They similarly controlled mastic sales in Egypt and Syria for ten years from January 1396, for an annual sale of 114 *kantars*, for the price of 190 gold *florins* per *kantar*. This indicates that Turchia and Romania were importing considerably more mastic than Egypt and Syria, and gives an idea of the price of mastic in Turkish markets in this period, for the mastic cannot have sold, at least under normal circumstances, for less than 25 *ducats* per *kantar*, and indeed should have sold for a price significantly more than this in order to make the deal attractive to the *apaltatores*.[50] Mastic was also imported by the Turks. In 1404 Cagi Mostaffa (Hacı Mustafa) bought thirteen boxes of mastic from Elias Sacerdotus to be handed over in Bergamo or Jasmati (?Çeşme).[51]

[44] 1337.pre–iv. = Zachariadou, *Trade and Crusade*, doc. 1337M, clause 28, pp. 199–200. This clause is repeated in the treaty of 1375 between Crete and Menteşe: 1375.iv.22 = *ibid.*, doc. 1375M, clause 28, p. 223. As it is a straight copy of the clause of the 1337 treaty, as are other clauses which are clearly no longer relevant, it seems probable that it is anachronistic and does not in fact reflect the situation in 1375.

[45] 1337.iii.9 = Zachariadou, *Trade and Crusade*, doc. 1337A, clause 11, p. 192 ; 1337.pre–iv. = *ibid.*, doc. 1337M, clause 22, p. 198; 1375.iv.22 = *ibid.*, doc. 1375M, clause 22, p. 222; 1403.vii.24 = *ibid.*, doc. 1403M, clause 22, p. 231 (doc.1403M DVL, clause 22, p. 231, uses the word *dacium* in place of *gabella*). 1407.vi.2 = *ibid.*, doc. 1407M, clause 22, p. 236 refers to no *amalium* on soap.

[46] Angeliki E. Laiou, *Constantinople and the Latins. The Foreign Policy of Andronikos II 1282–1328* (Cambridge, Mass., 1972), p. 149.

[47] Piloti, *L'Egypte*, pp. 71–2.

[48] Pegolotti, *Pratica*, p. 207. It sold there in the early part of the fourteenth century for four *soldi* per *centinaio*.

[49] Piloti, *L'Egypte*, p. 72. It sold there at the end of the fourteenth and beginning of the fifteenth centuries for 100 *ducats* per *cassa*.

[50] 1394.vi.17 = ASG, Notaio Donato de Clavaro, Sc.39, filza 1, doc. 224/299.

[51] 1404.xii.31 = ASG, Gregorio Panissario, sc.37, filza 1, doc. 49; Toniolo, *Notai Genovesi*, doc. 53, p. 106.

Other luxury items, such as gems, were traded round the eastern Mediterranean and brought into Turchia by western merchants. In 1439 a ruby weighing around 15 *karati* and valued at 100 *hyperpyra*, was sent to Edirne.[52] Some of this trade went through Chios, and gems leaving the island were placed under *gabella*.[53] Glass too was imported.[54]

Turchia was not just a market for imported luxuries; it also exported items such as spices. Antalya was a market for indigo, sold there by the *peso sotile*, henna, sold by the *calbano* (steelyard balance),[55] saffron and sesame.[56] The last two spices were exported from other parts of Turchia, including Alanya, Balat, where the Genoese were active in exporting these commodities, and Gelibolu.[57] The gum tragacanth too was exported from Antalya and 'draganti di Turchia' is listed in the manual of the Florentine merchant Francesco Balducci Pegolotti.[58] Tragacanth sold in Alexandria, Majorca and Venice.[59]

Antalya was also a market for pepper,[60] a commodity bought by the Genoese and other western merchants in various parts of Turchia and exported to cities in western Europe. Pepper from Theologos was imported into Genoa, where it was taxed on entry in 1377.[61] Pepper was also traded in Bursa[62] where it was sometimes bought by bartering. In 1439 Damian Spinola bought pepper there for Giacomo Badoer, bartering twenty-four sacks of canvas and five sacks of wool which had been sent to him for that purpose.[63] In 1437 Azi Baba, described variously as a Saracen ('sarain')[64] and as a Moor ('more'),[65] bartered five *kantar*s of pepper and musk for cloth valued at 717 *hyperpyra* 14 *karati*.[66] At other times pepper was bought with cash. In 1437 Elia Dedimari, a Jew, sold 20–25 *kantar*s of pepper to Antonio Contarini at 60 *hyperpyra* per *kantar* (5.45 *aspers*), for part of which sale he was to be paid 5,100 *aspers* (463 *hyperpyra* 15 *karati*).[67] These *aspers* were sent by Giacomo Badoer in Constantinople to Antonio

[52] 1439.ii.3 = Badoer, *Libro*, col. 199, p. 401, col. 386, p. 774.

[53] 1408.ii : Argenti, *Chios*, vol. I, p. 422. In 1381 there was a dispute involving pearls between merchants in Chios: 1381.ii.15 = ASG, Notario, Antonius Felani, C. 175, 110v–111r.

[54] E. Ashtor, *A Social and Economic History of the Near East in the Middle Ages* (London, 1976), p. 262.

[55] Pegolotti, *Pratica*, pp. 57–8.

[56] Piloti, *L'Egypte*, p. 60.

[57] Piloti, *L'Egypte*, pp. 60, 61, 62, 63, 73.

[58] Pegolotti, *Pratica*, pp. 294, 376.

[59] Pegolotti, *Pratica*, pp. 70, 123, 138.

[60] Pegolotti, *Pratica*, pp. 57–8. It was sold there by the *peso sotile*.

[61] 1377.viii.19 = Day, *Douanes*, vol. II, p. 928.

[62] 1436.xi.8 = Badoer, *Libro*, col. 33, p. 66, col. 33, p. 67; 1437.xii.28 = *ibid.*, col. 134, p. 270, col. 227, p. 457. There is a further entry connected with expense on the pepper: col. 134, p. 270, col. 290, p. 583.

[63] 1439.ii.26 = Badoer, *Libro*, col. 388, p. 778, col. 385, p. 773, col. 372, p. 747.

[64] 1437.xii.4 = Badoer, *Libro*, col. 148, p. 298.

[65] 1437.ix.17 = Badoer, *Libro*, col. 148, p. 299.

[66] 1437.xi.18 = Badoer, *Libro*, col. 148, p. 298, col. 111, p. 225, reading 'muscio' for 'musico'.

[67] 1437.viii.21 = Badoer, *Libro*, col. 93, p. 188, col. 92, p. 187. There is another entry for 19

Contarini in Bursa with orders that he should buy pepper.[68] There was a 1 per cent charge for the purchase of these *aspers* in Constantinople.[69]

There is some extant information for prices of pepper in Bursa in the late 1430s and on the expenses involved in purchase. Three prices are given by Badoer for 1436 and 1437 of 60, 63.3 and 69.5 *hyperpyra* per *kantar*, giving an average of 64.3 *hyperpyra*, which can presumably be used as a rough guide to pepper prices in this period. The expenses given for the same period were 4.5 per cent and 5 per cent of the purchase price, again a rough guide to what costs western merchants were likely to incur on pepper bought in Turchia.

In 1436 Christofal Bonifazio sent to Constantinople from Bursa 10 pounds (*pondi*) of pepper which he bought for 785 *aspers* (69.5 *hyperpyra*) per *kantar*. The gross weight of these sacks was 25 *kantars* 79 *rotoli*, the tare for the sacks was 82 *rotoli* and for dust at 1 per cent was 26, making a net weight of 24 *kantars* 71 *rotoli*. The expenses involved in the purchase were 16 *aspers* for cartage to his house, 10 *aspers* for storage, 100 *aspers* for ten sacks, 30 *aspers* for 15 ropes, 20 *aspers* for binding, 20 *aspers* for insurance ('siagardanà'), 40 *aspers* for weighing ('pexador'), eight *aspers* for the courier, and 75 *aspers* for cartage to the sea, 150 *aspers* for customs, 50 *aspers* for storage and provisions at 2 per cent, making 388 *aspers*. Thus the total expenses on pepper bought for 19,397 *aspers* were 907 *aspers*, or around 4.5 per cent.[70] The following year Christofal Bonifazio sent one pound (*pondo*) from Bursa, weighing 2 *kantars* 86 *rotoli* of Constantinople, 259 *rotoli* net weight of Bursa, costing 665 *aspers* per *kantar* (total of 1,722 *aspers*) to Constantinople. The expenses were 2 *karati* for sending the pepper from Bonifazio's house for weighing and back, 64 *aspers* (6 *hyperpyra*) for sending it to Constantinople, and 34 *aspers* (3.2 *hyperpyra*) for provisions. The total expenditure on the pepper purchased for 1,722 *aspers* (164 *hyperpyra*) was 98 *aspers* (173 *hyperpyra* 7 *karati*), or around 5 per cent.[71]

kantars 31 *rotoli* bought from Elia Dedimari by Giacomo Badoer, 1436.xi.15 = *ibid.*, col. 47, p. 94, col. 126, p. 255.

[68] 1437.vii.24 = Badoer, *Libro*, col. 47, p. 94, col. 92, p. 187.

[69] 1437.vii.24 = Badoer, *Libro*, col. 92, p. 186, col. 77, p. 157.

[70] 1436.xi.8 = Badoer, *Libro*, col. 33, p. 66, col. 33, p. 67. The *asper–hyperpyron* exchange rate is given as 11 *aspers* 4 *tornexi* to 1 *hyperpyron*. There are several other entries under the same date for pepper from Bursa but it seems that they are dealing with the same pepper. One is for 5 pounds (*pondi*) of pepper, gross weight 13 *kantars* 90 *rotoli*, tare for sack and rope 30 *rotoli*, at 6 *rotoli* per sack, tare for dust 14 *rotoli* at 1 per cent, net weight 13 *kantars* 46 *rotoli*, bought in Bursa by Christofal Bonifazio at the same rate of 785 *aspers* per *kantar* (68 *hyperpyra* 22.5 *karati*) (1436.xi.8 = *ibid.*, col. 33, p. 66, col. 33, p. 67). A second entry is again for 5 pounds of pepper, this time specified as being from the 10 pounds sent from Bursa by Christofal Bonifazio, gross weight of 13 *kantars* 18 *rotoli*, tare of 30 *rotoli* for the sacks and cords at 6 *rotoli* per sack, and 13 *rotoli* for dust, making a net weight of 12 *kantars* 75 *rotoli*, selling at 785 *aspers* per *kantar* (68 *hyperpyra* 22.5 *karati*) (1436.xi.8 = *ibid.*, col. 18, p. 36, col. 33, p. 67.) The figures in the two separate entries for 5 sacks each of pepper add up to the combined figure for the 10 sacks.

[71] 1437.xii.28 = Badoer, *Libro*, col. 134, p. 270, col. 227, p. 457. There is a further entry connected with expense on the pepper: col. 134, p. 270, col. 290, p. 583.

Turchia was an area of horse breeding and among the commodities it exported was livestock. Marco Polo commented on the outstanding breed of horses called Turki and excellent mules found in Turkomania (Anatolia) which sold for high prices.[72] A vital military asset, horses were much prized in Turchia and given as gifts. Mehmed Aydınoğlu sent an excellent horse to ibn Battuta as a present and Umur Aydınoğlu presented Şeyh Izz al-Din with three horses, all harnessed.[73] The Germiyan ambassador to Murad I gave good horses as *peşkeş*, and horses, together with mules and camels, were sent to him from the *sancakbeyis*.[74]

Both the beyliks of Menteşe and Aydın exacted export taxes on livestock leaving their territories. Horses exported from Menteşe by the Venetians, and presumably by other western merchants, were charged at the rate of 3 *aspers* per animal, and pack horses, asses or mules at 2 *aspers* per beast, the same rate being levied on cattle.[75] In Aydın too there was an export tax imposed on livestock exported by western merchants.[76]

Both the Genoese on Cyprus and the Venetians on Crete looked to Turchia as a source of horses. A supply of horses was important to Crete where, in 1356, the Venetian senate granted a total exemption from tax on all imports of horses and other beasts.[77] Venice assigned money to the authorities on the island for the purchase of horses, increasing the amount of money assigned for this in 1333 from 2,000 *hyperpyra* to 4,000 *hyperpyra* with instructions that the entente with the Ottoman ruler Orhan over the import into Crete of horses and corn was to be handled by the Cretan authorities.[78] In 1363 the Cretan authorities sought to have the 500 *hyperpyra* allocated to buying horses in Turchia increased to 1,000 *hyperpyra*, as 500 *hyperpyra* was considered insufficient.[79] The numbers bought could be fairly large. In 1383 there was a proposal in Cyprus to buy 200 horses from Anatolia (probably from Karaman)[80] and in the early 1360s the authorities on Crete bought 500 horses from Turchia.[81]

The Turks were not always willing to export their horses. In 1365 the Hospitallers were forced, due to Turkish annoyance over the capture of

[72] Marco Polo, *The Travels of Marco Polo*, trans. Aldo Ricci, with introduction and index by Sir E. Dennison Ross (London 1931), p. 50. While admiring the horses, Marco Polo was not so impressed by the people. They were, he said, 'a primitive people and dull of intellect'.

[73] ibn Battuta, *Voyages*, vol. II, pp. 302, 307, 311.

[74] Aşıkpaşazade, *Altosmanische Chronik*, p. 52, 53; Aşıkpaşazade, *Tevarih-i al-i 'Osman*, pp. 56, 57; Neşri, (*Menzel, Cod.*), pp. 55, 56; Neşri, *Kitab-ı Cihan-nüma*, pp. 204, 206.

[75] 1331.iv.13 = Zachariadou, *Trade and Crusade*, doc. 1331M, clause 3, p. 187; 1337.pre–iv. = *ibid.*, doc. 1337M, clause 20, p. 198; 1375.iv.22 = *ibid.*, doc. 1375M, clause 20, p. 222; 1403.vii.24 = *ibid.*, doc. 1403M, doc. 1403M DVL, clause 20, p. 230; 1407.vi.2 = *ibid.*, doc. 1407M, clause 20, p. 236.

[76] 1353.iv.7 = Zachariadou, *Trade and Crusade*, doc. 1353A, clause 19, p. 214.

[77] 1356.vii.7 : Thiriet, *Régestes*, vol. I, doc. 300, pp. 82–3.

[78] 1333.xi.16 : Thiriet, *Régestes*, vol. I, doc. 38, pp. 30–1.

[79] 1363.vi.8 : Thiriet, *Régestes*, vol. I, doc. 410, pp. 106–7.

[80] 1383.viii.1 = ASG, Notario, Giovanni Bardi, C. 381, fos. 148r–151r.

[81] 1363–5 = Andraea Naugerii, 'Historia Veneta', in *RIS*, vol. XXIII, col.1049.

Alexandria that year by King Peter of Cyprus, to buy horses in Apulia rather than Turchia.[82] Some years later the Venetians sent an ambassador to the emir of Theologos to try and persuade him to reconsider his restriction on the trade in these animals.[83]

Apart from livestock, Turchia also exported skins and hides, which, in Menteşe and Aydın, were not, for the Venetians, to be placed under *apalto*.[84] It seems that there was some sort of restriction in Menteşe over the sale of tanned hides (*pellamen*) and leather (*corame*), for permission was granted to Venetians trading there to buy them in the territories and markets of Menteşe, and not merely from the butchers.[85] The Genoese too traded in hides, exporting tanned leather from Balat.[86] Tanned leather and goatskin (*pele de chastron*) were exported from Gelibolu,[87] and sheepskin (*montonine*) and leather (*chordoani*) from Bursa and Edirne.[88] Goatshide was produced in Anatolia and goats' hair, which sold well in Turchia, was used by the Turks to make cloths and ropes for their Arab horses.[89] Named Turkish merchants occasionally appear in the sources trading in hides with western merchants. In 1438 Azi (?Aziz), a Turk, sold to Jeronimo Badoer 800 'pele de chastron de Mar Mazor crude' for 16 *hyperpyra* per *kantar*.[90]

Turks were also involved in other capacities in the trade in hides, acting for example as carriers. In 1437 a Turk called Jascia (?Yahya), a carrier, was involved with Sulia dal Mistrini, also described as a carrier, in the sale to an agent of Badoer of 20 bales of sheepskin ('pelle de chastron'), containing 1,000 hides, for which Sulia received, for carterage of 700 hides, weighing 33 *kantars*, at 5 *aspers* per *kantar*, 14 *hyperpyra* 21 *kantars*,[91] and Jascia, for

[82] 1365.xii.4, Anthony Luttrell, 'The Hospitallers of Rhodes Confront the Turks: 1306–1421' in Philip F. Gallagher (ed.), *Christians, Jews and Other Worlds. Patterns of Conflict and Accommodation*, (New York, London, 1988), p.113, n. 55, citing the archives in Malta.

[83] 1400.viii.19 : Thiriet, *Régestes*, vol. I, doc. 988, pp. 12–13.

[84] 1337.iii.9 = Zachariadou, *Trade and Crusade*, doc. 1337A, clause 11, p. 192; 1337.pre–iv. = *ibid.*, doc. 1337M, clause 22, p. 198; 1375.iv.22 = *ibid.*, doc. 1375M, clause 22, p. 222; 1403.vii.24 = *ibid.*, doc. 1403M, clause 22, p. 231; 1407.vi.2 = *ibid.*, doc. 1407M, clause 22, p. 236.

[85] 1331.iv.13 = Zachariadou, *Trade and Crusade*, doc. 1331M, clause 14, p. 189;

[86] Piloti, *L'Egypte*, p. 73.

[87] Piloti, *L'Egypte*, pp. 62, 63. 1438.xi.26 = Badoer, *Libro*, col. 277, p. 556, col. 197, p. 397. In 1438, seventy 'pele bianche' from Gelibolu were exported from Constantinople.

[88] 1438.xi.4 = Badoer, *Libro*, col. 277, p. 556, col. 266, p. 535, (one bale of 'montonine bianche' was sold in Bursa and six bales in Edirne); 1438.x.14 = *ibid.*, col. 154, p. 310, col. 266, p. 535, (fourteen bales of 'montonine bianche' were sent to Constantinople from Bursa); 1438.xii.22 = *ibid.*, col. 306, p. 615, ('montonine e chordani vermei abude de Adrenopoli'); 1439.ii.26 = *ibid.*, col. 414, p. 830, col. 367, p. 737, ('montonine bianche' sold in Edirne); 1439.ix.20 = *ibid.*, col. 358, p. 718, col. 234, p. 471, (1,000 'montonine' sold in Edirne, cost, including expenses, 3,176.5 *aspers* (310 *hyperpyra*)).

[89] Pegolotti, *Pratica*, p. 379.

[90] 1438.iii.7 = Badoer, *Libro*, col. 196, p. 394, col. 186, p. 375.

[91] 1438.iv.30 = Badoer, *Libro*, col. 56, p. 112, col. 3, p. 7. The *asper–hyperpyron* exchange was 11 *aspers* 2 *tornexi* to 1 *hyperpyron*.

carterage of 300 hides, weighing 14 *kantars*, at 5 *aspers* per *kantar*, 6 *hyperpyra* 7 *karati*.[92]

From Badoer's accounts it is possible to build up some guide to prices of hides sold in Turchia in the late 1430s. These were on average around 3.5 *aspers* per piece for sheepskin (*montonine*) and around 10 *aspers* for leather (*chordoani*). Sheepskins sold in 1437 for 4 *aspers* each, the price including unspecified expenses to bring them to Constantinople,[93] 4 *aspers* each,[94] the same rate in Bursa,[95] and 3 *aspers* each.[96] The following year sheepskins were sold in Bursa for 3.5, 3.25, and 3 *aspers* each.[97] In 1438, 584 white sheepskins were sold in Edirne for 3 *aspers* (2.85 *hyperpyra*) each.[98] In the same year Pipo de Jachomo bought various amounts of sheepskin in Turchia, possibly in Edirne,[99] paying 3.75 *aspers* (0.28 of a *hyperpyron*) each for red sheepskin[100] and 3 *aspers* (2.85 *hyperpyra*) each in Edirne for white sheepskin.[101] Leather was more expensive, selling for 9 aspers per piece in Edirne,[102] with red leather fetching 11.5 *aspers* per piece.[103] Goatskin (*pele de chastron*) was slightly cheaper than sheepskin (*montonine*), selling in 1437 for 2 *aspers* each.[104]

Badoer's accounts also give an idea of the expenses incurred by western merchants buying and exporting hide from Ottoman territories. These were, on average, in the region of 13 per cent of the purchase price. In 1438, 2,075 sheepskins were bought in Bursa by Christofal Bonifazio for 6,571 *aspers*, being sold at 3.5, 3.25 and 3 *aspers* each, and sent from there to

---

[92] 1438.iv.30 = Badoer, *Libro*, col. 56, p. 112, col. 36, p. 73. The *asper–hyperpyron* exchange was 11 *aspers* 1.5 *tornexi* to one *hyperpyron*.

[93] 1437.iii.16 = Badoer, *Libro*, col. 61, p. 122, col. 57, p. 115. The *asper–hyperpyron* exchange rate was 100:9.

[94] 1437.iii.16 = Badoer, *Libro*, col. 61, p. 122, ('montonine vermeie'). The *asper–hyperpyron* exchange rate was 100:9.

[95] 1437.vii.23 = Badoer, *Libro*, col. 61, p. 122, col. 33, p. 67 ('montonine vermeie'). The exchange rate was 11:1.

[96] 1437.iii.16 = Badoer, *Libro*, col. 61, p. 122, col. 57, p. 115, ('montonine bianche chonza de foia solamente'). The *asper–hyperpyron* exchange rate, although not given here, was 100:9 for the total of 30 *aspers* is given as the equivalent of 2 *hyperpyra* 17 *karati*.

[97] 1438.ix.18 = Badoer, *Libro*, col. 266, p. 534, col. 225, p. 453.

[98] 1438.x.20 = Badoer, *Libro*, col. 266, p. 534, col. 232, p. 467.

[99] That his purchases were made in Turchia is clear from the exchange rate given for *aspers* (10.5:1), this being the rate of exchange for Turkish *aspers*. Other entries for goods sent by Pipo de Jachomo at the same date place him in Edirne. He may therefore well have bought the hides and leather there, although this is not specified in the text.

[100] 1438.viii.18 = Badoer, *Libro*, col. 197, p. 396, col. 230, p. 462. The *asper–hyperpyron* exchange rate was 10.5:1.

[101] 1438.x.20 = Badoer, *Libro*, col. 266, p. 534, col. 230, p. 463. The *asper–hyperpyron* exchange rate was 10.5:1.

[102] 1438.viii.18 = Badoer, *Libro*, col. 197, p. 396, col. 230, p. 462.

[103] 1437.iii.16 = Badoer, *Libro*, col. 61, p. 122, col. 57, p. 115. The *asper–hyperpyron* exchange rate was 100:9. The entry of col. 57, p. 115 gives an incorrect total.

[104] 1438.iv.30 = Badoer, *Libro*, col. 56, p. 112, col. 17, p. 35. The sale consisted of 20 bales of 'pelle de chastron', containing 1,000 hides.

Constantinople.[105] The expenses incurred by Bonifazio in Bursa were 103 *aspers* for transporting them to his house, for tying them and for rope, 75 *aspers* for carterage at the rate of 10 *aspers* per *soma*, 248 *aspers* for weighing ('peazo') and customs at 35 *aspers* per *soma*, 60 *aspers* for storage at 4 *aspers* per *tango*, and 131 *aspers* and for provisions at 2 per cent. Thus the total expenses were 617 *aspers* on a purchase price of 6,571 *aspers*, (652.8 *hyperpyra*) or 9.4 per cent.

On top of this figure should be added other expenses involved in transporting the hides to Constantinople. The freightage charged for 3 *tangi* of sheepskins, made up of 450 skins, and transported by Statopira, a boatman ('barcharuol'), was 1 *hyperpyron* 18 *karati*.[106] The freightage charge for a further 5 *tangi*, consisting of 639 sheepskins, paid to Vasilicho, a boatman ('barcharuol'), was 2 *hyperpyra* 12 *karati*, and the cost of porterage ('chamali') was 8 *karati*. The cost of porterage for a further 6 *tangi*, sent by the boat ('barcha') of Manguzo, from Bursa, was 5 *karati*, while the freight charge for the remaining *tango* sent from Bursa on the boat ('gripo') of Piero 'varoter', and for porterage ('chamalo') was 13 *karati*.[107] Thus the total freightage costs for transporting 2,075 hides from Bursa to Constantinople was 5 *hyperpyra* 8 *karati* which, if added to the 617 *aspers* (58.76 *hyperpyra*, i.e. *c*.58 *hyperpyra* 18 *karati*) expended in Bursa makes a total expenditure of 64 *hyperpyra* which gives a total percentage expense charge of 9.8 per cent on an initial purchase of 6,571 *aspers* (652.8 *hyperpyra*).

The percentage figure from the same period for expenses on hide purchased in Edirne is considerably higher. In 1438 Pipo de Jachomo bought in Edirne 584 white sheepskins at 3 *aspers* each (2.85 *hyperpyra*), making a total of 1,752 *aspers* (166.86 *hyperpyra*).[108] The expenses on this purchase in Edirne were 4 *hyperpyra* 6 *karati* for freightage and porterage for six bales, 14 *hyperpyra* for provisions and 10 *hyperpyra* for 40 *pichi* of canvas, rope and tying the bales, for carriage to the port and onto the ship, making a total of 28 *hyperpyra* 6 *karati*[109] on a purchase of 1,752 *aspers* (166.86 *hyperpyra*), or *c*.17 per cent, which seems rather high.

In 1437 twenty bales of goatskin, containing 1,000 hides were sold at 2 *aspers* each, making a total of 2,000 *aspers*, and associated expenses were 87 *aspers* for porterage, tying and ropes, 40 *aspers* for brokerage (*sansaria*) at 1 per cent and provisions at 1 per cent, 24 *aspers* for weighing and 8 *aspers* for storage, a total for expenses of 159 *aspers* (14.3 *hyperpyra*). Other expenses were 19 *karati* for unloading at the warehouse and reloading on the boat

---

[105] 1438.ix.18 = Badoer, *Libro*, col. 266, p. 534, col. 225, p. 453.
[106] 1438.viii.7 = Badoer, *Libro*, col. 225, p. 452.
[107] 1438.ix.18 = Badoer, *Libro*, col. 225, p. 452, col. 227, p. 457. The *asper–hyperpyron* exchange rate was 10.5:1.
[108] 1438.x.20 = Badoer, *Libro*, col. 266, p. 534, col. 230, p. 463. The *asper–hyperpyron* exchange rate was 10.5:1.
[109] 1438.x.20 = Badoer, *Libro*, col. 266, p. 534, col. 232, p. 467.

('barcha'), and 6 *hyperpyra* 18 *karati* for port entrance and taxes to the Greeks, making a total of 7 *hyperpyra* 13 *karati*.[110] Total expenses were thus 21.8 *hyperpyra* on a total purchase price of 2,000 *aspers* (180 *hyperpyra*) or 12 per cent in line with the percentage expenses in Bursa in the following year.

There are also instances of the export from Turchia of horse and cattle hides.[111] In 1437 one of the commodities bought by Antonio da Negroponte in Samsun was thirty-three pieces of tanned oxhide, which cost 714 *aspers* (37.57 *hyperpyra*) and which he resold in Trabzon at 65 and 75 *aspers* of Trabzon per piece, making a total of 1,708 *aspers* (42.7 *hyperpyra*).[112] Before expenses Antonio therefore made 5.13 *hyperpyra*, approximately 13.5 per cent. In 1438 Pipo de Jachomo sent fifteen oxhides from Turchia to Constantinople at a cost, including both purchase and transport expenses, of 22 *hyperpyra* 12 *karati*. If one calculates at approximately 13 per cent for expenses, the hides must have cost in the region of 19.6 *hyperpyra* or 1.3 *hyperpyra* per hide. In Constantinople they were valued at 1.5 *hyperpyra* each.[113] Other tanned oxhides in Constantinople sold in the same period for 1 *hyperpyron* 18 *karati* (1.75 *hyperpyra*).[114]

Furs too were exported from Gelibolu and into Constantinople,[115] from Stalimini[116] (Limni, Lemnos) and from Samsun where, in 1437, twenty-six marten and four tanned 'funie'(?) were bought for 445 *aspers* (23 *hyperpyra* 10 *karati*).[117] Samsun also exported hair. In 1437, 304 *dexena* of hair, at 22 *aspers* (1.15 *hyperpyra*) per *dexena*, were bought there by Antonio da Negroponte for a total of 680 *aspers* (35.78 *hyperpyra*) and then sold by him in Trabzon for 2,038 Trabzon *aspers* (50.95 *hyperpyra*,)[118] approximately 42 per cent more than its sale price in Samsun. If one judges roughly from the expenses incurred on hide, the expenses may have been in the region of 13 per cent of the purchase price, making the mark-up on the hair fairly high, at 29 per cent of the original purchase price. This must indicate either that it was an expensive commodity *per se*, which seems unlikely in a country that

---

[110] 1438.iv.30 = Badoer, *Libro*, col. 56, p. 112, col. 17, p. 35.
[111] Pegolotti, *Pratica*, p. 85 lists goods, including horse hides, from Turchia, Rhodes, Syria, Egypt and Armenia paying the *missa* tax in Cyprus.
[112] 1437.xii.18 = Badoer, *Libro*, col. 152, p. 306, col. 152, p. 307.
[113] 1438.x.20 = Badoer, *Libro*, col. 215, p. 432, col. 230, p. 463.
[114] 1438.vii.1 = Badoer, *Libro*, col. 215, p. 432.
[115] Piloti, *L'Egypte*, p. 62.
[116] 1398.i.10 = ASG, Notario, Giovanni Bardi, C. 382, fo. 45r.
[117] 1437.xi.28 = Badoer, *Libro*, col. 102, p. 206, col. 152, p. 307. The exchange rate given on col. 102 is 17 *aspers* of Samsun to 1 *hyperpyron* so the exchange should have been for 445 *aspers* 26.17 *hyperpyra*. A note in the text states that the original figure was 26 *hyperpyra* 4 *karati* and that it was corrected to 21 *hyperpyra* 10 *karati*. The usual exchange rate at this time was 19 *aspers* per *hyperpyron*, calculating by which 445 *aspers* would equal 23.42 *hyperpyra*. In fact the rate of 19:1 is given on col. 152.
[118] 1437.xii.18 = Badoer, *Libro*, col. 152, p. 306, col. 152, p. 307. The exchange rate of Samsun *aspers* per *hyperpyron* was 19:1, and for Trabzon *aspers* per *hyperpyron*, 40:1.

produced vast quantities of livestock and would thus have had large reserves of hair at its disposal or, much more likely, that it was sought after in Trabzon, where the terrain of the small state was not so suited to livestock rearing as were the lands of Turchia. The people of Trabzon may perhaps have used the hair, as the Turks did, for making ropes and coverings for horses.[119]

Another agricultural export from Anatolia was foodstuffs such as pulses which were sold in Antalya[120] and, together with grain, were charged an export tax for Venetians in Aydın of 4 per cent.[121] In Menteşe, Venetians paid on exported pulses at the rate of 1 *asper* per *modium* throughout the fourteenth and into the fifteenth centuries.[122] The Hospitallers too bought victuals in Anatolia.[123]

One commodity that was exported from Turchia was timber. There was a ship-building industry in Antalya and timber from there was exported to Cairo,[124] as was pitch ('pece'),[125] which sold in Antalya by the steelyard balance.[126] On occasion Turkish rulers banned the export of timber from their territories to the west for the emir of Theologos, despite granting freedom of trade to the Venetians in 1400, refused to extend this to timber.[127] In 1379 the pope granted the Hospitallers permission to import corn and other foodstuffs from Anatolia, provided that there was no timber traded in return.[128] This would seem to indicate that timber was sometimes imported into Turchia. However, this seems unlikely as the Hospitallers would hardly have been trading timber with their enemies, even in return for foodstuffs and, in any case, Turchia was an exporter of timber and so not likely to be in need of supplies from outside. The explanation may be that this phrase is merely a formula included in such types of papal permissions, but without meaning.

Wax was exported from Anatolia, from Theologos, where it was taxed on

---

[119] Pegolotti, *Pratica*, p. 379.

[120] Pegolotti, *Pratica*, pp. 57–8. They were sold there by the *moggio* and the *ghilla*.

[121] 1353.iv.7 = Zachariadou, *Trade and Crusade*, doc. 1353A, clause 19, p. 214: 'frumentum vel alia victualia vel legumina'.

[122] 1331.iv.13 = Zachariadou, *Trade and Crusade*, doc. 1331M, clause 3, p. 187; 1337.pre–iv. = *ibid.*, doc. 1337M, clause 20, p. 198; 1375.iv.22 = *ibid.*, doc. 1375M, clause 20, p. 222; 1403.vii.24 = *ibid.*, doc. 1403M, clause 22, p. 230; 1407.vi.2 = *ibid.*, doc. 1407M, clause 22, p. 236.

[123] Luttrell, 'Hospitallers', pp. 35, 113 and n. 55, citing the archives in Malta. That the Hospitallers exported foodstuffs from Turchia is shown by their difficulties in 1365 when, due to Turkish anger over the fall of Alexandria, they were forced to bring victuals from Apulia instead.

[124] Piloti, *L'Egypte*, p. 61. See also p. 73 where he talks of Rhodians going to Turchia to get timber which they took to Egypt, a trade which was by now no longer going on.

[125] Piloti, *L'Egypte*, p. 61.

[126] Pegolotti, *Pratica*, p. 34.

[127] 1400.viii.19 : Thiriet, *Régestes*, vol. II, doc. 988, p. 12.

[128] 1379.viii.6, Anthony Luttrell, 'Intrigue, Schism, and Violence among the Hospitallers of Rhodes: 1377–1384', *Speculum* 41 (1966), 35.

exit at 2 per cent,[129] and from Antalya where it was sold by the *peso sotile*.[130] At the end of the fourteenth and beginning of the fifteenth centuries it was exported from Anatolia, from Antalya, Alanya, Balat, and from the western parts of the empire, from Gelibolu and from Albania and Greece and Thessaloniki.[131] The Genoese were active in trading it from Balat[132] as were the Venetians, for whom wax was not placed in *apalto* in the beyliks of Menteşe and Aydın.[133] Some of the wax from Ottoman lands was shipped to Venice.[134] In 1381 a Genoese ship sailing from Theologos, and Alexandria and Beirut, carried wax as part of its cargo.[135] In 1402 wax was bought for Conradus de Pestino for Lodisius.[136] In 1437 Ramadan of Samsun sold 10 *kantar*s 57 *rotoli* gross of wax, tare for the sacks and ropes of 34 *rotoli*, 'tara de fondi' at 4.5 *rotoli* per *kantar*, a total of 45 *rotoli*, leaving a net weight of 19 *kantar*s 78 *rotoli* at 22.5 *hyperpyra* per *kantar*.[137] Wax was still being traded by western merchants after the fall of Constantinople, for Florentines were buying it in Bursa in the 1470s.[138]

As in the case of hides and pepper, the accounts of Badoer for the late 1430s enable one to gain a rough idea of expenses involved in the wax trade in Ottoman territories. In 1438 Agustin di Franchi bought 3 sacks of wax in Gelibolu for 1,369 *aspers* (124.45 *hyperpyra*). The expenses consisted of 6 *aspers* (0.5 of a *hyperpyron*) for cartage and weighing ('chamali e pexador'), 5 *aspers* (0.46 of a *hyperpyron*) for brokerage ('sansaria'), 23 *aspers* (2 *hyperpyra*) for sacks, ropes and bagging, 5 *aspers* (0.46 of a *hyperpyron*) for bribing the weighing official ('magnaria al pexador'), 26 *aspers* (2.36 *hyperpyra*) for the 2 per cent customs tax, 9 *aspers* (0.8 of a *hyperpyron*) for storage and 27 *aspers* (2.45 *hyperpyra*) for provisions at 2 per cent. The total expenses were thus 101 *aspers* (9.18 *hyperpyra*) on a purchase price of 1,369 *aspers* (124.45 *hyperpyra*), or 7.4 per cent, less than the apparent average for hide and slightly more than that for pepper in this period.[139]

While the accounts of Badoer give specific information for the late 1430s, similar information is apparently lacking for the earlier period. However,

[129] Pegolotti, *Pratica*, p. 56.
[130] Pegolotti, *Pratica*, pp. 57–8.
[131] Piloti, *L'Egypte*, pp. 60, 61, 62, 63, 69.
[132] Piloti, *L'Egypte*, p. 72.
[133] 1337.iii.9 = Zachariadou, *Trade and Crusade*, doc. 1337A, clause 11, p. 192; 1337.pre–iv. = *ibid.*, doc. 1337M, clause 22, p. 198; 1375.iv.22 = *ibid.*, doc. 1375M, clause 22, p. 222; 1403.vii.24 = *ibid.*, doc. 1403M, clause 22, p. 231; 1407.vi.2 = *ibid.*, doc. 1407M, clause 22, p. 236.
[134] 1438.iii.15 = Badoer, *Libro*, col. 195, p. 392, col. 191, p. 385.
[135] 1381.ii.15 = ASG, Notario, Antonius Feloni, C. 175, fos. 110v–111r.
[136] 1402.v.30 = ASG, San Giorgio, Sala 34 590/1306 (Peira Massaria), fo. 72v.
[137] 1437.vi.6 = Badoer, *Libro*, col. 71, p. 144, col. 48, p. 97.
[138] *Benedetto Dei, La Cronica dell'anno 1400 all'anno 1500*, ed.Roberto Barducci with preface by Anthony Molho (1990), p. 141.
[139] 1437.viii.5 = Badoer, *Libro*, col. 191, p. 384, col. 175, p. 353.

Badoer shows that items that do not appear in large numbers in other sources were being traded and were presumably bought and sold in similar quantities in the preceding century.

Certain commodities dominated the trade between the Turks and the western merchants. Of the exported commodities, the most significant were grain, slaves and alum while the most traded import was cloth.

CHAPTER 4

Slaves

The slave trade was of major importance in the eastern Mediterranean in the fourteenth and first half of the fifteenth centuries, with the main markets in the coastal towns of Anatolia, in Pera, on Crete, Chios, Cyprus, Rhodes and Naxos. Naxos in particular was an important slave market where Turks sold those they had captured in their raids which extended all over the Aegean.[1] The trade was not restricted to Anatolia and the islands but spread across the Mediterranean to Egypt and further to western Europe as far as Catalonia, with slaves from the markets of the eastern Mediterranean appearing in cities such as Genoa and Venice. Of the Latin merchants involved in this trade, the Genoese were extremely active,[2] channelling slaves from the Black Sea through to the Mamluk sultanate and largely dominating the slave trade in the eastern Mediterranean. The Venetians were also heavily involved, as were various other Latins such as merchants from other Italian cities, the Hospitallers, Catalans, Anconitans, merchants from Marseilles and other parts of France. The Turks too traded in slaves and Turchia had flourishing slave markets. However, the activities of the Turkish merchants could not be compared with those of the two main protagonists: Genoa and Venice.

Turchia appears to have had slave markets active from the beginning of the fourteenth century onwards. Various Venetian notarial deeds give enactments of slave sales conducted in Crete in the first part of the century in which the vendor had originally bought the slave in Turchia.[3] Menteşe

---

[1] C. Verlinden, 'Le recrutement des esclaves à Venise aux XIVe et XV siècles', *Bulletin de l'Institut Historique Belge de Rome* 39 (1968), 88.

[2] Several of the merchants trading in slaves in Constantinople in the 1430s were Genoese: Bernardo Bonavita, Baoder, *Libro*, col. 178, p. 358; Polo Doxia, *ibid.*, col. 49, p. 99, col. 135, p. 272; Lodovigo Guazego, *ibid.*, col. 135, p. 272; Paris Ganbon, *ibid.*, col. 288, p. 578.

[3] 1301.x.7: Verlinden, 'Recrutement', p. 86, Rugerius de Rugerio, who in August 1301 sold a slave bought from the Turks, sold in October of the same year a female Greek slave whom his son had bought from the Turks in Turchia; 1301.v.15 = Benvenuto de Brixano, *Benevenuto de Brixano, notaio in Candia (1301–1302)*, ed. T. Morozzo della Rocca, Fonti relativi alla storia di Venezia, Archivi notarili (Venice, 1950), no. 119, p. 46, Hemanuel Vergici, active in April and May 1301 selling slaves bought from the Turks, sold a slave in May of that year whom he had bought with him from Turchia; 1301.vi.6 = Benvenuto de

and Aydın both had slave markets. Ibn Battuta, who travelled in Anatolia in the early 1330s, bought a young Christian girl in Theologos for 40 *dinars*[4] and Demetrius Kydones, the Byzantine statesman who lived from *c.* 1322 to 1400, refers to the slave markets there.[5] Sultanhisar (Nyssa), inland from Balat, had a slave market, or at least slaves were sold there, for in 1303 a Greek female from Kadı Kalesi (Ania), close to both Theologos and Sultanhisar, was bought there from the Turks.[6] Slaves were also exported from Foça to Sicily.[7] Under the Ottomans too Balat (Palatia) was an exporting port for slaves.[8] There were also markets at Antalya and slaves were exported from there and from Alanya (Candelor). In 1313 a female slave who had been bought at Antalya by an inhabitant of Rhodes was manumitted in Rhodes.[9] Fethiye (Meğri, Makri) too apparently was a slave market at an early date, for in 1300 two inhabitants of Candia contracted to take cloth to Meğri to sell it there and then with the money from the cloth to buy three females whom they were to send back to Crete.[10] Slaves were also sold in Saruhan and Karası[11] in great numbers for according to al-'Umarī, an official in the Mamluk chancery in Cairo who wrote, among other things, an account of Anatolia and who died in 1349, the constant inflow of prisoners of war ensured that slaves in the principality of Karası were very numerous, attracting merchants who arrived daily and lived off this traffic in slaves.[12] Kydones refers to the slave markets of Magnesia.[13]

Brixano, *Notaio in Candia*, no. 172, p. 65; 1303.vii.16 in C. Verlinden, 'La Crète, débouché et plaque tournante de la traite des esclaves aux XIVe et XVe siècles' in *Studi in onore di A. Fanfani* (Milan, 1962), vol. III, p. 609, a Greek slave whom the son of the seller had bought in Turchia sold in Candia; 1304.xii.12 : Verlinden, 'Recrutement', 87, Francesco Catalano sold a female Greek slave he had bought when he was in Turchia; 1304.vi.4 in Verlinden, 'Crète', p. 611, sale of six Greek slaves whom the seller had bought from the Turks in Turchia; 1304.x.12 in *ibid.*, p. 612; 1304.x.7 in *ibid.*, p. 612, sale of seven slaves bought from the Turks in Turchia; 1312.ix.25 : ASV Not. Martino Doto in Verlinden, 'Recrutement', 89, manumission of a Greek slave from Rhodes, originally bought in Turchia. In 1330 a Greek, bought in Turchia, was freed in Crete, 1330.vi.28 in Verlinden, 'Crète', p. 626. In 1331 three women and their three children, originally from Negroponte, were sold in Candia. They had been sent from Turchia by the agent of the seller: 1331.iii.26 in *ibid.*, p. 626.

[4] Ibn Battuta, *Voyages*, p. 309.
[5] Kydones, Demetrius, *Oratio pro subsidio Latinorum*, ed. J. P. Migne *Patrologica Graecia*, vol. CLIV, col. 981/982.
[6] 1305.v.27 in Verlinden, 'Crète', p. 613.
[7] 1439.iii.5 = Badoer, *Libro*, col. 304, p. 610, col. 248, p. 499: 'per ser Tomà Spinola dal bancho, i qual me fexe scriver Piero Chapelo per segurtà fata a Zuan Mozenigo da Modon e Aluvixe Falier, zoè a ser Tomà Spinola per so nome, su teste chargade per i diti su la nave patron Zuan Bonifatio, di poi che l'averà fato vela de le Foie finchè la serà zonta in Zezilia, a 9 per col. fo de perp. 200'.
[8] Pilotti, *L'Egypte*, p. 60.
[9] 1313.v.25 in Verlinden, 'Crète', p. 622.
[10] 1300.iii.2 = Pietro Pizolo, *Pietro Pizolo, notaio in Candia*, vol. I (1300), ed. S. Carbone, Fonti per la Storia di Venezia, Archivi notarili (Venice, 1978), no. 140, pp. 70–1.
[11] Kydones, *Pro subsidio Latinorum*, col. 981/982; S. I. Kourouses, Μανουὴλ Γαβαλᾶς εἶτα Ματθαῖος μητροπολίτης Ἐφέσου (1271/2–1355/60 (Athens, 1972), p. 236.
[12] Al-'Umarī, 'Voyages', p. 367.
[13] Kydones, *Pro subsidio Latinorum*, col. 981/982.

Markets also existed in Bursa and on the southern shores of the Black Sea. Slaves were taken from the Crimea to Sinop and Samsun and to Bursa.[14] As the Ottoman empire grew so did the locations of Turkish-controlled slave markets. Gelibolu was an important market to which Christian slaves were brought from the European part of the Ottoman empire and from where they were exported.[15] In the 1430s slaves were sold in Üsküp and Edirne and in the area of Belgrade.[16]

Many of the slaves sold in the markets of Turchia and on the Aegean islands during the fourteenth century were Greek Christians, captured by the Turks and traded not only by them but also by fellow Christians. In 1351 the expedition of Paganino Doria resulted in the capture of Marmaraereğlisi (Heraclea), on the Sea of Marmara between Silivri and Tekirdağ, and the enslavement of 766 Greeks who were subsequently sold in the slave market at Pera.[17] Ibn Battuta described Umur Aydınoğlu, the hero of the *Düsturname*, in which Enveri, writing in the second half of the fifteenth century, praised his many exploits against the Latins, as constantly fighting the infidel, making incursions in the area of Constantinople with his warships and taking slaves.[18] The slave markets of Karası were kept well supplied with a constant stream of prisoners taken in war.[19]

The numbers captured by the Turks were considerable, and Turkish raiding was a major problem for the Latins. Marino Sanudo Torsello, the Venetian author of the *Liber Secretorum Fidelium Crucis* who lived between *c.* 1270 and *c.* 1343, recorded 25,000 people taken prisoner by Turks during the period 1331–2.[20] A major battle could result in a large crop of captives. In this respect the Ottomans did well out of the battle of Nikopolis in 1396 which, according to Aşıkpaşazade, left no one in either Anatolia or Rumeli without a slave.[21] An unnamed Turk was able to send the Mamluk sultan, Barquq, a present of 200 Christians from among the captives he had taken.[22]

It was not only in major battles that Christians fell into Turkish hands. There were, of course, many more small-scale encounters. In the 1331 treaty

[14] Balard, *Romanie génoise*, vol. II, p. 828, n. 100, referring to the period 1410–11.
[15] Pegolotti, *Pratica*, pp. 14–15, 62; Aşıkpaşazade, *Altosmanische Chronik*, p. 50, l. 9, *Tevarih-i al-i 'Osman*, p. 54, ll. 15–16.
[16] Aşıkpaşazade, *Altosmanische Chronik*, pp. 113, 114, 115; Aşıkpaşazade, *Tevarih-i al-i 'Osman*, pp. 125, 126, 127; Piloti, *L'Egypte*, pp. 14–15.
[17] Balard, *Romanie génoise*, vol. I, pp. 303–4. Towards the end of the century it became less acceptable to enslave Orthodox Christians and was forbidden: *ibid.*
[18] Ibn Battuta, *Voyages*, p. 311.
[19] Al-'Umarī, 'Voyages', p. 367.
[20] 1332.iv.4 = Sanudo in Fr. Kuntsmann, *Studien über Marino Sanudo den Aelteren, Abhandlungen der historischen Classe der königlich bayerischen Akademie der Wissenschaften* (Munich, 1855), vol. VII, no. 5, p. 797 (letter from Sanudo to the king of France).
[21] Aşıkpaşazade, *Altosmanische Chronik*, p. 61, l. 7, Aşıkpaşazade, *Tevarih-i al-i 'Osman*, p. 66, ll. 17–18.
[22] Piloti, *L'Egypte*, pp. 109–10. Piloti met some of them. All were young, beautiful and hand-picked, ('tous estoyent josnes, beaulx et tous eslus').

between Menteşe and Marino Morosini, the duca di Candia, Orhan, the ruler of Menteşe, agreed to release all those taken from Crete and who were then in his hands or those of his subjects.[23] In a later treaty between the duca di Candia and Menteşe there is a clause dealing with the problem of slaves from Crete in the lands of Menteşe. This time the emir Musa agreed to hand over to the duca's ambassador, Pietro Badoer, a number of slaves from among twenty-four who had been abducted from Setia (in eastern Crete) by Turks of Menteşe.[24] In a later period, Ambrogio Bernichono di Arenzano opened a court case over a slave of his whom the Ottomans had captured while fighting in the gulf of Büyükçekmece (the Gulf of Atira) just south of Istanbul between Küçükçekmece (Rhegion) and Silivri (Selembria).[25] Life for those who had escaped from Turkish captivity was apparently not always easy, and some at least received hand-outs. Money was given, 'per amor de Dio', in Constantinople in 1439 to a 'poveromo' who had been rescued from the hands of the Turks.[26]

Enslavement through capture was not just a one-way process, for the Latins too captured Turks and other Muslims whom they then sold into captivity. In the early fifteenth century the king of Cyprus seized in successive raids 1,500 subjects of the Mamluk sultan to boost his labour force in the sugar plantations on Cyprus.[27] In the same period a corsair, Petro de Laranda, seized a Mamluk ship at Antalya (Setalia) which he sold together with the 150 Saracens on board to the duke of Naxos, Jacopo de Crispo.[28] One of the accusations levelled against the former *podestà* of Pera, Lodisio Banoso, in 1402 was that he had accepted money from Leondario Grecho, factor of the Byzantine emperor, for certain Turks, captured by Leondario outside the walls of Pera 'in the place where the Jews are buried'.[29]

Greek slaves were common in the courts of the various beyliks at the beginning of the century. Mehmed, the emir of Aydın, had Greek pages in his palace at Birgi in the 1330s. Among the parting gifts he gave to the traveller ibn Battuta was a Greek slave called Mīhail. Mehmed's son, Umur, also presented ibn Battuta with a slave when ibn Battuta visited him at İzmir. The slave was a young Christian called Nicola.[30]

The Turks were active traders, selling Greek slaves to Latin merchants who had no scruples over buying and selling Orthodox Christians. There are various extant slave sales recorded in Candia in the early 1300s in which

[23] 1331.iv.13 = Zachariadou, *Trade and Crusade*, doc. 1331M, clause 2, p. 187.
[24] 1358.x.13 = Zachariadou, *Trade and Crusade*, doc. 1358/1359M, clause 4, pp. 217–18.
[25] 1403.xi.23 = ASG, San Giorgio, Sala 34 590/1307, fo. 21v. See also 1403.xii.7 = *ibid.*, fo. 23r.
[26] 1439.iii.22 = Badoer, *Libro*, col. 327, p. 656, col. 258, p. 519.
[27] Piloti, *L'Egypte*, pp. 78–9.
[28] Piloti, *L'Egypte*, pp. 95–6.
[29] 1402.v.30 = ASG, San Giorgio, Sala 34 590/1306, fo. 72v.
[30] Ibn Battuta, *Voyages*, p. 309.

Greek slaves bought from the Turks were sold in Crete.[31] Later, as the Ottomans advanced, the importance of captives from the Balkans in the slave markets increased. In the early 1380s many Bulgars were bought from the Ottomans by Latin merchants and subsequently sold in Candia.[32] Export taxes on slaves were imposed by both Menteşe and Aydın in treaties with the duca di Candia.[33] From the 1353 treaty it is clear that the Turks of Aydın were trading in slaves with the Genoese as well as with the Venetians, and one may presume that the Turks of Menteşe did likewise.

The Ottomans too were involved in the slave trade including the trade of slaves to Egypt. Muslim slave merchants were active at the court of the Ottoman ruler, in Edirne and Gelibolu, where they bought young slaves, sometimes as many as 100 or 200, whom they transported to Cairo where they were sold to the Mamluk sultan. These slaves were shipped from Gelibolu on Muslim vessels, or sometimes on those of Christians 'malvais et mal disposés'.[34] As relations between the Ottomans and the Genoese were generally good these erring Christians may well have been Genoese.

It is possible that the Ottomans pursued a more active trade policy than that followed by the emirs of Menteşe and Aydın. One of Bayezid's demands in his peace proposal presented to the Hospitallers in 1393 was that he should be able to sell slaves in Rhodes without any restrictions.[35] This implies that the Ottomans, in contrast to the Turks of Menteşe and Aydın, sold slaves to Latins not merely in their own markets in Turchia, but actively went out to the markets on the Aegean islands to sell. As the Muslim merchants buying slaves in the markets in Turchia for the Mamluk sultanate travelled with their merchandise to Cairo,[36] and as some of these

---

[31] 1304.xi.9 in Verlinden, 'Recrutement', 86–7 (a Greek female bought from the Turks); 1305.v.27 in Verlinden, 'Crète', p. 613 (sale of Maria de Romania de loco qui dicitur Ania, quam emi in Nasso de turchis); 1305.vi.2 in *ibid.*, p. 613 (Greek bought from Turks); 1305.vii.1 in *ibid.*, p. 614 (Costa of Chios, bought from the Turks, sold in Candia); 1305.xi.20 in *ibid.*, p. 615 and Verlinden, 'Recrutement', 88 (Eudoxia of Samos, bought originally from the Turks, bought by an inhabitant of Coron in Crete); 1306.iii.2 in *ibid.*, and Verlinden, 'Crète', p. 615 (female Greek, Erini, de loco Theologo, bought from the Turks). Other slaves, probably Greek judging by their names, were sold by the Turks: 1301.iv.8 = Benvenuto de Brixano, *Notaio in Candia*, no. 1, p. 5 (Georgius); 1301.v.1 = *ibid.*, no. 68, p. 29 (Maria); 1301.vii.9 = *ibid.*, no. 222, p. 82 (Herinim); 1301.viii.1 = *ibid.*, no. 256, p. 95 (Maria). One merchant, Hemanuel Vergici, seems to have been particularly active, selling in April 1301 five slaves whom he had bought from the Turks and one in May, 1301.iv.8 = *ibid.*, no. 4, p. 6 (Anna); 1301.iv.9 = *ibid.*, no. 10, p. 8 (Maria bought from the Turks); 1301.iv.9 = *ibid.*, no. 11, p. 8 (from the Turks); 1301.iv.19 = *ibid.*, no. 46, p. 21 (Herinim from the Turks); 1301.v.15 = *ibid.*, no. 120, pp. 46–7 (Cally from the Turks).
[32] ASV, Notario Manoli Bresciano in Verlinden, 'Recrutement', 165.
[33] 1331.iv.13 = Zachariadou, *Trade and Crusade*, doc. 1331M, clause 3, p. 187; 1353.iv.7 = *ibid.*, doc. 1353A, clause 19, p. 214.
[34] Piloti, *L'Egypte*, pp. 14–15. Piloti describes the merchants as 'payens' which I take to mean here Muslim.
[35] Luttrell, 'Hospitallers', pp. 96–7, citing a document from the Malta archives.
[36] Piloti, *L'Egypte*, p. 15.

merchants may well have been Ottomans, it is possible that this too indicates a more adventurous trade policy than that of the beyliks.

Apart from selling, the Turks were apparently buyers of slaves, although presumably they were not as active in this field as they were as slave sellers since their territorial expansion ensured them of a constant source of slaves as booty. A Genoese document of 1413, enacted in Chios, makes it clear that the Genoese traded in slaves with the Ottomans in Turchia. Simon de Serra appointed Giovanni di Babaino as procurator to retrieve two of his slaves who had fled from Chios to Turchia. If Giovanni was unable to recover these slaves, he was to get the price for them that those holding the slaves, subjects of the lords of Turchia, were accustomed to pay for slaves acquired thus or transported there by the Genoese.[37] Genoese transporting of slaves into Turchia is also attested in the Massaria of Caffa for 1410 to 1411 which give various references to slaves being taken from the Crimea to Sinop, Samsun and Bursa where presumably they were bought by the Ottomans. In the same period 1,080 slaves were taken from Caffa to the southern shores of the Black Sea.[38] In a Genoese document of 1431 Batista Macio acknowledged having taken twenty men from Lo Vati near Sevastopolis to Liminia in Turchia.[39] Batista had contravened a decree, issued in Caffa a year earlier, forbidding the taking of men from there to Turchia and was petitioning for this to be excused on the grounds that he did not know of the decree at the time of his transgression.[40]

Turks were themselves also commodities. They were bought and sold often by Genoese merchants, particularly in the slave markets of Chios and Genoa,[41] where 2.4 per cent of the slaves known to have been sold in the Genoese slave market between 1300 and 1408 were Turks,[42] as well as in

---

[37] 1413.vii.5 = ASG, Notaio, Giovanni Balbi, Sc. 46, filza 1 doc. 17. 'precium et preciam quod et que detentores eorum in locis Turchie et subditi dominis Turchie soliti sunt solvere ilis ad quorum vertutem sclavi ad partes illas fugiunt seu converti sunt con Januensibus'.

[38] Balard, *Romanie génoise*, vol. II, p. 828, n. 100.

[39] Panaretos, the fifteenth-century chronicler of Trabzon, mentions the emirs of Limnia: Panaretos, *Eustathii Metropolita Thessalonicensis Opuscula accedunt Trapezuntinae Historiae Scriptores Panaretus et Evgenicus*, ed. T.F. Tafel (Frankfurt am Main, 1832), p. 369, l. 89. They were probably the Tacüddinoğulları, who were active in the area of Terme (Themiskyra) and Çarşamba, just east of Samsun: Donald Edgar Pitcher, *An Historical Geography of the Ottoman Empire* (Leiden, 1972), p. 31.

[40] C.1431 = ASG, San Giorgio, Sala 39, busta 88, doc. 440.

[41] eg. 1360.x.20 = ASG, Notai Ignoti XVIII.10, Raffaele di Casanova, fourth page, *recto*, enactment of the sale of a fifteen-year-old male Turkish slave, called Nicola, for 47 *florins*, enacted in Chios; 1404.v.15 = ASG, Notaio, Gregorio Panissario, Sc. 37, filza 1, doc. 82, Jane Crossecheri [? Crossorheri, or Crossoiheri] de Folia Vetera, sold to Nicolao de Mareo, a twenty-five-year-old male Turkish slave called Mithare for 21 gold *ducats*, enacted in Chios; 1423.v. = ASG, Notaio, Giovanni Labaino, Sc. 40, filza 1, doc. 383, 1423.v.c.9 = *ibid.*, doc. 381, 1423.v.11 = *ibid.*, doc. 382, <1423>.v.14 = *ibid.*, doc. (no number). Other sales were enacted in Genoa, e.g. 1370.ii.14 = ASG, Notaio, Donato de Clavaro, Sc. 39, filza 1, doc. 374, sale of female Turkish slave of about twenty-five years, for 45 Genoese pounds.

[42] Balard, *Romanie génoise*, vol. II, p. 800.

Crete,[43] Famagusta[44] and Constantinople.[45] The presence of Turkish slaves in Crete in the early fourteenth century is further attested by the order of the duca di Candia, Jacopo Barozzi, in 1301 that anyone helping Turkish, Greek or Saracen slaves to escape from the island would be fined 50 *hyperpyra* per slave.[46]

Turks continued to be sold as slaves in the markets of Crete throughout the fourteenth century.[47] Turkish slaves also appear in Venice in the fifteenth century.[48] In 1400 nine Turkish heads were listed among goods received from the ship of Giovanni Obizio of Venice, whose ship sailed from Venice to Ibiza. The Turks were forwarded to Valencia for sale, with a letter describing one of the slaves as a woman who could 'sew and do everything ... Your money will be well placed in her.'[49] Turkish slaves appear too in Pera.[50]

The numbers of Turkish slaves on the Aegean islands were sometimes considered a security risk. The Hospitallers on Rhodes controlled the movements of their Turkish slaves within the town.[51] In 1357 a decree was issued in Rhodes forbidding the keeping of Turkish slaves within the

---

[43] 1300.v.30 = Pietro Pizolo, *Notaio in Candia*, vol. I, no. 539, pp. 246–7, sale of three Turkish slaves 'nomine unus Ysilami quem vis clamare Vaxili et alius Feramardo quem vis clamare Georgium et alius Isa quem vis clamare Michali'; 1301.vi.10 = Benvenuto de Brixano, *Notaio in Candia*, no. 174, pp. 65–6, the sale of a Turkish slave called Mamut, who was sold to Magister Marco, the plague doctor (Medico plagarum); 1301.viii.5 = *ibid.*, no. 263, p. 97, the sale of a female Turk called Berta. There is reference to a Turkish slave in Crete in 1271, Verlinden, 'Crète', p. 594; 1303.v.10 in *ibid.*, p. 609, a Genoese merchant, Nicolao de Sauro, sold his male Turkish slave in Candia; 1303.vii.20, 1303.ix.12, 1303.xii.17, 1304.v.11, 1304.ix.5 (though Verlinden suggests that from the name this slave, although described as Turkish, was in fact Greek) in *ibid.*, p. 609; 1305.vi.8, 1305.vi.10 in *ibid.*, p. 613. There is also a manumission of a Turkish slave in Candia, 1312.x.23 in *ibid.*, p. 619.

[44] 1301.iii.1 = Lamberto di Sambuceto in C. Desimoni, 'Actes passés à Famagouste de 1299 à 1301 par devant le notaire génois Lamberto di Sambuceto' in *Archives de l'Orient Latin* (Brussels, 1964), vol. II, no. 255, pp. 302–3; 1301.iii.1 = *ibid.*, no. 256, pp. 303–4; 1301.iii.8 = *ibid.*, no. 270, pp. 321–3; 1301.iii.28 = *ibid.*, no. 293, pp. 351–3; 1301.v.22 = *ibid.*, no. 380, pp. 456–7; 1301.iv.1 = *ibid.*, no. 331, pp. 396–7; 1301.iv.11 = *ibid.*, no. 340, pp. 404–5; 1301.vii.27 = Lamberto di Sambuceto in Romeo Pavoni, *Notai Genovesi in Oltremare. Atti Rogati a Cipro da Lamberto di Sambuceto (Gennaio–Agosto 1302)*, CSFS (Genoa, 1957), no. 20, pp. 26–7 refers to a slave from Cassaria (?Kayseri); 1301.vii.27 = *ibid.*, no. 21, pp. 27–8; 1301.ix.2 = *ibid.*, no. 78, pp. 105–6; 1301.ix.28 = *ibid.*, no. 168, pp. 206–7; 1302.iii.14 = *ibid.*, no. 122, pp. 151–2; 1302.viii.8 = *ibid.*, no. 281, pp. 336–9.

[45] 1305.vi.8 and 1305.vi.10 in Verlinden, 'Crète', p. 613, two Turks who had been sold in Constantinople were sold again in Crete.

[46] Verlinden, 'Crète', p. 605.

[47] 1329.vi.29 in Verlinden, 'Crète', p. 626, sale of a Turk bought in Caffa; 1331.x.1 in *ibid.*, p. 627; 1332.iii.24 in *ibid.*, p. 627; 1381.xi.9 in *ibid.*, p. 635, sale of three Turks from Alto Loco; 1382.iv.30 in *ibid.*, p. 638; 1382.v.23 in *ibid.*, p. 640.

[48] Verlinden, 'Recrutement', pp. 84, 171. Verlinden, *ibid.*, 171–2, gives examples of Turkish slave sales in Venice in 1410, 1418, 1428, 1434, 1444 and 1456.

[49] 1400.ix.1 = Iris Origo, *The Merchant of Prato, Francesco di Marco Datini* (London, 1957), p. 99 and note 41, citing Archivio Datini.

[50] 1403.xii.1 = ASG, San Giorgio, Sala 34 590/1307, fo. 44r, a court case over Turkish slaves. 1403.xii.3 = *ibid.*, fos. 58v–59r, a case concerning a Turkish slave who had fled from Pera.

[51] Luttrell, 'Hospitallers', p. 87.

fortified town or sending them with the Brethren's horses to collect grass or hay. One Turkish slave was however permitted to each hostel.[52] In Crete there was a series of instructions from the senate concerning Turkish slaves on the island. Before 1313 there was a ban imposed on importing slaves except Turks and Tatars. This was perhaps a defensive measure occasioned by fear of a Greek revolt and directed against Greek slaves.[53] Later, however, fear of the Turks resulted in various controls. In 1341 the Venetian authorities ordered that only those Turks captured in attacks could be brought into Crete and that these captives had to be taken out of the island after six months. Various penalties were imposed on those bringing in any Turks who had not been captured and on anyone buying such a Turk.[54] Towards the end of the century the senate gave instructions that all captured Turks were to be sent to Crete where they were to work only for the commune. If any official used these Turks for his own purposes he was to be fined 5 *hyperpyra* per slave.[55] In 1363 the Venetian senate doubled the penalty for contravention of the law on Turks being sold as slaves in Crete, as the numbers of Turkish slaves were considered too great.[56] Even when in pressing need of slaves, the Cretan authorities, while encouraging the importation of slaves into the island, prohibited the import of Turks.[57] A few years later, however, the Venetian senate ordered the authorities in Negroponte to send twenty-five Turks to work in Crete.[58] In the early fifteenth century shortage of labour was also a problem on Cyprus.[59]

That the number of Turkish slaves was also high in Pera seems possibly indicated by a court case of 1403 over the imprisonment of a female Saracen who was in prison together with many other Turkish slaves.[60]

Clearly the slave trade was a profitable enterprise both for the Turks and for the Latin merchants. It is however extremely difficult to establish a clear

---

[52] A. Luttrell, 'Slavery at Rhodes: 1306–1440', *Bulletin de l'Institut Historique Belge de Rome* fasc. 46–7 (1976–7), 86–7.

[53] This ban was revoked in 1313. 1313.x.1 = Paola Ratti Vidulich, *Duca di Candia Bandi (1313–1329)* (Venice, 1965), no. 1, p. 5.

[54] 1341.iii.6 = S. Theotokes, Ἱστορικὰ Κρητικὰ Ἔγγραφα ᾗκδιδόμενα ᾗκ τοῦ Ἀρχείου τῆς Βενετίας Μνημεῖα τῆς, Ἑλληνικῆς, Ἱστοίας Academy of Athens, (Athens, 1933–1937), vols I/2, II.1–2 vol. II/I, no. 25, pp. 205–6. See also 1357.vi.26 = *ibid.*, II/2, no. 5, pp. 51–2.

[55] 1393.iii.11 = H. Noiret, *Documents inédits pour servir à l'histoire de la domination vénitienne en Crète de 1380 à 1485* (Paris, 1892), p. 55.

[56] 1363.vi.8 : Thiriet, *Régestes*, vol. I, no. 410, pp. 106–7; 1363.vi.8 = Theotokes, Ἱστορικὰ Κρητικά vol. II/2, no. 12, p. 110.

[57] 1393.iii.11 = Noiret, *Documents*, pp. 54–5.

[58] 1405.xii.15 = Noiret, *Documents*, p. 163.

[59] The king of Cyprus, in reply to the ambassadors of the Mamluk sultan who were endeavouring to arrange for the ransom of a large number of the sultan's subjects, seized in successive raiding by the king, said that he needed those he had seized to work the land: 'le roy respondist que lez .M. et .v.C. Sarrasins qu'il avoit prins estoit pou au grant besoing que l'isole de Chipre en avoit: car elle avoit grant besoing de laboreus qui laborassent lez terres pour faire sucre' (Piloti, *L'Egypte*, p. 79).

[60] 1403.xi.13 = ASG, San Giorgio, Sala 34 590/1307, fo. 57v. But see Balard, *Romanie génoise*, vol. I, p. 306.

picture of slave prices in Turchia and the other markets of the eastern Mediterranean. Various factors affected the price of slaves in general, such as age, looks and health. The condition of a slave at purchase was very important and accusations of imperfections could lead to court action. In 1423 a case was tried in Genoa over the sale of a female slave, described as a Bulgar from Turchia. The case arose because the slave had suffered from 'falling sickness' ('morbus caducus'), presumably epilepsy, since she had received a blow on the head when captured. She had been in Turchia, sold in Chios and transported from there by ship to Genoa. The case was an attempt to have the sale declared invalid because of the contention that the slave had already been ill at the time of purchase.[61]

Among the various specific factors influencing the price rate in Anatolia in this period were political developments in the area which affected not only the local markets but those further away. Prices in Genoa, for example, rose at the beginning of the fourteenth century to between 15 and 16 *libri*[62] as a result of the Venetian–Genoese war of Curzola (1294–9) which cut easy communications between Italy and the markets of the eastern Mediterranean. The later war between Genoa and Venice, the war of Chioggia, as well as troubles in Caffa with the Tatars of Solgat caused a price increase between 1375 and 1385 to 62 *libri* for female slaves and 54 for male. Some years later Ottoman success and that of Timur again interrupted the trade and caused another price rise.[63]

Natural disasters too disturbed the slave trade. A letter sent to the merchant Francesco Datini from Genoa in 1393 informed him that there would be only a few slaves from Romania because of the outbreak of plague there.[64] Another factor that affected the price of Turkish slaves in Genoa was that Turkish and Saracen slaves were apparently less valued on the Genoese market, particularly at the beginning of the fourteenth century, than Bulgars, Russians, Circassians and Tatars.[65]

One of the factors accounting for fluctuating prices through the fourteenth and first half of the fifteenth centuries was the quantity of slaves on the market. At the end of the thirteenth century the price of a Turkish slave

---

[61] 1423.v. = ASG, Notaio, Giovanni Labaino, Sc. 40, filza 1, doc. 383, 1423.v.c.9 = *ibid.*, doc. 381, 1423.v.11 = *ibid.*, doc. 382, <1423>.v.14 = *ibid.*, doc. (no number).

[62] Around 1300 11 Genoese *soldi* were equal to 1 *hyperpyron*: Spufford, *Handbook*, p. 288; Balard, *Romanie génoise*, vol. II, p. 653.

[63] Balard, *Romanie génoise*, vol. II, pp. 814–15.

[64] I. Origo, 'The domestic enemy: Eastern slaves in Tuscany in the fourteenth and fifteenth centuries', *Speculum* 30 (1955), 331, referring to a letter of 1393.ii.17 from Datini to his wife Margherita in which he said that he had heard from Genoa that there would be few slaves arriving from Romania 'for they say that in that country there are many dead and dying from the plague, and those who do come die on board'.

[65] Balard, *Romanie génoise*, vol. II, p. 811. Slave prices also varied in the Mamluk sultanate according to the origin of the slave. Tatars were the most expensive (130–40 *ducats*), followed by Circassians (110–20 *ducats*), Greeks (90 *ducats*), Albanians, Dalmatians and Serbs (70–80 *ducats*) (Piloti, *L'Egypte*, p. 15).

fell below that of a sheep as a result of the military successes of the Byzantine general Philanthropenos.[66] In 842/1438–9, conquests, this time those of the Ottomans, again caused the price of slaves to fall so that beautiful young females sold, in lots of three, for only 100 *akçes* (*c*.9.5 *hyperpyra*).[67] The Ottoman success of 841/1437–8 in Hungary resulted in so much booty that a four-year-old boy was sold at Üsküp for 20 *akçes* (*c*.1.9 *hyperpyra*).[68] In the same year the Ottoman chronicler Aşıkpaşazade himself captured five slaves whom he sold in Üsküp for 900 *akçes* (*c*.85.7 *hyperpyra*)[69] while, in the following year, he sold captives in Edirne for 100 *akçes* for two, and 100 *akçes* for three slaves (*c*.9.5 *hyperpyra*).[70] The Belgrade market seems to have been less affected by the numbers of captives for Aşıkpaşazade bought a six- to seven-year-old boy there for 100 *akçes* (*c*.9.5 *hyperpyra*), while female slaves fetched 150 *akçes* (*c*.14.3 *hyperpyra*).[71] These figures, particularly that of 100 *akçes* for three females, are extremely low. Even if one does not accept their accuracy at face value but allows for some exaggeration, they still show to what an extent a glut on the market could push prices down.

Slaves were clearly an important source of income in Turchia, and both Menteşe and Aydın imposed export duties on them. Slaves exported from Menteşe were taxed in 1331 at the rate of 10 *aspers* per slave,[72] the same rate applying in 1407,[73] while those from Aydın too were taxed under the 1353 treaty between the emir Hızır and the duca di Candia although no specific rate is given, the treaty only specifying that the Venetians were to pay on slaves at the same rates as the Rhodians and the Genoese.[74]

It has been argued on the basis of the treaties between Menteşe, Aydın and Venice that slaves were sold in Menteşe for an average of 24 *hyperpyra* (12 *ducats*),[75] as this was the fine imposed on anyone abducting a slave and payable to the slave's master, while that in Aydın was perhaps around 30

---

[66] Planoudes, *Mamimi monachi Planudis epistolae*, ed. M. Treu (Bresiau, 1890), letter 78, p. 99.

[67] Aşıkpaşazade, *Altosmanische Chronik*, p. 117, 5–6, Aşıkpaşazade, *Tevarih-i al-i 'Osman*, p. 128, ll. 15–16. The Istanbul edition says slave girls sold for this figure, while the Giese edition specifies that they were sold in threes for 100 *akçes*.

[68] Aşıkpaşazade, *Altosmanische Chronik*, p. 114, l. 16, Aşıkpaşazade, *Tevarih-i al-i 'Osman*, p. 126, l. 18.

[69] Aşıkpaşazade, *Altosmanische Chronik*, p. 115, ll. 8–9, Aşıkpaşazade, *Tevarih-i al-i 'Osman*, p. 127, ll. 9–10.

[70] Aşıkpaşazade, *Altosmanische Chronik*, p. 113, ll. 20–21, Aşıkpaşazade, *Tevarih-i al-i 'Osman*, p. 125, ll. 21–22.

[71] Aşıkpaşazade, *Altosmanische Chronik*, p. 113, ll. 12–13, Aşıkpaşazade, *Tevarih-i al-i 'Osman*, p. 125, ll. 15. The Istanbul edition does not give the age of the slave, nor the price for females.

[72] 1331.iv.13 = Zachariadou, *Trade and Crusade*, doc. 1331M, clause 3, p. 187.

[73] 1407.vi.2 = Zachariadou, *Trade and Crusade*, doc. 1407M, clause 20, p. 236.

[74] 1353.iv.7 = Zachariadou, *Trade and Crusade*, doc. 1353A, clause 19, p. 214.

[75] I give throughout the actual figure as it appears in the original source and convert it, where necessary, into *hyperpyra* and *ducats* for ease of comparison. During most of the fourteenth century the ratio of *ducat* to *hyperperon* was approximately 1:2, and for the end of the century and the beginning of the next was 1:3.

hyperpyra (15 *ducat*s), the amount of the fine imposed in the 1348 treaty with Hızır.[76] However, a young Greek female was sold at Theologos in the early 1330s for 40 gold *dinar*s (92 *hyperpyra*, 46 *ducat*s).[77] Presumably she was particularly attractive, but even so the discrepancy between the proposed average for Aydın in 1348 and ibn Battuta's purchase price is considerable. The same discrepancy appears for slaves sold in Menteşe. Two Greeks were sold in Balat (Palatia) in 1355 for 92 *hyperpyra* (46 *ducat*s), again in sharp contrast to the suggested average price based on the fines imposed in the treaty.[78] Fines in general do not seem a reliable guide for slave prices, particularly in view of the fine of 50 *hyperpyra* per slave imposed by the duca di Candia, Jacopo Barozzi, in 1301 on anyone helping Turkish, Greek or Saracen slaves to escape from the island.[79] In comparison the average price for slaves on the Cretan market in the early fourteenth century was 8 *hyperpyra* (4 *ducat*s) for males and 17 *hyperpyra* (8.5 *ducat*s) for females.[80] Clearly the fine here bears very little relation to the average sale price.

One might be able to suggest some sort of price guide by looking at what was paid for slaves, originally bought from the Turks and subsequently sold in Crete. (See tables 4.1 and 4.2.)

The Latin merchants who had bought the slaves from the Turks expected to make a profit by selling them in Crete. The prices therefore should reflect both the cost of transporting the slaves and the profit margin set by the merchants. The average price of slaves originally bought in Turchia and sold in Crete was approximately 17 *hyperpyra* (8.5 *ducat*s) per slave. This average is probably applicable only to females as all but one of the slaves in the list of those from Turchia sold in Crete are women, the resulting average figure tallying with that of the average female price on the Cretan market. Therefore the price in Turchia for, presumably, females must have been less than 17 *hyperpyra* (8.5 *ducat*s). The average price of a male slave on the Cretan market in the early fourteenth century was 8 *hyperpyra* (4 *ducat*s).[81] Presumably, therefore, the average price of male slaves in Turchia was less than this figure.

By the 1330s slave prices in Turchia had presumably risen, for it is likely that the increased strength of the beyliks would have been reflected in their ability to insist on higher prices for the goods they sold. At the same time Menteşe imposed an export tax on slaves taken from its territories under its treaty with Venetian Crete. Orhan imposed a tax of 10 *asper*s (0.88 of a

---

[76] Zachariadou, *Trade and Crusade*, p. 162; 1337.pre iv.= *ibid.*, doc. 1337M, clause 18, pp. 197–8; 1348.viii.18 = *ibid.*, doc. 1348A, clause 23, p. 210; 1375.iv.22 = *ibid.*, doc. 1375M, clause 18, p. 221; 1403.vii.24 = *ibid.*, doc. 1403M and doc. 1403M DVL, clause 18, p. 230; 1407.vi.2 = *ibid.*, doc. 1407M, clause 18, p. 236.

[77] Ibn Battuta, *Voyages*, p. 309.

[78] Zachariadou, *Trade and Crusade*, p. 163, n. 680.   [79] Verlinden, 'Crète', p. 605.

[80] Zachariadou, *Trade and Crusade*, p. 161.   [81] Zachariadou, *Trade and Crusade*, p. 161.

Table 4.1. *Prices of Turkish slaves sold in Crete, 1301*

Date	Description	Price	Source
1301.vi.10	1 male	27 *hyperpyra* 2 *grossi*	Benvenuto de Brixano, *Notaio in Candia*, no. 174, pp. 65–6
1301.viii.5	1 female	22 *hyperpyra*	*ibid.*, no. 263, p. 97

Table 4.2. *Prices of slaves bought originally from Turks and sold in Crete, 1301 and 1304*

Date	Description	Price	Source
1301.iv.8	1 male	14 *hyperpyra*	Benvenuto de Brixano, *Notaio in Candia*, no. 1, p. 5
1301.iv.8	1 female	18 *hyperpyra*, 1 *grosso*	*ibid.*, no. 4, p. 6
1301.iv.9	1 female	25 *hyperpyra*	*ibid.*, no. 10, p. 8
1301.iv.9	1 female	28 *hyperpyra*	*ibid.*, no. 11, p. 8
1301.iv.9	1 female	27 *hyperpyra*	*ibid.*, no. 46, p. 21
1301.iv.27	1 female	20 *hyperpyra*	*ibid.*, no. 63, p. 27
1301.v.1	1 female	14 gold *hyperpyra*	*ibid.*, no. 68, p. 29
1301.v.15	1 female	18 *hyperpyra*	*ibid.*, no. 119, p. 46
1301.v.15	1 female	18 *hyperpyra*	*ibid.*, no. 120, pp. 46–7
1301.vi.6	1 female	6 *hyperpyra*	*ibid.*, no. 172, p. 65
1301.vii.9	1 female	15 *hyperpyra*	*ibid.*, no. 222, p. 82
1301.viii.1	1 female	17 *hyperpyra*	*ibid.*, no. 256, p. 95
1304.x.7	1 female, Greek	9 *hyperpyra*	Verlinden, 'Recrutement', 86
1304.xi.8	1 female, Greek	15 *hyperpyra*	*ibid.*, 86
1304.xii.12	1 female, Greek	11 *hyperpyra*	*ibid.*, 87

hyperpyron, 0.44 of a *ducat*) per slave taken out of the beylik while that for horses was 3 *aspers* (0.26 of a *hyperpyron*, 0.13 of a *ducat*) per animal and for cattle 2 *aspers* (0.16 of a *hyperpyron*, 0.08 of a *ducat*).[82] If, as would seem reasonable to assume, a similar tax was imposed by the emir of Menteşe on other western merchants, this tax would presumably be reflected in the prices of slaves bought in Turchia and sold elsewhere by western merchants. Therefore one may assume that by the 1330s the prices paid for slaves in Turchia was higher than that paid at the beginning of the century.

The proposition that there was a rise in prices is supported by the rise in slave rates in Crete where, in the 1330s, the average price for women was between 31 and 55 *hyperpyra* (15.5 and 27.5 *ducats*) and for men between 25 and 36 *hyperpyra* (12.5 and 18 *ducats*).[83] Thus the prices in Crete had increased in the thirty years from the beginning of the century by approximately 100–300 per cent for female slaves and by 300–450 per cent for men. Such a price rise in Crete over such a short period is striking. It is in part explained by the increase in demand for slaves on the island and by the greater organisation of the Cretan market,[84] but this does not seem perhaps sufficient to account for such an increase. It may also be partly explained by the political development in Turchia at that time. The Turkish beyliks were becoming more powerful political units, more stable and more able to hold their own in the international market, while at the same time Turchia continued to be an important slave market, constantly replenished with slaves brought in from the incessant Turkish raids and conquests. Perhaps the high price in Crete for slaves in the 1330s is a reflection of this increased Turkish muscle.

Prices in Crete do not appear to have risen during the middle years of the century and in the 1360s the average price of a female slave was 35 *hyperpyra* (17.5 *ducats*).[85] This is surprising when one considers how eager the Venetian senate was to import slaves to work the land, Crete suffering from an acknowledged lack of manpower, and in view of the effect of the Black Death on slave markets in general.[86] While it is true that the Black Death wiped out slave owners as well as slaves, thus reducing the number of potential buyers, the plague must have carried off a higher proportion of the weaker and undernourished members of the society, including slaves, than of those in a fitter condition and with the ability to escape the approaching plague by moving elsewhere. After the outbreak of the Black

---

[82] 1331.iv.13 = Zachariadou, *Trade and Crusade*, doc. 1331M, clause 3, p. 187. One should however note that the same rate was levied in the 1407 treaty between Crete and Menteşe, 1407.vi.2 = *ibid.*, doc. 1407M, clause 20, p. 236, thus possibly undermining the significance of the rate as a guide to slave prices.

[83] Zachariadou, *Trade and Crusade*, p. 161.

[84] *Ibid.*   [85] *Ibid.*

[86] After the scarcity caused by the Black Death, the council of the *Rogati* offered rewards for those who found slaves who had fled: Paola Ratti Vidulich, *Duca di Candia, Quatenus (1340–1350)* (Venice, 1976), pp. 129–30.

Death prices in Genoa increased steeply to an average between 1350 and 1360 of 55 *libri* for women, 35 *libri* for men. Perhaps this apparent stability in the slave price on Crete is again connected with political developments in Turchia, or rather within the Ottoman state, for by the 1360s the state was expanding rapidly and possibly creating a glut of slaves on the markets in the eastern Mediterranean. After around 1360 the prices did fall in Genoa due to the large number of slaves on the market and settled at between 37 and 40 *libri*.

At the same time however the strength of the new Ottoman state should have ensured that it was able to charge more than the less powerful beyliks. Certainly by the 1380s the average price in Crete of female slaves had risen considerably to 96 *hyperpyra* (48 *ducats*),[87] representing a 275 per cent increase on the average price in the 1360s, with men fetching an average of 64 *hyperpyra* (32 *ducats*).

With these apparently huge percentage increases in prices through the fourteenth century one must bear in mind that they may not have been real increases but rather, in part at least, the result of currency devaluation. The Genoese pound, for example, lost 50 per cent of its value against silver and 33 per cent against gold during the fourteenth century.[88] Similarly the ratio of *ducat* to *hyperpyra* was approximately 1:2 for most of the fourteenth century, but 1:3 for the end of the century and the beginning of the next.[89]

The price of slaves sold in Crete may form some sort of guideline to slave prices in Turchia. If one turns to the average prices in the slave market on Chios, however, the picture seems surprisingly different. Between 1359 and 1412 the average price, which did not fluctuate greatly nor vary between the sexes, was 60 to 70 *hyperpyra* (20 to 35 *ducats*) for the first part of the period, 90 to 105 *hyperpyra* (30 to 35 *ducats*) for the end of the century and the beginning of the next.[90] Chios is in this respect different from the markets in Crete and Genoa. It seems odd, considering the various political upheavals affecting prices in markets in the same area, that prices did not rise too in Chios, particularly in view of the island's proximity to Turchia and the strength of its trade links with Turkish territory. Fluctuations on the Turkish market should therefore appear also on Chios. That there was no increase in Turkish slave prices does not seem credible, but it is hard to explain why such increases were not represented in Chian prices. Perhaps this is a reflection of the randomness of extant sources rather than a genuine reflection of the position at that time. The Chian slave market also differed from the markets of Genoa and Crete in that there was no apparent distinction made between male and female prices. In Genoa female slaves

[87] Zachariadou, *Trade and Crusade*, p. 162.   [88] Balard, *Romanie génoise*, vol. II, p. 814.
[89] Bertelé, 'Iperpero byzantino', 84.   [90] Balard, *La Romanie génoise*, vol. I, pp. 309–10.

were always more expensive than male.[91] This is also true of slaves in Crete.[92]

Another important market in the region was Constantinople. Prices charged there may be taken as some sort of guide to Turkish slave prices, for the Constantinople market would presumably not have been so divergent from Turkish markets, and its prices thus not extremely different from those charged in Turchia. The average slave price in Constantinople in the 1430s seems to have been in the region of 97 *hyperpyra* for all slaves, female slaves again fetching more than males, on average 108 *hyperpyra* to 101 *hyperpyra*.[93] These figures are in line roughly with those for Chios at the end of the fourteenth century of 90–105 *hyperpyra* and with the price on Crete in the same period for female slaves of around 96 *hyperpyra*, though considerably more than the male slave price there of 64 *hyperpyra*. These figures seem to indicate a certain stability in the slave market, with no great fluctuations in price between the end of the fourteenth century and the 1430s, or, even if there was a sharp price increase or decrease at some time during this period, it was temporary.

In order to gain some comprehension of the real value of slaves it is perhaps useful to compare their prices with those of other commodities on the market. Professor Balard has calculated that in comparison with grain, slaves in Genoa were an expensive commodity.[94] Slaves were certainly of greater value than livestock exported from the beylik of Menteşe as the export tax imposed on them in 1331 was 10 *aspers* per slave while that for horses was 3 *aspers* (0.26 of a *hyperpyron*, 0.13 of a *ducat*) per animal, and for cattle 2 *aspers* (0.16 of a *hyperpyron*, 0.08 of a *ducat*).[95] However, the tax rate may not be an altogether reliable guide as over seventy years later the same rate was again imposed on exported slaves.[96]

Apart from straightforward buying and selling, slaves represented another form of income generation: ransom. This was used not only between Christians and Muslims but also between Christians and fellow Christians. In 1301 Notara Sevasto, the son of Paulus Notaropulus, was sold by Filipo Bicontolo, Nicolao de La Fasina, Marcelino de Ancona and Andrea Çerbino who had captured him rebelling against the doge and commune of Venice. When his ransom arrived 6,050 *hyperpyra* were to be handed over for him.[97] The ransom clearly represented a profit, as in August of the same year Michaele, the son of Giovanni Maselo, sold to

[91] Balard, *Romanie génoise*, vol. II, p. 812.
[92] Zachariadou, *Trade and Crusade*, pp. 161–2.   [93] See appendix 2 below.
[94] Balard, *Romanie génoise*, vol. II, p. 815.
[95] 1331.iv.13 = Zachariadou, *Trade and Crusade*, doc. 1331M, clause 3, p. 187.
[96] 1407.vi.2 = Zachariadou, *Trade and Crusade*, doc. 1407M, clause 20, p. 236.
[97] 1301.vii.5 = Benvenuto de Brixano, *Notaio in Candia*, nos. 215, 216, 217, p. 79. See also 1301.viii.6 = *ibid.*, no. 281, pp. 103–4; 1301.viii.6 = *ibid.*, no. 282, p. 104; 1301.viii.21 = *ibid.*, no. 305, p. 112. In documents 281 and 305 the captured man is called Michaele Notara and in 282 Michaele Notara Sevasto, most probably the title Σεβαστός.

Giovanni Bicontolo the whole of his part of the profit which was to accrue from the ransom of Notara Sevasto.[98] In the same year, 1301, Phylipachis de Caristo sold two slaves, with the proviso that should they wish to ransom themselves through their relatives, they should be allowed to do so.[99] A similar clause was included in the deed of sale enacted again by Phylipachis in the same month when selling a Greek whom he had captured in Samos. If the slave's father or any of his relations should wish to ransom him, then this was to be agreed to.[100] The same condition was imposed on the sale of a female Greek slave from Samos, sold in Candia in 1300.[101]

Ransoming also took place between Turks and Latins, with Latins arranging ransoms from those held by the Turks and vice versa. In 1369 a ransom of 130 *ducats* was paid to Turks for three Venetians,[102] while, several years later, Nicolao Maximo was ransomed for 150 *ducats*, a large sum indicating his importance.[103] Expenses incurred by Petro de Groto in ransoming one of his slaves of Caffa from the Turks appears in the account books of the commune of Genoa for 1392.[104] In 1408 a Greek woman was in Genoa making arrangements about the money she owed for being ransomed from the Turks.[105] Sometimes those ransomed merely ending up swapping masters. In 1304 two Greeks of Leros, enslaved by the Turks, agreed to be the slaves of the inhabitant of Candia who had ransomed them,[106] and in the same year another Greek acknowledged himself to be the slave of Filippo de Milano who too had arranged his ransom.[107]

It seems that this system of ransoming was also used by the Turks to ransom back from the Christians. In 1403 Giovanni Centuriono made a complaint against Giuliano de Levanto, accusing him of taking from his house without his knowledge or permission his two Turkish slaves, whom he had bought from Guillielmo de Turino, and first imprisoning them and then selling one of them and sending the other to Genoa. Giovanni called for Giuliano to be made to pay the ransom of 2,000 *aspers* for each of these slaves and the 1,000 *aspers* which he had paid to Leonardo Constantio for a slave of his whom they had sent to Turchia to get the ransom for the slaves.[108] From this it appears that Giovanni was intending to ransom his Turkish slaves and in order to do so had sent another of his slaves,

[98] 1301.viii.6 = Benvenuto de Brixano, *Notaio in Candia*, no. 282, p. 104.
[99] 1301.vii.16 = Benvenuto de Brixano, *Notaio in Candia*, no. 236, p. 87.
[100] 1301.vii.9 = Benvenuto de Brixano, *Notaio in Candia*, no. 220, p. 81.
[101] 1300.iii.7 = Pietro Pizolo, *Notaio in Candia*, no. 173, p. 85.
[102] 1369.ix.6 : Elisabeth Santschi, *Regestes des arrêts civils et des Mémoriaux (1363–1399) des Archives du Duc de Crète*, Bibliothèque de l'Instut Hellénique d'Etudes Byzantines et Post-byzantines de Venise 9 (Venice, 1976), no. 170, p. 39.
[103] 1394.iv.6 : Santschi, *Regestes*, no. 354, p. 90.
[104] 1392.iv.19 = ASG, Antico Comune 22, fos. 76, 194.
[105] 1408.v.19 = ASG, Notario, Johannis de Alegro, C.472, fo. 273r–v.
[106] 1304.v.8 in Verlinden, 'Crète', p. 611.
[107] 1304.vii.6 in Verlinden, 'Crète', p. 612.
[108] 1403.xii.4 = ASG, San Giorgio, Sala 34 590/1307, fo. 58r.

presumably either Turkish or Turkish speaking, to Turchia to organise payment. Possibly Giuliano paid the 1,000 *aspers* to Leonardo Constantio for the slave's passage.

In the same year Giuliano di Palma made a complaint against the ex-*podestà* Janoto Lomellino. According to Giuliano, he had nine Turkish slaves whom he and his partners (*socii*) had captured and whom Giuliano had bought from his partners. Of these, two were in his own house, the other seven having escaped from prison. Giuliano accused Janoto of sending his officials to take the two slaves from his house against his will. Giuliano was therefore claiming the 3,000 Turkish silver *aspers* he was expecting as ransom from the slaves' relations.[109] From a further document on the case it appears that Giuliano had had nine Turkish slaves in prison but that they had escaped. Giuliano managed to recapture three, of whom one had broken his leg falling from the walls of Pera in his attempt to flee and died in Giuliano's house. Giuliano kept the remaining two slaves in his house expecting the ransom of 1,500 *aspers* each from their relations. These two were removed from Giuliano's house on orders of the then *podestà* and put into prison.[110]

In reply to these charges Janoto Lomellino, claiming that Bartolomeo Rubeo was in fact *podestà* at the time, said it was known that Giuliano had committed many acts of piracy against the Turks and had disregarded the orders of the *podestà*. Giuliano had, according to Janoto, received under promise the said Turks and their ransom which they gave to him. Not content with this ransom, he had kept the slaves to sell them. Peace had then been arranged with the Turks[111] under which it was agreed that all Turks and especially those who were detained by Giuliano were to be released. Janoto and the *podestà* Bartolomeo took the slaves held by Giuliano and handed them over to the ambassadors of the Turks who had come to complete the peace.[112] In evidence Giuliano de Levanto confirmed that the slaves were handed over to a certain Turk who came to ask for them. Giuliano explained that he had not actually seen the handover himself but had been told about it by his partner (*socius*) Giovanni de Monte, who had freed the slaves on the orders of Janoto.[113]

While it is thus clear that ransoming between the Turks and the Latins, as a two-way process, did take place, the mechanism by which it was organised is very obscure. It seems possible that in the case of Latins ransoming from the Turks, people, either going to Turchia or sent there specially, were charged with paying the ransom and, possibly, collecting the person

---

[109] 1403.xii.1 = ASG, San Giorgio, Sala 34 590/1307, fo. 44r.
[110] 1403.xii.12 = ASG, San Giorgio, Sala 34 590/1307, fo. 45r.
[111] This is presumably in connection with the interregnum following Bayezid's defeat at the battle of Ankara in 1402.
[112] 1403.xii.4 = ASG, San Giorgio, Sala 34 590/1307, fo. 44r–v.
[113] 1403.xii.12 = ASG, San Giorgio, Sala 34 590/1307, fo. 45v.

ransomed. In 1327 Andreas de Raynaldo, who was about to set out for Turchia, received from a Greek in Crete 55 *hyperpyra* for the ransom of his daughter, a slave in Turchia of a Turkish paşa called Murad.[114] As for Turks ransoming from the Latins it seems possible that the ambassadors were used as intermediaries. This was certainly the case when the Mamluk sultan Barsbay (1422–37) dispatched an ambassador to endeavour to ransom 1,500 of his subjects seized by the king of Cyprus.[115] The Turkish slaves held in Pera in 1403 were, on the conclusion of peace, handed over to the Turkish ambassadors,[116] while the Turkish ambassador, Petro Longo, was to receive from the *podestà* Dexerino de Podio payment for a Turkish or Bulgar slave who had fled from Turchia to Chios and was then in the possession of Michaele Neamonitus.[117]

Apart from these official channels it appears that people may have acted on their own. Giovanni Centuriono sent a slave to Turchia to organise the ransoming of the Turkish slaves he held.[118] In 1413 Simon de Serra appointed a procurator to recover his two slaves who had fled from Chios to Turchia. The procurator, Giovanni de Babaino, was to track down whoever was holding them, to sell them and to send the money back to Simon.[119] Although this is not a case of ransoming, presumably the same procedure would have been used in locating those missing. The ransom could also be arranged through the slave concerned who then presumably furnished the information necessary to contact his or her relations. In 1403 Giuliano di Palma sued Janoto Lomellino for the 3,000 *asper*s he had agreed as ransom with his two Turkish slaves and their relatives.[120]

It seems also that Turks who had money, or goods, with them could pay their own ransom. In the case against Janoto Lomellino brought by Giuliano di Palma in 1403, Janoto alleged that the Turks whom Giuliano held had paid their own ransom to him, but that, finding this ransom insufficient, Giuliano had detained them for sale.[121] This seems to have applied not only to Turks. In 1300 a Greek female slave from Samos was sold in Crete with the proviso that should she wish to ransom herself so that she could return to Samos, then the buyer was to accept this.[122] It may be that the sum required from the slave as a ransom was high, for in Majorca,

[114] 1327.viii.16, Verlinden, 'Crète', p. 625.
[115] Piloti, *L'Egypte*, pp. 79, 95–103.
[116] 1403.xii.4 = ASG San Giorgio, Sala 34 590/1307, fo. 44r–v.
[117] 1403.x.3 = ASG, Notaio, Gregorio Panissario, Sc. 37, filza 1, doc. 21.
[118] 1403.xii.4 = ASG, San Giorgio, Sala 34 590/1307, fo. 58r.
[119] 1413.vii.5 = ASG, Notaio, Giovanni Balbi, Sc. 46, filza 1, doc. 17. Giovanni de Babaino was not apparently successful for in 1414.vi.13 = *ibid.*, doc. 293, Simon appointed another procurator to find his missing slaves.
[120] 1403.xii.1 = ASG, San Giorgio, Sala 34 590/1307, fo. 44r.
[121] 1403.xii.4 = ASG, San Giorgio, Sala 34 590/1307, fo. 44r–v.
[122] 1300.iii.7 = Pizolo, *Notaio in Candia*, no. 173, p. 85.

for example, at the beginning of the fourteenth century slaves wishing to ransom themselves had to pay very highly indeed.[123]

Ransoming was therefore an alternative way of earning money from slaves, as opposed to selling them. Presumably, ransoming could be more lucrative on occasion for, while there were many slaves on the market, the relatives concerned wanted only one particular person back. Therefore the ransom demanded could be much higher than the price of the slave as a commodity. This certainly seems to have been the case with Maghribians captured by Catalans or vice versa at the end of the thirteenth and beginning of the fourteenth centuries.[124] It seems that the Genoese, and presumably other Latins, carried out raids in which they took captives whom they then imprisoned while contacting their relations and organising a satisfactory ransoming. Turkish slaves were certainly present in the prison in Pera at the beginning of the fifteenth century. Guillielmo de Turino was accused of imprisoning the slaves of Giuliano de Levanto before selling one and sending the other to Genoa.[125] Giuliano di Palma kept in prison nine Turkish slaves whom he and his partners (socii) had captured.[126] Another document of the same period refers to many Turkish slaves in the prison in Pera.[127] If the slaves were not kept there for this purpose it is difficult to think up any other explanation.

Even without imprisonment slaves seem to have had a somewhat miserable existence which presumably accounts for the great prevalence of runaway slaves, a constant theme in the relations between the Turks and the Genoese and Venetians in the fourteenth and fifteenth centuries. The Arab traveller ibn Battuta also suffered from the problem of escaping slaves while travelling in Anatolia in the 1330s. When staying at Manisa, in the beylik of Saruhan, one of his slaves fled in the direction of Phokaea, together with another slave and ibn Battuta's horses. They were, however, all recaptured and returned to ibn Battuta the following day.[128]

The problem of slaves running away either from Turks to Latins or vice versa appears at the very beginning of the fourteenth century. In 1301 Jacopo Barozzi, the duca di Candia, imposed a fine of 50 hyperpyra per slave on anyone helping Turkish, Greek or Saracen slaves to escape from Crete.[129] As the average price for slaves on the Cretan market in the same period was 8 hyperpyra (4 ducats) for males and 17 hyperpyra (8.5 ducats)

---

[123] C. E. Dufourcq, 'Prix et niveau de vie dans les pays catalans et maghribins à la fin du XIIIe et au début du XIVe siècles', Le Moyen Age, 4th series, 20 (1965), 502–3. Among the examples Dufourcq gives is that of a woman bought for 460 sous who had to pay a ransom of 920 sous.

[124] Dufourcq, 'Prix et niveau', 501–4. On occasion the ransom was incomparably higher than the slave price by as much, according to Dufourcq, as ten times.

[125] 1403.xii.4 = ASG, San Giorgio, Sala 34 590/1307, fo. 58r.

[126] 1403.xii.12 = ASG, San Giorgio, Sala 34 590/1307, f.45r.

[127] 1430.xi.13 = ASG, San Giorgio, Sala 34 590/1307, fo. 57v.

[128] Ibn Battuta, Voyages, pp. 313–14.   [129] Verlinden, 'Crète', p. 605.

for females[130] the scale of the problem for the Cretan authorities is obvious. This problem recurs in Venetian treaties throughout the fourteenth century. A clause of the 1337 treaty between the duca di Candia and İbrahim, emir of Menteşe, stated that if a slave fled taking goods with him, the goods were to be restored though the slave remained free; and if a master or pilot of a ship knowingly took a slave on board, he was to pay 12 *florins* to the slave's master.[131] This clause is repeated in the 1375 treaty between Ahmed, emir of Menteşe, and the duca di Candia[132] with similar clauses appearing in the 1403 and 1407 treaties between İlyas, emir of Menteşe and the duca di Candia.[133] Musa, emir of Menteşe, made a treaty in 1358 with the duca di Candia in which he promised to hand over to the duca's ambassador certain slaves whom he had in his lands, to search diligently for the rest of these slaves, still missing, and to hand them back should they be found.[134] A clause dealing with runaway slaves also appears in the 1348 treaty between the Sancta Unio and Hızır of Aydın which specified the payment of 15 *florins* by the party that received a runaway slave to the party from whom the slave had fled. Any goods the slave had taken from his master were to be handed back.[135]

The problem of runaway slaves also forms a clause in the 1387 treaty between the Ottoman sultan Murad and the Genoese commune. The significance of the problem is apparent from the fact that this is one of the few detailed and most extensive clauses in the treaty. The Genoese agreed that if any slave fled from Murad to Pera, that slave was to be handed over to the *podestà* who was to pay the price of the slave to the master plus 100 *hyperpyra*. Murad, for his part, undertook to return all slaves who fled from their Genoese masters into Turchia or Grecia, that is areas which had come under Ottoman domination, unless the slave was recognised to be a Muslim, in which case Murad was to pay a fair price for the slave concerned.[136] An entry in the deliberations of the Venetian senate in the same year as the treaty shows that the Venetians were anxious that the issue of runaway slaves from Ottoman lands should not be a cause of friction between Venice and the sultan, although Venice, while professing innocence, was undoubtedly profiting from the situation. The Venetian envoy was instructed that should Murad complain of Venetian ships accepting his

[130] Zachariadou, *Trade and Crusade*, p. 161.
[131] 1337.pre iv = Zachariadou, *Trade and Crusade*, doc. 1337M, clause 18, pp. 197–8.
[132] 1375.iv.22 = Zachariadou, *Trade and Crusade*, doc. 1375M, clause 18, p. 221.
[133] 1403.vii.12 = Zachariadou, *Trade and Crusade*, doc. 1403M and doc. 1403M DVL, clause 18, p. 230; 1407.vi.2 = *ibid.*, doc. 1407M, clause 18, p. 236.
[134] 1358.x.13 = Zachariadou, *Trade and Crusade*, doc. 1358/1359M, clause 4, pp. 217–18.
[135] 1348.viii.18, = Zachariadou, *Trade and Crusade*, doc. 1348A, clause 23, p. 210.
[136] 1387.vi.8 = ASG, Archivio Segreto, Materie Politiche 2729, doc. 26; Kate Fleet, 'Treaty', clause 7, p. 15. See also the 1380 treaty between Genoa and the Han of Solgat in which a clause deals with the capture and return of each side's runaway slaves, C. Desimoni, 'Trattato dei genovesi col Khan dei Tatari nel 1380–1381, scritto in lingua volgare', *Archivio Storico Italiano* 20 (1887), 164.

slaves on board and transporting them elsewhere against his wishes, he was to assure Murad that Venetian ships and citizens were forbidden from loading his slaves and that it was in no way the intention of Venice to act in such a manner.[137]

The problem continued into the reign of Bayezid and beyond. In 1390 there was a dispute over payment for alum occasioned by the flight of certain slaves from Turchia to Phokaea;[138] and in 1403 the *podestà* of Chios, Dexerino de Podio, agreed to pay 25 *florins* to Petro Longo, 'ambassador of the Turks', for a Turkish or Bulgar slave who had recently fled from Turchia.[139] In the same year Batista Spinolla, procurator of Ricardo de Vindobonis, sued Giuliano de Levanto over a Turkish slave whom Ricardo had left in Giuliano's care and who had fled.[140] In 1413 Simon de Serra appointed a procurator to retrieve his two slaves who had fled from Chios to Turchia.[141]

Not all slaves tried to escape from their owners. There is one particularly tragic case of a runaway slave who actually tried to run back to his master. In 1401 Ambrogio Bernichono de Arenzano was obliged by the *Capitanei* Ettore de Flisco and Ottobono Giustiniano to sail with his ship from Pera against the Turks in the gulf of Büyükçekmece (the Gulf of Atira in Grecia), south of Istanbul between Küçükçekmece (Rhegion) and Silivri (Selembria). While he was there one of his slaves, a twenty-five-year-old Tatar called Asperto, was captured by the Turks. After about a year the slave managed to escape from the Turkish commander Şerefedin (Sarafadinus) and reached Pera on board a ship from Gallacia, that is from the Iberian peninsula. Unfortunately the Gallacians then wished to sell him. Asperto appealed to three friends of Ambrogio who interceded with the *podestà* on his behalf, pointing out that he could not be sold as he had not been captured by the Gallacians and was in fact the slave of Ambrogio. The *podestà*, however, paid no attention and had Asperto imprisoned. Despite further remonstrances from Ambrosio's friends, the *podestà* handed Asperto over to the Gallacians to do with him what they wanted. Ambrogio in turn sued the *podestà* for the 200 *hyperpyra* at which Asperto was valued.[142] In evidence, Enrico Baldinelo, appearing for Ambrogio, said that he had gone to a castle

---

[137] 1387.x.3 = J. Chrysostomides (ed.), *Monumenta Peloponnesiaca. Documents for the History of the Peloponnese in the 14th and 15th Centuries* (Camberley, 1995), no. 35, p. 83.

[138] 1394.ii.18 = ASG, Notaio, Donato de Clavaro, Sc. 39, filza 1, doc. 97/240.

[139] 1403.x.3, ASG, Notaio, Gregorio Panissario, Sc. 37 filza 1, doc. 21; = Toniolo, *Notai Genovesi*, doc. 22, pp. 74–5. This is presumably the same person as Pietro Longo Candiotto who appears in Gerardo Sagredo's account of the battle of Ankara of 1402 and who, with the army of Bayezid, fled after the battle to Constantinople, was ambassador of Süleyman in 1409, proclaimed peace in Albania, and in the following year was consul in Theologos: see M. M. Alexandrescu-Dersca, *La campagne de Timur en Anatolie (1402)* (Variorum Reprints, London, 1977), p. 129 and n. 2.

[140] 1430.xii.3 = ASG, San Giorgio, Sala 34 590/1307, fos. 58v–59r.

[141] 1413.vii.5 = ASG, Notaio, Giovanni Balbi, Sc. 46, filza 1, doc. 17.

[142] 1403.xi.23 = ASG, San Giorgio, Sala 34 590/1307, fo. 21r.

which the Turks then called Cotolo on business for the commune of Pera in connection with the current war between Pera and the Turks.[143] Ambrogio, then in Pera, had asked Enrico to find out if there was there a Tatar slave, captured by the Turks. When Enrico arrived, he had made enquiries and had, in the presence of some Turks, seen a Tatar slave who said he belonged to Ambrogio. He had asked the slave why he did not escape, to which the slave had replied that he would willing do so if possible and return to Pera, search for Ambrogio and stay with him.[144]

The concern over recovering escaped slaves indicates their value in the economy of the late medieval Mediterranean world and highlights their considerable importance as a commodity in the trade between the Turks and the Genoese, a trade in which the Turks took part both as traders and as trade items.

---

[143] This presumably refers to the period of confusion following the defeat of Bayezid by Timur in 1402, before the treaty of early 1403 made between Süleyman and various Christian powers including Genoa.

[144] 1403.xii.7 = ASG, San Giorgio, Sala 34 590/1307, fo. 23r.

CHAPTER 5

Grain

Grain was one of the most important commodities in trade between the eastern Mediterranean and the western city states in the fourteenth and first half of the fifteenth centuries, even being regarded by Marcha di Marco Battagli da Rimini, the fourteenth-century author of a chronicle from 1212 to 1354, as the cause of the western crusade against Aydın in 1344.[1] It was a trade in which Genoese merchants played a major role. According to Professor Balard, 'Pour Gênes, plus peut-être que pour aucune autre ville de l'Occident médiéval le commerce du blé est un commerce de masse.'[2] Genoese dominated the Bulgarian and Black Sea areas supplying grain to Constantinople[3] and were among the western merchants who replaced the Byzantines in trading grain from the ports of Mesembria and Anchialos, on the Black Sea south of Varna, where the Genoese of Pera became particularly active.[4] Genoa had not only to supply the city itself but also on occasion her colonies. Pera needed a constant supply of grain and suffered at times a dearth, as at the beginning of the fifteenth century, a situation which often led to profiteering.[5]

Before looking at the grain trade between the Genoese and the Turks it is essential to consider exactly what kind of cereals were traded. The most common terms used in Latin sources are *frumentum*, *granum* and *bladum*. These terms appear to mean grain in general and to be at first glance

---

[1] G. Carducci and V. Fiorini (eds.), 'Marcha di Marco Battagli da Rimini (1212–1354)', in *RIS* XVI/3 (Città di Castello, 1912), pp. 50–1.

[2] Balard, *Romanie génoise*, vol. II, p. 750.

[3] Balard, *Romanie génoise*, vol. II, p. 756.

[4] A. Laiou, 'The provisioning of Constantinople during winter 1306–1307', *Byzantion* 37 (1967), 92.

[5] In the inquiry into their conduct, two ex-officials of Pera, Ettore de Flisco and Ottobono Giustiniano, were accused, among other things, of bringing grain from Chios to trade in Pera, 1402.v.30 = ASG, San Giorgio, Sala 34 590/1306, fo. 101v. There were various other accusations concerning Ettore and Ottobono involving grain. Petro Natono complained of being forced by them to carry grain free of charge from Chios to Pera, = *ibid.* and 1402.v.26 = *ibid.*, fo. 97r. They also were charged with selling grain in Constantinople and of profiting, together with the Byzantine emperor and his factor Leondarius, in selling grain, 1402.v.26 = *ibid.*, fo. 97r; 1402.v.27 = *ibid.*, fo. 97v, 1402.v.30 = *ibid.*, fos. 101v, 102r.

interchangeable.[6] In the two versions of the chronicle written by Jan Jacopo Caroldo, one refers to *biave* and the other to *frumenti*.[7] In a report on the situation in Romania made to the Venetian signoria by a Genoese, Jacopo de Orado, in September 1401, Jacopo reported that there was much 'bladorum' in Caffa selling at the rate of 'modium frumenti aspros centum'.[8] G. T. Dennis translates *bladorum* here as 'wheat' and *frumentum* as 'grain'. However, a clause in the 1331 treaty between Venice and Menteşe might perhaps be taken to indicate that the term *bladum* was more general in meaning than *frumentum*, as the first phrase refers to 'bladi et leguminum, bobum, equorum et sclavorum' whereas the sentence in the same clause which specifies the tax rates to be paid refers to 'frumento ... ordeo ... legumine', so distinguishing two types, grain/wheat/corn and barley, presumably covered in the previous phrase by the word *bladum*.[9] That there could be a difference between *frumentum* and *bladum* seems confirmed by a clause in the 1278 list of complaints by Venetians against Byzantium. Stefano Gondem went to Constantinople with his ship loaded with 'frumento et ordeo' but was prevented from selling or doing anything with 'ipso blando'. He, in consequence, suffered loss, the greater part of the 'frumentum et ordeum' being destroyed. Stefano claimed damages for his ship and for the 'frumento et ordeo'.[10] Here it appears as if *bladum* was a more general term than *frumentum* and could mean both grain/corn and barley. In both the 1277 chrysobul of Michael VIII and in the treaty of 1285 between Venice and Byzantium, Venetians were granted freedom to enter the empire from the Black sea 'cum frumento vel blado ... et frumento seu alio blado'.[11] *Frumento* was thus here a type of *blado* while *blado* had a

---

[6] Charlton T. Lewis and Charles Short, *A Latin Dictionary* (Oxford, 1907) define *frumentum* as corn, grain and *granum* as grain, seed, small kernel; R. E. Latham, *Dictionary of Medieval Latin from British Sources* (London, 1975), defines *bladum* as corn, grain, especially wheat; Evans in his edition of Pegolotti, *Pratica*, p. 414 defines *biado* as grain and *granum* as wheat, p. 420. J. F. Neirmeyer, *Mediae Latinitatis Lexicon Minus* (Leiden, 1976) defines *bladum* as (a) bread-corn (wheat, rye, spelt), (b) wheat; *frumentum* as wheat; *granum* as (a) corn, (b) wheat.

[7] J. Chrysostomides, 'Studies on the chronicle of Caroldo, with special reference to the history of Byzantium from 1370 to 1377', *Orientalia Christiana Periodica* 35 (1969), 176–7.

[8] 1401.ix.10 = G. T. Dennis, 'Three reports from Crete on the situation in Romania', *Studi Veneziani* 12 (1970), 246, no. 1, clause 7.

[9] 1331.iv.13 = Zachariadou, *Trade and Crusade*, doc. 1331M, clause 3, p. 187: 'duo per centinario, excepto comerclo et solutione bladi et leguminum, bobum, equorum et sclavorum. Et non debeant solvere in omnibus terris dicti admirati comerchium vel dacia nisi una vice, etiam si ipsi portarent merces suas in pluribus terris. Et de frumento debeant solvere aspros duos pro modio et de ordeo et legumine asprum unum pro modio et de bove aspros duos, de equos aspros tres et de sclavo aspros decem pro quolibet predictorum.'

[10] 1278.iii. = G. L. Tafel and G. M. Thomas, *Urkunden zur älteren Handels- und Staatsgeschichte der Republik Venedik mit besonderer Beziehung auf Byzanz und die Levante. vom neunten bis zum Ausgang des fünfzehnten Jahrhunderts*, Fontes Rerum Austriacarum, Diplomataria et Acta (Vienna, 1857), vols. I–III (vol. III = 1256–99): vol. III, no. 370, p. 240.

[11] 1277.iii.19 = Tafel and Thomas, *Urkunden*, vol. III, no. 368, p. 144; 1285.vi.15 = *ibid.*, no. 378, p. 332.

more general meaning. That this was so is confirmed in a document of 1345 in which the Venetian senate, discussing the Byzantine attempt to impose tax on grain imported from Turchia, referred to 'frumentum et omni aliud bladum'.[12] In the complaint of Petro Castolum and Andrea Vendelino against the Byzantines, their ship was loaded with 'frumento et milio et fabis'. The ship was captured at Ania and taken to Butrino, on the Greek coast opposite Corfu, and almost all the 'blando' offloaded. The merchants lost 'frumenti, milio et fabis'. Afterwards the ship 'cum aliqua parte dicti blandi' was returned and they included in their claim for damages the expenses incurred in recovering 'dicta navi et blando illo pauco'.[13] Here too *bladum* does appear to have a more general meaning than *frumentum*, including on this occasion grain/corn, millet (*milium*) and beans (*faba*). From these examples it appears that *bladum* was a general term for grain while *frumentum* was more specific, meaning wheat.

Granum was commonly used and seems to be equivalent to *frumentum*. It is translated by Evans as wheat.[14] That *granum* was distinct from *bladum* is indicated by the different treatment in Pegolotti of two distinct commodities. Pegolotti refers to *biado* being sold in and exported from Theologos while also discussing the expenses involved in taking *grano* out of the same area.[15]

It is quite clear that *ordeum* and *frumentum* were distinct commodities, though often cited together in the sources. The phrase 'frumento et ordeo' appears in the complaint of Giovanni Barocio, robbed when going to Negroponte with his ship loaded with 'frumento et ordeo et aliis mercationibus' and in a complaint by Giovanni de Pagano whose ship too was loaded with 'frumento et ordeo'.[16] In the treaties between Venice and Menteşe of 1331, 1337, 1375, 1403 and 1407 *frumentum* was charged a customs tax of 2 *aspers* per *modio* while *ordeum* was charged at a rate of 1 *asper* per *modio*.[17]

Granum was also something clearly different from *ordeum*. In the 1387 treaty between Murad I and the Genoese, the Genoese were to be taxed at a reduced rate for 'grani ordei milli et aliorum leguminum'.[18] *Bladum* too was distinct from *ordeum*. In the complaint of Antonio Squaia against the customs officials of Mesembria over 'frumento et ordeo pro comerclo,

---

[12] 1345.i.24 = J. Chrysostomides, 'Venetian commercial privileges under the Palaeologi', *Studi Veneziani* 12 (1970),332, doc. 3.

[13] 1278.iii. = Tafel and Thomas, *Urkunden*, vol. III, no. 370, pp. 243–4.

[14] Pegolotti, *Pratica*, p. 420.   [15] Pegolotti, *Pratica*, p. 56.

[16] 1278.iii. = Tafel and Thomas, *Urkunden*, vol. III, no. 370, pp. 180, 233. See also *ibid.*, p. 240.

[17] 1331.iv.13 = Zachariadou, *Trade and Crusade*, doc. 1331M, clause 3, p. 187; 1337.pre-iv. = *ibid.*, doc. 1337M, clause 20, p. 198; 1375.iv.22 = *ibid.*, doc. 1375M, clause 20, p. 222; 1403.vii.24 = *ibid.*, doc. 1403M, doc. 1403M DVL, clause 20, p. 230; 1407.vi.2 = *ibid.*, doc. 1407M, clause 20, p. 236.

[18] 1387.vi.8 = ASG, Archivio Segreto, Materie Politiche, 2729, no. 26; Fleet, 'Treaty', clause 5, p. 15.

accepto sibi de ipso blando per illos de Mesembria et de ordeo multo sibi accepto per lo Mangatriarcha ... , et propter moram, quam fecerat ibi per VIII dies mandato dicti Mengatriarche cum alio blando contra suam voluntatem', *bladum* and *ordeum* appear as two distinct items.[19]

Of the three terms commonly used in the Latin sources, *frumentum* and *granum* appear to have had the same meaning, wheat, while *bladum* was a wider term for grain in general. It is not possible to be precise about the type of grain involved when the term used is *bladum* or *semen*, another term similar in scope, as in the phrase 'frumentum et alia semina'.[20] But the two words commonly applied in the Latin sources to grain exported from Turchia, *granum* and *frumentum*, allow one to suggest that what western Anatolia exported mostly was wheat, together with barley (*ordeum*). That western Anatolia was predominantly a wheat- and barley-producing area is supported by Aşıkpaşazade's reference to Bayezid's troops buying wheat ('buğday') and barley ('arpa') in Konya around 797–8/1394–5.[21] This is also supported by Gregoras's use of the word σῖτος when talking of the grain of Turchia.[22]

Perhaps of the two, wheat was the more important.[23] In the early part of the reign of Mehmed II, the sultan ordered infidels of the *hass* villages of Constantinople and Galata to plant one *mudd* of wheat, 0.5 of barley and 0.5 of oats each.[24] Apart from showing that these were presumably the common grains grown in this period, it also gives an idea of the importance of wheat. A Venetian document of 1345 too perhaps allows one to argue that what western Anatolia exported particularly was wheat for the word used for grain exported from Turchia was *frumentum*, the word *bladum* being used for the Byzantine empire. The Venetian senate was concerned that Venetian merchants were being charged *comerchium* unjustly in Phokaea on 'frumento nato in partibus Turchie'.[25]

[19] 1278.iii. = Tafel and Thomas, *Urkunden*, vol. III, no. 370, p. 246. *Mangatriarcha* was the Greek official, *Megatriesarcham, ibid.*.

[20] 1304.iii. = Belgrano, 'Documenti', no. 10, p. 109.

[21] Aşıkpaşazade, *Altosmanische Chronik,*, pp. 64–5; Aşıkpaşazade, *Tevarih-i al-i 'Osman*, pp. 71–2.

[22] Gregoras, *Historia*, vol. II, p. 687, l. 1.

[23] This was certainly the case in north-eastern Anatolia in the area round Tokat where in c.1455 wheat formed 45 per cent and barley 20 per cent of total agricultural production in Cinife, while in Venk at the same date wheat formed 65.5 per cent and barley 30.7 per cent of total production. The figures for Yıldız c.1455 were 63.5 per cent for wheat and 36.4 per cent for barley. See Huri İslamoğlu-İnan, 'State and Peasants in the Ottoman Empire: A Study of Peasant Economy in North-Central Anatolia during the Sixteeneth Century', in İslamoğlu-İnan, *World-Economy*, p. 142.

[24] Post-1354.iv.18 or end of 1458 = Robert Anhegger and Halil İnalcık, *Kanunname-i Sultani ber Muceb-i 'Örf-i 'Osmani II Mehmed ve II Bayezid devirlerine ait yasakname ve kanunnameler*, Türk Tarih Kurumu Yayınlarından, eleventh series 5 (Ankara, 1956), no. 37, p. 51; Nicoră Beldiceanu, *Les actes des premiers sultans conservés dans les manuscrits Turcs de la Bibliothèque Nationale à Paris I*, Ecole Pratique des Hautes Etudes, VIe section (Paris–The Hague, 1960–64) vols. I–II, vol. I, no. 38, pp. 119–20.

[25] 1345.i.24 = Chrysostomides, 'Venetian commercial privileges', doc. 3, p. 332.

It is possible that Aydın may have been predominantly a wheat-producing area. While wheat and barley appear in the treaties between Venice and Menteşe throughout the fourteenth century, grain is not mentioned in the 1337 treaty between Aydın and Venice while in that of 1353 the clause concerning tax on grain refers to 'frumentum vel alia victualia vel legumina' which were charged at 4 per cent.[26] Could this mean that while Menteşe produced and exported wheat and barley, Aydın produced only wheat, or that it was wheat alone that was exported by the Venetians? This relies on the word *victualia* meaning something different from grain. But in a clause in the 1387 treaty between Murad I and the Genoese *victualia* is used clearly meaning grain. Under this clause the Genoese were granted freedom to 'victualibus honerari solvendo ... pro quolibet modio Romanie grani ordei milli et aliorum leguminum illud quod solvent Saraceni Greci Veneti et allteri qui minus solvent'.[27]

Western Anatolia was an important source of grain in the eastern Mediterranean and one that the Genoese, and other western city states, used constantly. The *Officium Victualium* of Genoa sent representatives in 1374–5 to buy grain in Turchia, concluding a 4,000-*mine* contract with one of them, Lanzarotto Cattaneo, and instructing another, Leonardo Tartaro, to buy in Turchia barley and grain at whatever price he wished.[28] The Genoese were certainly buying wheat, barley and millet from the Ottomans in 1387.[29] By analogy with the treaties between Venice and the emirs of Menteşe and Aydın, it would seem reasonable to assume that for the Genoese too, grain was an important item in their trade with these beyliks.

Wheat and grain were sold in and exported from Theologos in the fourteenth century[30] and Genoese merchants are known to have exported grain from there,[31] as they did from Phokaea, another important grain-export port in western Anatolia. Grain from both Phokaea and Theologos was imported into Genoa in 1381, 1382, 1384, 1391 and 1393.[32] Anatolian grain also was exported from there to places in the eastern Mediterranean. In 1381 Steffano and Carolo Cataneo acting for Rafaele de Castro bought 1,800 *modii* of wheat from Phokaea which they transported to Famagusta and handed over to Precivali Cibo, *podestà* and consilius of the state of Cyprus, in accordance with the agreement made for the commune with Rafaele.[33]

[26] 1353.iv.7 = Zachariadou, *Trade and Crusade*, doc. 1353A, clause 19, p. 214.
[27] 1387.vi.8 = ASG, Archivio Segreto, Materie Politiche, 2729, doc. 26; Fleet, 'Treaty', clause 5, p. 15.
[28] Balard, *Romanie génoise*, vol. II, pp. 752, 759, citing ASG, Manoscritti no. 104.
[29] 1387.vi.8 = ASG, Archivio Segreto, Materie Politiche, 2729, no. 26; Fleet, 'Treaty', clause 5, p. 15.
[30] Pegolotti, *Pratica*, pp. 55, 56.
[31] 1344.viii.9 : Balard, Laiou and Otten-Froux, *Documents*, no. 46, pp. 27–8.
[32] Balard, *Romanie génoise*, vol. II, p. 754.
[33] 1382.xi.7 = ASG, Antico Comune, 16 (Communis Ianuae Massaria), fo. 64r. One *modio* of

Grain was also exported from the Black Sea region, Torpeto Malocello, for example, being sent by the *podestà* of Pera to buy 2,000 *mines* of grain for Genoa in Caffa, the Black Sea or Phokaea in 1389,[34] and from Thrace where ships loaded at Pannidos (modern Barbaros, just south of Tekirdağ).[35] Tarsus too was a grain market for the Genoese from an early date. In 1300 Antonio, son of Musso, went with 100 silver *bessant*s to buy grain in Tarsus and Armenia and return with it to Cyprus.[36] Antalya was also a market and export port for wheat and barley in the first half of the fourteenth century,[37] and it would seem reasonable to assume that Genoese merchants were involved there too in the grain trade.

The Genoese on Chios were active in buying grain from the Turks. In 1414 Sipahi Bayezid ('Sapihi Bayezit quondam Jhacsi, Turchus de Cazali isich obasi'), a Turk of some importance to judge from his title, acknowledged to the notary Giovanni Balbi, acting for Domenico Giustiniano, that he had received full payment for all the goods, monies and wheat which he, 'Sapihi Bayaxit', had on any occasion sold to Domenico. The document was enacted in Chios and the witnesses included one Greek, Micalli Verioti de Fliis Veteribus Grecho and two Turks, Bayrambey Turcho de Smirris (İzmir) quondam Ezedim ('İzeddin), Elies (İlyas) Turcho de Smrris (İzmir) quondam Tagdira (?) and the interpreter, Cristoforo Picenino, 'interpetre cive Chii', who translated from Turkish into Latin at the request of Sipahi Bayezid.[38] The document reads as if Sipahi Bayezid had been in the habit of providing Domenico with goods and that this was a general statement to the effect that Domenico now owed nothing for any of the deals. Its importance is perhaps reinforced by the large number of witnesses (seven).

In the same period Cüneyd Bey, the ruler of Aydın at that time, was involved in selling grain to Chios, a trade which it would seem reasonable to assume was a useful source of income for him. In 1414 the *podestà* of Chios, Paulo de Montaldo, held an investigation into the tax position of the Jew Magister Moyses de Meir, citizen and inhabitant of Chios and a doctor ('fixitum'). Moyses was exempt from taxation but had been charged for payment he had made to Cüneyd Bey ('Jonayt Bey Turchus') and for wheat, which had been distributed by the officials for the provisioning of Chios.

Romania was equivalent to *c*.317 litres: E. A. Zachariadou, 'Prix et marchés des céréales en Romanie (1343–1405)', *Nuova Rivista Storica* 61 (Milan, 1977), 301–2.

[34] Balard, *Romanie génoise*, vol. II, p. 761.

[35] Balard, *Romanie génoise*, vol. II, p. 762. Two ships loaded grain at Pannidos and Phokaea.

[36] 1300.xii.2 = Lamberto di Sambuceto in Valeria Polonia, *Notai Genovesi in Oltremare. Atti Rogati a Cipro da Lamberto di Sambuceto (3 Iuglio 1300–3 Agosto 1301)*, CSFS 31 (Genoa, 1982), no. 139, pp. 155–6.

[37] Pegolotti, *Pratica*, p. 39.

[38] 1414.vii.16 = ASG, Notaio, Giovanni Balbi, Sc. 46, filza 1, doc. 311. See appendix 5 below, doc. 12. 'Jhacsi' is probably, by analogy with the Latin *Ihallabi* for *Çelebi*, a Latin rendering of a Turkish name beginning with Çe, while 'cazali', meaning a small settlement, shows that 'isich obasi' is a place name, of which the second word is probably *ovası* (? Ece Ovası, modern Eceabat, south of Gelibolu, opposite Çanakkale).

Moyses was absolved from these taxes, for receiving the wheat and for the money whether the money was handed to a Turk or was handed over by a Turk.[39]

Other western merchants, as well as the Genoese, frequented Turchia in search of grain. In the 1270s Venetians loaded wheat at Fethiye (Makre, Meğri, on the Turkish coast opposite Rhodes), for Giovanni Bembo, having sailed from Negroponte to Fethiye where he loaded wheat and wine, was attacked there and his cargo seized.[40] In the same period, grain was being sold at İncir Liman (Paralimine). In 1278 Nicolo Dente and Filippo Bono, needing to prepare their ship, offloaded, within the territories of the Byzantine emperor, their cargo of wheat from the Crimea which they intended to transport to Venice. When they wished to re-load and leave for Venice, they were prevented from doing so and the wheat was kept locked and under guard. Ultimately they were able to obtain imperial permission to sell, but sold at a loss at İncir Liman.[41]

The Venetians also bought and exported wheat and barley from the emirates of Aydın and Menteşe.[42] In 1376 the Genoese, annoyed by the Venetian seizure of Tenedos, attacked Venetian ships sailing from Crete to Theologos to load grain.[43] From an early date, the Venetians entered into negotiations over grain exports with the Ottomans. In 1333 the signoria decided that officials of Crete should themselves handle the agreement with Orhan for the import into Crete of horses and grain.[44] Apart from the regions of western Anatolia, other areas under Ottoman control were grain markets for western merchants. In 1437 Antonio de Negroponte bought 26 *moza* of grain ('fromenti') in Samsun at 85 *aspers* of Samsun, equivalent, at an exchange rate of 19 *aspers* of Samsun to 1 *hyperpyron*, to 116.3 *hyperpyra*.[45]

Some of the grain exported by the Venetians from Turchia was imported into Constantinople, for in 1342 the Venetians were complaining of Byzantine attempts to tax them on grain they had imported from Phokaea and other places, formerly Byzantine but by then in Turkish hands.[46] The Venetians were still complaining about this matter three years later.[47]

Among other westerners who traded in Turkish grain were the Hospital-

---

[39] 1414.iii.18 = ASG, Notaio, Giovanni Balbi, Sc. 46, filza 1, doc. 288. See appendix 5 below, doc. 10.

[40] 1278.iii = Tafel and Thomas, *Urkunden*, vol. III, no. 370, pp. 196–7.

[41] 1278.iii = Tafel and Thomas, *Urkunden*, vol. III, no. 370, p. 266.

[42] 1331.iv.13 = Zachariadou, *Trade and Crusade*, doc. 1331M, clause 3, p. 187; 1337.pre-iv. = *ibid.*, doc. 1337M, clause 20, p. 198; 1353.iv.7 = *ibid.*, doc. 1353A, clause 19, p. 214; 1375.iv.22 = *ibid.*, doc. 1375M, clause 20, pp. 221–2; 1403.vii.24 = *ibid.*, doc. 1403M, doc. 1403M DVL, clause 20, p. 230; 1407.vi.2 = *ibid.*, doc. 1407M, clause 20, p. 236.

[43] 1376 = Chrysostomides, 'Caroldo', 176–7.

[44] 1333.xi.16 : Thiriet, *Régestes*, vol. I, doc. 38, pp. 30–1.

[45] 1437.xii.18 = Badoer, *Libro*, col. 152, p. 306.

[46] 1342.iii.16 = Chrysostomides, 'Venetian commercial privileges', no. 2, pp. 330–1.

[47] 1345.i.24 = Chrysostomides, 'Venetian commercial privileges', no. 3, pp. 331–3.

lers and the Ragusans. Prompted by the problems besetting the Hospitallers – disease, depopulation and Turkish attacks – Pope Clement VII in 1379 granted the Hospitallers the right to import grain and other foodstuffs from Turchia.[48] Ragusan merchants were active in Antalya in the mid-fifteenth century. In 1451 a Ragusan was to buy grain in Antalya and take it to Alexandria.[49] Two years later, in 1453, the emir of Alexandria forced a Ragusan merchant to take 500 *ducats* to buy a cargo of grain in Cyprus and Antalya and transport it to Alexandria. When the merchant did not reach his destination, the emir forced another Ragusan to pay half the cost of 100 *ribebe* of grain which the emir should have received.[50] The Byzantines also imported grain from Turchia into the empire, though by now rarely.[51]

The Turchian market was not always able to supply requirements. The Genoese had on occasion to provide Cyprus with grain when Famagusta was not able to obtain enough on the local markets or import sufficient from Turchia. Sicilian grain was sent to Cyprus in 1383, 1386, 1388, 1390, 1391, 1392, 1393, 1394 and 1397.[52] Crete, on the other hand, was itself a grain-producing area and thus only rarely imported grain from the west.[53] At the beginning of the fifteenth century bad harvests in Romania and Turchia forced Chian merchants to go to Apulia for grain. In 1404 they even went as far as Catalonia.[54]

While it is clear that Turchia was an important grain-supplying region, it was perhaps of the three main sources of grain in the eastern Mediterranean – Thrace, the Black Sea region and Turchia – the least important, the Black Sea, being much more of a bulk supplier. This is reflected in a letter dated May 1347 and sent from Crete by the merchant Vannino Fecini to Pignol Zucchello, a merchant based in Venice and active in the first half of the fourteenth century, in which Fecini comments, after quoting the price of grain in Crete and Balat (Palatia), that he believes the market for grain and other commodities was now better because peace had been made in Tana and many ships had gone there.[55] In 1384 Phokaea and Theologos provided Genoa with 3,710 *mines* of grain in comparison, in the same year, with 31,919 from Romania and 31,344 from Caffa. These figures together made up 77 per cent of the known grain imports for that year.[56] According to Professor Balard's figures, grain from Phokaea in 1391 made up 0.5 per cent

---

[48] 1379.viii.6 = Luttrell, 'Intrigue', 35.

[49] 1451.i.18 : Krekić, *Dubrovnik*, no. 1201, p. 368.

[50] 1453.i.5 : Krekić, *Dubrovnik*, no. 1258, pp. 379–80.

[51] Gregoras, *Historia*, vol. II, pp. 686–7.

[52] Balard, *Romanie génoise*, vol. II, p. 764.   [53] Zachariadou, 'Prix', p. 292.

[54] Balard, *Romanie génoise*, vol. II, pp. 764–5, citing ASG, Notaio, Gregorio Panissario.

[55] 1347.v.16 = Zucchello, *Lettere*, no. 36, p. 73: 'ma io credo che ora megliora merchato di formento e d'assai altre cose perochè la pacie de la Tana è fatta, e molte navi so' andate dentro'.

[56] Balard, *Romanie génoise*, vol. II, p. 760 and n. 121, citing ASG, Antico Comune, Magistrorum rationalium.

of the grain imported into Genoa that year and 9 per cent for 1392/3. Phokaea grain does not figure in his table for 1390.[57] There thus seems to be a considerable fluctuation in the amount imported, from 0 per cent in 1390 to 9 per cent in 1392/3. Ottoman activity in this period was undoubtedly disrupting the grain trade. However, the explanation for this fluctuation may lie more in the randomness of the sources than in the political situation, for if the fluctuation was due to Ottoman advances one might expect a decline from 1390 to 1392/3 rather than an increase in grain exports.

The importance of Turchia as a grain market fluctuated according to external factors such as the accessibility of other grain-producing areas or according to internal political events such as attack or Ottoman activity. Difficulties in other grain-supplying regions or times of scarcity resulted in an increase in the amount of grain exported from Turchia. In 1269, a year of famine in Italy, Genoese and Venetian merchants exported grain into Italy from Turchia.[58] In 1343 the troubles in the Crimean region with the Tatar han resulted in the decline of that region as a source of grain, the han forbidding export from his territories, and the subsequent rise in the importance of Turchia as a market. But in 1347 this importance declined because of the reopening of Tana.[59] In 1386 Caffa, at war with the Tatars of Solgat, was forced to import grain from, among other places, Turchia, and at this time only Turchia and Cyprus were good grain markets.[60]

Local political events also affected Turchia as a market for grain. In 1344 Turchia became closed to western merchants, as a result of the increase of Aydın's military power from 1341 and the deteriorating relations between Aydın and the western states. A crusade was organised to counter the threat posed by Aydın and an attack launched on the beylik in the summer of 1344. The port of İzmir was occupied in October. In a letter written from Candia and dated 5 October 1344, the merchants Domino Pingniuolo, Giannino Pingniuolo and Franciescho Bartolomei reported that there was at that time no movement to or from Turchia.[61] A total break in trade relations did not, however, persist for long and by the spring of the following year Venetian merchants were once more trading in western Anatolia.[62] Relations were

[57] Balard, *Romanie génoise*, vol. II, p. 762.

[58] Martin da Canal, 'La cronique des Veniciens' in *Archivio Storico Italiano* 8 (Florence, 1845), 650, 654. According to G. I. Bratianu, 'La question de l'approvisionnement de Constantinople à l'époque byzantine et ottomane', *Byzantion* 5 (1929–30), 96, citing da Canal, this is the first time that the Venetians and the Genoese imported into Italy from, among other places, Turchia. But 650 has nothing about Turks and neither 650 nor 654 mention Genoese: 'Tatars, Alan, Giquis, Rous, Turs, Armins et Gres donerent la vitaille as Veneciens a celui tens' (654).

[59] 1347.v.16 = Zucchello, *Lettere*, no. 36, p. 73.

[60] Balard, *Romanie génoise*, vol. II, p. 761, citing 1386.ix.4, AS Prato, Carteggio Pisa da Genova, no. 508.

[61] 1344.x.5 = Zucchello, *Lettere*, no. 9, p. 25.

[62] 1346.iii.17 = Zucchello, *Lettere*, no. 24, p. 54.

apparently not put on a firm footing again until the enactment of a treaty between Aydın and Venice in 1353.

Ottoman advances and the consequent political upheaval of the 1390s reduced the reliability of Turchia as a secure source of grain. From 1394 the Genoese could no longer rely on the eastern grain markets and it was not until 1402 that Turkish grain shipped from Chios once again appeared in the Genoese markets. Traffic in Turkish grain remained sluggish for several years, not really picking up until around 1406. But by then the Genoese had started looking west for supplies, deterred from the markets of western Anatolia and the Black Sea by the new political conditions.[63] According to Professor Balard, there was nothing as irregular as the eastern grain trade at end of fourteenth century.[64]

Apart from the instability caused to markets by Ottoman territorial advances, absorbing as they did the grain-growing regions of the beyliks, it appears that the Ottomans, apparently in contrast to the emirs of Menteşe and Aydın, controlled and manipulated the markets, actively seeking to use their economic muscle to improve their relations with western states. One way in which they did this was to control the flow of goods. Bayezid certainly controlled the export of grain from his territories. In 1390 a Venetian citizen, Lodisio Bragadino, brought a complaint before the *podestà* of Pera, Antonio Leardo, against Jane de Draperiis, *burgensis* of Pera. Lodisio had bought grain from Jane but Jane had, according to the complaint, failed to hand over part of the grain at the agreed time and agreed place. Lodisio therefore requested that Jane hand over 1,000 *modio* of grain in Pannidos (modern Barbaros) or one of the ports of Greece where ships customarily loaded or in Turchia 'videlicet in locis et scalis dominacionis domini Ihallabi turchi, videlicet a Buccha Avis citra'. Lodisio further requested that Jane hand over 2,000 *modio* of grain at Lo Porro or Pannidos or some other place in Greece where ships customarily loaded 'videlicet a Bucha Avis citra' or in loading places of Turchia ('in locis Turchie carregatoriis') but specifies in only one or two of these places, in Camalı (just south of Gelibolu) or this side of Scorpiata ('Scorpiata citra') (on the coast opposite Tenedos), it being known that Lodisio always had free passage from these places for that quantity of grain.[65] This presumably means either that these two Turkish ports, Camalı and Scorpiata, as distinct from other Turkish ports, were always open, or that Lodisio had some special arrangement either with Bayezid or with some local official. If the latter, it would be most interesting to know how such arrangements were

[63] Balard, *Romanie génoise*, vol. II, p. 763.
[64] Balard, *Romanie génoise*, vol. II, p. 768.
[65] 1390.iii.2 = Musso, *Navigazione*, no. 5, pp. 236–40: 'ipsis duobus locis comprehensis, ita quod semper libere dictus Lodisius a dictis locis de dicto frumento supradicte quantitatis liberam habeat'.

come to, whether they were official or whether Lodisio had bribed an individual official.[66]

In 1390, after his capture of Menteşe and Aydın, Bayezid forbade the export of grain.[67] He also imposed a ban on grain export from Macedonia.[68] In 1400 the emir of Aydın (Theologos), described as Lord Zalapi (i.e. Çelebi), son of Bayezid, identified by Professor Thiriet as probably Süleyman, then governor of Aydın,[69] but by Professor Zachariadou as probably Ertoğrul,[70] sent ambassadors to Crete to tell the Venetians of his friendly feelings towards them. His ambassadors were to reassure the Venetians that their ships were welcome to trade in Aydın and export whatever goods they wished with the exception of cereals, timber and horses. In return, the emir requested Venetian support in any power struggle with his brothers. Venice, pleased with the emir's friendly attitude, advised the Cretan authorities to send an ambassador instructed to try and procure freedom of trade for horses and grain. In the event of a struggle with his brothers, the ambassadors were to restrict themselves to offering the emir asylum either in Crete or in some other Venetian territory.[71]

One can compare the policy of the Ottomans with that pursued in 1343 by the Tatar han who, in his struggle with the Venetians, forbade the export of grain from his state.[72] The han forced western merchants out of the ports on the Black Sea under his control, so driving the Venetians out of Tana. In retaliation, the Venetians imposed a ban on their merchants' entering the han's territory. The subsequent prohibition on the export of grain enforced by the han resulted in an immediate scarcity of the commodity in Constantinople. The situation persisted for two years, the Genoese refusing to join the Venetians in their proposed commercial boycott of Tatar lands, until lack of grain forced the Venetians to capitulate. In 1347 the Venetians reversed the prohibition on trade in Tatar territories and, shortly afterwards, a treaty was concluded between them and the han.[73]

It is interesting to speculate on whether there was any economic policy similar to Ottoman control of the flow of grain followed by the emirs of

[66] See Kate Fleet, 'Ottoman grain exports from western Anatolia at the end of the fourteenth century', *JESHO* 40, 3 (1997), 283–93.

[67] Dukas, *Historia Byzantina*, p. 47, ll. 11–13; Dukas, *Historia Turcobyzantina*,, p. 75, ll. 16–17; Dukas, *Decline and Fall*, p. 81; Chrysostomides, *Monumenta Peloponnesiaca*, doc. 68, p. 138, n. 2.

[68] Freddy Thiriet, *La Romanie vénitienne au Moyen Age. Le développement et l'exploitation du domaine colonial vénitien (XII–XV siècles)* (Paris, 1975), p. 364.

[69] Thiriet, *Régestes*, vol. II, p. 12.

[70] E. A. Zachariadou, 'Ertogrul Bey il sovrano di Teologo (Efeso)', *ASLSP* 79, n.s. 5 (Genoa, 1965) 158.

[71] 1400.iii.19 : Thiriet, *Régestes*, vol. II, doc. 988, pp. 12–13; Noiret, *Documents*, pp. 110–11; Iorga, *Notices et Extraits*, vol. I, Paris and Bucharest, 1899, p. 102.

[72] 1344.xii = Morozzo della Rocca, 'Notizie da Caffa' in *Studi in onore di A Fanfani* (Milan, 1962), vol. III, doc. 5, p. 281; 1345.i.26 = *ibid.*, doc. 6, p. 285.

[73] Zachariadou, 'Prix', 295–6; 1344.xii = Morozzo della Rocca, 'Notizie', doc. 5, p. 281; 1345.i.26 = *ibid.*, doc. 6, p. 285.

Menteşe or Aydın, or if there was any difference in the policy pursued by the two beyliks. In this respect it may be significant that in Menteşe the tax charged on grain remained the same throughout the fourteenth century. Bearing in mind the fluctuations of the market and the great importance, on occasions, for western states of grain exports from western Anatolia, coupled with the effect of inflation, it seems remarkable that the same figure should have been levied from the treaty of 1331 up to that of 1407. This might perhaps be taken as indicative of a lack of firm economic management by Menteşe and a willingness to accept a position favourable to Venice rather than, when possible, to dictate terms to her. Aydın, on the other hand, may have been more dominant in its handling of the grain trade. There was certainly no trade in the area in 1344 at the time of the crusade launched by western states against the beylik.[74] Perhaps, in a move similar to that of the Tatar han in the same period, the emir of Aydın prohibited the export of grain from his territories. That there was at this time a breach of treaty arrangements is clear from Marcha di Marco Battagli da Rimini and it was presumably the Turks of Aydın who broke the arrangement as the response, again according to Marcha di Marco Battagli da Rimini, was the western crusade against İzmir.[75] It would certainly not have been in western interests to lose this source of grain.

Fluctuations in the price of grain from Turchia were due in large part to the availability of the commodity, which depended on the political position at the time. The actions of the Tatar han in 1343 against the Venetians resulted in an immediate scarcity of grain which the Venetians were forced to make up by importing from Anatolia, causing a price rise. Once peace had been made in Tana in 1347, however, ships were able to return to the area and the price dropped in Romania from 8 or 9 *hyperpyra* per *mogio* to 5 to 6 *hyperpyra* per *mogio*.[76] In Crete and Constantinople prices of grain were high in 1343–7, then fell, rising again in the 1390s. This seems, as Professor Zachariadou has suggested, to be the result of the political position in one of the main grain-supplying regions, western Anatolia.[77] In 1386 Caffa, occupied with fighting the Tatars of Solgat, was not able to supply grain to Genoa and the price in Sicily rose to 50 per cent above the normal cost.[78]

The level of Turkish activity had a direct impact on grain prices. In the 1390s the difficult situation for Constantinople, under siege by Bayezid since 1391, was reflected by high prices in Pera.[79] Fear of Turkish attack

[74] 1344.x.5 = Zucchello, *Lettere*, no. 9, p. 25.
[75] Carducci and Fiorini (eds.), 'da Rimini', pp. 50–1
[76] 1347.v.16 = Zucchello, *Lettere*, no. 36, p. 73.
[77] Zachariadou, *Trade and Crusade*, p. 164.
[78] Balard, *Romanie génoise*, vol. II, p. 761 and n. 124, referring to the archives of Prato.
[79] 1392.x.11 = Paola Massa, 'Alcune lettere mercantile toscane da colonie genovesi alla fine del trecento', *ASLSP* n.s. 11, fasc. 11 (1971), 357, no. 2.

resulted in a short supply of foodstuffs in Pera in 1392 as people's attention was distracted from harvesting and trading. The slowdown in trading activity was reflected in the availability of goods and in prices.[80] The price of grain of 20 *hyperpyra* in 1399–1400 was due, according to Dukas, to the Turkish siege of Constantinople. In 1402 the price had once again fallen and grain now fetched between 7 and 8 *hyperpyra* in Constantinople[81] and 8 *hyperpyra* in Pera.[82]

Grain was subject to various taxes in western Anatolia, the most important of which was customs. Grain exported from Aydın in about the 1320s was charged, presumably for Latins, at the rate of 4 per cent while in Antalya in the same period the rate, again presumably for Latins, was 6 *aspers* per *modio*.[83] It is possible that in 1337 the rate on grain in Aydın, paid by the Venetians, was 6 per cent as this was the rate applied to those commodities measured by the *seruch*.[84] There is, however, no clause specifying a charge on grain in the treaty of that year. From 1331 to 1407 the rate in Menteşe for Venetians was 2 *aspers* per *modio* for wheat and 1 *asper* per *modio* for barley and legumes.[85] The Ottomans too charged a special rate for grain. Under the treaty enacted in 1387 between Murad I and the Genoese it was stipulated that the Genoese were to pay on each Romania *modio* of wheat, barley and millet, at the same rate as that paid by the Arabs (or Muslims), Greeks, Venetians and others who were granted a reduced rate.[86] The rate paid by the Genoese on grain in the reign of Murad I was perhaps half a *hyperpyron* per *modio*, since in 1384 the Venetian senate instructed its ambassador to Murad, Marino Malipetro, to try and persuade Murad to agree to Venetians loading and exporting grain from his ports without paying any tax. If however Murad would not agree, Marino Malipetro was instructed to accept a rate not higher than half a *hyperpyron*

---

[80] 1392.x.5 = Massa, 'Lettere', no. 1, p. 356: 'Le cose di qua stanno a l'usato: nulla o pocho si fa di mercantia, prima perchè s'atendea i' re d'Ungheria con grande sforzo in questo inperio; e però le cose stanno sospese; ora si dice se ne torna, che sarebe ria nuova, ma non è certa. Apresso, la moria ci fa grande danno; Idio ce ne deliveri. Per la prima cagione le vettuarie ci sono in carestia e penso le navi verrano vote, non perchè le ricolte non sieno grandi e buone, ma le novità tenghono gli uomini di qua sospesi. La cera vale perperi 29 o meglo, ch'è gran carestia e al pregio val costà non vi si può mettere simile. La più parte di cose si traghono di qua sono in carestia perchè non c'è incetta nessuna.'
[81] 1402.x.12 = Gerardo Sagredo in Alexandrescu-Dersca, *Campagne de Timur*, p. 134.
[82] Tommaso da Molina in Alexandrescu-Dersca, *Campagne de Timur*, p. 140.
[83] Pegolotti, *Pratica*, pp. 56, 58.
[84] 1337.iii.9 = Zachariadou, *Trade and Crusade*, doc. 1337A, clause 7, p. 191. The *seruch* seems to have been a capacity measure used for grain which may have been, according to Professor Zachariadou's calculations, the equivalent of 60–2 litres; *ibid.*, p. 149.
[85] 1331.iv.13 = Zachariadou, *Trade and Crusade*, doc. 1331M, clause 3, p. 187; 1337.pre-iv = *ibid.*, doc. 1337M, clause 20, p. 198; 1375.iv.22 = *ibid.*, doc. 1375M, clause 20, pp. 221–2; 1403.vii.24 = *ibid.*, doc.1403M, doc. 1403M DVL, clause 20, p. 230; 1407.vi.2 = *ibid.*, doc. 1407M, clause 20, p. 236.
[86] 1387.vi.8 = ASG, Archivio Segreto, Materie Politiche, 2729, no. 26; Fleet, 'Treaty', clause 5, p. 15.

per *modio*.[87] The clause in the 1387 treaty makes it clear that Murad did not in fact agree to any such exemption.

In 1390 the Venetian ambassador, Francesco Quirino, after paying his respects and passing on the condolences of the commune of Venice for the death of Murad, was ordered to attempt to persuade Bayezid to grant Venice freedom from tax when exporting grain from his ports. If Bayezid was not agreeable, then Querini was to accept a tax of up to 1 *hyperpyron* per *modio*, while assuring the Ottoman ruler that the grain was for Venice or Venetian territories only.[88] Grain was now at a premium as Bayezid, who had recently conquered two very important sources of grain, Aydın and Menteşe, had forbidden its export from these areas.[89] In 1403 Süleyman charged the Latins and Greeks exporting grain from his territories, that is the European section of the by now fragmented empire, at the rate of 1 *hyperpyron* per *mozo* of Constantinople.[90]

During the reign of Mehmed II, imported grain was charged on the seller in Istanbul at the rate of 4 per cent, 'Edrene 'adeti üzre' (according to the custom of Edirne).[91] This presumably means that the rate of 4 per cent was that charged when the empire had its capital at Edirne before the conquest of Constantinople. After January 1476 4 per cent was levied on grain imported into various ports from Istanbul to the borders of Aydın from Muslims and tributaries, while 5 per cent was charged on non-tributaries.[92] It is interesting, when comparing these figures, that 4 per cent was charged on export in Aydın, presumably on Latins, in approximately the 1320s and the same rate of 4 per cent was charged, this time for imported grain, before 1476 under the Ottomans or, after January 1476, 5 per cent for non-tributaries and 4 per cent for Muslims and tributaries. If one compares the rates given in *aspers* or *hyperpyra* per *modio*, that of Antalya, 6 *aspers* per *modio* (equivalent roughly to 0.5 of a *hyperpyron*),[93] during approximately the 1320s, is high in contrast with that of Menteşe which remained at 2 *aspers* per *modio* of grain and 1 *asper* per *modio* (*c*.0.1 of a *hyperpyron*) of barley and legumes from 1331 until 1407. The Ottomans in contrast probably charged between 0.5 of a *hyperpyron* and 1 *hyperpyron* under

---

[87] 1384.vii.22 = G. Thomas, *Diplomatarium Veneto-Levantinum* (Venice, 1890–9), vols. I–II: vol. II, no. 116 p. 194.

[88] 1390.iii.6, ASV, Senato, Misti 41, fo. 59r = Chrysostomides, *Monumenta Peloponnesiaca*, no. 68, p. 138.

[89] Dukas (Bekker), p. 47, ll. 11–13; Dukas, *Historia Byzantina*, p. 75, ll. 16–17; Dukas, *Decline and Fall*, p. 81; Chrysostomides, *Monumenta Peloponnesiaca*, doc. 68, p. 138, n. 2.

[90] 1403 = Dennis, 'Treaty', clause 13, p. 79.

[91] 1476.i.14 = Anhegger and İnalcık, *Kanunname*, no. 33, pp. 44–5; Beldiceanu, *Actes*, vol. I, no. 33, clause 2, p. 109; 1476.i.14 = Anhegger and İnalcık, *Kanunname*, no. 34, p. 47; Beldiceanu, *Actes*, vol. I, no. 34, clause 2, pp. 111–12.

[92] Post 1476.i.28 = Anhegger and İnalcık, *Kanunname*, no. 35, pp. 47–8; Beldiceanu, *Actes*, vol. I, no. 36, clause 4, p. 114.

[93] 22.6 *akçe* to the *ducat*, 1 *ducat* to 2 *hyperpyra*, thus 5.65 *akçe* to 0.5 of a *hyperpyron*: see Zachariadou, *Trade and Crusade*, p. 140, basing her argument on al-'Umarī.

Murad I and levied 1 *hyperpyron* under Süleyman. This is in sharp contrast to that charged in Menteşe, which also contrasts with the higher rate charged in Antalya, though this too was lower than that levied in the Ottoman empire.

Apart from customs, grain was subject to various other taxes, one of which was brokerage (*senseraggio*). Pegolotti gives taxes rates for *assaggio* in Antalya of 1 *asper* per *moggio* of wheat[94] while *senseraggio* was paid in Constantinople on wheat and grain at 4 per cent.[95] A market charge also existed in Antalya in the same period of 3 *aspers* per *moggio* of wheat for the market ('fonda').[96] Wheat was charged a warehouse rent in Theologos at a rate of one-fifth of a gold *florin* per month per 100 *moggia* for the *loghiera* in the warehouse.[97] In Antalya the charge for warehouse rent was 1 *asper* per *moggio* of wheat which included a charge for transporting the grain from land to the ship.[98] There was also a charge for transporting in Theologos where hiring animals to take the wheat out of the city to the sea, 9 *miglia* by land, cost 2.5 gold *florins* per 100 *moggia*.[99]

Grain was essential for the survival of the western city states and was, in consequence, an extremely important element in their trade. Although Turchia was not perhaps the most important grain source for states such as Genoa and Venice, it nevertheless supplied large quantities and, when political factors affected other suppliers, became a source of the utmost importance.

[94] Pegolotti, *Pratica*, p. 58. [95] Pegolotti, *Pratica*, p. 45.
[96] Pegolotti, *Pratica*, p. 58. [97] Pegolotti, *Pratica*, p. 56.
[98] Pegolotti, *Pratica*, p. 58. [99] Pegolotti, *Pratica*, p. 56.

CHAPTER 6

Wine

Wine was one of the important commodities in the trade with Turchia and was apparently much consumed by the Turkish rulers of the time, even the pious Umur Aydınoğlu being a wine drinker. While in the beylik of Saruhan before setting out on *gaza*, he drank wine with the sons of Saruhan, Atmaz and Orhan,[1] and wine was drunk at the feast celebrating the defeat of the *tekfur* of Eğriboz (Euboea, Negroponte).[2] When, in response to Kantakuzenos's request for help, Umur went to Didimotiho (Dimetoka, Didymoteichon), Kantakuzenos laid on a feast for him such that the wine flowed in abundance. Umur however passed the time more piously in prayer.[3] The Ottoman ruler Mehmed II was not, however, given to wine and did not, according to Nicola Sagundino, indulge in wine drinking as was the habit of his people.[4]

Wine was a commodity of great significance in the trade of the eastern Mediterranean and the Black Sea, being imported from southern Italy, Provence, Crete and Cyprus, famous for its wines in the Middle Ages. One of the most sought-after wines was malvoisie, a sweet wine made for export in Crete. The name, which in English became malmsey, was used by this period to mean a type of wine rather than specifying its origin, namely from Monemvasia (Malvasia).[5] For the Genoese wine was 'un des produits de base du commerce génois en Romanie' and one in which they made considerable profits.[6] Their trade in wine extended beyond Romania to the lands of the Mongols with whom they used it as a means of payment and exchange for goods such as spices, silks and precious stones which they exported to the west.[7]

---

[1] Enveri, *Le destan d'Umur Pacha (Dusturname-i Enveri). Texte, translation et notes*, ed. I. Melikoff-Sayar, (Paris, 1954), p. 60.
[2] Enveri, *Destan*, p. 70.   [3] Enveri, *Destan*, p. 95.
[4] 1454.i.25 = Nicola Sagundino in Agostino Pertussi, *La Caduta di Costantinopoli* (Milan, 1976), vol II, *L'eco nel Mondo*, p. 130.
[5] Piloti was granted the privilege of importing to Alexandria five *bottes* of malvoisie a month by the Mamluk sultan Faraj: Piloti, *L'Egypte*, pp. 102–3.
[6] Balard, *Romanie génoise*, vol. II, pp. 845–6.
[7] Balard, *Romanie génoise*, vol. II, p. 845.

The wine trade in Anatolia was two way, for at the same time as importing wine Turchia was also a producer. Vines were cultivated there and both grapes and wine were exported. Ibn Battuta in his description of Theologos referred to the vineyards along both banks of the river.[8] Black dried grapes were exported from Balat and the surrounding area at the end of the fourteenth and beginning of the fifteenth centuries.[9] Grapes were also exported from Gelibolu and imported into Constantinople from Turchia.[10] Seven *bote* of dried grapes (*zebibo*), weighing 63 *kantars*, were sold in Samsun at 62 and 72 *aspers* per *kantar* for a total of 4,210 *aspers* which was equivalent to 221.5 *hyperpyra*.[11] They were loaded onto the ship of Galeoto Lumelin (Lomellini) and the expenses associated with their shipment listed as 137 *hyperpyra* 17 *karati*.[12] These grapes were from Lichomidia (?Nicomedia, İzmit) and were sold by a Turk called Amet (Ahmed) who bartered them for cloth.[13] The value of the grapes is given here as 2 *hyperpyra* per *kantar*, a total of 127 *hyperpyra*. This is less than their sale value in Samsun which was between 3.3 and 3.8 *hyperpyra* per *kantar*, calculating at the rate of 19 Samsun *aspers* per *hyperpyron*. Thus the market value of the grapes was higher than that with which they were credited for the purpose of bartering.

As well as exporting grapes, Anatolia also produced and exported wine. Much of the wine production was probably in the hands of Christians, for Timurtaş appears to have forbidden Christians from selling wine when he was Mongol governor in the 1320s.[14] Both Fethiye (Makre, Meğri) and Ania (Kadı Kalesi, south of Theologos) were wine-producing areas in the thirteenth century, and the Venetians exported wine from there[15] while the Byzantines taxed the export of wine from Ania.[16] Wine came from Trilia, İncir Liman (Paralime, Liminia) and Giresun (Kerasunt, on the Black Sea

---

[8] Ibn Battuta, *Voyages*, p. 309.

[9] Piloti, *L'Egypte*, p. 61: 'cebibo noires, qui sont roisons de quaresme'.

[10] Piloti, *L'Egypte*, pp. 62–3. The raisins were 'armelins', a type of Egyptian raisin.

[11] 1437.xii.18 = Badoer, *Libro*, col. 44, p. 89.

[12] 1436.i.20 = Badoer, *Libro*, col. 44, p. 88, col. 43, p. 87.

[13] 1436.i.14 = Badoer, *Libro*, col. 43, p. 86, col. 42, p. 85; col. 42, p. 84, col. 13, p. 27.

[14] S. Vryonis, *The Decline of Medieval Hellenism* (Berkeley, 1971), p. 225, citing Karim al-Din Mahmud, a contemporary of the events, who stated that Timurtaş imposed what ibn Arabi had advised the sultan Kaykaus I (1211–20). Among ibn Arabi's advice was that Christians not be allowed to sell wine.

[15] 1278.iii = Tafel and Thomas, *Urkunden*, vol. III, no. 370, p. 159 ff. Giovanni Bembo went c.1275 from Negroponte to 'Macrem de Turchia' and loaded wine and grain (pp. 196–7); Michaele de Verona sailed to Ania about the same time to load wine (p. 239); Nicolao Dente and Filippo Bono, again around the same period, also went to Ania for wine (p. 254).

[16] 1278.iii = Tafel and Thomas, *Urkunden*, no. 370, p. 239: Michaele de Verona complained of being made to pay *commerchium* by the emperor's officials in Ania of 18 *hyperpyra* for 2 *viatici* ('fuisse comerclatum per comerclarios, qui ibi erant [i.e. in Ania] ... pro duobus viaticis in XVIII yperperis'). *Ibid.*, p. 254: Nicolao Dente and Filippo Bono complained of the same thing, also in Ania ('comerclatis in Ania per comerclarios domini Imperatoris ... dixere dicti judices, debere reddi VIII yperpera, que solverint pro ipso comerclo').

coast west of Trabzon) and was sold in Pera and Caffa.[17] Wine from Trilia was also sold in Tana.[18] Cappadocia too was a famous wine-producing area in the thirteenth century and the Ottoman sultan Mehmed II is reputed to have drunk the wine of Beyşehir while campaigning in that area.[19] It seems possible that wine was sold in Aydın to Latins as a clause in the 1348 treaty between Hızır and the *Sancta Unio* allowed any of its galleys to come to the beylik and sell and buy anything that was necessary for provisioning, such as bread, wine, meat and all other victuals, without paying any *comerclum* or other tax.[20] As the clause specifies goods, among them wine, necessary for provisioning, it seems that these goods were bought by the galleys rather than sold.

Apart from producing and exporting wine, Anatolia was an importer, presumably of better quality wine than the home-grown product. The Genoese were involved in this trade, shipping wine from Naples into Theologos.[21] Greeks too traded wine, for in 1437 Dimitri Argiti de Chandia imported it into Gelibolu.[22]

Wine imports into Anatolia in the fourteenth century were taxed. Wine brought into Theologos paid 1 gold *florin* per *botte di Napoli*,[23] while in Menteşe wine was taxed at the rate of 50 *aspers* per *vegete*,[24] the rate remaining unaltered throughout the fourteenth and into the fifteenth centuries.[25] In the 1337 treaty between Hızır of Aydın and the duca di Candia all goods were exempt from import tax for Venetians except soap and wine. Wine was to be charged at the rate of 1 *florin* per *vegeta de Neapoli*.[26] In the 1353 treaty between Hızır and Marino Morosini, the duca di Candia, wine was taxed at the rate of 1 *florin* per *buta de mena*.[27] It may be significant that under the treaty of 1337 the goods upon which import tax exemption specifically was not to apply were soap and wine but not cloth, a major western import. This perhaps may be due to the fact that, presumably, neither soap nor wine were imported in the quantities that cloth was and that therefore the Venetians were prepared to give way over an import tax on these commodities, but were unwilling to see a similar tax applied to cloth.

[17] Balard, *La Romanie génoise*, vol. II, p. 844.   [18] Pegolotti, *Pratica*, p. 24.

[19] Vryonis, *Decline*, p. 483; Babinger, *Mehmed*, p. 399.

[20] 1348.viii.18 = Zachariadou, *Trade and Crusade*, doc. 1348A, clause 19, p. 209.

[21] Musso, *Navigazione*, pp. 169–70.

[22] 1437.iii.31 = Badoer, *Libro*, col. 125, p. 252.

[23] Pegolotti, *Pratica*, p. 56.

[24] The *vegeta* was the same as the *buta de mena de Napoli* and was a common wine measurement in Romania: see Zachariadou, *Trade and Crusade*, p. 149. A *buta* was between 501 and 515 litres: see Schilbach, *Metrologie*, pp. 112, 135.

[25] 1337.pre-iv. = Zachariadou, *Trade and Crusade*, doc. 1337M, clause 22, p. 198; 1375.iv.22 = *ibid.*, doc. 1375M, clauses 22, p. 222, 28, p. 223; 1403.vii.24 = *ibid.*, doc. 1403M, clause 22, p. 231; 1407.vi.2 = *ibid.*, doc. 1407M, clause 22, pp. 236–7.

[26] 1337.iii.9 = Zachariadou, *Trade and Crusade*, doc. 1337A, clause 7, p. 191.

[27] 1358.iv.7 = Zachariadou, *Trade and Crusade*, doc. 1353A, clause 20, p. 214.

Wine was also taxed in Chios and New Phokaea. From 1351 to the beginning of the fifteenth century, the rate in Chios was 0.5 of a *florin* per *vegete*.[28] In New Phokaea at the beginning of the fifteenth century, a *comerchium* of 4 *florins* per *vegete* was charged.[29] Working on the basis of 1 *ducat* to *c.*23 *aspers* for the 1330s and to *c.*31 *aspers* at the end of the fourteenth century,[30] one sees that for the first half of the fourteenth century the tax was *c.*23 *aspers* or 1 *ducat* in Aydın, 50 *aspers* or *c.*2 *ducats* in Menteşe and 11.5 *aspers* or 0.5 of a *ducat* in Chios. For the end of the fourteenth century and the beginning of the fifteenth the rate in Menteşe was 50 *aspers* or *c.*1.5 *ducats*, in Chios *c.*15.5 *aspers* or 0.5 of a *ducat* and in New Phokaea *c.*124 *aspers* or 4 *ducats*. These figures show that the rate in Menteşe was considerably more than that in Aydın while that charged in New Phokaea was extremely high in comparison with that of Chios and the beyliks. The Chian rate was the best, being substantially less than that of the other three places. It is interesting that the rates both in Menteşe and Chios remained the same in the fourteenth and early fifteenth centuries.

Imported wine went through the hands of tax farmers in the beyliks of Menteşe and Aydın. According to Pegolotti wine brought into Theologos was subject to *appalto* or *gabella*.[31] In Aydın wine was subject to *appalto* before 1337. A clause in the treaty of that year between Menteşe and the duca di Candia stated that if the emir of Aydın, Hızır, made an agreement with the Venetians under which wine, soap and alum remained subject to *appalto* then Ibrahim, emir of Menteşe, was at liberty to impose *appalto*, on alum in Balat only, though not on wine and soap. If Hızır removed *appalto* from alum, wine and soap, Ibrahim would not impose it on alum.[32] Aydın did in fact lift *appalto* for the Venetians from wine and soap in 1337[33] though not from alum, which was exempted under the treaty of 1358.[34] The linking here of commercial policy in Menteşe with that of Aydın is interesting, showing, as it does, that the beyliks were, to some extent, in competition with each other over attracting western merchants while at the same time being aware that neither beylik need concede much more than the other. The fact that Menteşe was prepared to maintain the exemption for Venetian subjects from *appalto* on wine and soap, regardless of what

---

[28] 1404.xii.15 = Argenti, *Chios*, vol. II, pp. 161, 164, 165, 166; 1405.xi.26 = *ibid.*, p. 172.

[29] 1405.ii.14 = Argenti, *Chios*, vol. II, p. 171.

[30] The comparative rates are based on al-'Umarī's rate of one *akçe* to 0.75 of a *dirhem*, and the rate given in a court decision in Crete of one *ducat* per 30 or 32 *akçe*: see Zachariadou, *Trade and Crusade*, pp. 140–1 and Santschi, *Regestes*, n. 354, p. 90. Professor Zachariadou calculated the duty in Menteşe as 1.66 *florins* for 50 *akçe* in comparison with that charged in Aydın. However, as the rate given for Aydın appears in the treaty of 1353 it would seem better to calculate at the rate based on al-'Umarī rather than that for the end of the century: see Zachariadou, *Trade and Crusade*, p. 157.

[31] Pegolotti, *Pratica*, p. 56.

[32] 1337.pre iv. = Zachariadou, *Trade and Crusade*, doc. 1337M, clause 28, pp. 199–200.

[33] 1337.iii.9 = Zachariadou, *Trade and Crusade*, doc. 1337A, clause 11, p. 192.

[34] 1358.x.13 = Zachariadou, *Trade and Crusade*, doc. 1358/1359M, clause 8, p. 218.

Aydın did, while maintaining the right to impose it on alum indicates that the income from alum was more important, as one would expect, than that from either wine or soap. The concession was thus worth making as it did not deprive the state of much income.

In Menteşe, Venetian merchants continued to be able to trade in wine without the imposition of *appalto* throughout the fourteenth and into the fifteenth centuries.[35] In Chios and New Phokaea wine was subject to the *gabella*. In the report of Gregorio di Marsupino to Marshal Boucicault in 1404 dealing with tax in Chios and the rights of the Maona in New Phokaea, reference is made to 'cabelle' imposed in Chios on wine imported into the island. This *gabella* existed also in 1351.[36] In response to Gregorio's report, Marshal Boucicault refers in his order to the 'cabelle seu Introytus' of 0.5 of a florin per *vegete* of wine.[37]

It has been stated that the emirs of Menteşe and Aydın reserved the wine trade as a monopoly.[38] However, it may be that the emirs had a right of state intervention rather than placing the commodity under a monopoly. It certainly was subject to restrictions. In Menteşe in 1331 the emir had the right to first pick of any wine imported into the beylik. Merchants were permitted to unload their wine and take it to 'domum suam'. If the *namatari* of the emir wanted to buy the wine and came to an agreement with the vendor, the *namatari* had ten days in which to pay for the wine and take possession of it. If the deal had not been settled by the end of this period the vendor was then free to sell his wine as he wished.[39] The meaning of the title *namatari* is unknown. Professor Zachariadou has suggested that it may come from the Persian *name*(letter) and *-dar* (bearer),[40] while Dr Zhukov has proposed that it is derived from the Greek word *nama* which, he says, was used in Byzantium for communion wine and which he suggests may in colloquial speech well have meant wine in general.[41] The word *nama,* however, meant something poured or flowing. Porphyrogenitos, when referring to the communion, used the word *nama* for wine, but its significance in this context was that it was something poured, a libation, not that it was wine.[42] Therefore this explanation of the title *namatari* is not

---

[35] 1337.pre iv. = Zachariadou, *Trade and Crusade*, doc. 1337M, clause 22, p. 198; *ibid.*, doc. 1375M, clauses 22, p. 222 and 28, p. 223. 1403.vii.24 = *ibid.*, doc. 1403M, clause 22, p. 231 and doc. 1403M, DVL, clause 22, p. 231. Doc. 1403M refers to *gabella* and doc. 1403M, DVL to *datium*.

[36] 1404.xii.15 = Argenti, *Chios*, vol. II, pp. 161, 164, 165, 166. The rate is repeated in 1405.xi.26 = *ibid.*, p. 172.

[37] 1404.xii.16 = Argenti, *Chios*, vol. II, p. 167. This phrase is repeated in a list of taxes paid in New Phokaea, 1405.ii.14 = *ibid.*, p. 170.

[38] Zachariadou, *Trade and Crusade*, p. 171.

[39] 1331.iv.13 = Zachariadou, *Trade and Crusade*, doc. 1331M, clause 13, pp. 188–9.

[40] See Zachariadou, *Trade and Crusade*, p. 135 and n. 577.

[41] Zhukov, Эгейкие Эмираты, p. 84.

[42] Porphyrogenitos, *De Ceremoniis*, I, p. 134, 25. I am grateful to Miss Chrysostomides for her advice on this point.

credible. As an alternative derivation, Dr Zhukov has pointed out that it might be a distortion of the title *amaldar-i emir* or tax farmer.[43] This however seems unlikely, as in this case it would be hard to explain the initial *n* of the word *namatari*, particularly in view of the use of the word *amalim* in the treaty of 1407 between Menteşe and Crete, which seems to be the Latin form of the Arabic *'amal.*

In any case it is clear that the *namatari* was a state official and that in Menteşe the state could, if it so wished, intervene in transactions over wine. If, however, the emir was not interested in buying, any restriction over sale was lifted. This is the same process as that employed by the emir of Menteşe over other goods imported into his state. If the emir wished to buy any merchandise bought into the beylik by Venetian merchants he could purchase within three days, provided there was an agreement with the merchant over the price. If, however, no agreement was reached within this period the merchant was then free to sell his goods to whomsoever he wished.[44] This seems more a right of intervention in the market than a state monopoly.

However, monopolies were used by the later Ottomans who imposed state monopolies on various commodities, as they did for example on timber in the second half of the fifteenth century when the monopoly on the timber trade between Antalya and Egypt was farmed out to individuals.[45] Wine may have been a monopoly in Aydın, for Hızır granted the monopoly on selling wine to merchants in Theologos (Ephesus) to the widow of the last Byzantine governor there who kept a tavern on the outskirts of the city.[46]

---

[43] Zhukov, Эгейкие Эмираты, p. 84.
[44] 1331.iv.13 = Zachariadou, *Trade and Crusade*, clause 4, p. 188.
[45] Halil Inalcık, 'Bursa and the commerce of the Levant', *JESHO* 3/2 (1960), 147.
[46] Ludolphus de Sudheim, *Ludolphi rectoris ecclesiae parochialis in Suchem, De itinere Terrae Sanctae liber*, ed. F. Deycks, in *Bibliothek des Litterarischen Vereins XXV* (Stuttgart, 1851), p. 25.

CHAPTER 7

Alum

A major commodity in Genoese trade with Anatolia in the later Middle
Ages was alum, a colourless crystalline substance procured from certain
rocks, which was used for a variety of industries and also in medicine, and
was extremely important in the European cloth industry, where it was used
in dyeing as a fixer and for cleansing fibres.[1] A further benefit for merchants
was that alum acted as ballast in their ships.[2]

The process involved in producing alum was fairly lengthy and consisted
of a series of boilings, soakings and dryings.[3] Two basic grades of alum
were produced: rock alum and grain alum. Rock alum, the best and most
expensive type, was that which stuck to the basin edges in the last stage of
the processing, while the alum at the bottom of the basin was called *allume
corda* or *allume di fosso* and was a poor-quality alum.[4] This was grain alum
(*allume minuto*), and was the alum of everyday use.[5] *Allume di sorta della
buona luminiera* was second-quality alum, made up of two-fifths rock and
three-fifths grain alum.[6]

According to Pegolotti, the bigger (*grosso*) and less grainy (*minuto*), the
whiter, brighter, clearer and cleaner of stones and sandy soil the alum was,

---

[1] Alum was also used in the leather industry, in making certain types of glass and in the sugar
industry: Suraiya Faroqhi, 'Alum production and alum trade in the Ottoman empire (about
1560–1830)', *WZKM* 71 (1979), 154–5; Zachariadou, *Trade and Crusade*, p. 167; Balard,
Romanie génoise, vol. II, p. 769; W. Heyd, *Histoire du Commerce du Levant au Moyen-Age*,
(Amsterdam, 1967), vols.I–II: vol. II, p. 570; Jean Delumeau, *L'alun de Rome XVe–XIXe
siècle*, Ecole Pratique des Hautes Etudes – VIe section, Centre de Recherches Historiques,
Ports-Routes-Trafics XIII (Paris and The Hague, 1962), p. 14; Léone Liagre, 'Le commerce
de l'alun en Flandre au Moyen Age', *Le Moyen Age* 61 (1955), 177–9.

[2] Faroqhi, 'Alum production', 153.

[3] Pegolotti, *Pratica*, pp. 367–8; Dukas, *Historia Byzantina*, p. 160, l. 12 – p. 161, l. 7; Dukas,
Historia Turcobyzantina, p. 205, ll. 7–19; Dukas, *Decline and Fall*, p. 148.

[4] Pegolotti, *Pratica*, p. 368.

[5] Marie-Louise Heers, 'Les Génois et le commerce de l'alun à la fin du Moyen Age', *Revue
d'Histoire Economique et Sociale* 32 (1954), 38, n. 26; Léone Liagre-de Sturler, *Les relations
commerciales entres Gênes, la Belgique et l'Outremont d'après les archives notariales génoises
(1320–1400)* (Brussels and Rome, 1969), vols. I–II: vol. I, p. cxxxix, n. 3.

[6] Pegolotti, *Pratica*, pp. 411–12.

the better it was.[7] The quality of alum varied according to where it came from.

Mining, production and export of alum in Anatolia was very much in the hands of the Genoese who, from an early date, dominated this trade. William of Rubruck, who was in Konya in 1255, met a Genoese merchant there, Nicolao de Santo-Siro, who, together with a Venetian called Benefatio de Molendino, had a monopoly of all the alum in Turchia, the sultan selling only to them. In consequence the price was, according to Rubruck, about 22 per cent higher than it should have been.[8] In the early fourteenth century the Zaccaria family, later followed by the Cattanea della Volta, controlled alum extraction. After 1346, the Maona of Chios was predominant, controlling Phokaea and neighbouring islands. Ten years later, in 1356, the Gattilusio family, having established themselves on Lesbos, controlled the alum production there and on the other islands in the northern Aegean. It was through them that the Genoese gained the farms of the mines in Turchia.[9] Towards the middle of the fifteenth century the Genoese merchant Francesco de Draperiis gained a position of great importance in the alum trade[10] and various Genoese families, such as the Lomellini, the Doria, the Paterio, the Adorno, the Salvaigo and the Pallavicini, together with the Giustiniani, dominated alum export to the west.[11]

Alum extraction and export was sometimes in the hands of a partnership of western merchants, as it was in 1416 in Phokaea[12] and again in 1437 when a partnership farmed the alum under Murad II.[13] The size of such partnerships varied, Domenico Doria, for example, creating a small partnership in the 1440s to trade 8,000 *kantars* of alum per annum from Grecia and Turchia,[14] while a very large partnership of 500,000 *kantars*, in which

---

[7] Pegolotti, *Pratica*, pp. 368–9, 369–70.

[8] William of Rubruck, *The Mission of Friar William of Rubruck. His Journey to the Court of the Great Khan Mönke, 1253–1255*, trans. Peter Jackson, introduction, notes and appendices by Peter Jackson with David Morgan (London, 1990), p. 273; Corpus Christi College, Cambridge MS 66A, fos. 109r col. 1 – 109v col. 1; Corpus Christi College, Cambridge, MS 181, fo. 396. Nicolao and Benefatio increased the price so that alum which should have cost 15 *besants* sold for 50 *besants*. Balard, *Romanie genoise*, vol. II, p. 770, n. 4 considers this to be alum from Kütahya which was closer to Konya than Karahisar. But Rubruck refers to all Turchia.

[9] Heers, 'Commerce de l'alun', 32.

[10] Francesco de Draperiis appears in various transactions entered into the accounts of Giacomo Badoer dealing with alum (1439.iii.21 = Badoer, *Libro*, col. 310, p. 622), oil (1437.ix.-. = *ibid.*, col. 45, p. 90, col. 99, p. 201, of Messina, 1437.vii.5 = *ibid.*, col. 47, p. 94, col. 66, p. 133, of Coron), wax, a slave (1437.xii.10 = *ibid.*, col. 143, p. 288), sugar (1436.ii.14 = *ibid.*, col. 45, p. 90) and copper (1437.xii.18 = *ibid.*, col. 143, p. 288). He was a banker, being described as 'Franzesco Drapieri banchier' or 'Franzesco Drapieri dal bancho' (e.g. *ibid.*, col. 47, p. 94, col. 143, p. 288, col. 148, p. 298) and dealt in letters of exchange, 'letera de chanbio' (1437.vii.3 = *ibid.*, col. 143, p. 288, 'una letera de chanbio da Veniexa', 1439.iii.20 = *ibid.*, col. 320, p. 643, again a letter of exchange from Venice).

[11] Heers, 'Commerce de l'alun', 34, 38–9.   [12] Heers, 'Commerce de l'alun', 34.

[13] Heyd, *Histoire du commerce*, vol. II, p. 40.

[14] 1448.i.4 in Heers, 'Commerce de l'alun', 37.

Francesco de Draperiis owned half the capital, was formed in 1449. By this time there was apparently a problem of over-production and falling prices, and this partnership was formed in an attempt to control the situation. It negotiated an agreement with the lord of Lesbos, paying him 5,000 gold *ducat*s of Chios a year in return for a moratorium on processing alum in Mitylene.[15]

While the trade in alum was largely in the hands of the Genoese, Turks too traded in this commodity. When he was *appaltator* of Phokaea, that is an official appointed by the Chian government to collect the tax on alum there, Francesco de Campis bought 100 *kantar*s of alum for 50 *ducat*s from a Turk. Apparently the alum was never delivered, and the Turk refused to hand back the money because of certain slaves, presumably his own, who had fled from Turchia to Phokaea. Francesco, by now ex-*appaltator*, requested, in a case of arbitration in Chios, that he be paid the money he had handed over to the Turk, and the government of Chios agreed to 40 gold *ducat*s being paid to him, Francesco ceding his rights against the Turk to the government of Chios. The 40 *ducat*s were to be paid by the current *appaltator*s from the money they had to deliver to the government of Chios and they were to make up this money in the following four months.[16]

Anatolia was one of the principal alum-producing areas, exporting it to the east, to Egypt and Syria, and the west.[17] Alum was exported to Cyprus, for ships carrying alum from Turchia paid the *missa* tax there.[18] Turkish alum went further west and into northern Europe, even reaching as far as England. It was traded in Bruges, appearing there in a list of alums dating from the first part of the fourteenth century.[19] In 1400 Antonio Cataneo was the owner and captain of a ship hired to take alum from Turchia to Bruges.[20] L'Ecluse, in the south-west Netherlands, just north-east of Bruges, was also a destination and market for Turkish alum as were

---

[15] Heers, 'Commerce de l'alun', 31–2, 39–42. First payment under the Mitylene agreement, 1450.x.1 = Argenti, *Chios*, vol. III, doc. 128, pp. 598–9.

[16] 1394.ii.18 = ASG, Notaio, Donato de Clavaro, Sc. 39, filza 1, doc. 97/240.

[17] Heers, 'Commerce de l'alun', 45–9; Dukas, *Historia Byzantina*, p. 161, ll. 9–12; Dukas, *Historia Turcobyzantina*, p. 205, ll. 21–23; Dukas, *Decline and Fall*, p. 148.

[18] Pegolotti, *Pratica*, p. 85. He describes a tax called *missa* which was imposed for keeping the sea around Cyprus safe and was paid by the masters of ships carrying merchandise from Turchia, Rhodes, Armenia, Syria and Egypt. If the master of the ship was Genoese or Venetian he did not pay the tax, as Venetians and Genoese were free from *comerchium* in Cyprus. In this case the tax was paid by the merchant whose goods were carried on the ship. Among the goods taxed was alum, taxed at 6 *karati* per sack. As Rhodes, Armenia, Syria and Egypt were not alum-producing areas, the alum in question must have come from Turchia. It seems reasonable that alum exported from Antalya went to Cyprus, or Syria and Egypt. See *ibid.*, p. 370.

[19] Pegolotti, *Pratica*, pp. 243–4. These alums presumably also appeared in England as the equivalent of the Bruges *carica* of alum was given by Pegolotti for London.

[20] 1400.v.28 = Renée Doehaerd and C. Kerremans, *Les relations commerciales entres Gênes, la Belgique et l'Outremont d'après les archives notariales génoises, 1400–1440* (Brussels and Rome, 1952), no. 2, p. 23.

Middelburg, in the south-west Netherlands, Sandwich and Southampton. In 1343 158 *kantar*s of 'aluminis turcheschi' together with some Kütahya alum *en route* for L'Ecluse were part of a security put up in Genoa.[21] In 1371 alum from Turchia appears in a list of goods taken from English ships or seized in Flanders and sold in L'Ecluse;[22] in 1388 and 1398 alum was loaded in Turchia for L'Ecluse or Middelburg[23] and in 1393 alum from Turchia went to Southampton, Sandwich or L'Ecluse.[24] Later, in 1417, a ship with a cargo of merchandise including alum loaded at Old and New Phokaea was to go to L'Ecluse, calling at various ports *en route* including Southampton, provided that the Genoese and the English were at peace.[25] Spain also imported Turkish alum. In 1332 a request was made to Alfonso III, king of Aragon, for the return of alum of Turchia, confiscated in Roses.[26]

One of the main centres for alum production in Anatolia was Phokaea. The Genoese were established there[27] from 1275[28] or before, when the alum mines there were granted by Michael VIII to Benedetto Zaccaria and his brother Manuel.[29] The Zaccaria family control ended in 1314 with the death of Nicolino, and they were succeeded in Phokaea by the Cattaneo della Volta family. Phokaea reverted to Byzantine control in 1336[30] but from 1346 the Maona of Chios assumed control there, and the area remained in Genoese hands until 1445. Under the Maona of Chios the alum mines of Phokaea were farmed out, the mines being auctioned approximately every ten years.[31]

[21] 1343.iv.10 = Liagre-de Sturler, *Relations commerciales*, vol. no. 127, pp. 155–8.

[22] In 1371.viii.1 the English destroyed a Flemish fleet in the Channel. In reprisal, goods seized from the English were sold in L'Ecluse. There is an inventory of these goods dated 1371.viii.25 in the Bruges Archives: Liagre, 'Commerce de l'alun', 191 and n. 65. She refers to Gilliodts Van Severn, *Inventaire des Archives de la Ville de Bruges*, vol. II, no. 6, p. 118.

[23] 1388.i.13 = Liagre-de Sturler, *Relations commerciales*, vol. II, no. 503, p. 659; 1388.iv.7 = *ibid.*, doc. 521, pp. 682–3; 1398.x.8 = *ibid.*, no. 623, p. 825 (for L'Ecluse only).

[24] 1398.vi.28 = Liagre-de Sturler, *Relations Commerciales*, no. 565, pp. 746–51.

[25] 1417.i.6 = Doehaerd and Kerremans, *Relations commerciales*, no. 230, pp. 253–7.

[26] Francesco C. Casula, *Carte Reali Diplomatiche di Alfonso III il Benigno, Re d'Aragon Riguardanti l'Italia* (Padua, 1970), no. 521, p. 296.

[27] There were two Phokaeas, the original Old Phokaea north of the Gulf of İzmir, and New Phokaea, built on the coast at the foot of the alum mountains. New Phokaea was established by the Genoese because of Turkish raiding. Dukas, *Historia Byzantina*, p. 161, l. 5 – p. 162, l. 15; Dukas, *Historia Turcobyzantina*, p. 205, l. 26 – p. 207, l. 18; Dukas *Decline and Fall*, pp. 148–9.

[28] Michel Balard, 'The Genoese in the Aegean (1204–1566)', *Mediterranean Historical Review* 4 (June 1989), 161 says the date was undoubtedly 1267. Heers, 'Commerce de l'alun', 31, gives it as 1275, as does Pachymeres, *George Pachymeres, De Michaele et Andronico Palaeologis libri XIII*, ed. I. Bekker, CSHB (Bonn, 1835), vols. I–II: vol. I, p. 419, l. 10. Balard, *Romanie génoise*, vol. II, pp. 770–1, basing himself on two notary deeds, says the date must be pre-1268. Liagre, 'Commerce de l'alun', 179, dates it to 1264.

[29] Dukas, *Historia Byzantina*, p. 161, ll. 12–15; Dukas, *Historia Turcobyzantina*, p. 205, ll. 24–6; Dukas, *Decline and Fall*, p. 148; Pachymeres, vol. I, p. 420, ll. 5–6.

[30] Balard, *Romanie génoise*, vol. II, p. 778; Heers, 'Commerce de l'alun', 31, gives the date as 1340.

[31] Heers, 'Commerce de l'alun', 32.

Ramon Muntaneer, the author of a chronicle of the Catalan expedition in the east, described Phokaea in the early fourteenth century as a town of 3,000 Greeks busy in the production of alum.[32] There was clearly a high level of production which, according to Pegolotti, amounted to 14,000 Genoese *kantars* per annum.[33] In the first half of the fifteenth century it was the main alum mine in Anatolia, producing a yearly total of 750 tons.[34] A Genoese notary deed of 1452 gives the production figure for the mines of Phokaea in that period as around 15,800 *kantars* per annum.[35]

Phokaea alum was used to make a mixture of two-fifths rock and three-fifths *allume corda* and was very similar to second-quality alum (*allume di sorte della buona luminiera*).[36] Used by French, German, English, Italian, Spanish, Arab, Egyptian and Syrian dyemakers,[37] it was traded locally and exported to the west, selling in Constantinople, Pera,[38] Chios,[39] Bruges,[40] Middelburg[41] and l'Ecluse.[42] Its importance is clear from Dukas, according to whom every ship in the early fifteenth century sailing westwards from there carried a cargo of alum.

Alum mines in Phokaea were, at least on occasion, owned or leased by the *appaltatores*. It seems that their ability to lease them out was controlled by the authorities on Chios for in 1394 Francesco de Campis, the ex-*appaltator* of Phokaea, was granted permission from Chios to lease to Nicolao Paterio, one of the current *appaltatores*, an alum works which he owned in Phokaea, for the period in which Nicolao held office. In return,

---

[32] R. Muntaner, *L'expediciò dels Catalans a Orient*, ed. Lluis Nicolau d'Olwer, Els nostres clàssics 7 (Barcelona, 1926), p. 156.

[33] Pegolotti, *Pratica*, p. 369.   [34] Faroqhi, 'Alum production', 161.

[35] 1452.x.14 = Heers, 'Commerce de l'alun', 36–7. Balard, *Romanie génoise*, vol. II, pp. 773, 775 has questioned the accuracy of Pegolotti's production figures, pointing out that Pegolotti gives exactly the same figure for Karahisar alum. In this context the figure from Bernardo de Ferrari is particularly interesting in that it is close to that of Pegolotti. But Heers, 'Commerce de l'alun', 37 n. 20 points out that this was the minimum. De Draperiis refers to fraud of 6 per cent, so that without fraud this figure would be 17,300 *kantars* per annum.

[36] Pegolotti, *Pratica*, p. 369.

[37] Dukas, *Historia Byzantina*, p. 161, ll. 9–12; Dukas, *Historia Turcobyzantina*, p. 205, ll. 21–3; Dukas, *Decline and Fall*, p. 148.

[38] Pegolotti, *Pratica*, p. 43.

[39] 1405.iv.4 = Doehaerd and Kerremans, *Relations commerciales*, nos. 11, 12, pp. 13–17, sale of 3,000 *kantars* of grain alum of Phokaea in Chios; 1413.xii.18 = *ibid.*, no. 167, pp. 159–60, 10,000 *kantars* of alum being loaded in New Phokaea and Chios; 1426.v.26 = *ibid.*, no. 305, pp. 338–9, alum loaded in Phokaea, some of which was offloaded in Chios.

[40] Pegolotti, *Pratica*, p. 244; Doehaerd and Kerremans, *Relations commerciales*, no. 261, pp. 289–91, 2,126 *kantars* of grain alum of Phokaea were in Bruges.

[41] 1388.viii.18 or 28 = Liagre-de Sturler, *Relations commerciales*, vol. II, no. 526, pp. 691–5, 3,000 *kantars* were loaded in New Phokaea and 490 *kantars* in Old Phokaea for Middelburg. This document gives the loading times for the alum as eight days in New Phokaea and four days in Old Phokaea; 1439.xi.9 = Doehaerd and Kerremans, *Relations commerciales*, no. 805, pp. 630–3, 11,000 *kantars* or more of Phokaea alum was to be shipped to L'Ecluse or Middelburg.

[42] 1426.v.26 = Doehaerd and Kerremans, *Relations commerciales*, no. 305, pp. 338–9, 9,000 *kantars* of alum from Phokaea were shipped to L'Ecluse. 1439.xi.9 = *ibid.*, no. 805, pp. 630–3, 11,000 *kantars* of Phokaea alum were to be shipped to L'Ecluse or Middelburg.

Nicolao was to pay 400 gold *ducat*s, or 350 *kantar*s of rock alum if Francesco preferred, as surety, the *ducat*s or alum being returnable when Nicolao handed back the alum works to Francesco at the end of his period in office. Presumably Francesco would have used the money or alum for trading during the period in which the mine was let. Whether he chose alum or cash presumably depended on how easily he could dispose of the alum and on how much money he was likely to make on it. As he owned an alum mine and had been an *appaltator* in Phokaea, he could be presumed to have been active in the alum trade.

Alum could also be used in place of cash for purchasing an alum mine, for if Francesco wished to sell his alum works to Nicolao, Nicolao was bound to buy it for 300 *kantar*s of rock alum, Francesco returning the 400 *ducat*s given him by Nicolao when Francesco originally handed the works over to him.[43] Nicolao Paterio also bought another alum mine in Phokaea in the same year for 400 gold *ducat*s.[44]

Other sources of alum included that of the Black Sea region at Karahisar (Koloneia, modern Şebinkarahisar).[45] The Genoese were exporting alum from there before *c.*1275[46] and presumably controlled the trade of Karahisar alum to Europe throughout the fourteenth century, when they were the dominant force in the Black Sea.[47] These activities clashed with the interests of the Zaccaria of Phokaea who, in order to protect their own alum monopoly, sought to have an interdict applied against the alum of Karahisar to prevent its export to the west. In 1275 they obtained an agreement to this effect from the Byzantine emperor, Michael VIII. But the Genoese government was not happy and the interdict was quashed.[48]

Karahisar alum was the best type of alum produced in Turchia. There were three grades: rock alum which was the most valuable; second-quality alum (*allume di sorta della buona luminiera*), made up of two-fifths rock and three-fifths *allume corda*, a grain alum (*allume minuto*); and *allume corda*, which was the most grainy type of alum.[49] Annual production was 14,000 Genoese *kantar*s.[50] It was exported from Giresun (Kerasunt, Chisenda), on the Black Sea coast west of Trabzon, a seven-day journey from Karahisar[51] and was sold in Constantinople and Pera[52] and in markets further west, for Karahisar alum appears in the accounts of Bruges for 1312, valued at 40 *denari*.[53]

Another source of alum was Kütahya, in western Anatolia, south-east of

[43] 1394.ii.18 = ASG, Notaio, Donato de Clavaro, Sc. 39, filza 1, doc. 97/240.
[44] 1394.iii.19 = Argenti, *Chios*, vol. I, p. 488.
[45] Zachariadou, *Trade and Crusade*, p. 168, n. 709.
[46] Balard, *Romanie génoise*, vol. II, p. 773, says it was pre-March 1274.
[47] Zachariadou, *Trade and Crusade*, p. 167.
[48] Balard, *Romanie génoise*, vol. II, pp. 776–7.
[49] Pegolotti, *Pratica*, p. 369.   [50] *Ibid.*   [51] *Ibid.*
[52] Pegolotti, *Pratica*, p. 43.
[53] Liagre, 'Commerce de l'alun', 187 and n. 65.

Bursa. Pegolotti describes Kütahya alum (*allume dal cotai e d'Altoluogo*) as being 'grossetto' and 'minuto' mixed together, similar to Ulubat (Ulek Abad) alum but more grainy (*minuto*), and close to Phokaea alum in quality. Twelve thousand Genoese *kantar*s per annum were produced, and alum was exported through Theologos and Balat with 4,000 *kantar*s going out through Antalya.[54] It sold in Constantinople and Pera.[55] According to Professor Balard,[56] the alum referred to as alum of Christo is the same as Kütahya alum, as is the alum noted by William of Rubruck towards the mid-thirteenth century as coming from mines in the sultanate of Iconium.[57] Kütahya alum was pledged in Genoa in 1343 as part security for 396 *florins*. It was on a *cocha* due to leave Genoa for L'Ecluse, calling at Maiorca, Cadiz and Malaga.[58]

Mention is made in Genoese notary deeds of alum of Scorpiata. Scholars are divided as to whether this could be taken as evidence that the alum originated from Scorpiata or that simply it was exported from there. According to Professor Balard, the Genoese began to go to Scorpiata for alum from 1380.[59] He questions whether this alum represented local production from mines previously unknown or whether the alum was in fact from mines close to the Sea of Marmara, at Ulubat (Ulek Abad, Lopadion) and Kapıdağ (Cyzicus), which the Genoese had brought overland to avoid a passage through the straits. Professor Balard concludes that the alum was probably from local mines, pointing out that if the Genoese had wished to avoid a passage through the straits and were using Scorpiata solely as a place from which to collect alum, they would surely have been more likely to have selected Edremit (Adramyttion), altogether more accessible than Scorpiata.[60]

In support of this one could argue that Scorpiata clearly had drawbacks as a loading site, being a beach not a port,[61] and therefore loading and

---

[54] Pegolotti, *Pratica*, p. 43.

[55] Pegolotti, *Pratica*, p. 369. Pegolotti does not specify how often the 4,000 *kantar*s went to Antalya but it may well have been a per annum figure as are his production figures.

[56] Balard, *Romanie génoise*, vol. II, p. 773, n. 21.

[57] William of Rubruck, *Mission*, p. 273; Corpus Christi College, Cambridge MS 66A, fo. 109r col. 1 – 109v col. 1; Corpus Christi College, Cambridge MS 181, fo. 396. But see Heyd, *Histoire du commerce*, vol. II, p. 567.

[58] 1343.iv.10 = Liagre-de Sturler, *Relations commerciales*, vol. I, doc. 12, pp. 155–8.

[59] Balard, *Romanie génoise*, vol. II, p. 774. Professor Balard does not give his reasons for this dating. If it is based on lack of documents referring to Scorpiata prior to 1380, surely this could simply be fortuitous, no documents happening to have survived. It seems to me unlikely that one could in fact be so precise over the dating here.

[60] *Ibid.*

[61] 1408.x.24 = ASG, Notaio, Giovanni Balbi, Sc. 46, filza 1, doc. ?386. The captain in this deed said that he was unable at that moment to collect alum from Scorpiata because the weather/season was such that he could not go to Scorpiata, it being a beach. It was contested that the alum left in Scorpiata was in danger of deterioration and 'other things' (although it was also contested that the alum was safe and well looked after), perhaps futher indicating Scorpiata's difficulties as a loading place: 1408.x.13 = *ibid.*, doc. 397.

unloading would have been hampered both by location and by weather conditions. In 1393 Scorpiata is specifically excluded in an agreement over loading goods including alum in a port in Turchia. Manuel Doria promised to go with his ship to Chios and to wait there for two days to be told by the hirer, Michaele Lomellino, which port in Turchia, including Mytilene, he was to go to. Manuel stated, however, that he was not held to go to Scorpiata, even if told to do so. The document gives no indication as to why Manuel was not prepared to go to Scorpiata, but it may well have been that his refusal was in some way connected with difficulties of loading or landing there.[62] That Scorpiata was not ideal is confirmed by a notary deed of 1404 in which a captain of a ship agrees to go to Scorpiata or another place nearby better suited to loading.[63]

While one can convincingly argue that Scorpiata had its drawbacks as a loading site, this does not necessarily mean that the alum exported from there was from a previously unknown local source, as Professor Balard has concluded. The name Scorpiata when applied to alum may well refer to Scorpiata as the export port and not the place of origin of this alum. Evidence for such an argument may be adduced from the fact that Pegolotti refers to Kütahya alum variously as 'allume dal Cotai e d'Altoluogo', 'allume del Cotai, cioè d'Altoluogo' and 'allume di Coltai d'Altoluogo'.[64] However, he explains that the alum of Kütahya was sometimes called alum of other Turkish places or alum of Theologos (Altoluogo) but that its correct name was Kütahya (Coltai) because it came from the area of Kütahya.[65] As Theologos was one of the ports for Kütahya alum[66] perhaps this is why it was sometimes called 'allume d'Altoluogo'. This may well also explain the name 'alum of Christo' referring to Kütahya alum,[67] where again the name of the export port and not that of the origin is used.

Thus, by the same token, the alum of Scorpiata could have come from somewhere else, such as Kütahya. Against this, however, is the fact that it would seem strange to take the alum to Scorpiata rather than to the nearer and more accessible and suitable ports of Balat and Theologos, from which Kütahya alum was in fact exported. More plausibly, the alum of Scorpiata might have originated in the nearby alum-producing areas of Ulubat or Kapıdağ. Two Genoese notary deeds refer to the alum of Scorpiata as 'bad'

---

[62] 1393.vi.28 = Liagre-de Sturler, *Relations commerciales*, vol. II, no. 565, pp. 746–51.
[63] 1404.xi.4 = Doehaerd and Kerremans, *Relations commerciales*, no. 10, pp. 11–13, 'ad La Scorpiata, vel alium locum eidem vicinum magis habile ad levandum et onerandum onus infrascriptum . . . in dicto loco Scorpiate vel alio loco eidem vicino magis abili ad levandum'.
[64] Pegolotti, *Pratica*, pp. 43, 293.
[65] Pegolotti, *Pratica*, p. 369.   [66] *Ibid.*
[67] Balard, *Romanie génoise*, vol. II, p. 773, n. 21 says that the alum of Christo is without doubt Kütahya alum. Balard identifies Christo as, in all probability, the port of Dioshieron near Theologos.

rock alum ('bruta'), perhaps adding weight to this supposition,[68] since Pegolotti describes the alum from Kapıdağ as 'poco e molto laida' (small and foul), one of the three worst sorts.[69]

Professor Balard further argues that the frequent mention of Scorpiata alum between 1384 and 1409 leads one to conclude that there must have been alum-producing mines there which came to compete with the mines of Phokaea.[70] This seems too strong a conclusion to make on the evidence available, particularly bearing in mind that the alum of Scorpiata may well have got its name from the port and not the place of origin. The Genoese archival material seems more plentiful for the 1390s than for the earlier period, and this alone could account for the apparent upsurge in material relating to Scorpiata.

Whether there was or was not a new source of alum in Scorpiata it is certainly clear that alum was sold and exported from there. In 1384 there is a reference to a cargo of alum loaded in Pera or Scorpiata, insured for 125 Genoese pounds, which was to be unloaded in either L'Ecluse, England or Middelburg,[71] and four years later alum was loaded in Scorpiata for L'Ecluse.[72] In 1404, 10,000 *kantars* of alum were to be loaded in Scorpiata for Southampton and La Crussa.[73] In 1408 there was a sale of 4,999 *kantars* and 50 *rotoli* of alum – 3,000 *kantars* of grain alum and 1,999 *kantars* and 50 *rotoli* of rock alum – in Scorpiata where the ship was to spend twelve days loading alum and other merchandise.[74] The documents dealing with

---

[68] 1408.x.22 = ASG, Notaio, Giovanni Balbi, Sc. 46, filza 1, doc. 388, 'aluminum de rocha bruta'; 1408.x.24 = *ibid.*, doc. ?386, 'aluminum bruti'.

[69] Pegolotti, *Pratica*, p. 369.

[70] Balard, *Romanie génoise*, vol. II, p. 774. He refers to ASG, Not. Cart. 311, fos. 154r, 155r; ASG, Notai, Gregorio Panissario, doc. 118; ASG Notai, Giovanni Balbi, 1408.x.13, 17, 22; Liagre-de Sturler, *Relations commerciales*, docs. 457, 499, 500. But the Balbi documents all refer to the same alum (and interestingly Balard does not refer to the other documents in this series, 1408.viii.14 and 1408.x.24). Similarly docs. 499 and 500 in Liagre-de Sturler both deal with the same cargo of alum. Do these references in fact amount to frequent mention, sufficient to allow Professor Balard to draw his conclusion about the importance of a mine in the Scorpiata area?

[71] 1384.x.29 = Liagre-de Sturler, *Relations commerciales*, vol. II, no. 457, pp. 606–7.

[72] 1388.i.2 = Liagre-de Sturler, *Relations commerciales*, vol. II, no. 499, pp. 654–5; 1388.i.3 = *ibid.*, no. 500, pp. 655–6.

[73] 1404.xi.4 = Doehaerd and Kerremans, *Relations commerciales*, no. 10, pp. 11–13. La Crussa is Pegnitz: *Orbis Latinus. Lexikon lateinischer geographischer Namen des Mittelalters und der Neuzeit*, ed. Graesse, Benedicts and Pechl (Braunschweig, 1972), vols. I–III: vol. I, p. 597.

[74] ASG, Notaio, Giovanni Balbi, Sc. 46, filza 1. In the sale document, doc. 397, 1408.viii.14, the amount of alum sold is 2,000 to 2,500 *kantars* of rock alum, whatever the whole amount was, and *c.*3,000 *kantars* of grain alum. In doc. 397, 1408.x.13, the first in a series of documents concerning a dispute over the sale, the amount appears as 5,500 *kantars*, as it does in doc. 396, 1408.x.17. Doc. 388, 1408.x.22, is more precise. It says that the sale was of 5,000 *kantars*, 3,000 of grain alum and 2,000 or more of rock alum. But it also says that 1,561 *kantars* and 50 *rotoli* of rock alum were loaded and 3,000 *kantars* of grain alum and 438 *kantars* of rock alum were left behind in Scorpiata. These figures are repeated in doc. ?386, 1408.x.24, although in the second reference to the amount loaded the document misses out the 50 *rotoli*. It also makes the total 5,000 *kantars* though it must have been 4,999 *kantars* and 50 *rotoli*. Heers, 'Commerce de l'alun', 35, refers to the sale as being of 5,500

this sale and the subsequent dispute[75] show that the Florentines too were involved in buying and exporting alum from Scorpiata, since the alum in question was sold by a Genoese, Fillipo Lomellino, to two Florentine merchants, Petro de Ticio and Gieronimo Bartolo, who were to pay half the price of the alum in Florentine cloth. It is interesting to note the large amount of alum bought at Scorpiata in these documents, particularly when compared with Pegolotti's annual production figures for Phokaea and Karahisar of 14,000 *kantars* per annum.[76]

Alum was also produced in various other places in Anatolia. Ulubat (Ulek Abad, inland from the Sea of Marmara, west of Bursa) alum (*allume lupaio* or *allume lupaio turchesco*) was sold in Constantinople and Pera.[77] It was 'allume grossetto', heavier than that of Kütahya and was exported through Trilia (Triglia). The annual production figure was 10,000 Genoese *kantars*.[78] It was clearly traded to Bruges, as it appears in a list of alum values there.[79] Camalı, just south of Gelibolu, also had mines producing excellent rock alum and the Genoese merchants were active there.[80] Alum from Kapıdağ (Cyzicus, west of Bursa on the coast of the Sea of Marmara) (*allume Chisico*) was one of the three worst sorts together with ?Diaschila alum (*allume ghiaghillo*) and *allume corda*.[81] It was used for tanning hides and was 'small and foul' ('poco e molto laida').[82] It too is listed among the alums in Bruges.[83]

The export of alum from Anatolia was subject to tax. It would seem from Pegolotti that the tax on alum exported from Theologos was 4 per cent, as he states that, with the exception of wax, all goods paid at this rate.[84] From the various treaties with the Venetians it is known that alum in the beyliks of Menteşe and Aydın was placed under *appalto*, that is, it was tax farmed. In the treaty of 1337 between Giovanni Sanudo, duca di Candia, and İbrahim, emir of Menteşe, and in the treaty between Sanudo and Hızır of Aydın in the same year, alum is listed as one of the goods on which the Venetians did not have to pay *appalto*. This is presumably a concession specially for the Venetians and therefore one can presume that generally the *appalto* was applied to alum. This point is further strengthened by clause 28 of the treaty where İbrahim stated that he would impose *appalto* on alum in

kantars of alum with payment in cloth. But, as shown above, the amount must have been 4,999 *kantars* and 50 *rotoli* and the payment was for half the amount in cloth. There were 100 *rotoli* in one Genoese *kantar*: Schilbach, *Metrologie*, pp. 188, 189.

[75] The series of documents about this sale are 1408.viii.14 = ASG, Notaio, Giovanni Balbi, Sc. 46, filza 1, doc. 384; 1408.x.13 = *ibid.*, doc. 397; 1408.x.17 = *ibid.*, doc. 395; 1408.x.17 = *ibid.*, doc. 396; 1408.x.22 = *ibid.*, doc. 388; 1408.x.24 = *ibid.*, doc. ?386.

[76] Pegolotti, *Pratica*, p. 369.   [77] Pegolotti, *Pratica*, p. 43.
[78] Pegolotti, *Pratica*, p. 369.   [79] Pegolotti, *Pratica*, p. 243.
[80] Balard, *Romanie génoise*, vol. II, p. 774 and n. 23, citing ASG, Not. Cart. no. 445/2.
[81] Pegolotti, *Pratica*, pp. 43, 293, 369.
[82] Pegolotti, *Pratica*, p. 369. Pegolotti says that many alums were called 'cassico' because of their smallness and foulness.
[83] Pegolotti, *Pratica*, p. 243.   [84] Pegolotti, *Pratica*, p. 56.

Balat if Hızır of Aydın concluded a treaty with Crete but continued to make alum subject to *appalto* in Aydın.[85]

It would appear that at some time between 1337 and 1358 *appalto* was imposed on alum in Menteşe since Musa, emir of Menteşe, undertook in his treaty of 1358 with the duca di Candia, Pietro Badoer, to lift *appalto* on alum.[86]

In the treaty of 1375 between Ahmed, emir of Menteşe, and Giovanni Gradenigo, duca di Candia, the clause of the 1337 treaty relating to non-payment of *appalto* for alum is repeated. However, the 1375 treaty is largely a word-for-word copy of the 1337 treaty, of which it was a renewal. In some clauses, for example 26 and 27, where the oaths of İbrahim and his nobles are copied exactly, the content is clearly completely out of date, and this therefore casts doubt on the reliability of the other clauses. One has to wonder whether they were merely mindless copying or whether they, or at least some of them, were relevant to conditions in 1375.[87] Under the 1403 treaty between İlyas, emir of Menteşe and the duca di Candia, Marco Falier, there was to be no *datium* imposed on alum.[88] The 1407 treaty, this time between İlyas, emir of Menteşe, and the new duca di Candia, Leonardo Bembo, refers to no *amalim* being imposed on alum, meaning that, for the Venetians, it was not subject to *appalto*.[89]

*Gabella*s and *introytus* were charged on alum in Phokaea, which taxes were collected by the *appaltatores*. It appears that, at least for the end of the fifteenth century, the *appaltatores* were entitled to some tax concessions on alum which they acquired during their period in office as they were able to export it without paying any 'new taxes' on it.[90]

It seems that under the Ottomans alum was farmed out to the Genoese. Dukas, for example, refers to Giovanni Adorno, the new *podestà* of Phokaea, who, in *c*.1415,[91] 'according to ancient custom', went to present himself to Mehmed I and made the 'customary obeisance'. In return for the

---

[85] 1337.pre-iv = Zachariadou, *Trade and Crusade*, doc. 1337M, clause 22, p. 198, clause 28, pp. 199–200; 1337.iii.6 = *ibid.*, doc. 1337A, clause 11, p. 192.

[86] 1358.x.13 = Zachariadou, *Trade and Crusade*, clause 8, p. 218.

[87] 1375.iv.22 = Zachariadou, *Trade and Crusade*, doc. 1375M, pp. 222–3.

[88] 1403.vii.24 = Zachariadou, *Trade and Crusade*, doc. 1403M DVL, clause 22, p. 231. Doc. 1403M has 'gabelam' in place of 'datium', clause 22, p. 231.

[89] 1407.vi.2 = Zachariadou, *Trade and Crusade*, doc. 1407M, clause 22, p. 236.

[90] 1394.ii.18 = ASG, Notaio, Donato de Clavaro, Sc. 39, filza 1, doc.97/240. The *appaltatores* in question were granted this tax concession because this was an established practice: 'Et hec ut supra declaramus [referring to the concession] cum cognoverimus sic temporibus retro-actis usitatum fuisse.' Francesco, ex-*appaltator*, had however to pay *gabellas* and *introytus* on alum which he had put in Phokaea after he had ceased being *appaltator* unless Domenico Giustiniano, *podestà* of Chios, certified that the alum had been sent to Phokaea for a legitimate reason. He had to pay on alum put in Phokaea by him after Nicolao had taken over the *appaltatorship*, as others paid it.

[91] Dukas, *Historia Byzantina*, p. 164, l. 8; Dukas, *Historia Turcobyzantina*, p. 209, l. 18; Dukas, *Decline and Fall*, p. 150. Dukas says that this happened six years before the death of Mehmed. Mehmed I died in 824/1421.

rights to farm alum, which he 'finally' obtained from the sultan, he had to pay 20,000 gold coins per annum for the ten years of his period in office. On Mehmed's death the money went to his successor, Murad II, Adorno again making obeisance before the sultan. Adorno had fallen behind on his payments because of the Genoese–Catalan wars which prevented the export of alum westwards and, apparently, because of the heavy cost of mining the alum. Murad II waived debts on alum in return for a passage across the straits in his fight with the rival claimant to the throne, Mustafa.[92]

Under Mehmed II too the Genoese were tax farmers of alum. In 1452 Francesco de Draperiis made an arrangement with Paris Giustiniano, Paulo Bocardo and Benedetto Salvaigo. These three merchants gave Francesco 400 pieces of Genoese cloth worth around 5,000 gold *ducats* of Chios (*c*.7,000 Genoese *ducats*) which he was allowed to take to Edirne, and promised him a further 45,000 Turkish *aspers* (7,000 gold *ducats* of Chios, 9,800 Genoese), paid in Edirne, if he secured the tax farm of the mines of Greece and Turchia from Mehmed II.[93] In 1454 Mehmed II's fleet appeared off Chios with instructions that if 40,000 gold coins owed by the Chian authorities for alum to Francesco de Draperiis (who in turn appears to have owed this sum to the sultan) was not paid, the island was to be attacked.[94]

It is very difficult to give an accurate and detailed picture of the price of alum in this period.[95] Apart from the usual problem over currency exchange ratios and the correspondence between different measurements, there is the added problem of not always knowing what sort of alum is involved when a price is given. Although on occasions the sources specify, for example, rock alum, often they give a price for unspecified alum only.

---

[92] Dukas *Historia Byzantina*, p. 163, l. 19 – p. 165, l. 24, p. 178, l. 2 – p. 179, l. 9; Dukas, *Historia Turcobyzantina*, p. 209, l. 9 – p. 211, l. 19, p. 225, l. 24 – p. 227, l. 12; Dukas, *Decline and Fall*, pp. 150–1, 158; Aşıkpaşazade, *Altosmanische Chronik*, bab 87, p. 88; Aşıkpaşazade, *Tevarih-i al-i 'Osman*, p. 99. According to Dukas, the amount owed was *c*.27,000 gold coins. See also Dukas, *Historia Byzantina*, pp. 162–3, Dukas, *Decline and Fall*, p. 149, where he refers to a treaty made with Saruhan and the annual payment from Phokaea to him of 15,000 *lepta*.

[93] 1452.x (?).28 = Argenti, *Chios*, vol. III, no. 222, pp. 658–9; Heers, 'Commerce de l'alun', 50, n. 64 dates this document to 1451.xii.28. She refers to the price of alum as fixed at 0.45 of a *ducat* which represented 26,000 *kantars* of alum. However, no figure is given in the document. At the same time, without knowing what sort of alum was involved it would be difficult to be precise about what the money paid by Paris and his partners represented in terms of alum. All one can say is that the three Genoese merchants involved considered an investment of 12,000 gold *ducats* of Chios (16,800 Genoese *ducats* – 140 Genoese *ducats* to 100 Chian *ducats*: Heers, 'Commerce de l'alun', 40, n. 39) worthwhile in order to gain control of the alum coming from the mines of the Turkish sultan. It would be very helpful to know how long Francesco's arrangement with the sultan was made for. Unfortunately the document gives no indication of this.

[94] Dukas *Historia Byzantina*, p. 322, ll. 10–19, p. 327, ll. 20–2; Dukas, *Historia Turcobyzantina*, p. 402, ll. 12–19, p. 411, ll. 19–20; Dukas, *Decline and Fall*, pp. 246–7, 250.

[95] See appendix 3 below.

This problem is compounded by the fact that alums from different regions varied in price.[96]

As Professor Zachariadou has pointed out, there appears to have been a considerable increase in alum prices in the eastern Mediterranean during the fourteenth century. In 1336, 5.5 *kantar*s of alum was sold for 1 *ducat*. At the end of the fourteenth century alum fetched in the region of 0.5 of a *ducat* per *kantar*. It seems that this increase took place at the end of the century rather than being a progressive development, something reflected in the Genoese slave market where prices remained without fluctuation throughout the century, increasing only at the end.[97] Both Professor Zachariadou and Professor Balard have attributed this increase to Ottoman activity, Professor Zachariadou ascribing it to Ottoman policy and Professor Balard to Ottoman advance at the end of the century.[98] While it is true that Ottoman advance was no doubt a disruptive factor, it is not likely to have been the sole reason for an increase in price, for, had it been, one would perhaps have expected to see a decrease in price after the collapse of the Ottoman state in 1402.[99] In fact prices appear to have remained fairly stable, even rising slightly.

A combination of Ottoman advance and subsequent Ottoman policy probably largely explains the increase in alum prices in Anatolia at the end of the fourteenth century. In 1381 the Ottomans took the alum-producing region of Kütahya and, at the beginning of the 1390s, annexed Menteşe and

---

[96] Pegolotti, *Pratica*, pp. 243–4. In a list of alum values in Bruges the various alums are said to be 2 *soldi* of the silver *tornesi grossi* cheaper or more expensive than each other. Unfortunately part of the text is missing and so no actual price is given. The alums listed are Cyzicus alum, Ulubat alum, second-quality alum, Phokaea alum and rock alum.

[97] Balard, *Romanie génoise*, vol. II, pp. 780–1. Liagre-de Sturler, *Relations commerciales*, vol. I, p. cxl also considers the prices stable. Balard, *Romanie génoise*, p. 57, in quoting prices for alum at the end of the fourteenth century, refers to ASG, Not. Donato di Chiavari, 1394, n. 240; Not. Gregorio Panissario doc. 70, 135 (date = 1405.18.4, in Doehard and Kerremans, *Relations commerciales*, no. 11); D. Gioffre, 'Atti rogati in Chio nella seconda metà del XIV secolo' in *Bulletin de l'Institut Historique Belge de Rome* 34 (1962), 324, 359. Professor Balard here refers to grain alum. But Donato di Chiavari 1394 doc. 240 (1394.ii.18) refers either to alum or rock alum, not to grain alum. As Professor Balard specifically states that the rock alum price is for 1398 (i.e. not from Donato de Clavaro, of 1394) while he quotes the rest, at the end of the fourteenth century, as grain prices (i.e. thus including the Donato de Clavaro reference), Professor Balard must here be mistaken, quoting a rock alum price as a grain alum price. Further, the prices Professor Balard quotes, grain alum from between 12 *sous* 6 *deniers* (i.e. 0.5 of a *ducat*) and 18 *sous* 9 *deniers* (0.75 of a *ducat*) per *kantar*, rock alum at 45 *sous* (1.72 *ducat*s) in 1398, do not tie in with the price in Donato de Clavaro, 1394, where the price for alum, type unspecified, was 4 to 5 gold *ducats* per *kantar* (and so presumably, judging from the price, rock alum). The other alum referred to was rock alum.

[98] According to Zachariadou, *Trade and Crusade*, p. 169, the increase in the price of alum during the fourteenth century was a direct result of Ottoman policy. Balard, *Romanie génoise*, vol. II, p. 718 regards the 'temporary rise' in alum prices at the end of the fourteenth century as caused by the Ottoman advance.

[99] Dr Colin Imber, verbal communication, has suggested rather that one might expect a rise post-1402, in view of the insecurity of the period.

Aydın and thus gained control of the export ports of Theologos and Balat. The Ottomans were therefore in a position to control alum exports and prices. The fact that prices apparently did not rise earlier in the century suggests that the beyliks were insufficiently powerful to increase substantially the prices paid by western merchants for alum in their territories. The change after the Ottoman take-over suggests a more dynamic economic policy, necessarily supported by considerably greater military strength.

The Ottomans, having established their position in these areas, did seek to control the alum trade. After annexing Kütahya in 1381, Murad imposed restrictions on alum export, as is indicated by the Venetian senate's instructions to its ambassador in 1384 to try and ensure that Venetians could load and export rock alum in Murad's territories. At the same time the ambassador was to request a reduction in the price of alum fixed by the sultan.[100] A Genoese notary deed from this period makes it clear that trading alum in Turchia was then not always easy.[101] The document refers to the goods of the late Nicolao de Oliva, the executor of whose will, Giovanni de Bulgaro, had been unable to carry out his functions as *fideicommissor* because of 'various impediments and the great diversity of his trade'. He had particular difficulty in Pera and Turchia because of the distances involved, the dangers and the abundance of his goods. Giovanni in consequence appointed two agents to deal with all Nicolao's affairs and to receive all the alum that Giovanni Demerode had in Turchia and that from the goods of the late Nicolao and to sell it, investing or lending the money from the sale.

According to Dr Zhukov, the Ottoman take-over of Kütahya in 1381 resulted in an almost complete paralysis of the alum trade in Menteşe and Aydın, forcing the Genoese to obtain alum from areas under Ottoman control, in particular, in the period 1384–1409, from Scorpiata. This discontinuance of the transit trade, again according to Dr Zhukov, deprived the emirs of Aydın and Menteşe of an important source of foreign currency, which in turn resulted in the intensification of the unequal balance of trade with the Latin states of the Levant.[102] There are, however, various factors which argue against this assessment of the situation after 1381. First, it relies partly on the assumption that Scorpiata became a centre of either alum trade or production after 1384 and, as has been argued above, this does not seem necessarily established. Further, there was clearly still an alum trade with western merchants in the beyliks during the 1380s and 1390s, apart from the trade in other commodities which is known to have existed. While it seems fairly clear that Ottoman control resulted in a tougher trade policy, as is evidenced by the Venetian senate's request to

[100] 1384.vii.22 = Thomas, *Diplomatarium*, vol. II, no. 116, p. 194.
[101] 1381.ii.28 = ASG, Notario, Antonius Feloni, C. 175, fos. 114r–115r.
[102] Zhukov, Эгейские Эмираты, p. 100.

Murad for a reduction in alum prices and its concern over its citizens' ability to load and export this commodity, trade relations were very much in Ottoman interests and continued under them. It does not seem possible therefore to refer to a paralysis in transit trade, nor to ascribe this as a cause for any worsening balance of trade between western states and the beyliks.

At the beginning of the fifteenth century the price of alum was slightly higher, per-*kantar* prices ranging from 0.75 of a *ducat* in 1405, c.0.66 for rock and c.0.33 for grain in 1408 and 0.7 in 1412. The price appears to have risen again by the late 1430s, though not by much, for per-*kantar* prices in Constantinople then varied between *c*.1.25 *ducat*s and *c*.1.7. By 1450, however, prices appear to have declined again, hitting a level similar to that of the 1390s. In 1448 1 *kantar* sold for 0.375 of a *ducat*, and more than 0.5 in 1449 and 1450. After 1453 eastern alum became uncommon in European markets and the price correspondingly increased fivefold.[103] By 1462 the Ottoman empire was receiving as much as 300,000 gold *ducat*s per annum from alum sales to the west.[104]

The trade in alum sheds light on Ottoman trade policy in various ways. The rise in alum prices at the end of the century and the apparent restrictions imposed by Murad on Venetian trade in alum indicate that the Ottomans pursued a more hard-edged trade policy than that of the weaker beyliks, using their increasing political strength as a base from which to exercise greater economic dominance. Ottoman rulers were prepared to use western merchants, farming out their alum resources particularly to the Genoese, thus benefiting from a guaranteed income without much effort. The Ottomans, as well as exerting control, were also prepared to give concessions in order to foster trade. They did not apparently in general impose restrictions on alum export[105] and allowed some ports to be free. In 1408 Scorpiata appears to have been a free port, since a sale of alum there is described as being free from all expenses and *anaris* according to the custom of Scorpiata.[106]

---

[103] Delumeau, *L'alun*, p. 19; Heers, 'Commerce de l'alun', 53.
[104] Liagre 'Commerce de l'alun', 194.
[105] Faroqhi, 'Alum production', 153. She in fact says that the Ottomans never forbade alum export.
[106] 1408.viii.14 = ASG, Notaio, Giovanni Balbi, Sc. 46, filza 1, doc. 384: 'libera et expedita ab omnibus expensis et anaris secundum consuetudinem loci predicti Schorpiate'.

CHAPTER 8

Cloth

Cloth was an important commodity, and figured heavily in trade and in other transactions. Rich fabrics were much valued and given as presents, as bribes and as rewards for favours. The Genoese often made presents of fabrics to the Ottoman ruler, and European cloth appears in lists of expenses of the Genoese commune for their embassies to the Ottomans or for embassies received from the Ottoman ruler. In 1390 cloth was to be given to 'Jalabi' (Çelebi, Bayezid I), costing 7 *hyperpyra*,[1] in 1391 seven pieces of Florentine cloth were given to Bayezid's ambassador, Serefedinus (Şerefedin), at a cost of 19 *hyperpyra*, 6 *karati*,[2] and in the following year seven pieces of red cloth costing 21 *hyperpyra* were given to 'Momico turco domini Jhalabi Capitaneo Grecie', meaning the *beylerbeyi* of Rumeli and in consequence an extremely important government official. It is indicative of the importance the Ottomans attached to their relations with the Genoese that the *beylerbeyi* of Rumeli took part in an embassy.[3] In 1392 on two separate occasions, seven pieces of Florentine cloth were given to envoys of Bayezid, once to Bagadus and once to Tangriberinis de Viso, at a cost of 21 *hyperpyra*.[4] In that same year, an envoy of Bayezid, who brought news of the king of Hungary, was given seven pieces of cloth, at a cost to the commune of 17 *hyperpyra* 12 *karati*.[5] It is interesting that of these six examples of cloth being presented to a representative of the Ottoman ruler, five were gifts of seven pieces of cloth, while the remaining example is for an unspecified amount. If this is not merely an irrelevant coincidence, it must indicate either that, for some reason, seven was considered a suitable number of pieces for gifts on this type of occasion, or that seven pieces represented a certain measurement, such as a bundle.

Apart from presenting cloth to visiting Ottoman ambassadors, the Genoese commune spent money on cloth for garments for their own

[1] 1390.iii.31 = ASG, San Giorgio, Sala 34 590/1304, fo. 25v.
[2] 1391.xii.19 = ASG, Antico Comune, 22, fos. 70, 192.
[3] 1392.1.16 = ASG, Antico Comune, 22, fos. 74, 193.
[4] 1392.ii.24 = ASG, Antico Comune, 22, fos. 76, 193; 1392.v.23 = *ibid.*, fos. 78, 196.
[5] 1392.x.15 = ASG, Antico Comune, 22, fos. 88, 175.

officials sent on embassies to the Ottoman court. In 1392 the commune paid 18 *hyperpyra* 10 *karati* for six pieces of 'red cloth for a garment'.[6] One of the expenses of an embassy of Stephanus Rex sent to Bayezid was for a cloth garment.[7] Thirteen pieces of vermilion Florentine cloth for two garments for an embassy to Bayezid cost 36 *hyperpyra*, 3 *karati*.[8] In the same year one expense of an embassy to Bayezid was for six pieces of red cloth for a garment, at a cost of 16 *hyperpyra* 9 *karati*.[9] Six pieces of red cloth for a garment for an embassy to Bayezid cost the commune 32 *hyperpyra* 12 *karati*.[10]

The Turks too used cloth as a suitable gift for visiting dignitaries and on embassies. When the Germiyan ambassador, İshak Fakıh, went on an embassy to Murad I, he took with him as a gift (*peşkeş*) Denizli cloth.[11] This was an important embassy, as it was for the proposing of a marriage alliance between the daughter of the ruler of Germiyan and Murad I's son Bayezid.[12] In the 1330s Umur Aydınoğlu gave the Arab traveller ibn Battuta, who travelled in Anatolia in the 1330s and who visited the court of Umur, a parting gift of a piece of gilded silk called 'annah'[13] as well two garments of damask, made of silk from Baghdad, Tabris, Nishapur and China.[14] It seems that Turkish cloth was also suitable for horses. Giacomo Badoer covered his horse, which he presented to Antonio Contarini, with a 'coverta turchesca'.[15]

Apart from its use for ceremonial presentation, cloth could be used in other arrangements. Fabrics formed part of the repayment of a loan from the Ilhanids taken out by the Seljuk rulers 'Izz al-Dīn and Rukn al-Dīn and the vizier Şams al-Dīn Baba Tughrā'ī.[16] Cloth was also involved in dealings between Genoese officials and the commune of Pera and the Byzantine emperor when it was given as a reward for services rendered. In 1402 in the enquiry into the conduct of Ettore de Flisco and Ottobono Giustiniano, reference is made to them having received Florentine cloth for a garment for each of them from the Byzantine emperor in return for their requesting various people to lend the emperor money.[17] In a not dissimilar way, the

---

[6] 1392.vi.17 = ASG, Antico Comune, 22, fo. 128.

[7] 1392.vi.20 = ASG, Antico Comune, 22, fos. 81, 84.

[8] 1392.v.25 = ASG, Antico Comune, 22, fo. 174; 1392.v.5 = *ibid.*, fo. 81.

[9] 1392.vi.17 = ASG, Antico Comune, 22, fos. 84, 92.

[10] 1392.vi.17 = ASG, Antico Comune, fos. 84, 197.

[11] Aşıkpaşazade, *Altosmanische Chronik*, p. 52; Aşıkpaşazade, *Tevarih-i al-i 'Osman*, pp. 56–7; Neşri, *Menzel, Cod.* p. 56; Neşri, *Kitab-ı Cihan-nüma*, p. 204.

[12] Aşıkpaşazade, *Altosmanische Chronik*, p. 52; Aşıkpaşazade, *Tevarih-i al-i 'Osman*, p. 56; Neşri, *Menzel, Cod.* p. 55; Neşri, *Kitab-ı Cihan-nüma*, vol. I, p. 204.

[13] Ibn Battuta, *Voyages*, p. 309.   [14] Ibn Battuta, *Voyages*, p. 311.

[15] 1439.ii.25 = Badoer, *Libro*, col. 380, p. 763.

[16] Cahen, *Pre-Ottoman Turkey*, p. 332.

[17] 1402.v.30 = ASG, San Giorgio, Sala 34 590/1306, fo. 102r: 'habuisse a dicto domino imperatore certum panum florentie pro una gona pro quolibet ipsorum. Et hoc quia ipsi Hector et socius rogabant diversis personis, tam civibus Janue quam burgensibus Peyre quod ipsi prestarent ipsi domino imperatori aliquam quantitatem peccunie.'

Ottomans too used cloth as a form of bribe. During the period of struggle between the sons of Bayezid, Mustafa attacked Bursa whereupon the top men there gathered together money and 100 pieces of cloth (*kumaş*) which they sent with Ahi Ya'kub and Ahi Kadem to present to Mustafa's *lala*, Şarapdar İlyas. The presents were accepted and a settlement arranged.[18]

Cloth was a major item in trade between Turchia and the western city states. Expensive fabrics were imported into Anatolia which, in turn, was a producer and exporter both of raw materials and of expensive, worked tissues. Marco Polo referred to the manufacture of beautiful carpets and rich, high-quality silks of various colours and talked of the Armenians of Erzincan making a beautiful buckram.[19] Piloti, referring to the period at the end of the fourteenth and beginning of the fifteenth centuries, wrote of carpets exported from Antalya and Alanya and of the Genoese exporting them from Balat.[20] Sivas and Kastamonu produced woollen goods in the mid-thirteenth century.[21] Denizli, in south-west Turkey, produced good-quality cloth, white and marked (i.e. with a sign) used for the kaftan (*sırtak tekele*) worn over a robe of honour.[22] The edging for such robes was made from the red cloth produced in Alaşehir.[23] Cloth was exported from Balat and other places in Turchia in bales[24] while Erzincan buckram was sold in wooden boxes by tenths of pieces in Pera and Constantinople,[25] and in Pisa.[26] In France, Turkish camelot cloth became so widespread that by the end of the Middle Ages even the poorer element of society was clothed in it.[27] Anatolia also exported covers for horses. In 1438 the merchant Giacomo Badoer imported into Constantinople from Bursa a cover for his horse costing 60 *asper*s (5.7 *hyperpyra*).[28] This may perhaps be the same as the 'coverta turchesca' on his horse when he presented it to Antonio Contarini a few months later.[29]

---

[18] Aşıkpaşazade, *Altosmanische Chronik*, p. 90; Aşıkpaşazade, *Tevarih-i al-i 'Osman*, p. 101; Neşri, *Menzel, Cod.* p. 152; Neşri, *Kitab-ı Cihan-nüma*, p. 568.

[19] Marco Polo, *Le livre de Marco Polo citoyen de Venise conseiller privé et Commissaire impérial de Khoubilaï-Kaàn rédigé en français sous sa dictée en 1298 par Rusticien de Pise*, ed. M. G. Pauthier (Paris, 1865), vol. II, pp. 37–8: 'draps de soie de diverses couleurs moult beaux et moult riches, en moult grant qualité'. The buckram made in Erzincan was 'les meilleurs bouguerans du monde': Marco Polo, *Travels*, p. 50.

[20] Piloti, *L'Egypte*, pp. 60, 73.

[21] Cahen, *Pre-Ottoman Turkey*, p. 320, referring to the *Risāla* of Ibn Kiya Mazandaranī.

[22] The Ottoman word is *bezler*, a linen, hempen or cotton cloth: Aşıkpaşazade, *Altosmanische Chronik*, p. 52, 9; *Tevarih-i al-i 'Osman*, p. 56, ll. 17–18; Neşri, *Menzel, Cod.* p. 55, ll. 20–1; Neşri, *Manisa, Cod.* p. 85, 1; *Kitab-ı Cihan-nüma*, p. 204, 5.

[23] Aşıkpaşazade, *Altosmanische Chronik*, p. 52, l. 10; *Tevarih-i al-i 'Osman*, p. 56, l. 18; Neşri, *Menzel, Cod.* p. 55, l. 21; Neşri, *Manisa, Cod.* p. 85, l. 2; Neşri, *Kitab-ı Cihan-nüma*, p. 204, ll. 6–7.

[24] Piloti, *L'Egypte*, pp. 61–2: 'couvertures par balles ... fautres de laine'.

[25] Pegolotti, *Pratica*, p. 36.   [26] Pegolotti, *Pratica*, p. 208.

[27] Robert Lopez, Harry Miskimin and Abraham Udovitch, 'England to Egypt, 1350–1500: Long-term Trends and Long-distance Trade', in Cook (ed.), *Economic History*, p. 105.

[28] 1438.xii.28 = Badoer, *Libro*, col. 301, p. 604.

[29] 1439.ii.25 = Badoer, *Libro*, col. 380, p. 763. The exchange rate is given as 10.5:1.

Western merchants came to the Near East to buy raw silk for the developing European silk industry, an industry in which Genoa played a dominant role.[30] After the Black Death, the much-reduced population turned increasingly to luxuries, one of the manifestations of which was the wearing of silk garments. In England the silk industry grew steadily throughout the fourteenth and first part of the fifteenth centuries.[31] Presumably this upsurge in the wearing of silk increased the demand for the raw material and thus boosted the silk markets of Turchia, predominantly that of Bursa, the Turkish centre of the trade. At the same time, however, while the European silk industry continued to develop after the Black Death, the main Italian centre, Lucca, which had by the thirteenth century a well-established silk industry,[32] never recovered its former strength.[33]

Silk was much traded in Turchia by western merchants who exported it from ports such as Antalya and Alanya, from where it was shipped to Constantinople and Alexandria,[34] and frequented Bursa, a major silk emporium to which came the raw silks of Astarabad and Gilan which were then exported westward, to Venice and to Lucca, the centre of the European silk industry in the fourteenth century. Johannes Schiltberger, captured at the battle of Nikopolis in 1396 only returning to his homeland in 1427, refers to silk from 'Schurban' being worked in Damascus, Caffa and Bursa, thus possibly implying that the silk trade and silk industry of Bursa were comparable to those of these other two cities.[35] Turchia exported both Iranian silk brought into the country and traded with western merchants in Turkish markets, particularly Bursa, and Turkish silk known as *seta turci*.[36] Turkish silk was sold in Pisa[37] and appears in Pegolotti in two lists of silk, 'Nomora di seta' and 'tare di seta'.[38]

Silk often made up part of the merchandise of Genoese merchants, or those acting as Genoese citizens. In 1402 Ettore de Flisco took in Trabzon two or three *fardelli* of silk which belonged to a dead Armenian who was treated as Genoese. This seems from context to mean that Ettore, as a Genoese representative, laid claim to the silk while he was in Trabzon from Caffa on business of the commune.[39] Some years later Petro Drago de

[30] Lopez, Miskimin and Udovitch, 'England to Egypt', p. 114.
[31] Lopez, Miskimin and Udovitch, 'England to Egypt', pp. 99–100, 104–5.
[32] Ashtor, *Social and Economic History*, p. 263.
[33] Lopez, Miskimin and Udovitch, 'England to Egypt', p. 114.
[34] Piloti, *L'Egypte*, pp. 60, 63.
[35] Johann Schiltberger, *The Bondage and Travels of Johann Schiltberger, a Native of Bavaria, in Europe, Asia and Africa 1396–1427*, ed. and trans. Commander J. Buchan Telfer (London, 1879), p. 34.
[36] Pegolotti, *Pratica*, pp. 430, 212, 301.   [37] Pegolotti, *Pratica*, pp. 208–9.
[38] Pegolotti, *Pratica*, pp. 297, 300.
[39] 1402.v.30 = ASG, San Giorgio, Sala 34 590/1306, fo. 102r: 'se tractabat pro Januense'. The granting of Venetian citizenship to Greek subjects of the Byzantine emperor was a constant bone of contention between Venice and Constantinople. Successive emperors complained of

Sanguines, heir of Batisto Drago, acknowledged in Caffa that he had received all goods and monies of the late Batisto held by Prospero Adorno including a *fardeletus* and two *fardelli* of silk ('cete') held by the agent of Prospero Adorno in Amasra (Samachi), on the Black Sea coast east of Zonguldak.[40]

Turchia was a cotton-producing and exporting area, particularly high-quality cotton being grown in the Çukurova plain, between Adana and Tarsus, which remained one of the major cotton-producing areas in the sixteenth and seventeenth centuries, together with the *sancaks* of Aydın, Saruhan and Kütahya.[41] Cotton was traded in Antalya where it was sold by the *stadera* (steelyard balance),[42] and in Bursa where, in the later part of the fifteenth century, Benedetto Dei mentioned its sale to Florentines.[43]

Cotton was exported from Turchia to both southern and northern Europe.[44] Turkish cotton was traded in France where 'cotone turchiescho' is listed among goods in Avignon sold in August 1392. The value of this cotton was entered as 30 *florins*, while that of the 'cotone asciano' was 45 *florins*, of the 'cotone damano' 40 *florins* and of the 'cotone alessandrino' 36 *florins*.[45] One of the Anatolian export ports for cotton was Foça, from where cotton was sent westwards as far as Spain. In the 1430s it was shipped from there to Ancona[46] and Majorca.[47] The scale of cotton exports from Foça, or perhaps the volume of commodities handled there in general, may be gauged from the problem of overloading. In 1438 Alesandro Zien was unable to load 49 *kantar*s of cotton in Foça, leaving them there with Pantalon Guardato. Most of the cotton was to be sent on to Ancona the following year.[48] This was presumably because there was no space available for this cotton, indicating in turn that the volume of exports from Foça was greater, on occasion, than the capacity of the shipping available.

The Venetians invested heavily in the Levantine cotton trade, exporting

---

lost tax revenue due to their nationals claiming Venetian nationality: Chrysostomides, 'Venetian commercial privileges', 276–89.

[40] 1410.x.7 = ASG, Notaio, Giovanni Labaino, Sc. 40, filza 1, doc. 15. In the manuscript the scribe first wrote 'turchia' and then crossed it out and wrote 'Samachi'.

[41] There was also, in this later period, cotton production in Erzıncan, Malatya and Alanya. Centres of production of cotton cloth (*bez/boğası*) in the sixteenth and seventeenth centuries were the *sancaks* of Aydın, Hamid and İçel. According to Professor Faroqhi, it seems possible that in some areas of Anatolia in the sixteenth century commercialized weaving was fairly widespread and aimed not just at local consumption but also for the Istanbul market. There seems in that period to have been a fairly lively trade in cotton thread: Suraiya Faroqhi, 'Notes on the production of cotton and cotton cloth in XVIth and XVIIth century Anatolia', *JEEH* 8, 2 (Fall 1979), 406–7, 11, 413.

[42] Pegolotti, *Pratica*, p. 58.   [43] Dei, *Chronica*, p. 141.

[44] Lopez, Miskimin and Udovitch, 'England to Egypt', p. 105.

[45] 1392.viii. = Jacques Heers, 'Il commercio nel Mediterraneo alla fine del sec. XIV e nei primi anni del XV', *Archivio Storico Italiano* 113 (1955), 162–4.

[46] 1439.vii.28 = Badoer, *Libro*, col. 320, p. 643 (Foie).

[47] 1438.i.22 = Badoer, *Libro*, col. 261, p. 524. The shipment was of 601 *kantar*s 31 *rotols* of cotton of Foça (Foie).

[48] 1439.iv.8 = Badoer, *Libro*, col. 318, p. 638, col. 224, p. 451, col. 376, p. 754.

mostly from Syria but also from Turchia and Grecia.[49] Turkish cotton was imported into Venice from Turchia[50] and from Crete.[51] The Genoese too were very active in the trade of Turkish cotton which was imported into Genoa. Thirty-seven sacks of cotton loaded in Balat (Palatia) on the *ligno* of Luchino Cibo, valued at 942 Genose pounds, were listed in the tax register of Genoa for 1377.[52] It is possible that three bales of cotton thread on a *cocha en route* for L'Ecluse from Genoa in 1343 were also from Turchia, since the bales were listed with 210 *kantars* of alum from Kütahya and Lipari and 158 *kantars* of Turkish alum. Together, the commodities were security for 396 *florins*.[53]

Other raw material exported from Turchia included unspun hemp which was exported from Theologos,[54] flax, sold in Antalya at the weight of the *stadera* (steelyard balance)[55] and muslin.[56] Wool was exported from Antalya, Alanya, Balat and other places in Turchia[57] and exported to Constantinople and Pera where washed and unwashed Turkish wool was sold.[58] In the 1430s western merchants bought it in the western parts of the Ottoman empire, from Tekirdağ (Rodosto),[59] Edirne[60] and Gelibolu[61] and the surrounding area, including Megalicharia and Malchara (just northeast of İspata),[62] where high-quality wool was produced. Bortolamio da

[49] Eliyahu Ashtor, 'Underdevelopment in the pre-industrial era. The case of declining economies', *JEEH* 7 (1978), 300–1.

[50] 1408.i.17 = C. N. Sathas, *Documents inédits relatifs à l'histoire de la Grèce au Moyen Age* (Paris, 1881), vol. II, no. 460, pp. 219–20; 1409.vii.18 = *ibid.*, no. 472, p. 226; 1406.iii.4 = *ibid.*, no. 364 p. 135.

[51] In 1347 ten sacks of Turkish cotton, weighing 1,712 lbs were sent from Candia to Venice: 1347.ix.18 = Zucchello, *Lettere*, no. 46, p. 92; 1347.ix.20 = *ibid.*, no. 48, p. 93; 1347.ix.22 = *ibid.*, no. 50, p. 95; 1347.ix.23 = *ibid.*, no. 51, p. 100.

[52] 1377.viii.9 = Day, *Douanes*, vol. II, p. 693. The tax owed was 18s 10d.

[53] 1343.iv.10 = ASG, Notario, Tommaso de Casanova, fos. 269v–270r in Liagre-de Sturler, *Relations commerciales*, vol. I, no. 127, pp. 155–8.

[54] Pegolotti, *Pratica*, pp. 55–7.

[55] Pegolotti, *Pratica*, p. 58.

[56] 1438.viii.8 = Badoer, *Libro*, col. 227, p. 456, col. 61, p. 123, (12 *casete* of *veli* were sent to Constantinople from Bursa); 1347.i.9 = *ibid.*, col. 125, p. 252, col. 160, p. 323, (4 *casete* of *veli crespi* were sent from Bursa at 51 *hyperpyra* per *caseta*).

[57] Piloti, *L'Egypte*, pp. 60, 62. Piloti refers to 'soye ... laine soubtile' from Antalya and Alanya.

[58] Pegolotti, *Pratica*, p. 34.

[59] 1438.iii. = Badoer, *Libro*, col. 100, p. 202, dealing with an expense incurred on 'lana da Rodosto'; 1438.iii.20 = *ibid.*, col. 197, p. 396.

[60] 1438.xii.3 = Baoder, *Libro*, col. 292, p. 586, col. 244, p. 491, col. 268, p. 238 (fourteen sacks of fine wool ('lana fina') of Edirne, weighing 40 *kantars* net, sold in Constantinople for 10 *hyperpyra* per *kantar*); 1437.i.24 = *ibid.*, col. 173, p. 348 (refers to ten sacks of wool weighing 21 *kantars* at the weight of Edirne presumably meaning that Edirne, or somewhere in that region, was its place of origin or place of sale).

[61] 1437.iii.13 = Badoer, *Libro*, col. 40, p. 80, col. 306, p. 615, refers to buying wool in Gelibolu. 1437.iii.13 = *ibid.*, col. 41, p. 82: 'per el viazo di Garipoi per un sacho di lana vergato e j. tamexo chonprò Zorzi' (total = 1 *hyperpyron* 4 *karati*); 1437.iii.13 = *ibid.*, col. 63, p. 126, (eleven sacks of wool in Gelibolu cost 1,408 *aspers*).

[62] 1437.iii.13 = Badoer, *Libro*, col. 63, p. 126, col. 55, p. 111.

Modena bought wool there described as being of the best type. This wool was later exported to Venice[63] as was part of the seventy-nine sacks of wool, fifty-one of unwashed wool and twenty-eight of washed wool, bought in Gelibolu by Agustin di Franchi in 1438.[64]

Various expenses were involved in exporting wool from Ottoman territories in the late 1430s, much of which went on carterage and freightage, porters, guides and horses for collection of the wool and boats to transport it to Constantinople, and general living expenses. Money was also paid out for sacks and expenses related to packing the wool, as well as on salaries. In 1437, 26 aspers were given to Bortolamio da Modena who, together with Zorzi Morexini, bought wool in Gelibolu for Giacomo Badoer, for part of the salary Zorzi was to have in Gelibolu. Bortolamio's own salary for the twenty-nine days he spent collecting the wool amounted, at the rate of 2 ducats per month, to 4 hyperpyra while a salary of 4 hyperpyra, 12 karati had to be paid for twenty-five days for a servant to serve in the place of Zorzi.[65] There were also expenses for weighing and customs, and also for bribing the Turkish officials. In 1438, money was listed in Badoer's accounts for a bribe to the weighing official and money changers of 40 aspers (3.8 hyperpyra). The total purchase price for the wool was 4,818 aspers and thus the bribe represented approximately 0.8 per cent of the purchase price; 105 aspers (10 hyperpyra) was also set aside to bribe the subaşı.[66] Gifts too were taken apparently as bribes, for one of the expenses incurred on the purchase of wool in Tekirdağ was 1 hyperpyron 6 karati for soap and other things which were to be given as presents, presumably as bribes, to officials.[67]

By comparing the prices and expenses given by Badoer for wool sales it is possible to obtain some idea of what percentage of the purchase price the expenses represented. In 1438 a company was formed with a capital of 5,200 Turkish aspers (around 483.7 hyperpyra) to buy wool in Tekirdağ.[68] Their total expenses on a purchase of 5,200 aspers (c.483.7 hyperpyra) came to 14.75 hyperpyra, around 3 per cent of the purchase price.[69] This figure seems very low when compared to other percentage figures from the same period. Expenses on wool bought in Edirne in 1437 and sent to Trabzon[70] were as much as 23 per cent, for on a purchase of ten sacks of wool,

[63] 1437.iii.24 = Badoer, Libro, col. 21, p. 42, col. 63, p. 127.

[64] 1438.ix.18 = Badoer, Libro, col. 247, p. 496, col. 175, p. 353; 1439.ii.26 = ibid., col. 403, p. 808.

[65] 1437.viii.17 = Badoer, Libro, col. 63, p. 126, col. 88, p. 179.

[66] 1438.x.16 = Badoer, Libro, col. 247, p. 469.

[67] 1438.iii.20 = Badoer, Libro, col. 197, p. 396.

[68] Three thousand Turkish aspers worth was bought at the rate of 11 aspers 'mancho tornexi 5' per hyperpyon and a further 2,200 at the rate of 10.75 aspers per hyperpyron.

[69] 1438.iii.20 = Badoer, Libro, col. 197, p. 396. The expenses were 8 hyperpyra for carterage and three horses at 1 hyperpyron per day, 5 hyperpyra 12 karati on the freight charge for a boat (barcha) to take the wool from Tekirdağ to Constantinople, and 1 hyperpyron 6 karati for gifts, presumably meaning bribes.

[70] 1437.ix.22 = Badoer, Libro, col. 51, p. 102, col. 116, p. 235.

weighing 23 *kantars* of Edirne and sold at 40 *aspers* (3.6 *hyperpyra*) per *kantar*, making a total purchase price of 920 *aspers* (82.8 *hyperpyra*), the expenses amounted to 211 *aspers* (20 *hyperpyra* 10 *karati*.)[71] This figure is in line with those for wool purchases in Gelibolu the following year: fifty-one sacks of unwashed wool were bought for 4,818 *aspers* with expenses amounting to 1,232 *aspers*, and twenty-eight sacks of washed wool were sold for 3,143 *aspers* with expenses of 806 *aspers*. In both cases the expenses amount to approximately 25.5 per cent of the purchase price.[72]

As well as exporting raw material and fabrics, Turchia also imported cloth both from the east and the west. Silk fabrics and brocade such as *kamkha* stuffs came in from Baghdad[73] and worked silk was imported from Alexandria.[74] Iranian merchants came to Bursa to sell their silk and other expensive commodities such as Chinese porcelain, musk and rhubarb from China and Central Asia and bought there European cloth, precious velvets and brocades, and woollens which they took back with them to Iran.[75] Linen came from Upper Egypt and fine cloth worked in Alexandria was exported to Anatolia.[76]

Turchia, and indeed the Near East as a whole, was very much a market for imported European cloth, not merely luxury fabrics but also of other materials. Florentine cloth was imported in great quantity into the Levant.[77] In Egypt the wearing of clothes made from European cloth became fashionable, as is attested by Leonardo Frescobaldi, a Tuscan pilgrim who passed through Cairo in 1384 on his way to the Holy Land. He described the costume of the women he saw there, stating that their dresses were mostly of well-worked silk, under which they wore either Rhenish cloth or high-quality Alexandrian linen.[78] Referring to roughly the same period, the Egyptian chronicler al-Maqrizi wrote that Egyptians began wearing European cloth, particularly woollens, at the beginning of the fifteenth century.[79]

Many different types of European cloth arrived in the markets of Turchia. At the beginning of the fourteenth century Gabriel de Pinu took

---

[71] 1437.ix. = Badoer, *Libro*, col. 116, p. 234, col. 57, p. 115. The exchange rate was 9 *hyperpyra* per 100 *aspers*; 73 *aspers* (8 *hyperpyra*) were listed for unspecified expenses and 138 *aspers* (12 *hyperpyra* 10 *karati*) for porterage at 6 *aspers* (0.5 of a *hyperpyron*) per *kantar*.
[72] 1438.ix.18 = Badoer, *Libro*, col. 247, p. 496, col. 175, p. 353.
[73] Ashtor, *Social and Economic History*, p. 262.
[74] Piloti, *L'Egypte*, p. 36.
[75] H. İnalcık, 'The Ottoman Economic Mind and Aspects of the Ottoman Economy', in Cook, *Economic History*, p. 211.
[76] Piloti, *L'Egypte*, p. 35.
[77] Ashtor, 'Underdevelopment', 305–6.
[78] Frescobaldi, *Visit to the Holy Places*, p. 47.
[79] *Al-Khitat*, vol. I, p. 217, cited in Ashtor, 'Underdevelopment', 298, which also cites the French translation in R. Dozy, *Dictionnaire détaillé des noms des vêtements chez les Arabes* (Amsterdam, 1845), p. 128.

cloth of Chalons from Cyprus to Alanya.[80] Silk came into Turchia from Chios where it was taxed on export from 1354.[81] Camlets were imported from Cyprus into Antalya[82] where merchants traded pistache-green, scarlet and yellow cloths and *panni gentili*, buckram, a fine material, camlets (*cambellotti*), and woollens such as *scarlattini*, a fine woollen cloth, cloths of Lombardy, Narbonne[83] and Perpignan.[84] Azure, turquoise, emerald green, pistache-green and scarlet cloths, Perpignans, cloth of Toulouse and dyed woollens of Florence, coloured in the manner of Narbonnes, cloth of Chalons and cloth of Narbonne all appeared in the market of Theologos.[85] In 1394 one bale of tafeta was loaded onto the ship of a Genoese merchant in Chios bound for Theologos.[86] In 1437 four bales containing thirty-two pieces of cloth were imported into Constantinople. Sixteen of them were destined for Grecia and sixteen for Turchia.[87]

One of the main markets was Bursa. It is difficult to gauge the exact amount of cloth imported, but Florentine cloth was certainly being brought into the city in the 1430s.[88] Cloth, however, did not always sell well there. Three Florentine cloths were, for example, sent back to Constantinople unsold in 1438,[89] as were two turquoise Florentine cloths, one green Florentine cloth and one scarlet cloth of Mantua. The reasons for this are not clear. The cloth in the latter example may have been defective or it may simply not have sold. Whatever the case, this deal must have been rather expensive for the merchant, as expenses involved in sending it to Bursa amounted to 8.45 *hyperpyra* while those for sending it back came to 67 *asper*s (6 *hyperpyra* 9 *karati*).[90] Bursa was not just a market where western merchants could sell, but also one where they could buy imported western cloth. In 1438 Christofal Bonifazio bought a piece of camlet in Bursa for 60

[80] 1305ı.viii.7 = Lamberto di Sambuceto in Michel Balard, *Notai Genovesi in Oltremare. Atti Rogati a Cipro da Lamberto di Sambuceto (31 Marzo–19 Iuglio 1305, 4 Genaio–12 Iuglio 1307), Giovanni de Rocha (3 Agosto 1308–14 Marzo 1310)*, CSFS 43 (Genoa, 1984), no. 28, pp. 48–9.

[81] Argenti, *Chios*, vol. I, pp. 427–8.

[82] Pegolotti, *Pratica*, pp. 57–8, presumably from Cyprus as they had to be sealed with the seal of Cyprus.

[83] According to Evans, the name was sometimes used rather as an indication of quality than of geographical origin: Pegolotti, *Pratica*, p. 425.

[84] Pegolotti, *Pratica*, pp. 57–8. The term *panni pirpignani* had by the fourteenth century ceased to have any geographical connection, the cloth in fact coming from Florence (*ibid.*, p. 425).

[85] Pegolotti, *Pratica*, pp. 55–8.

[86] 1394.ix.24 = ASG, Notaio Donato de Clavaro, Sc. 39, filza 1, doc. 182.

[87] 1437.ix.19 = Badoer, *Libro*, col. 108, p. 218.

[88] 1436.ix.4 = Badoer, *Libro*, col. 14, p. 28; 1437.iii.16 = *ibid.*, col. 54, p. 109; 1437.iii.16 = *ibid.*, col. 61, p. 122, col. 14, p. 29.

[89] 1438.x.14 = Badoer, *Libro*, col. 261, p. 524.

[90] 1438.ix.13 = Badoer, *Libro*, col. 240, p. 482, col. 227, p. 457; 1438.xii.29 = *ibid.*, col. 306, p. 614, col. 240, p. 483; 1438.xii.28 = *ibid.*, col. 61, p. 123.

aspers (5.7 *hyperpyra*) which was sent to Venice as a present for Giacomo Badoer's brother Jeronimo.[91]

European cloth was also imported into the markets of Edirne and Tekirdağ, Samsun and Sinop. In 1436 Andrea Rixa, a Greek who lived in Edirne, owed money for cloth.[92] In 1438, thirty-eight pieces of white damascene with gold and silk brocade were imported from Constantinople to Edirne by Jachomo de Chanpi[93] and 1.5 pieces of black cloth, valued at 3 *hyperpyra* 9 *karati*, were imported into Tekirdağ.[94] In 1436 one bale of cloth was loaded in Constantinople for Sinop.[95] Samsun seems to have been an active cloth market and much cloth was shipped there from Constantinople. Four cloths, three of which were scarlet and one green, were loaded in 1436 onto the ship of Galeoto Lomellino for Samsun.[96] The following year sixty pieces of bocasin sold there at various prices, totalling 1,184 *aspers* (62.3 *hyperpyra*); two pieces of camlet, one blue and one black, were sold for 126 *aspers* (6.6 *hyperpyra*), and taffeta for 70 *aspers* (3.7 *hyperpyra*).[97] The camlets and taffeta were bought by Antonio da Negroponte, who was taking goods to Samsun and Trabzon, for his own use. The bocasin was sold in Trabzon for 2,773 *aspers* (69.3 *hyperpyra*, 40 Trabzon *aspers* to 1 *hyperpyron*), making a difference of 7 *hyperpyra* between the sale price in Samsun and the more expensive price in Trabzon.

Cloth came into Turchia from other parts of the Aegean. Irish saye was shipped from Famagusta to Rhodes and Turchia. In 1361 Manulio Verigo de Candida received thirty-eight pieces of *saia d'Irlanda*, valued at 570 silver *bessants* of Cyprus, from Michalio Marino de Candida. These pieces he was to add to those already in his possession, making a total of seventy-six pieces. With these he was to go to Rhodes, or Milas, north-east of Bodrum, or Theologos or Balat where he was to sell the cloth. He was then to buy goods to the value of the 570 silver *bessants* at which the cloth was valued, and which he would receive from the sale, and send the goods he bought back to Michalio in Famagusta, where Michalio would sell them. Any profit over and above the initial 570 silver *bessants* was to be split between them, a quarter going to Manulio and three-quarters to Michalio. After buying commodities in Rhodes or Milas or Theologos or Balat, Manulio was to go to Antalya to buy goods, and from there sail to Cyprus, to

[91] 1438.xii.28 = Badoer, *Libro*, col. 301, p. 604, col. 227, p. 457. The exchange rate given is 10.5 *aspers* to 1 *hyperpyron*.
[92] 1436.xi.1 = Badoer, *Libro*, col. 37, p. 74.
[93] 1438.x. = Badoer, *Libro*, col. 244, p. 490.
[94] 1438.vii.9 = Badoer, *Libro*, col. 197, p. 396, col. 188, p. 379.
[95] 1436.ix.7 = Badoer, *Libro*, col. 7, p. 14, col. 13, p. 27.
[96] 1436.ii.12 = Badoer, *Libro*, col. 44, p. 88, col. 13, p. 27.
[97] 1437.xii.18 = Badoer, *Libro*, col. 152, p. 306, col. 152, p. 307. The exchange rate for Samsun *aspers* to *hyperpyron* is given as 19:1.

Paphos or Limassol or Kyrenia, where he was to spend the remaining money, presumably trading, before returning to Famagusta.[98]

As with all other commodities, the Genoese were heavily involved in the importation of cloth into Turchia. As early as the end of the thirteenth century cloth was being traded there by the Genoese from Caffa. In 1290 Babillano de Nigro received in accommodation from Conrado Pichamillio 638 Genoese pounds, 16 *soldi*, 6 *denari* invested in 155 pieces of cloth of Champagne. Babillano was to sail from Caffa with the cloth to trade it in Turchia.[99] Genoese merchants brought cloth into Balat[100] and into Theologos, which was apparently one of the principal destinations of cloth imported by Genoese merchants. In 1377 Domenico Cattaneo hired a *cocha* and loaded, among other things, 100 pieces of cloth. The *cocha* was to sail via Gaeta and Naples to Chios and Theologos.[101] In the same year bundles of saye and cloth were sent to Theologos from Genoa.[102] Several years later, in 1382, twenty pieces of cloth of Beovays were loaded in Genoa for Theologos.[103] In 1394 a bale of camlets was loaded in Chios onto the *cocha* of Bernarbono Dentuto to be taken to Theologos.[104] It appears that Bernarbono was also to load in Theologos cloth imported there by a recently deceased merchant, Veri Francisco Fori de Florai, whose will declared that he had left in Theologos, with a Genoese, Bartholomeo de Castro, one bale of cloth of eight pieces of wide English cloth which was to be loaded in Theologos on the *cocha* of Bernarbono Dentuto and taken to Rhodes. Veri confirmed that he had loaded in Chios on the *cocha* of Bernarbono Dentuto six bales containing fifty-two pieces of wide English cloth and a *fardello*, also containing the same type of cloth. They were to be shipped to Rhodes.[105]

Genoese cloth was also traded into Turchia. In 1452 cloth of Genoa of various colours formed part of negotiations over the tax farm of alum mines. Three merchants, Paris Giustiniano, Paulo Bocardo and Benedetto Salvaigo, offered 400 pieces, worth c.5,000 Chian gold *ducat*s, as part payment to Francesco de Draperiis if he was successful in renewing from the Ottoman sultan the *appalto* of alum mines in Turchia and Grecia. The

[98] 1361.xi.1 = Nicola de Boateriis, *Nicola de Boateriis, Notaio in Famagosta e Venezia (1355–1365)*, ed. Antonio Lombardo, Fonti per la Storia di Venezia, Sez. III, Archivi Notarili (Venice, 1973), no. 114, p. 116.

[99] 1290.v.23 = G. I. Bratianu, *Actes des notaires génois de Péra et de Caffa de la fin du treizième siècle (1281–1290)*, Académie Roumaine, Etudes et Recherches 2 (Bucharest, 1927), no. 330, p. 297.

[100] Piloti, *L'Egypte*, p. 72.

[101] 1377 = Musso, *Navigazione*, pp. 169–70.

[102] Day, *Douanes*, vol. II, p. 737.

[103] 1382.vi.7 = ASG, Notario, Giovanni Bardi, C. 381, fo. 4r–v.

[104] 1394.ix.24 = ASG, Notaio, Donato de Clavaro, Sc. 39, filza 1, doc. 182.

[105] 1394.xi.9 = ASG, Notaio, Donato de Clavaro, Sc. 39, filza 1, doc. 197. I presume from the date of this document that the voyage referred to is the same as that which appears in doc. 182 (1394.ix.24).

cloth could be taken by Francesco, at the risk of the receiving merchants, to Edirne.[106] The cloth may have been intended as a gift for the Sultan or as part of Francesco's payment. The three merchants undertook to settle 45,000 Turkish *akçe*s in Edirne if Francesco was successful in obtaining the alum tax farm. The fact that Edirne is specifically mentioned as the place to which Francesco could take the cloth, as well as the place of settlement, may indicate that the sultan was in Edirne at this time. On the other hand, it may be that the reason Francesco was to go to Edirne was to sell the cloth, which would indicate that Edirne was an important cloth market.

Some markets clearly were very important cloth centres. Bursa, during the fourteenth century the economic centre of the Ottoman empire upon which the trade routes of Anatolia converged, was a major cloth market. Something is known of how the Bursa silk market worked in the later fifteenth century and it seems reasonable to assume that the same system had been in operation there for some time, since Bursa had by then been in Ottoman hands for well over a century. On arrival, silk was transported to the caravanserai with the *mizan* (balance) for silk, the only place where sales were permitted. Sales were under the control of the *kethüda* (steward) and the *simsar* (broker) who appointed the *dellal* (broker, who collected the brokerage tax, the *dellaliyye*). No sale could be transacted or silk spun without the *simsar*'s permission, and he too prevented any attempt by the merchants to increase the weight of their silk by making it wet. After the sale, the *simsar* issued a document certifying full payment of tax without which the owner of the silk could not leave the caravanserai. The *kethüda* placed under seal the money from sales due to the sultan and oversaw the activities of the *simsar*. All sales had to be transacted in the presence of both officials.[107]

The market of Antalya had special requirements and the merchants there preferred to buy certain cloths in certain lengths, Lombardy in 40 piece lengths and cloth of Narbonnes and Perpignan in 200-piece lengths.[108] Cloth had to be coloured, with good bright scarlets, yellows and pistache-greens. All cloths had to be sheared once, that is with half nap. Soft cloths and *scarlattini*, a fine woollen cloth, had to be sheared in the same way once, but done well on the inside. Buckram and camlets were sold there by the piece. Woollens too were sold by piece or by cut such as *scarlattini*, which was sold by cut or by the *braccia*.[109]

In Theologos too, cloth was sold by certain measurements. Cloth of Chalons was to be sold in 20-piece lengths, while that of Narbonne had to be sold there in 18-*ancone* lengths of Theologos or 12 *canne* of Cyprus.

[106] 1452.x.28 = Argenti, *Chios*, vol. III, pp. 658–9.
[107] Halil İnalcık, 'Bursa I:xv asır sanayi ve ticaret tarihine dair vesikalar' in *Belleten* 24, 93 (1960), 58; N. Beldiceanu and Irène Beldiceanu-Steinherr, *Deux villes de l'Anatolie Préottomane: Develi et Qarahisar d'après des documents inédits* (Paris, 1973), pp. 109–11.
[108] Pegolotti, *Pratica*, p. 58.   [109] *Ibid.*

Woollens were sold there by the measurement called the *accono*. One cloth of Narbonnes was equivalent to 18 *ancone* of Theologos while one *canne* of Florence was one and five-twelfths of an *ancone*.[110]

Although the Turkish merchants who bought cloth from the westerners in Turchia are usually anonymous in western sources, they do occasionally appear by name. In 1436 a Turk called Ahmed from Lichomidia (?Nicomedia, İzmit) bartered 63 *kantar*s 50 *rotoli* of dried grapes of Lichomidia, valued at 2 *hyperpyra* per *kantar* for two cloths, one green and one turquoise, valued at 52.5 *hyperpyra* per piece.[111] In the same year Jael, factor of Muxalach (?Mu'ala') bought twelve cloths, eight scarlet, two turquoise and two green, at a cost of 815 *hyperpyra* 21 *karati*.[112]

It seems that trading cloth was a profitable business.[113] In 1436 four cloths were valued in Constantinople at 47.5 *hyperpyra* per piece (*peza*). The same cloth sold in Samsun for 21 Turkish *ducat*s per piece, or 756 *aspers*.[114] Calculating at 11 Turkish *aspers* per *hyperpyron*, the cloth cost in Samsun was c.67 *hyperpyra* per piece, or around 19.5 *hyperpyra* per piece more than in Constantinople, an increase of approximately 40 per cent. While it is true that this increase must have covered transport costs, insurance, customs and other charges, it still seems a considerable mark-up and indicates how rewarding trading cloth into Turchia must have been for western merchants. Expenses could have been in the region of 7 per cent of the sale price, for in 1438 white damascene with gold brocade was taken by Jachomo da Chanpi to Edirne. Expenses on taking the cloth there amounted to 10 *hyperpyra* (*c.*105 *aspers*) with an additional expense in Edirne of 219 *aspers* (*c.*21 *hyperpyra*). The cloth sold for 4,680 *aspers* (*c.*446 *hyperpyra*), thus making the expenses *c.*7 per cent of the sale price.[115]

Of the taxes that affected cloth, one of the most important for import–export was customs. What customs were specifically charged on cloth, either imported or exported, in the period before 1453 is not known for certain. It may have been a commodity which was not charged at any

[110] Pegolotti, *Pratica*, p. 55.
[111] 1436.i.14 = Badoer, *Libro*, col. 42, p. 84, col. 13, p. 27, col. 43, p. 86, col. 42, p. 85. But there is a difference in the figures given. The two entries giving the amount of cloth have a total of 105 *hyperpyra*, the two dealing with the quantities of grapes have 127 *hyperpyra*.
[112] 1436.x.7 = Badoer, *Libro*, col. 13, p. 27.
[113] See appendix 4 below.
[114] 1436.ii.12 = Badoer, *Libro*, col. 44, p. 88, col. 13, p. 27 (in Constantinople); 1437.xii.18 = *ibid.*, col. 44, p. 89 (in Samsun). The exchange rate was given as 36 *aspers* per Turkish *ducat*.
[115] 1438.x. = Badoer, *Libro*, col. 244, p. 490, 1439.iii.5, 1439.iii.12 = *ibid.*, col. 244, p. 491. The listed expense of 10 *hyperpyra* was for ' la mia provixion, per provixion de achatar e vender e mandar in Andr[enopoli] e scuoder la moneda, e spexa fata in pano, inzerado e canevazo e taole e per far ligar el damascin brochà'. The damascine sold in Edirne for 4,680 *aspers*, at the rate of 120 *aspers* per *picho* from which 219 *aspers* on expenses were deducted, leaving a total of 4,461 *aspers*. The expenses were made up of a *comerchium* of 2 per cent making 93 *aspers*, brokerage at 0.5 per cent making 23 *aspers*, 10 *aspers* for storage and 93 *aspers* for provisions. The rate of exchange for the *aspers* was 10.5 *aspers* two *tornexi* per *hyperpyron* for 3,000 *aspers* and 10.5 *aspers* 4 *tornexi* per *hyperpyron* for 1,461 *aspers*.

specific rate but was included in commodities in general, for it appears in the treaties between Aydın and Venice and in those between Menteşe and Venice as merely one of various listed commodities upon which a flat rate customs charge was levied. On the other hand, it is perhaps a little surprising that, being an item of such importance in trade between Turchia and the various western states, it did not attract a special customs charge, such as that applied to grain, livestock or slaves. The absence of any such rate can perhaps be explained by the haphazard nature of the sources that have survived from the earlier period, although this argument is of course rather open to question. If one however looks at Ottoman sources for the second half of the fifteenth century, one sees that in this period at least cloth, both imported and exported, did attract a specific customs rate. For the period c.1453 to 1482 Latins paid on imported cloth either 4 per cent,[116] 5 per cent[117] or, in the case of the Genoese and Venetians in Bursa, 3 per cent.[118] If cloth was charged a special customs rate in the Ottoman empire before 1453 the most likely rate, judging from the these figures, was probably therefore something between 3 per cent and 5 per cent for Latin merchants.

Other taxes charged on cloth included brokerage. *Senseraggio* was paid in Constantinople and Pera on camlets where they were charged at a rate of 4 *karati* per 100 *hyperpyra*, the same rate applying to silks and cloth of gold.[119] In the later fifteenth century, brokerage tax (*dellalık*) was farmed out, as it was for example in 1476 on cloth (*kumaş*) and broadcloth (*çuka*) in Istanbul and Galata.[120] *Bac*, the tax taken at the *mizan*, was charged under Mehmed II on cloth at the rate of 2 *akçe* per *yük*,[121] a measure used for silk, among other commodities, and described by Professor İnalcık as 'one of the most varied and imprecise measures in the Ottoman empire'.[122]

---

[116] Post 1453.v.29 = Anhegger and İnalcık, *Kanunname*, no. 36, pp. 49–50; Beldiceanu, *Actes*, vol. I, no. 37, clause 2, pp. 116–18; 1476.i.28/ii.6 = Anhegger and İnalcık, *Kanunname*, no.53, p. 74; Beldiceanu, *Actes*, vol. I, no. 54, clause 5, p. 147; 1481.viii.26/ix.24 = Anhegger and İnalcık, *Kanunname*, no. 55, p. 79; Beldiceanu, *Actes*, vol. I, no. 56, clauses 1, 2, 3, p. 151; 1482.i.20 = Anhegger and İnalcık, *Kanunname*, no. 56, p. 80; Beldiceanu, *Actes*, vol. I, no. 57, clauses 3, 4, pp. 152–3.

[117] Post-1476.1.28 = Anhegger and İnalcık, *Kanunname*, no. 35, pp. 47–8; Beldiceanu, *Actes*, vol. I, no. 36, clause 4, p. 114.

[118] 1454–63 or 1479–81 = Anhegger and İnalcık, *Kanunname*, no. 30, pp. 40–1; Beldiceanu, *Actes*, vol. I, no. 30, clauses 2, 3, pp. 104–5. Imported cloth (*kumaş*) was charged in Bursa at the rate of 3 per cent on Muslims, tributaries and infidel merchants from Venice, Genoa, Chios and other places, indigenous infidels being exempt. On export cloth, 3 per cent was levied in Bursa from Muslims, tributaries, indigenous infidels and infidel merchants from Venice, Genoa, Chios and other places: 1454–63 or 1479–81 = Anhegger and İnalcık, *Kanunname*, no. 30, pp. 40–1; Beldiceanu, *Actes*, vol. I, no. 30, clauses 2, 3, pp. 104–5.

[119] Pegolotti, *Pratica*, p. 45.

[120] 1476.i.28/ii.6 = Anhegger and İnalcık, *Kanunname*, no. 53, pp. 73–4; Beldiceanu, *Actes*, vol. I, no. 54, clause 1, p. 146.

[121] İnalcık, 'Ticaret tarihine dair vesikalar', 57.

[122] Halil İnalcık, '*Yük (Himl)* in the Ottoman Silk trade, Mining and Agriculture' in İnalcık, *The Middle East and the Balkans*, p. 432.

Tax collection on cloth was probably handled in the fourteenth and first half of the fifteenth centuries by tax farmers. Linen was apparently usually under tax farmers in Aydın, but was exempted for the Venetians under their treaty with Hızır in 1337.[123] The situation was the same in Menteşe, where too the Venetians were exempt.[124] According to Professor Zachariadou, there was an attempt to impose a monopoly on imported textiles, but this was unsuccessful. To support this, she refers to the treaties of 1337 between Venice and Aydın and Venice and Menteşe. This, however, relies on interpreting *appalto/gabella* as monopoly which it does not seem to have meant.[125]

Tax collection on cloth after 1453 was handled by tax farmers. In 892/ 1486–7, for example, the collection of tax, which would have included the *bac* collected on cloth, at the *mizan* of Bursa was farmed out.[126] In 883/ 1478–9 the tax farm on the measuring of cloth in Bursa was sold for 58,800 *akçe* or 1,200 gold *florins*.[127]

In this lucrative trade there was always a temptation for some merchants to attempt to defraud the tax officials. One of the ways in which fraud was attempted over cloth sales in the later part of the fifteenth century was an arrangement between a Muslim and an infidel whereby they agreed to declare the infidel's cloth (*kumaşlar*) as belonging to the Muslim, thereby avoiding the customs payable by a non-Muslim. Such fraud, punishable by the *yasak kulu*,[128] was presumably not new but practised earlier in the century.

On an individual level, disputes between Genoese merchants and Turks went to arbitration. In 1414 a Genoese citizen, Raffaele Centurionis, and Giovanni Paterio, a citizen of Chios, agent for Alemano Sofiano of Old Phokaea and acting also for 'Catip Bassa Turchus de Bergamo' (Katib Paşa from Bergama, in western Anatolia near the coast opposite Mitylini), went to arbitration in Chios over the sale made that year in which Raffaele had bought cotton from Alemano and Katib Paşa.[129]

Unfortunately this document gives no details, as it is merely a preparatory agreement to go to arbitration rather than being part of the case itself. It does, however, show that disputes between Genoese and Turkish traders did go to arbitration under Genoese jurisdiction. It would be interesting to

---

[123] 1337.iii.9 = Zachariadou, *Trade and Crusade*, doc. 1337A, clause 11, p. 192.

[124] 1337.pre-iv. = Zachariadou, *Trade and Crusade*, doc. 1337M, clause 22, p. 198; 1375.iv.22 = *ibid.*, doc. 1375M, clause 22, p. 222; 1403.vii.24 = *ibid.*, doc. 1403M, 1403M DVL, clause 22, p. 231; 1407.vi.2 = *ibid.*, doc. 1407M, clause 22, p. 236.

[125] Zachariadou, *Trade and Crusade*, p. 170.

[126] İnalcık, 'Ticaret tarihine dair vesikalar', 57.

[127] İnalcık, 'Ticaret tarihine dair vesikalar', 60. The exchange rate was 1 *florin* to 49 *akçe*.

[128] 1482.i.20 = Anhegger and İnalcık, *Kanunname*, no. 56, p. 80; Beldiceanu, *Actes*, vol. I, no. 57, clause 6, p. 153.

[129] 1414.iv.2 = ASG, Notaio, Giovanni Balbi, Sc. 46, filza 1, doc. 286. See appendix 5, doc. 11 below.

know if this was always the case or if on occasion such disputes were settled under Turkish jurisdiction in this period. Here perhaps the sale took place in Chios and the case was therefore to be heard there. It does seem that there were controls over where the case could be heard. In 1413 Hacı Satıoğlu, ambassador of Cüneyd, the ruler of Aydın at that time, appeared before the *podestà* of Chios to protest over a court case involving one of Cüneyd's subjects, Hacı Sarti, who was claiming against the *fedeicommissors* of the late Sorleone Salvaigo. As Hacı Sarti had been unable to attend the court, for unspecified reasons, the case had been postponed for one year. Hacı Sarti was, however, still unable to appear in court and had heard that the Genoese authorities now wished to have the case tried in Genoa. Cüneyd's ambassador protested to the *podestà* that this was unjust ('iniuriose et cavilose').[130] It is not clear whether the phrase means actually unlawful, or if it simply means that insisting on trying the case in Genoa would be unjust, presumably as Hacı Sarti would be unable to attend and would therefore receive no legal redress. That Turks did have legal rights against Genoese citizens in Genoese courts is clear from the case in Pera against Ottobono Giustiniano and Ettore de Flisco. Turks with any complaints against the former authorities in Pera were requested to come forward.[131]

If there were disputes over sales in Turchia, it would be interesting to know before whom they were settled. Disputes between Genoese and other European merchants were, judging from a document enacted in Turchia in 1383, settled before Genoese officials. Rodol Dalan Theotonito,[132] servant of Hernes, brought a case before the court of the *capitaneus* and *consilium* against a Genoese citizen, Quilico Gentile, accusing Quilico of having, out of 'boldness and arrogance', struck him on the hands with a shoe, and then in the eye with his fist, drawing blood, and then on the head three or four times. When questioned, Quilico replied that in fact Rodol had hit him on the ear with the back of his hand and that he, Quilico, had not touched Rodol with his shoes. Quilico was ordered by the *capitaneus* and *consilium* to put up 200 gold *florins* as bail and Luca Gentile interceded for him.[133]

Presumably it would have been very much in the interests of the Genoese to have any disputes involving their nationals tried before their own courts. Whether they were, or were not, able to ensure this must have depended on the strength of the Turks with whom they were dealing. Thus, perhaps, disputes in the earlier part of the fourteenth century in the beyliks would have gone before Genoese officials. On the other hand, it seems highly unlikely that, under the early Ottomans, Genoa would have been able to

---

[130] 1413.viii.28 = ASG, Notaio, Giovanni Balbi, Sc. 46, filza 1, doc. 255. See appendix 5, doc. 9 below.
[131] 1402.x.30 = ASG, San Giorgio, Sala 34 590/1306, fos. 16r–17r.
[132] The name Theotonito may mean that he was Teutonic, this being a Greek rendering.
[133] 1383.vii.20 = ASG, Notario, Giovanni Bardi, C. 381, fo. 146v.

enforce such a control. This obviously concerns only individual complaints between merchants and not disputes with state officials.

Cloth was a commodity of considerable importance in the trade of Turchia in the fourteenth and first half of the fifteenth centuries. In general, raw materials, such as cotton and wool, were exported westward and finished products, the various European cloths, imported. It was not, however, totally an exchange of raw materials and finished products, for Turchia also produced its own luxury cloths and exported silks. As a major item of trade, cloth must have generated a great deal of income both for individual merchants and for the state through the collection of customs.

CHAPTER 9

Metals

Any study of the metal trade into Anatolia is severely hampered by lack of data. This is due not only to the haphazard survival of documents, something which affects all research into all aspects of this area and period, but also to the banning by governments and church of Christian trading of metals with the infidel. The arms trade is particularly difficult to trace. Weapons clearly did arrive in Anatolia. Aşıkpaşazade refers to there being no firearms in the reign of Bayezid, but plenty in the time of the sultans Murad II and Mehmed II.[1] The Genoese were known to be importing large quantities of arms into the Levant,[2] though this does not mean that they were necessarily trading them with the Turks.[3] So far no reference to arms trading with the Turks has been found in the Genoese sources for this period. An added complication when tracing the movement of metals is the fact that the origin of the metals traded is often not given.

Nevertheless, there clearly was a metal trade between western merchants and Muslim powers for the constant repetition of papal bans against the export to the infidel of forbidden commodities, that is foodstuffs and war materials including metals, is an indicator of a persistent trade, conducted in defiance of papal prohibition[4] and, one must assume, therefore profitable.

Iron, a major import from the west, and goods made from iron were one of the most important commodities traded by the Genoese.[5] Western merchants seem to have been largely unconcerned by religious scruple over this commerce. Pope Gregory XI was obliged, in 1373, to direct a threat of

---

[1] Aşıkpaşazade, *Altosmanische Chronik*, p. 60, Aşıkpaşazade, *Tevarih-i al-i 'Osman*, p. 66, ll. 3–4.

[2] Balard, *Romanie génoise*, vol. II, pp. 782–3, 840–1.

[3] For the trading of guns into the Ottoman empire in the fifteenth century see Gàbor Àgoston, 'Ottoman artillery and European military technology in the fifteenth and seventeenth centuries', *Acta Academiae Scientiarum Hungaricae* 47 (1994), 15–48. See also Colin Heywood, 'Notes on the production of fifteenth century Ottoman cannon', in *Proceedings of the International Symposium on Islam and Science (Islamabad)* (Islamabad, 1981).

[4] Governments too forbade such exports. The Venetians banned the export of iron and plough shears: 1389.vi.22 = Chrysostomides, *Monumenta Peloponnesiaca*, no. 51, p. 112.

[5] Balard, *Romanie génoise*, vol. II, pp. 782–3, 840–1.

excommunication against those Christians who were trading iron to the Turks.[6] Papal permission, granted in 1363, to the Hospitallers to import foodstuffs from the Turks, contained the proviso that the Hospitallers should not, in return, trade war materials, including iron.[7] It is unlikely that the Hospitallers supplied their enemies with weapons, this clause being probably a stock phrase used by the popes when granting such permission. However, this does show how much of a threat the trade in war materials, largely metals, was considered to be by the church.

Regardless of papal sentiment, iron was sold throughout the Levant, in Lesser Armenia,[8] Crete,[9] Constantinople, Pera[10] and Caffa,[11] and in Turchia, in Antalya[12] and Bursa.[13] Iron wire (*fil de fero*) fetched 1 *hyperpyron* per bundle (*mazo*) in Bursa in the late 1430s,[14] the price being comparable with that of iron wire on its way to Caffa in the same period.[15] In Caffa itself the price was slightly higher at around 1.2 *hyperpyra* per *mazo*.[16]

Iron was not the only metal brought into the eastern Mediterranean, for lead too came in from the west, traded from Ragusa to Alexandria, to the Levant and into Syria[17] and sold in the markets of Alexandria,[18] Crete, Pera and Constantinople,[19] from where it was taken to Crete.[20] It sold too in

---

[6] 1373.v.15 : G. Mollat, *Lettres secrètes et curiales du Pape Grégoire XI (1370–1378)*, Bibliothèque des Ecoles Françaises d'Athénes et de Rome, 3 fascicles (Paris, 1962–5), fasc. I, no. 1798, p. 252.

[7] 1363.vii.17 = Michel Hayez, *Urbain V (1362–1370), lettres communes*, Bibliothèque des Ecoles Françaises d'Athénes et de Rome (Paris, 1964–72), vol. II, fasc.I–IV, no. 6420, p. 207.

[8] Pegolotti, *Pratica*, p. 59.   [9] Pegolotti, *Pratica*, p. 105.

[10] Pegolotti, *Pratica*, p. 33. *Fil de fero* was sold in Constantinople: 1436.vi.26 = Badoer, *Libro*, col. 29, p. 58, col. 68, p. 137; 1437.vi.23 = *ibid.*, col. 68, p. 136, col. 137, p. 277.

[11] 1437.vii.1 = Badoer, *Libro*, col. 79, p. 160, col. 68, p. 137; 1437.ix.19 = *ibid.*, col. 79, p. 160, col. 68, p. 137; 1437.xii.5 = *ibid.*, col. 154, p. 310, col. 79, p. 161; 1438.iv.29 = *ibid.*, col. 196, p. 394, col. 189, p. 381; 1439.i.15 = *ibid.*, col. 367, p. 737, seems to be coming back from Caffa: 'per fil de fero che me fo tornà de Caffa'; 1439.iii.5 = *ibid.*, col. 325, p. 652, also seems to be returning from Caffa: 'fil de fero barilli 3 dixe eser mazi 416 ... mandadome de Chafa'. This presumably means that it was not sold, since there is an entry on the same day for expenses for the *barili* 'andar e retornar'.

[12] Pegolotti, *Pratica*, p. 58: sold by 'peso del calbano, cioè la stadera'.

[13] 1439.vii.8 = Badoer, *Libro*, col. 325, p. 652; 1439.ii.15 = *ibid.*, col. 348, p. 698, col. 325, p. 653.

[14] 1439.iii.7 = Badoer, *Libro*, col. 329, p. 660, col. 325, p. 653.

[15] 1437.vii.1 = Badoer, *Libro*, col. 79, p. 160.

[16] 1437.xii.5 = Badoer, *Libro*, col. 79, p. 161.

[17] 1359.viii.30 : Kerkić, *Dubrovnik*, doc.241, p. 203; 1410.vi.25 : *ibid.*, doc. 585, pp. 259–60 refers to 1,230 pieces of lead at a weight of 143,465 Ragusan pounds; 1389.vi.23 : *ibid.*, doc. 392, p. 228, refers to 231 pieces of lead weighing 23,500 pounds 'ad pondus grossum Venetiarum', and to 714 pieces of lead weighing 100,945 pounds at the weight of Ragusa; 1377.xi.29 : *ibid.*, doc. 330, p. 218.

[18] Pegolotti, *Pratica*, p. 70; 1347.viii.11 = Zucchello, *Lettere*, doc. 44, p. 87.

[19] Pegolotti, *Pratica*, pp. 105, 33. Lead of 'every region' was sold in Pera and Constantinople. 1437.viii.27 = Badoer, *Libro*, col. 95, p. 192, col. 50, p. 101; 1438.iii.21 = *ibid.*, col. 83, p. 168, col. 62, p. 125.

[20] 1438.iii.21 = Badoer, *Libro*, col. 198, p. 398, col. 62, p. 125.

Turchia and the Genoese traded it in Balat around the end of the fourteenth and beginning of the fifteenth centuries.[21]

Other metals were also shipped into the Levant. The Venetians traded tin into Alexandria and Syria[22] and, like iron and lead, it too appeared in the markets of the eastern Mediterranean, in Alexandria,[23] Beirut,[24] Damascus,[25] Crete, Lesser Armenia and Constantinople and Pera, where tin 'of every region' was sold.[26] The Genoese imported it into Balat[27] and it was also sold in Antalya.[28] Copper was brought into the Levant from Ragusa[29] and into Egypt from Venice, and sold in Alexandria.[30] Frescobaldi travelled from Venice to Alexandria on a ship whose cargo, loaded in Venice, included copper.[31]

It has been assumed that the trade in metals from the west into Turchia was of greater significance or volume than the sources appear to show, due to its illegality and consequent concealment combined with the haphazard survival of data. However, the comparatively scanty evidence on the trading of metals may suggest that there was not in fact a large commerce in these commodities. If its illegality had been a factor of such importance, metals would presumably not have appeared at all in lists of commodities exported eastwards. Further, Turchia does not appear always to have been a sure market for metals, for on occasion imported metals remained unsold there,[32] indicating that Turchia was not suffering from a dearth of metals, such as would have attracted a large flow of imports.

The most striking indication that the trade in imported metals was not perhaps as great as has sometimes been assumed was the fact that the Levant was in a position to export. One of the main commodities that the

---

[21] Piloti, *L'Egypte*, p. 72.

[22] 1400.viii.30 : Heers, 'Commercio', 167, 168.

[23] Heers, 'Commercio', 205; 1347.viii.11 = Zucchello, *Lettere*, doc. 44, p. 87.

[24] Heers, 'Commercio', 205.   [25] *Ibid.*

[26] Pegolotti, *Pratica*, pp. 70, 105, 59, 33; 1436.ix.6 = Badoer, *Libro*, col. 8, p. 16, col. 17, p. 35, col. 4, p. 9 (this presumably was imported into Constantinople because the costs cited included unloading); 1436.xi.4 = *ibid.*, col. 9, p. 18, col. 17, p. 35, col. 4, p. 9; 1436.ii.5 = *ibid.*, col. 50, p. 100, col. 50, p. 101; 1436.ii.22 = *ibid.*, col. 50, p. 100. col. 170, p. 343; 1436.iii.22 = *ibid.*, col. 49, p. 98, col. 50, p. 101; 1437.ix.19 = *ibid.*, col. 107, p. 216, col. 174, p. 351, col. 161, p. 325; 1437.x.17 = *ibid.*, col. 89, p. 180, col. 107, p. 217; 1437.x.17 = *ibid.*, col. 127, p. 256, col. 107, p. 217; 1437.xi.7 = *ibid.*, col. 128, p. 258, col. 107, p. 217; 1437.xii.5 = *ibid.*, col. 107, p. 216, col. 163, p. 329; 1437.xii.28 = *ibid.*, col. 168, p. 398, col. 107, p. 217; 1437.ii.4 = *ibid.*, col. 173, p. 348, col. 107, p. 217; 1437.ii.8 = *ibid.*, col. 175, p. 352, col. 107, p. 217; 1437.ii.10 = *ibid.*, col. 139, p. 280, col. 107, p. 217; 1438.iii.4 = *ibid.*, col. 107, p. 216, col. 28, p. 57.

[27] Piloti, *L'Egypte*, p. 72.   [28] Pegolotti, *Pratica*, p. 58.

[29] 1389.vi.23 : Krekić, *Dubrovnik*, doc. 392, p. 228 refers to 4,864 pieces of fine copper weighing 60,000 pounds 'ad pondus grossum Venetiarum' and 140 pieces of copper weighing 1,541 pounds.

[30] 1347.viii.11 = Zucchello, *Lettere*, doc. 44, p. 87.

[31] Frescobaldi, *Visit to the Holy Places*, p. 35.

[32] Three *barili* of *fil de fero* returning from Caffa, 1439.iii.5 = Badoer, *Libro*, col. 325, p. 652. 38 *mazi* of *fil de fero* imported into Bursa were left with Piero Palavexin, apparently unsold, 1439.ii.15 = *ibid.*, col. 348, p. 698, col. 325, p. 653., col. 388, p. 788, col. 348, p. 699.

Venetian galleys carried home from Romania was its metals.[33] Anatolia was after all a metal-producing and exporting country in its own right. It had metal resources, copper, iron and silver in particular.[34] There were silver mines at Bayburt, south-east of Trabzon, Gümüşhane (Argiron, south of Trabzon) and at Amasya.[35] Iron was produced around İzmir in Byzantine times.[36]

Copper was mined in north-east Anatolia in the region of Kastamonu, Sinop, Samsun and Osmancık and was of high quality, for Chalcocondyles described it as second only to that of Iberia.[37] These copper resources were a bone of contention between local rulers and the expanding Ottoman state. The copper mines around Kastamonu were initially, in the fourteenth century, in the hands of the local rulers, the İsfendiyaroğulları, control passing to the Ottomans at the end of the century when, in 1391, Bayezid I killed Süleyman Paşa, the İsfendiyaroğulları ruler of Kastamonu, and took over his territory.[38] Osmancık fell to Bayezid in the same period,[39] although he apparently failed to conquer Sinop.[40] He may however have exerted some control over the area for the ruler in Sinop, the son of Kötürüm Bayezid, former İsfendiyaroğulları ruler, was in some way subordinate to him.[41] That Bayezid exercised influence over Sinop is supported by Chalcocondyles who refers to Bayezid taking over the revenue of the copper mines there.[42]

[33] Heers, 'Commercio', 170. Both lead and copper were taken from Grecia back to Venice: *ibid.*, 169.

[34] For a discussion of mines in Anatolia and the Balkans see S. Vryonis, 'The question of Byzantine mines', *Speculum* 37 (1962), 1–17.

[35] Abu'l Fida, *Géographie d'Aboulféda*, ed. M. Rainaud and M. Le Bon Mac Guckin de Slane (Paris, 1840), p. 383; Aflaki, *Les saints des derviches tourneurs (Manaqib ul-'arifin)*, trans. Clément Huart (Paris, 1918) vols. I–II: vol. II, p. 380; ibn Battuta, *Voyages*, p. 293; al-'Umarī, 'Voyages', pp. 20, 31.

[36] Hélène Ahrweiler, 'L'histoire et la géographie de la région de Smyrne entre les deux occupations turques (1081–1317) particulièrement au XIIIe siècle', *Travaux et Mémoires* 1, Centre de Recherche d'Histoire et Civilisation Byzantines (Paris, 1965), 18.

[37] Chalcocondyles, *Historiarum Libri Decem*, ed. I. Bekker (Bonn, 1843), p. 498, l. 6.

[38] Imber, *Ottoman Empire*, p. 38 dates Süleyman's death to pre-July 1391. Neşri, dates Bayezid's conquest of Kastamonu to 795/1393: Neşri, *Menzel, Cod.* p. 77; Neşri, *Kitab-ı Cihan-nüma*, vol. I, p. 320. Aşıkpaşazade, dates it to between 797 and 798: Aşıkpaşazade, *Altosmanische Chronik*, p. 65, Aşıkpaşazade, *Tevarih-i al-i 'Osman*, p. 72. Süleyman was trading copper with Genoese merchants: 1390.i.11 = ASG, Notario, Donato de Clavaro, C. 476, doc. 26. A summary of this document is given in Balard, Laiou and Otten-Froux, *Documents*, no. 82, p. 37.

[39] Imber, *Ottoman Empire*, p. 39; Neşri, *Menzel, Cod.* p. 58; Neşri, *Kitab-ı Cihan-nüma*, p. 322.

[40] Imber, *Ottoman Empire*, p. 40.

[41] Aşıkpaşazade, *Altosmanische Chronik*, p. 65; Aşıkpaşazade, *Tevarih-i al-i 'Osman*, p. 72; Neşri, *Menzel, Cod.* p. 58; Neşri, *Kitab-ı Cihan-nüma,,* p. 322.

[42] Chalcocondyles, *Historiarum Libri Decem*, p. 185, l. 5, Chalcocondyles, *Historiarum Demonstrationes*, ed. E. Darkó (Budapest, 1922–7), vol. I, pp. 173–4. Chalcocondyles *Historiarum Libri Decem*, p. 489, l. 6, and *Historiarum Demonstrationes*, vol. II, p. 242 says that when Mehmed II conquered Sinop in the middle fifteenth century, the annual tax income from the mines was 50,000 gold pieces.

Towards the end of his reign, Bayezid also annexed Samsun[43] while Amasya was seized from Burhan al-Din in 1398.[44]

After the Ottoman collapse of 1402 Kastamonu and Samsun reverted to İsfendiyaroğulları control while Amasya remained in Ottoman hands.[45] Mehmed I campaigned against the İsfendiyaroğulları and took Samsun.[46] The İsfendiyaroğulları ruler became subordinate to Mehmed, retaining land round Sinop but surrendering the copper revenues of Kastamonu to the Ottoman ruler.[47] In the period of civil strife in 1421–2, the İsfendiyar ruler, Mübarizeddin, occupied Ottoman territory and, apparently, retook the copper-producing lands of Kastamonu.[48] This victory was in any case short-lived for in 1423[49] Murad II took Kastamonu and set the copper furnaces to work. The İsfendiyaroğulları ruler was once more reduced to vassal status in the area of Sinop.[50]

Mehmed II continued to control the copper mines of the area, taking Sinop in 1461.[51] The most important of the products of the Sinop region was, according to Kritovoulos, copper.[52] During his reign the area of Kastamonu was a producer of 'infinite' amounts of copper, extracted from quarries and mines there.[53] Its importance as a source of copper in this period is indicated by its being sold in *appalto* to two people, one of whom controlled the export via the sea and the other that via the land route. A good reserve of copper was always kept in the treasury.[54]

---

[43] Imber, *Ottoman Empire*, p. 41 dates this to, probably, 1398. His conquest of Samsun appears in Neşri, at the same time as the conquest of Kastamonu and Osmancık in 795/1392–3: Neşri *Menzel, Cod.* p. 58; Neşri, *Kitab-ı Cihan-nüma*, p. 322.

[44] Imber, *Ottoman Empire*, p. 40. Neşri, *Cod. Menzel*, p. 77, dates the conquest of Amasya to 794/1391–2.

[45] Imber, *Ottoman Empire*, p. 63.

[46] Aşıkpaşazade, *Altosmanische Chronik*, pp. 79–80; Aşıkpaşazade, *Tevarih-i al-i 'Osman*, pp. 89–90; Neşri, *Menzel, Cod.* p. 145; Neşri, *Kitab-ı Cihan-nüma*, pp. 540–2.

[47] Colin Imber dates Mehmed I's campaign to, probably, the second half of 1417: *Ottoman Empire*, p. 88 and n. 23.

[48] Imber *Ottoman Empire*, pp. 95–6.

[49] Imber, *Ottoman Empire*, p. 95 gives this date, although Vryonis, 'Byzantine mines', 10 dates the Ottoman conquest of Kastamonu to 1425.

[50] Aşıkpaşazade, *Altosmanische Chronik*, pp. 92–3; Aşıkpaşazade, *Tevarih-i al-i 'Osman*, pp. 104–5; Neşri, *Menzel, Cod.* pp. 153–4; Neşri, *Kitab-ı Cihan-nüma*, pp. 574–6.

[51] Aşıkpaşazade, *Altosmanische Chronik*, pp. 147–9; Aşıkpaşazade, *Tevarih-i al-i 'Osman*, pp. 154–5; Neşri, *Menzel, Cod.* pp. 190–2; Neşri, *Kitab-ı Cihan-nüma*, pp. 740–6. Aşıkpaşazade specifies that the income from the copper furnaces allocated to the Ottoman ruler was to be used if required.

[52] Kritovoulos, *De Rebus per Annos 1451–1467 a Mechemet II Gestis*, ed. V. Grecu (Bucharest, 1963), p. 275; Kritovoulos, *History of Mehmed the Conqueror. By Kritovoulos*, trans. C. T. Riggs (Westport, Conn., 1954), p. 166.

[53] Franz Babinger, *Die Aufzeichnungen des Genuesen Iacopo de Promontorio-de Campis über den Osmanenstaat um 1475*, Bayerische Akademie der Wissenschaften, philosophisch–historische Klasse Sitzungsberichte, Jahrgang 1956–8 (Munich, 1957), p. 67.

[54] *Ibid.*: 'de quali rami ne tiene sempre una ampla torre piena loco thesauri'. Copper from this area was used to mint money.

Apart from the mines in north-east Anatolia, the Ottomans also came to control the metal resources of the Balkans. After the battle of Kosovo in 1389 for example, the mines of that region fell into Ottoman hands.[55]

The Turks therefore had at their disposal their own metal resources. These resources, particularly copper, were exported from Turchia westwards, a trade in which, according to Professor Balard, the Genoese played a dominant role.[56] Lead was exported westwards and appears on ships of western merchants as an export commodity.[57] In the inventory of the goods of Bartolomeo Vignoso, for example, items being sent west included 50 *kantars* of lead.[58] Thessaloniki, under the Ottomans, exported lead which went via Crete to Alexandria[59] as did lead exported from Constantinople.[60]

Anatolia was a producer and exporter of copper which the Italian merchants bought in large quantities.[61] In 1403 Petro Falacha planned to sail from Caffa to Turchia to load copper and other goods.[62] Merchants also went from Pera to Sinop for copper.[63] Turkish copper may have been exported to Barcelona. In 1381 a ship mastered by Martino Umcentii and Alnardo Belegerio, both of Barcelona, was to sail from Chios to Theologos and from there to Alexandria or Beirut before going to Barcelona. It could load, among other things, copper in these places. The document does not specify which of the ports copper was to be loaded in but it could well have been Theologos.[64] Copper was sold in Antalya and although Pegolotti does not specify where the copper came from, it may, in the light of the evidence of Turkish copper production, have been produced in Turchia.[65]

Turks themselves traded in copper with the Genoese, the İsfendiyaroğulları, for example, selling Kastamonu copper to Genoese merchants. In 1390, Constantino de Groto, *burgensis* of Pera, brought a case for damages before the Genoese *podestà* in Pera, against Dagnano Spinulla and Petro de Groto, *burgenses* of Pera, *fideicommissors* of Raffaele Capello, also a *burgensis* of Pera. Constantino claimed that he and Raffaele Capello had made a *società* concerning 16,000 pounds of copper at the weight of Solimambasa

---

[55] Aşıkpaşazade, *Altosmanische Chronik*, p. 58; Aşıkpaşazade, *Tevarih-i al-i 'Osman*, p. 64.

[56] Balard, *Romanie génoise*, vol. II, p. 783.

[57] 1396.v.31 : Heers, 'Commercio', 173; 191 pieces of lead are listed on a ship arriving in Genoa from Romania.

[58] Balard, *Romanie génoise*, vol. II, p. 783.

[59] Piloti, *L'Egypte*, p. 63.

[60] 1437.ix.4 = Badoer, *Libro*, col. 62, p. 124, col. 95, p. 193. Lead was traded in Constantinople, 1437.viii.27 = *ibid.*, col. 50, p. 101, col. 95, p. 192.

[61] Ashtor, 'Pagamento', p. 370 and n. 3.

[62] 1403.xi.28 = ASG, San Giorgio, Sala 34 590/1307, fos. 40r–41r.

[63] Balard, *Romanie génoise*, vol. II, p. 784, n. 69 (1402).

[64] 1381.ii.15 = ASG, Notario, Antonius Feloni, C. 175, fos. 110v–111r; Balard, *Romanie génoise*, vol. II, p. 784 n. 72, in reference to this document, talks of Catalan merchants going to Chios to get copper for Alexandria. The document however makes it clear that the merchants, sailing from Chios, were to load copper in either Theologos or Beirut or Alexandria.

[65] Pegolotti, *Pratica*, p. 58.

Turchus, lord of Kastamonu (Süleyman Paşa, the İsfendiyaroğullari ruler). This weight was the equivalent of c.4,000 *kantar*s of Pera. Constantino bought the copper from Süleyman Paşa for 476,000 silver *aspers* of Kastamonu, a sum which Raffaele promised to settle with him. When, however, Constantino had requested settlement from Raffaele's agents, Dagnano and Petro, they had not paid it, thus resulting in a loss to Constantino.[66]

Turkish trading does not appear to have been restricted to regions of copper production, for Turkish merchants apparently traded the commodity further afield. In 1404 Cagi Mostaffa Turk of Bursa (Hacı Mustafa) acknowledged payment from the Jew Elias Sacerdotus for copper which he had handed over to Elias.[67] The Genoese document in which this was stated was enacted in Chios, which presumably indicates that this was where the copper had been delivered. Turkish merchants would therefore appear to have been trading copper in Chios in the early fifteenth century.

Much copper was sold in Constantinople[68] and was exported from there to Crete, Venice, Messina and Saragosa, Damascus, Beirut and Alexandria.[69]

---

[66] 1390.i.11 = ASG, Notario, Donato de Clavaro, C. 476, doc. 26. A summary of this document is given in Balard, Laiou and Otten-Froux, *Documents*, no. 82, p. 37.

[67] 1404.xii.31 = ASG, Notaio Gregorio Panissaro, Sc. 37, filza 1, doc. 48; Toniolo, *Notai Genovesi*, doc. 52, p. 105. These two merchants were also involved in a transaction over mastic which Elias was to hand over to Mustafa: 1404.xii.31 = *ibid.*, doc. 49; Toniolo, *Notai Genovesi*, doc. 53, p. 106.

[68] Pegolotti, *Pratica*, pp. 35, 59; 1436.ii.17 = Badoer, *Libro*, col. 38, p. 76, col. 39, p. 79; 1436.xii.3 = *ibid.*, col. 38, p. 76, col. 38, p. 77; 1436.xii.3 = *ibid.*, col. 39, p. 78, col. 38, p. 77; 1436.xii.4 = *ibid.*, col. 39, p. 78, col. 40, p. 81; 1437.iii.15 = *ibid.*, col. 55, p. 110, col. 55, p. 111, col. 17, p. 35; 1437.vi.7 = *ibid.*, col. 55, p. 110, col. 40, p. 81; 1437.vi.12, 17 = *ibid.*, col. 55, p. 110, col. 36, p. 73; 1437.vii.5, 15, 27 = *ibid.*, col. 55, p. 110, col. 75, p. 153; 1437.vii.12 = *ibid.*, col. 55, p. 110, col. 29, p. 59; 1437.iii.15, iv.22 = *ibid.*, col. 56, p. 112, col. 55, p. 111; 1437.iii.15 = *ibid.*, col. 56, p. 112, col. 4, p. 9; 1437.vi.7, vii.6 = *ibid.*, col. 56, p. 112, col. 72, p. 147; 1437.vi.7 = *ibid.*, col. 72, p. 146, col. 55, p. 111, col. 17, p. 35; 1437.vii.4 = *ibid.*, col. 72, p. 146, col. 5, p. 11; 1437.vii.5 = *ibid.*, col. 72, p. 146, col. 74, p. 151; 1437.vi.29 = *ibid.*, col. 76, p. 154, col. 74, p. 151; 1437.vii.3 = *ibid.*, col. 81, p. 164, col. 47, p. 95; 1437.vii.4 = *ibid.*, col. 81, p. 164, col. 81, p. 165; 1437.viii.7, ix.7 = *ibid.*, col. 81, p. 164, col. 91, p. 185; 1437.vii.8 = *ibid.*, col. 83, p. 168, col. 55, p. 111; 1437.vii.8 = *ibid.*, col. 83, p. 168, col. 80, p. 163; 1437.viii.7 = *ibid.*, col. 91, p. 184, col. 45, p. 91; 1437.ix.26 = *ibid.*, col. 120, p. 242, col. 119, p. 241; 1437.x.31 = *ibid.*, col. 130, p. 262, col. 101, p. 205, col. 141, p. 284, col. 101, p. 205; 1437.xi.15 = *ibid.*, col. 130, p. 262, col. 141, p. 285; 1437.x.31= *ibid.*, col. 141, p. 284, col. 101, p. 205, col. 137, p. 277, col. 121, p. 245, col. 100, p. 203; 1438.vii.8 = *ibid.*, col. 218, p. 438, col. 218, p. 439; 1438.vii.9 = *ibid.*, col. 218, p. 438, col. 120, p. 243; 1438.vii.18 = *ibid.*, col. 218, p. 438, col. 169, p. 341; 1438.viii.14 = *ibid.*, col. 227, p. 456, col. 35, p. 71; 1438.viii.14 = *ibid.*, col. 227, p. 456, col. 220, p. 443; 1438.xii.7 = *ibid.*, col. 291, p. 584, col. 291, p. 585; 1438.xii.5 = *ibid.*, col. 291, p. 584, col. 176, p. 355; 1439.vi.6 = *ibid.*, col. 331, p. 664, col. 133, p. 269; 1439.ix. = *ibid.*, col. 365, p. 732, col. 365, p. 733; 1439.ii.25 = *ibid.*, col. 401, p. 804, col. 401, p. 805; 1439.ii.26 = *ibid.*, col. 401, p. 804, col. 387, p. 777.

[69] 1436.xii.4 = Badoer, *Libro*, col. 39, p. 78, col. 40, p. 81 (Messina, Saragosa); 1437.iv.22 = *ibid.*, col. 55, p. 110, col. 55, p. 111 (Venice); 1437.xi.17 = *ibid.*, col. 142, p. 286, col. 143, p. 289, col. 137, p. 277, col. 121, p. 245, col. 100, p. 203 (Venice); 1437.xi.17 = *ibid.*, col. 117, p. 236, col. 142, p. 287; 1438.xii.7 = *ibid.*, col. 291, p. 584, col. 291, p. 585 (Beirut); 1437.iii.15, iv.22 = *ibid.*, col. 56, p. 112 and col. 55, p. 111 (Candia, Alexandria); 1437.vi.7, vii.6 = *ibid.*, col. 56, p. 112, col. 72, p. 147 (Candia, Alexandria); 1436.ii.22 = *ibid.*, col. 38, p. 76, col. 17, p. 35 (Messina); 1437.iv.22 = *ibid.*, col. 55, p. 110, col. 17, p. 35 (Alexandria); 1437.viii.2 = *ibid.*, col. 89, p. 180, col. 83, p. 169 (Candia).

While some of this copper came from the Balkans,[70] it seems highly possible that much of the copper on sale on the Constantinople market came from Anatolia.[71] Badoer refers to settling copper sales after the return of ships from the Black Sea, perhaps indicating that copper was being brought into Constantinople from the Kastamonu region.[72] Merchants did after all sail with cargoes of copper from Sinop to Pera.[73] The copper referred to by Piloti being sold 'en piatines' in Constantinople[74] may too well have originated in Anatolia, for Turchia was listed together with Tana, Caffa, Trabzon and Greece as the places from which the commodities listed by Piloti came.

In conclusion, it seems at least reasonable to suggest that the absence of references to a large volume of metal trading from the west into Turchia was due not to its illegality and gaps in extant data, but to the reality that there was no such volume. Anatolia did not necessarily need to import large quantities of metal, or at least not those it produced itself. In the case of the arms trade, perhaps weapons were not traded in concealed quantities but what was imported was technology and expertise. The cannons under Mehmed II that fired so effectively at the walls of Constantinople were cast by a Hungarian renegade.[75]

Precious metals too were traded in Anatolia. Silver and gold were traded as luxury items. These were, after all, items much sought after as tokens of wealth. At the end of the thirteenth century, the Byzantine general Philanthropenos sent silver and gold as part of the spoils of his fighting in Asia Minor back to Constantinople.[76] Around the same period, the *tekfur* of Bilecik (Greek Bekloma, east of Bursa, north-west of Eskişehir), sent, according to Neşri, whose reliability for this early period is a shaky, Köse Mihal to 'Osman to invite him to his wedding. Köse Mihal went bearing gifts of gold and silversmiths' tools.[77] In the 1330s, Mehmed Aydınoğlu, the ruler of Aydın, regarded silver as among those items suitable to give as presents to the traveller ibn Battuta.[78] He also gave silver pieces to ibn Battuta's companions on their departure.[79] There were gold and silver plates and spoons at the palace at Birgi.[80] Umur Aydınoğlu presented Şeyh

[70] 1438.vii.8 = Badoer, *Libro*, col. 218, p. 438, col. 120, p. 243, 'rame in tornexi vlachesci'.
[71] Both Thiriet, *Romanie vénitienne*, p. 427 and Balard, *Romanie génoise*, vol. II, p. 783, n. 68 say that Badoer dealt in copper from Kastamonu and refer to Badoer, *Libro*, col. 56. This reference, however, although dealing with copper, does not mention Kastamonu.
[72] 1439.vi.6 = Badoer, *Libro*, col. 331, p. 664 and col. 133, p. 269; 1437.iv.22 = *ibid.*, col. 55, p. 110, col. 55, p. 111.
[73] Balard, *Romanie génoise*, vol. II, p. 784, n. 69 (1402).
[74] Piloti, *L'Egypte*, pp. 62–3.
[75] Dukas, *Historia Byzantina*, pp. 247–8, Dukas, *Historia Turcobyzantina*, pp. 307, 309.
[76] Planoudes, *Epistolae*, letter 78, p. 99.
[77] Neşri, *Menzel, Cod.* p. 30; Neşri, *Kitab-ı Cihan-nüma*, p. 98.
[78] Ibn Battuta, *Voyages*, p. 302.
[79] Ibn Battuta, *Voyages*, p. 307.   [80] Ibn Battuta, *Voyages*, p. 304.

'Izz al-Dīn with silver vessels.[81] At the wedding in 783/1381–2 between Bayezid and the daughter of the emir of Germiyan there were gold and silver trays, silver ewers and pots, and gold coins.[82] Around the same period Aşıkpaşazade makes reference to silver and gold trays and bowls taken as spoil from a captured castle.[83] At the end of the fourteenth century, the Byzantine emperor sent 100 fish full of gold and silver to the Ottoman ruler Bayezid.[84] Even if this is more myth than reality, it still indicates the importance of gold and silver as tokens of wealth and power.

Gold was a commodity in the Turkish markets. Spun gold was sold in Antalya[85] and gold appeared too in the markets of Edirne. In 1438 3 *chanele* of gold thread was sold in Edirne, from the 10 *chanele* sent there. The figure entered is 9 *hyperpyra*, presumably the amount for which they were sold.[86] The remaining 7 *chanele* of gold thread were sent to Constantinople from Edirne by Pipo de Jachomo.[87] The 10 *chanele*, weighing 10 ounces of Constantinople, were sent by Asalon, son of Cain, a Jew, and were valued at 3 *hyperpyra* per ounce.[88] Spun gold of every region came to the markets of Pera and Constantinople where spun gold of Lucca, Genoa and Provence was sold.[89]

Silver too was traded in the markets of Turchia, selling in Antalya and in Theologos in pieces and bullion.[90] Silver items were also bought and sold. In 1358 Musa, emir of Menteşe, promised to pay the duca di Candia, Pietro Badoer, the remainder owed for silver/a silver object ('argentei') of the commune of Crete which Musa's father had received from Francisco Blanco when he was in Balat on negotiations for the commune.[91] In 1381 there was a dispute in Chios between two merchants from Barcelona and the Barcelonese masters of a ship. One of the matters of dispute concerned nine bales of cloth and some silver.[92] As this ship was on its way to Theologos and as the item together with silver in dispute was cloth, something much traded into Theologos, it seems possible that the silver may have been destined for Theologos.

It is possible that some silver was traded into this region from Chios, for

[81] Ibn Battuta, *Voyages*, p. 311.
[82] Aşıkpaşazade, *Altosmanische Chronik*, p. 53, Aşıkpaşazade, *Tevarih-i al-i 'Osman*, p. 57; Neşri, *Menzel, Cod.* p. 56, Neşri, *Kitab-ı Cihan-nüma*, p. 206.
[83] Aşıkpaşazade, *Altosmanische Chronik*, p. 55; Aşıkpaşazade, *Tevarih-i al-i 'Osman*, p. 60.
[84] Aşıkpaşazade, *Altosmanische Chronik*, p. 61; Aşıkpaşazade, *Tevarih-i al-i 'Osman*, pp. 67–8.
[85] Pegolotti, *Pratica*, p. 58.
[86] 1438. x.22 = Badoer, *Libro*, col. 230, p. 462, col. 89, p. 181.
[87] 1438.x.22 = Badoer, *Libro*, col. 113, p. 228, col. 89, p. 181.
[88] 1437.xii.17 = Badoer, *Libro*, col. 89, p. 180, col. 113, p. 115.
[89] Pegolotti, *Pratica*, p. 36.
[90] Pegolotti, *Pratica*, pp. 56, 58.
[91] 1358.x.13 = Zachariadou, *Trade and Crusade*, doc. 1358/1359M, clause 5, p. 218. The amount paid was 800 gold *florins* but this sum included a settlement for damages by Turks against Cretan subjects on the *grippa* of Leone Marmara.
[92] 1381.ii.15 = ASG, Notario, Antonius Feloni, C. 175, fos. 110v–111r.

no exemption was granted for silver or gold from the *gabella* of 0.5 per cent charged there on all merchandise carried by sea to Chios, Mitylene, Rhodes, Old and New Phokaea, Caffa and all places in Turchia.[93] Gold and silver could therefore have been imported into Anatolia from Chios, particularly as one of the other items specially mentioned as not being granted exemption was soap, an import into that region.

Apart from importing, Turchia also exported gold and silver. In 1377 Dutch gold (*aurepelium*) was imported from Balat into Genoa where it was taxed.[94]

There was thus a circular movement of metals round the eastern Mediterranean, flowing both into and out of Anatolia. Although it is generally assumed that the volume of metal traded into Turchia was larger than suggested by extant evidence, it seems possible at least to suggest that this was not in fact so and that lack of evidence in this case is due to there being a lack of anything to evidence. On the other hand, any conclusion must remain tentative as there is very little extant data from which one can gauge the extent of this trade or the details of its operation.

[93] 1408.ii, Argenti, *Chios*, vol. I, p. 422.
[94] 1377.viii.19 = Day, *Douanes*, vol. II, p. 874.

CHAPTER 10

The fall of Constantinople and Ottoman–Genoese relations after 1453

The fall of Constantinople was without doubt viewed by Latin contemporaries as a disaster of enormous magnitude. Piccolomini, later Pope Pius II, described the fall as the loss of one of the two eyes of the church.[1] The carnage shocked contemporaries who witnessed the streets running in blood and watched as bloated bodies floated like melons along the waters of the Dardanelles.[2]

While the fall was undoubtedly important and galvanised the west into more urgent calls for concerted action against the Turkish menace,[3] which never materialised, the actual impact of the conquest on economic relations was probably much more limited. Trade tends to continue under even the most difficult of circumstances. While the Turks massed before the walls of Constantinople, two merchants, Raffaele Vegerio and Michele Natono, dined on board Giovanni Caneta's ship where they haggled, unsuccessfully, over the price of a garment.[4] Aron Maiavello, observing the Turkish bombardment of the ships anchored at Constantinople, remarked, 'I am afraid that we shall lose the ship and the fish.'[5]

Ottoman policy pursued by Mehmed II in his relations with the Latins shows both the continuity of economic policy and the importance attached to such relations. It seems generally accepted now that 1453 does not

---

[1] 1453.vii.21 = Piccolomini in Pertusi, *Caduta*, vol. II, p. 56.

[2] Nicolò Barbaro, 'Giornale dell'assedio di Costantinopoli', in Pertusi, *Caduta*, vol. II, p. 35; Nicolò Barbaro, *Nicolò Barbaro. The Diary of the Siege of Constantinople 1453*, trans. J. R. Jones (New York, 1969), p. 67.

[3] The king of Cyprus sent an ambassador to the pope (Niccola della Tuccia in Pertusi, *Caduta*, vol. I, pp. 98–9), the Hospitallers approached both the pope (Niccola della Tuccia in Pertusi, *Caduta*, vol. I, pp. 98–9) and the margrave of Brandenburg (1453.vi.30 = Agostino Pertusi, *Testi inediti e poco noti sulla caduta di Constantinopoli: Edizione postuma a cura di Antonio Carile*, Il mondo medievale. Sezione di storia bizantina e slava (Bologna, 1983), p. 54), and Lauro Quirini wrote to Pope Nicholas V (1453.vii.15 = Quirini in Pertusi, *Testi inediti*, p. 66), all urging Christian action against the Ottomans (Pertusi, *Testi inediti*, p. 66). See also 1453.xii.10 = Belgrano, 'Documenti', no. 153, pp. 259–61.

[4] 1453.viii.23 = Ausilia Roccatagliata, *Notai Genovesi in Oltremare. Atti Rogati a Chio (1453–1454, 1470–1471)*, 35 (Genoa, 1982), doc. 18, pp. 22–4.

[5] 1453.xii.31 = Roccatagliata, *Chio*, doc. 65, p. 101.

represent a break in trade relations between the Ottoman state and those of western Europe.[6] However, many scholars argue that there was a decline in western trade with the Ottomans after this date.[7] Certainly by the end of the century Genoese notarial activity connected with trade in the Ottoman empire had tailed off.[8] However, the fact that by the end of the fifteenth century western traders were not as active within Ottoman lands as they had been earlier in the century does not necessarily have to be explained in terms of either the fall of Constantinople or Ottoman policy introduced by Mehmed II.

In general, the view that Ottoman conquest *per se* should have led to a decline in trade relations with western merchants does not, on the basis of existing evidence, seem convincing. The Ottomans had been taking over areas in which the Genoese traded for a considerable time. At the end of the fourteenth century the Ottoman ruler Bayezid had annexed two beyliks, Menteşe and Aydın, which were major trading partners of the Genoese and which had granted favourable trading privileges to western merchants. The Ottoman takeover did not lead to any decline, and favourable trading concessions continued under the new rulers. Later, with the fall of Thessaloniki in 1430, the Ottomans took over an extremely important commercial centre without adverse effects on trade. Trade was, after all, a big money spinner for the state and therefore not something to be discouraged. As Franz Babinger pointed out, Ottoman expansion, far from being detrimental to international trade, produced one great advantage in that it did away with numerous borders and resulted in one homogeneous trading zone in which only one set of import–export customs was due.[9]

The loss of Genoese colonies in the Levant to the Turks, in particular Pera and Caffa, has been cited as leading directly to the end of the Genoese

[6] Geo Pistarino, 'La caduta di Costantinopoli: da Pera Genovese a Galata Turca', in *La Storia Genovese. Atti del Convegno di Studi sui Ceti dirigenti nelle istituzioni della Repubblica di Genova. Genova 12–13–14 Aprile 1984*, vol. V, p. 30; Geo Pistarino, 'Tra i Genovesi dell'Oriente Turco dal tramonto del medioevo al primo tempo dell'età moderna', in *Atti dell'Academia Ligure di Scienze e Lettere, annata 1986* (Genoa, 1988), vol. XLIII, pp. 204, 208–9; Sandra Origone, 'Genova e i genovese tra la fine di Bisanzio e i Turchi', in *Atti dell'Academia Ligure di Scienze e Lettere, annata 1986* (Genoa, 1988), vol. XLIII, p. 390; Sandra Origone, 'Chio nel tempo della caduta di Costantinopoli', in *Saggi e Documenti II*, Civico Istituto Colombiano, Studi e Testi, Serie Storica 3 (Genoa, 1982), vol. I, pp. 148, 149, 196, 197; G. G. Musso, 'Nuovi documenti dell'Archivio di Stato di Genova sui Genovesi e il Levante nel secondo quattrocento', *Rassegna degli Archivi di Stato* 27 (1967), 445, 464, 479; G. G. Musso, 'Fonti documentarie per la storia di Chio dei genovesi', *La Berio* 8, 3 (1968) 8, 20–1; Rossana Urbani, 'Note d'archivio sui notai genovesi del' 400: l'attività di Bartolomeo Canessa', *La Berio* 11/1 (1971), p. 11.
[7] Eliyahu Ashtor states that while Italian trade in the Ottoman empire continued to flourish after 1453, it was not, after the fall, equal to what it had been before: Ashtor, 'Commercio italiano', pp. 44–7; see also Urbani, 'Bartolomeo Canessa', 11; Ausilia Roccatagliata, 'Nuovi documenti su Pera Genovese', in *Atti del convegno di Studi sui Ceti dirigenti; nelle istituzioni della Repubblica di Genova, Genova 29–30–31, maggio–1 giugno 1990*, vol. XI, p. 129.
[8] Pistarino, 'Caduta', p. 36.
[9] Babinger, *Mehmed*, p. 433.

trading presence within the empire. However, while these losses undoubtedly caused great inconvenience, in that they removed the security enjoyed
by the Genoese merchants, trade relations were not necessarily entirely
dependent on the presence of such trading bases. Latin trade with the
Mamluk empire or with Tunisia is evidence of this. The Latins who traded
so vigorously within Mamluk lands never had colonies there. In any case,
Genoa continued to hold Chios, a major trade base in the Levant, until well
into the sixteenth century.

The existing evidence does not support the view that there is any inherent
reason why any decline in Genoese trading activity within the empire should
necessarily be put down to Ottoman advance. The question remains to be
answered whether the fall of Constantinople in 1453 and the policies of
Mehmed II did in fact usher in a decline of Genoese–Ottoman trade
relations.

In the immediate aftermath of the fall of Constantinople, it was inevitable
that trade would have been adversely affected as merchants fled to the
islands, such as Chios,[10] and as much merchandise in the Genoese warehouses in Pera and in those of other Latins in different parts of the city went
up in flames, was looted by incoming Turkish soldiers or was simply stolen
by other westerners. One of the instructions to the Genoese ambassadors to
the Ottomans in early 1454 was to try and obtain a settlement for the
damages and losses sustained by the Genoese in Pera.[11] Turkish looting or
appropriation of goods was no doubt disruptive, Giovanni Caneta, for
example, claiming that one of the reasons he had sold wine belonging to
Michele Natono in Pera just after the fall was that, had he not sold it, the
Turks would have taken it.[12] In the chaos immediately after the conquest,
Latins too pilfered or simply sold goods they did not own. After the fall
part of Michele Natono's wine, marked with his name, had apparently been
sold by Carolo de Bozolo, who had the wine in his warehouse, to an
Armenian. Carolo was in the process of transferring the rest of the wine to
Lodisio Gattulusio's warehouse.[13] Giovanni Caneta and Francesco For-
cherio, using the house of Aron Maiavello, who was conveniently absent,
pilfered Aron's goods and used his house as a base to store other goods they
had come by unlawfully. Together with a locksmith and a *magister asie*,
whom they often entertained in Aron's house, they had gained access to the
warehouses.[14]

---

[10] The notary Lorenzo Calvi himself fled after the fall to Chios: Roccatagliata, 'Nuovi documenti', p. 127.

[11] 1454.iii.11 = Belgrano, 'Documenti', no. 154, p. 268.

[12] 1453.viii.23 = Roccatagliata, *Chio*, no. 18, pp. 22–4. This forms part of a series of documents dealing with a dispute over the sale of a garment: 1453.viii.18 = *ibid.*, no. 14, pp. 19–20; 1453.viii.18 = *ibid.*, no. 15, p. 20; 1453.viii.23 = *ibid.*, no. 16, pp. 20–1; 1453.viii.23 = *ibid.*, no. 17, p. 22; 1453.viii.23 = *ibid.*, no. 19, pp. 24–5.

[13] 1453.viii.23 = Roccatagliata, *Chio*, no. 18, pp. 22–4.

[14] 1453.xii.22 = Roccatagliata, *Chio*, no. 61, pp. 95–8.

The Turkish conquest also meant the death, capture[15] or disappearance of many Latins and Latin officials. Genoese merchants, seeing Constantinople crashing before them, rushed to the waterfront in search of ships on which to leave, deserting their merchandise and homes,[16] and when Mehmed entered Pera five days after the fall he found that many people had fled.[17] The Venetian *bailo*, his son and various Venetian officials were executed as were the Catalan consul and six or seven other Catalans.[18] In Pera, there was no *podestà* or *vicario* to dispense justice in the aftermath of the fall,[19] something that no doubt hampered commercial transactions and would certainly have been a problem in settling any disputes. In such conditions some temporary interruption in trade is easily explicable.

The situation in Pera continued to be difficult and the Genoese on Chios and Mitylene remained constantly anxious about Ottoman intentions.[20] In view of the weakened defensive position of Pera, with many of its walls razed, merchants were not so keen on bringing their goods into a city in which they could not guarantee their safety.[21] The authorities in Genoa referred to the 'bad treatment of our people of Pera by lo segnor Turco since the fall of Constantinople' and even discussed the possibility of discontinuing diplomatic relations.[22] Nearly two years after the fall Giovanni da Pontremoli was urging the merchant Battista Goastavino, in view of the dangerous position, to return to Genoa rather then remaining in Pera.[23]

Thus there were undoubtedly problems for the Genoese traders in the aftermath of the fall. But problems trading in Turchia were not new. In 1381 Giovanni de Bulgaro complained of being unable to carry out his functions as *fideicommissor*, particularly in Pera and Turchia, in part because of the dangers there.[24] Despite fluctuations in trade, something that could also occur at other times and for other reasons, such as an outbreak

---

[15] e.g.1453.xii.31 = Roccatagliata, *Chio*, no. 66, pp. 102–3, Petro di Cremona and his family were slaves of the Turks in Pera before they managed to escape.

[16] Dukas, *Historia Byzantina*, p. 296, ll. 19–25; Dukas, *Historia Turcobyzantina*, p. 373, ll. 9–13; Dukas, *Decline and Fall*, p. 230.

[17] Dukas, *Historia Byzantina*, p. 312, ll. 22 – p. 313, l. 2; Dukas, *Historia Turcobyzantina*, p. 393, ll. 12–14; Dukas, *Decline and Fall*, p. 240.

[18] Barbaro in Pertusi, *Caduta*, vol. II, p. 38; Barbaro, *Diary*, pp. 77–8; 1453.vi.23 = Belgrano, 'Documenti', no. 149, p. 231 (letter from Angelo Giovanni Lomellino, the ex-*podestà*).

[19] 1453.viii.23 = Roccatagliata, *Chio*, no. 18, pp. 22–4.

[20] Dukas, for example, refers to how on the sultan's preparation of a fleet in 1461 for an unknown destination, the Latins of the islands including Chios, Lemnos and Rhodes were in 'abject fear'. Dukas, *Historia Byzantina*, p. 314, ll. 15–18; Dukas, *Historia Turcobyzantina*, p. 427, ll. 24–7; Dukas, *Decline and Fall*, p. 258. Mitylene fell to Mehmed the following year.

[21] 1454.iii.11 = Belgrano, 'Documenti', no. 154, p. 266.

[22] 1453.<xii>.<25> = ASG, Archivio Segreto, Diversorum, 555, fos. 1r–2r.

[23] 1455.i.30 = Giovanni da Pontremoli in Domenico Gioffrè, *Letter di Giovanni da Pontremoli, mercante Genovese 1453–1459*, Collana Storica di Fonti e Studi 33 (Genoa, 1982), no. 27, p. 38.

[24] 1381.ii.28 = ASG, Notario, Antonius Feloni, C. 175, fos. 114r–115r.

of plague,[25] Genoese and other Latin traders were active in the Ottoman state after 1453 and indeed throughout Mehmed's reign.[26] Genoese merchants were operating very soon after the fall and many who had initially fled appear to have returned.[27] While many merchants were captured and had to organise a ransom, this process could be very speedy. Tommaso di Capriata was captured in Constantinople on Tuesday 29 May and ransomed on Thursday.[28] The ransom must have been equally quick for Giovanni Caneta, for he too was back in Pera by Sunday.[29] By no means everything was lost during the conquest. Bales of cloth were sent from Pera to Chios in November.[30] Goods, like people, were redeemed from the Turks,[31] letters of credit were exchanged, Gregorio Magnano agreeing to accept a letter of credit in Amasra for money owed him by Giovanni Guidice.[32] By the end of the year grain from Greece and Macedonia was being traded into Constantinople and Pera;[33] alum was being exported to Genoa at the beginning of 1454.[34] The Genoese ambassadors to the Turks in 1454 were instructed to negotiate as much wheat export as they could.[35] Life continued, houses in Pera were rented out or sold. In 1454 Magister Petro di Cremona instructed his procurators to rent out his houses and vineyards both within and without Pera[36] while Antonio di Cabella gave instructions for the sale of his small wooden house in the *bassali* of Pera, above the dockyards, to be sold.[37]

The Turks themselves took part in various aspects of this trade, including

---

[25] In 1455 the plague was very bad in Thrace and the sultan was on the move to avoid it, leaving Edirne and going to Plovdiv, which he also left as the plague reached the city, and set off for Sofia, Dukas, *Historia Byzantina*, p. 329, l. 17 – p. 330, l. 5; Dukas, *Historia Turcobyzantina*, p. 413, ll. 17–26; Dukas, *Decline and Fall*, p. 251.

[26] See, for example, the documents enacted in Pera and published by Ausilia Roccatagliata, *Notai Genovesi in Oltremare. Atti rogati a Pera e Mitilene*, vol. I, *Pera (1408–1490)*, vol. II, *Mitilene (1454–1460)* (Genoa, 1982).

[27] 1453.viii.16 = Iacopo Bracelli in Giovanni Balbi, *L'Epistolario di Iacopo Bracelli*, Collana Storica di Fonti e Studi, 2 (Genoa, 1969), no. 48, p. 103.

[28] 1453.xii.22 = Roccatagliata, *Chio*, no. 61, p. 96. Giacomo di Portovenere borrowed 65 *hyperpyra* to ransom himself, his wife and his sons from the Turks, 1454.i.29 = *ibid.*, no. 93, p. 156 and 1454.i.29 = *ibid.*, no. 94, p. 158.

[29] 1453.xii.22 = Roccatagliata, *Chio*, no. 61, p. 96.

[30] 1453.xi.6 = Roccatagliata, *Chio*, no. 38, pp. 56–7. Genuino de Saulo had his three bales of cloth opened in Chios before witnesses and an inventory drawn up. This cloth had been sent from Pera, where Genuino had entrusted it to Agostino Nicolao Saccerio, by Oliverio Doria and consigned to Agostino de Franchi. Presumably, as the cloth was opened and the inventory made on 6 November, the cloth was sent from Pera shortly beforehand.

[31] 1454.i.22 = Roccatagliata, *Chio*, no. 85, p. 137. Goods and garments of Andrea Campofregoso were redeemed from the Turks for 2,715 Turkish *aspers*.

[32] 1454.iii.1 = Roccatagliata, *Chio*, no. 126, pp. 224–6.

[33] 1454.i.15 = Roccatagliata, *Chio*, no. 79, pp. 126–7.

[34] 1454.ii.26 = Roccatagliata, *Chio*, no. 121, p. 217.

[35] 1454.iii.11 = Belgrano, 'Documenti', no. 154, pp. 268–9.

[36] 1454.ii.4 = Roccatagliata, *Chio*, no. 169, pp. 168–9.

[37] 1454.ii.26 = Roccatagliata, *Chio*, no. 124, pp. 222–3.

selling captives.[38] There were clearly commercial relations between the Genoese and the Turks immediately after the fall of the city. At some time before 15 January 1454, the *subaşı* of Constantinople, Süleyman Bey, rejected a letter of exchange from Odoardo Grillo who had given it to Paride de Mari to cover freight charges on grain of 3,467 *hyperpyra* 6 *karati*, loaded for either Constantinople or Pera. If the grain was unloaded at Constantinople, it was to be handed over to Süleyman Bey, if in Pera, to Cristoforo Pallavicino.[39] It is not clear from the document whether the *subaşı* here was acting as an official of state, accepting grain on its behalf for which he had agreed to pay the freight, or was acting as an individual merchant whose arrangement with Grillo included accepting letters of credit. If Süleyman Bey was in fact acting as an individual merchant, the arrangement over the letter of credit might suggest that he was acting as banker for Grillo,[40] which would in turn show a high level of Turkish–Genoese commercial co-operation. Individuals certainly did co-operate, as Giovanni Caneta's behaviour in Pera clearly illustrates. Very soon after the fall, he had returned home in the company of several Turks. Upon being asked by Tommaso di Capriata, 'Giovanni, what are you doing with these Turks?', he had replied that he was attempting to barter cloth for a purple Latin garment the Turks had in their possession.[41]

Extant Genoese archival material therefore establishes that trade continued after the fall of Constantinople. It is not possible, however, to argue, on the basis of this material that this trade was or was not less than it had been before the Ottoman conquest, as there is simply not sufficient extant data for a reliable quantitative study. However, this material does at least establish that Mehmed II did not, presumably, undertake any extreme anti-Latin policies vis-à-vis the western traders within his empire and any new policies he may have introduced were not sufficiently harsh to lead to an abrupt decline in this trade after 1453. Indeed Ottoman material shows that Latin merchants continued to be active throughout his reign.[42]

Genoese–Ottoman relations were based very firmly on mutual interest. The Genoese were essentially pragmatic in their dealings with the Turks, something which was no doubt encouraged by the fact that Genoese

---

[38] The Turk Kadı Hasan (Cagi Cassani) sold a Greek, described as his captive or slave, to two Greeks and an Armenian in Pera in August 1453: 1453.viii.4 = Roccatagliata, *Pera e Mitilene*, vol. I, *Pera*, no. 53, pp. 138–9.

[39] 1454.i.15 = Roccatagliata, *Chio*, no. 79, p. 127.

[40] Genoese merchants active in Ottoman territories did use letters of exchange during the reign of Murad II: see 1437.iii.31 = Badoer, *Libro*, col. 125, p. 252, col. 204, p. 411; 1438.iii.31 = *ibid.*, col. 125, p. 252, col. 186, p. 375; 1437.iv.30 = *ibid.*, col. 55, p. 110; 1437.ix.2 = *ibid.*, col. 125, p. 252; 1438.xii.3 = *ibid.*, col. 233, p. 468.

[41] 1453.xii.22 = Roccatagliata, *Chio*, no. 61, pp. 95–8.

[42] İnalcık, 'Ticaret tarihine dair vesikalar', no. 4, p. 70, no. 6, p. 71, no. 7, p. 72, no. 8, pp. 72–3, no. 10, p. 74, no. 13, p. 77, no. 16, pp. 78–9, no. 19, p. 80, no. 20, p. 80, no. 25, pp. 82–3, no. 29, pp. 85–6, no. 32, pp. 87–8, no. 34, pp. 88–9, no. 38, p. 94, no. 39, p. 94.

Turkish policy was largely dictated by the Genoese on the spot in colonies such as Pera and Chios rather than directed from Genoa itself.[43] Even during the siege of Constantinople, the Genoese of Pera managed to maintain their relations with the Turks, while, simultaneously, siding with the defenders of the city, sending letters urgently requesting help to Genoa, ambassadors to the sultan in Edirne to renew treaty relations and express undying friendship, soldiers to Constantinople, oil for Turkish cannons to the sultan's camp and betraying Longo Giustiniano's scheme to set fire to the Turkish ships.[44] Relations were such that when Turkish cannon sank a ship belonging to Genoese merchants of Pera, loaded with merchandise and ready to leave for Italy, the Perotes complained to the Turks. Explaining that they had not realised that the ship belonged to the Genoese of Pera, taking it rather as belonging to the enemy, the Turks assured them that, after the capture of the city, the merchants would be fully indemnified.[45] Once Constantinople had fallen, what the Genoese really wanted was to have Pera back and to continue trading as before, a situation for which they were quite prepared to pay tribute. Their overriding concern was to ensure freedom of movement and, in particular, access to and from the Black Sea.[46]

In the same way as it was very much in the interests of the Genoese to keep good relations with the new Turkish ruler, Mehmed too had a definite interest in keeping relations with the local Genoese running smoothly, and Genoese merchants frequented his court.[47] At the beginning of his reign the Genoese of Pera, of Chios and Mitylene and the Hospitallers of Rhodes all sent ambassadors bearing gifts and arranged agreements.[48] That Mehmed had no interest in losing merchants from Pera is made clear by the attempts of his vizier, Zaganos Paşa, to persuade the Genoese there not to flee, assuring them of Mehmed's friendly intentions and promising them better

[43] 1454.iii.11 = Belgrano, 'Documenti', no. 154, pp. 261–70.
[44] Dukas, *Historia Byzantina*, p. 265, ll. 10–11, p. 267, ll. 8–11, p. 275, ll. 10–20, p. 277, ll. 13–14; Dukas, *Historia Turcobyzantina*, p. 329, ll. 25–6, p. 333, 5–7, p. 343, l. 28 – p. 345, l. 4, p. 347, l. 13; Dukas, *Decline and Fall*, pp. 211, 212, 217, 218.
[45] Dukas, *Historia Byzantina*, p. 278, l. 8 – p. 279, l. 8; Dukas, *Historia Turcobyzantina*, p. 347, l. 29 – p. 349, l. 13; Dukas, *Decline and Fall*, p. 219.
[46] 1454.iii.11 = Belgrano, 'Documenti', no. 154, pp. 265–7.
[47] The Genoese authorities instructed their ambassadors to Mehmed in 1454 to talk to the Genoese at Mehmed's court, in particular to Francesco de Draperiis, who knew the Turkish court very well: 1454.iii.11 = Belgrano, 'Documenti', no. 154, p. 263. Francesco accompanied the Ottoman expedition against Chios and conducted the negotiations between the Turkish forces and the Latin defenders on Kos: Dukas, *Historia Byzantina*, pp. 322, 324; Dukas, *Historia Turcobyzantina*, p. 405, ll. 14–17, p. 407, ll. 25–6; Dukas, *Decline and Fall*, pp. 246–7, 248. Francesco appealed to the Sultan for help over a debt for alum he alleged was owed him by the Chians: Dukas, *Historia Byzantina*, pp. 327–8; Dukas, *Historia Turcobyzantina*, p. 405, ll. 14–17, p. 411, ll. 19–24; Dukas, *Decline and Fall*, pp. 246–7, 250.
[48] Dukas, *Historia Byzantina*, p. 233, ll. 3–8; Dukas, *Historia Turcobyzantina*, p. 291, ll. 3–6; Dukas, *Decline and Fall*, p. 191.

treaty arrangements than they had from the Byzantine emperor.[49] In a further attempt to keep the merchants in the city Mehmed, having entered Pera on the fifth day after the fall, ordered a census of property and possessions and promised that if the owners returned to the city within three months they would receive their goods back.[50] Mehmed's keen interest in trade and its attendant profits for the state treasury was recognised by Luciano Spinula and Balthasaro Marrufo, the Genoese ambassadors sent to the Ottoman court in early 1454 with instructions to persuade the sultan to restore Pera to Genoese control. They were to point out that the current situation in Pera was in the interests of neither the sultan nor the Genoese, but that were the city to be repaired and restored to them, it would once again flourish and the merchants would again bring in the array of goods usually imported from the west.[51]

In his treaties with the Genoese, and other Latin trading nations, Mehmed granted concessions. In the imperial decree (*aman-name*) issued to the Genoese of Pera on 30 May 1453, Mehmed granted them the right to sell their goods freely, as in all other parts of his lands, exemption from taxes except the *harac*, a legal authority of their own to deal with the affairs of the merchants, while he granted merchants from Genoa the right to come and go, provided they paid according to law and custom.[52] These commercial arrangements were not only limited to the Genoese, but were also extended to the Venetians, both in the treaty of 1454 and that of 1479 which ended the war begun in 1463.[53] The fact that Mehmed was prepared to give such concessions to the Venetians whose bargaining power was, after a sixteen-year war, reduced to almost nothing indicates the importance he attached to his trade relations with the west. Mehmed's relations with Florence were particularly good, granting her trading privileges in 1469. Under the 1479 arrangement the Hospitallers too received trading privileges. This, however, was, as the Hospitallers themselves realised, more of a stalling manoeuvre giving Mehmed time to organise for an attack than a genuine move motivated by desire for trade. There is, however, nothing in these treaties to indicate a major shift in policy vis-à-vis the western traders within Ottoman lands.

In considering the proposition that decline in western trading activity was due to Ottoman behaviour, one must examine whether Mehmed adopted any new economic policies which would have discouraged western merchant activity within his empire, activity that had flourished under his predeces-

---

[49] Dukas, *Historia Byzantina*, p. 296, l. 25 – p. 297, l. 10; Dukas, *Historia Turcobyzantina*, p. 373, ll. 13–21; Dukas, *Decline and Fall*, p. 230.

[50] Dukas, *Historia Byzantina*, p. 313, ll. 2–6; Dukas, *Historia Turcobyzantina*, p. 393, ll. 12–17; Dukas, *Decline and Fall*, p. 240; 1453.xii.22 = Roccatagliata, *Chio*, no. 61, pp. 96–7.

[51] 1454.iii.11 = Belgrano, 'Documenti', no. 154, pp. 265–7.

[52] 1453.v.30 = Belgrano, 'Documenti', no. 148, pp. 226–9.

[53] 1479.i.25 = F. Miklosich and J. Müller, *Acta et Diplomata Graeca Medii Aevi* (Vienna, 1870), vol. III, pp. 295–8.

sors. One aspect of economic policy of immediate relevance to western traders was customs tax. If Mehmed II, after his conquest of Constantinople in 1453, had brought in substantial rises to these rates, this might well have acted as a disincentive for western traders. The rates charged by the Ottomans in the fourteenth century are not known. The treaty between Murad I and the Genoese enacted in 1387 gives no rate but refers to customs as being paid by the Genoese according to custom.[54] For the fourteenth century it seems reasonable to suggest a general rate on Latins of around 2 per cent on both imports and exports, in line with that charged in Menteşe, in Aydın under the 1353 treaty, and for Cypriots in Antalya.[55] Under the treaty of 1403 made by Süleyman the rates again appear as those paid according to custom.[56] In the 1430s, a *comerchium* of 2 per cent was charged in Gelibolu,[57] in Edirne[58] and an import customs of 2 per cent in Samsun.[59]

Under Mehmed II customs rates charged on Latins were around 4 per cent or 5 per cent. Muslims and tributaries were charged in Gelibolu at a rate of 4 per cent and non-tributaries at not more than 5 per cent on both imports and exports;[60] in 1475, according to the income given by Jacopo di Promontorio, foreigners in Gelibolu and Istanbul paid 5 per cent customs on both imports and exports while subjects of the sultan paid 4 per cent.[61] In 1476 Muslims and tributaries paid 4 per cent on imports while non-tributary Franks and other infidels paid 5 per cent in various ports including Istanbul, Galata, Gelibolu, Çeşme and the two Phokaeas.[62] In 1481 non-Muslims and non-tributaries paid 4 per cent on imported goods and on merchandise transferred from one ship to another, tributaries 2 per cent and Muslims 1 per cent.[63] The same grading of customs rates also applied to

[54] 1387.vi.8 = ASG, Archivio Segreto, Materie Politiche, 2729, no. 26; Fleet, 'Treaty', clause 5, p. 15.

[55] Pegolotti, *Pratica*, pp. 41, 55–7, 58; Zachariadou, *Trade and Crusade*, 1331.iv.13 = doc. 1331M, clause 3, p. 187, 1337.iii.9 = *ibid.*, doc. 1337A, clauses 7, 13, pp. 191, 192–3, 1353.iv.7 = *ibid.*, doc. 1353A, clause 20, p. 214, 1375.iv.22 = *ibid.*, doc. 1375M, clause 21, p. 222, 1403.vii.24 = *ibid.*, doc. 1403M, clause 21, pp. 230–1, 1407.vi.2 = *ibid.*, doc. 1407M, clause 20, p. 236, 1414.x.17 = *ibid.*, doc. 1414M, clause 3, p. 238 (states that the *comerchium* on import and export was to be paid as it had been in the past).

[56] 1403 = Dennis, 'Treaty', 79.

[57] 1437.ii.17, 1437.viii.5 = Badoer, *Libro*, col. 175, p. 352, col. 125, p. 253; 1438.ix.18 = *ibid.*, col. 247, p. 496, col. 175, p. 353; 1438.viii.5 = *ibid.*, col. 191, p. 384, col. 175, p. 353.

[58] 1437.iv.30 = Badoer, *Libro*, col. 57, p. 114, col. 43, p. 87; 1438.viii.18 = *ibid.*, col. 230, p. 462, col. 89, p. 181; 1439.iii.12 = *ibid.*, col. 319, p. 640, col. 244, p. 491.

[59] 1436.xii.18 = Badoer, *Libro*, col. 152, p. 306, col. 44, p. 89.

[60] no date = Anhegger and İnalcık, *Kanunname*, no. 45, p. 63; Beldiceanu, *Actes*, vol. I, no. 46, clause 9, p. 135.

[61] Babinger, *Mehmed*, p. 63.

[62] Post 1476.i.28 = Anhegger and İnalcık, *Kanunname*, no. 35, pp. 47–8; Beldiceanu, *Actes*, vol. I, no. 36, clauses 2, 3, 4, pp. 11–14; 1476.i.28/ii.16 = Anhegger and İnalcık, *Kanunname*, no. 53, p. 74; Beldiceanu, *Actes*, vol. I, no. 54, clauses 2, 3, p. 146.

[63] 1481.viii.26/ix.24 = Anhegger and İnalcık, *Kanunname*, no. 55, pp. 78–9; Beldiceanu, *Actes*, vol. I, no. 56, pp. 151–2.

cloth[64] and to goods in general in Samsun and Sinop in 1482.[65] The rates were sometimes lower for in either 1454–63 or 1479–81, a rate of 3 per cent on cloth imported into Bursa was levied on Muslims, tributaries and infidel merchants from Venice, Genoa, Chios and other places.[66]

These figures seem to indicate that there was a substantial rise in customs taxes sometime after the 1430s, for Badoer quotes rates of 2 per cent while, under Mehmed Latin merchants paid generally 4 per cent or 5 per cent. That there was no rise in customs charges for over 100 years seems unlikely. It is probable that Bayezid, in taking over areas such as Menteşe and Aydın, did seek to increase the revenue at least slightly, bearing in mind that he did introduce various controls on the flow of goods, banning, for example, the export of grain from his territories. Similarly, it is hard to imagine that the much enlarged empire under Murad II charged the same rates as those of Murad I. One document from the reign of Mehmed II refers to 4 per cent being charged on Muslims and tributaries and not more than 5 per cent on non-tributaries in Gelibolu 'adet üzre' (according to custom).[67] 'adet üzre' may simply be formula here or may refer to what had been charged by the previous sultan. A more convincing explanation of the figures given by Badoer is that they represent a generous concession granted to favoured western merchants, such as the Genoese and the Venetians. Such a concession of 2 per cent or 3 per cent seems possible. In the early 1480s tributaries were charged at 2 per cent in contrast with the 4 per cent levied on non-Muslims and non-tributaries.[68] Perhaps western merchants such as the Genoese and Venetians were, in the 1430s, granted rates in line with those levied on tributaries in the early 1480s. One further argument against there being a significant rise in Ottoman customs charges under Mehmed II is that there does not appear to be any trace of complaints from Genoese merchants in extant archival material. Under such circumstances one would have expected the complaints to be vociferous.

Apart from customs charges, western merchants trading within the Ottoman empire were affected by state control of the flow of commodities. Under Mehmed II there was clearly control of goods. State monopolies were imposed on various commodities, such as timber in the second half of the fifteenth century when the monopoly on the timber trade between

---

[64] 1481.viii.26/ix.24 = Anhegger and İnalcık, *Kanunname*, no. 55, p. 79; Beldiceanu, *Actes*, vol. I, no. 56, clause 1, p. 151.

[65] 1482.i.20 = Anhegger and İnalcık, *Kanunname*, no. 56, p. 80; Beldiceanu, *Actes*, vol. I, no. 57, clause 2, p. 152.

[66] 1454–63 or 1479–81 = Anhegger and İnalcık, *Kanunname*, no. 30, pp. 40–1; Beldiceanu, *Actes*, vol. I, no. 31, clause 2, p. 104.

[67] no date = Anhegger and İnalcık, *Kanunname*, no. 45, p. 63; Beldiceanu, *Actes*, vol. I, no. 46, clause 9, p. 135.

[68] 1481.viii.26/ix.24 = Anhegger and İnalcık, *Kanunname*, no. 55, pp. 78–9; Beldiceanu, *Actes*, vol. I, no. 56, pp. 151–2; 1482.i.20 = Anhegger and İnalcık, *Kanunname*, no. 56, p. 80; Beldiceanu, *Actes*, vol. I, no. 57, clause 2, p. 152.

Antalya and Egypt was farmed out to individuals.[69] The sale of soap imported from the west and soap production at Foça were controlled.[70] However, such controls were not new. After his takeover of Kütahya in 1381, Murad I imposed restrictions on alum export. This affected Venetian merchants, for in 1384 the Venetian senate instructed its ambassador to ensure Venetian loading and exporting of rock alum from Ottoman territories, and to request a reduction in the price of alum fixed by the sultan.[71]

Under Murad I's son and successor, Bayezid, the grain trade was controlled and its export forbidden in 1390, after the Ottoman capture of Menteşe and Aydın.[72] Bayezid also forbade the export of grain from Macedonia.[73] That the export of grain from Turkish ports in this period was not always free is clear from a case brought before the *podestà* of Pera, Antonio Leardo, by a Venetian citizen, Lodisio (Alvise) Bragadino, against a Genoese *burgensis* of Pera, Jane de Draperiis. The dispute concerned grain sold by Jane to Lodisio which had not apparently been delivered at the agreed time or place. Lodisio therefore wanted the grain handed over at ports either in Grecia or in Turchia where he specified two places only, Camalı or this side of Scorpiata ('Scorpiata citra'), it being known that Lodisio always had free passage from these places for that quantity of grain.[74] This seems to indicate that, apart from the two ports of Camalı and Scorpiata, there was a restriction on grain exports from Turkish ports.[75] The reason why this did not apply to these two specific ports is not clear unless it was due to some personal arrangement which Lodisio had either with Bayezid or with a local official.

The prohibition on grain export, along with that of timber and horses, existed in 1400 when the emir of Aydın[76] approached the Venetians for support against his brothers in any potential power struggle. Through his ambassador in Crete he assured the Venetians that they were welcome to trade in the beylik, exporting whatever commodities they wished apart from

[69] İnalcık, 'Commerce', p. 47.

[70] İnalcık, 'Ticaret tarihine dair vesikalar', no. 9, p. 700; Marie Magdeleine Lefebvre, 'Quinze firmans du Sultan Mehmed le Conquérant', *Revue des Etudes Islamiques* 39, 9 (1971), 160–1.

[71] 1384.vii.22 = Thomas (ed.), *Diplomatarium*, vol. II, no. 116, p. 194.

[72] 1390.iii.6 = Chrysostomides (ed.), *Monumenta Peloponnesiaca*, no. 68, p. 138. Dukas, *Historia Byzantina*, p. 47, ll. 11–13; Dukas, *Historia Turcobyzantina*, p. 75, ll. 16–17; Dukas, *Decline and Fall*, p. 81; 1390.vi.28 = Noiret, *Documents*, p. 36, 1396.ii.17 = *ibid.*, p. 74, 1400.viii.16 = *ibid.*, pp. 110–11.

[73] Thiriet, *Romanie vénitienne*, p. 364.

[74] 1390.iii.2 = Musso, *Navigazione*, no. 5, pp. 236–40: 'ipsis duobus locis comprehensis, ita quod semper libere dictus Lodisius a dictis locis de dicto frumento supradicte quantitatis liberam habeat'.

[75] Fleet, 'Grain exports', 286.

[76] The emir, described as lord Zalapi (i.e. Çelebi), son of Bayezid, is identified by Thiriet as probably Süleyman, then governor of Aydın (Thiriet, *Régestes*, vol. II, p. 12), but by Zachariadou as probably Ertoğrul (Zachariadou, 'Ertogrul Bey', p. 158).

cereals, timber and horses. Venice advised the Cretan authorities to try and have this prohibition on horses and grain lifted.[77]

Economic policy under Mehmed II therefore does not appear to have differed greatly from that followed by his predecessors and cannot be viewed as a determining factor in any decline in trade relations between the Genoese and the Ottoman state. Indeed during Mehmed's reign trade with the Genoese continued and Italians were still in evidence at his court.[78] But by the end of the century there was a decline. While the Ottoman advance may have been on occasion disruptive, the lose of trading colonies discouraging,[79] and perhaps the imposition of the *cizye*[80] may have had some influence, these factors in themselves can hardly explain the movement of the Genoese out of the Ottoman market. Presumably this was due to other factors unconnected with any Ottoman policy and resulting more from Genoese motivation to find richer pickings in the newly discovered markets of the New World.

[77] 1400.iii.19 : Thiriet, *Régestes*, vol. II, doc. 988, pp. 12–13; Noiret, *Documents*, pp. 110–11.

[78] 1454.iii.11 = Belgrano, 'Documenti', no. 154, p. 263.

[79] Apart from the loss of such colonies, there was also the need to defend them. At the end of 1454 the Maona of Chios received permission from the authorities in Genoa to increase commercial taxes to raise money for defence against the Turks: Giustina Olgiati, 'I Genovesi in Oriente dopo la caduta di Costantinopoli', *Studi Balcanici – Quaderni di Chio* 8 (Rome, 1989) 58.

[80] Mehmed imposed the *cizye* when he took Mitylene in 1460, Tursun Bey, *The History of Mehmed the Conqueror by Tursun Beg*, ed. Halil İnalcık and Rhoads Murphey (Minneapolis and Chicago, 1978); fo. 102b, l. 13; Tursun Bey, *Tursun Bey Tarih-i Ebü'l-Feth*, ed. Mertol Tulum (Istanbul, 1977), p. 120.

Conclusion: The Latin contribution to the early Ottoman economy

In the period from the early establishment of the Ottoman state to the fall of Constantinople, the lands under Turkish control played a significant role in the economy of the eastern Mediterranean. Commerce with the Turks contributed considerably to the wealth of the state of Genoa. At the same time, the role of the Genoese merchant within the early Ottoman economy was important, and Genoese capital and know-how played a role in its development. Successive Ottoman rulers were eager to cultivate and encourage commercial relations with the Genoese and other Latin trading states, an attitude that is also evident after 1453.

The Genoese merchant was an integral part of the embryonic Ottoman economy, not merely as an outside factor coming, taking and leaving, but as one of the functionaries of the state, for Genoese and other Latin merchants operated as tax farmers for the Ottomans. That Latins were acting in such a capacity at an early date seems supported by a Venetian document from 1390. In March of that year Francesco Quirino received his instructions from the senate as Venetian ambassador to the Ottoman ruler Bayezid I. Quirino was to present the condolences of Venice for the death of Bayezid's father Murad I, to assure the new ruler of Venice's pleasure at his accession and to express the senate's desire to maintain good relations with him in the future.

Not unnaturally, one of the senate's main concerns was its trade relations with the Ottoman state. What Venice wanted, and what Quirino was instructed to try and obtain, was free access to Ottoman ports, no controls on grain exporting, and no tax on transactions within Ottoman territory. Envisaging that Bayezid might not grant an exemption from tax for Venetian grain exports, the senate gave Quirino instructions that he might accept a tax of up to 1 *hyperpyron* per *modio*. Quirino was also to ensure that, as in the days of Murad I, Venetian merchants could trade safely within Ottoman lands, with freedom of movement and security of persons and goods. He was to obtain letters from Bayezid to ensure that these merchants did not have to go through the hands of other Franks who had in the past mistreated Venetian subjects. It was better, the senate said, to go through the hands of the Turks than through the hands of such Franks. If Venetian merchants did have to deal with other people in the ports, they should have to deal through Venetians.[1]

These instructions given to Quirino concerning Venetian transactions in Turkish territory seem to mean that Franks were acting in some capacity for the Ottoman ruler in his ports, and that these Franks were not, at this point, Venetian, but, on the contrary, were hostile to Venetian interests. It also appears that Turks too were acting in the same capacity, at least on occasion, for the senate regarded it as preferable to go through Turkish hands rather than through those of the Franks. Further, the instructions indicate the possibility of Venetians acting in this capacity for if it proved necessary to go through agents Quirino was urged that these should be Venetian. Thus, presumably, Venetian agents were feasible, even if not acting as such here.

Although this document does not state in what capacity these Franks were acting, it seems highly likely that they were tax farmers. Aşıkpaşazade refers to a tax farmer ('amaldar') who was at Gelibolu at the beginning of the reign of Murad II.[2] It is very probable that tax farmers were operating in Ottoman territory at an earlier period. Again according to Aşıkpaşazade, the *pençik* tax, the taking of one slave out of every five captives,[3] and the imposition of a tax on slaves of 25 *akçe* per head[4] was introduced during the reign of Murad I when a certain Kara Rüstem from Karaman pointed out that the Ottoman ruler was losing revenue due to his failure to levy the *pençik*. Murad therefore allowed the introduction of both the *pençik* and the tax of 25 *akçe* per slave, and Kara Rüstem set himself up at Gelibolu to collect the tax. Kara Rüstem's position thus seems very much to have been that of a tax farmer who had gained the right from the Ottoman ruler to collect the tax. While, as Colin Imber has so sharply pointed out, Aşıkpaşazade was not a contemporary of the events in this period, and one cannot take his account of events as an undisputed truth, it is at least here an

---

[1] 1390.iii.6 = Chrysostomides (ed.), *Monumenta Peloponnesiaca*, no. 68, p. 138: 'non sit necesse nostratibus, qui ibunt in locis sibi subiectis quod vadant per manus aliquorum Franchorum qui emunt de suis scalis et qui temporibus retroactis non bene tractarunt nostros. Et sis potius contentus velle ire per manus Turchorum quam per manus talium Franchorum, reducendo tibi ad memoriam quod quando posses obtinere quod nostratos non haberent agere ad ipsas suas scallas cum aliquibus personis, et quando pur deberent agere cum aliquibus personis, ipsi haberent agere cum nostris, hoc summe nobis placeret.'

[2] Aşıkpaşazade, *Altosmanische Chronik*, bab 87, p. 88.

[3] See Cemal Kafadar, *Between Two Worlds. The Construction of the Ottoman State* (Berkeley, 1995), pp. 112–13 for details about the introduction of the *pençik*. Kafadar points out that this tax cannot have been taken during the period when Gelibolu was not in Ottoman hands, and therefore dates this introduction to post-1376/77 and the reconquest of the town by Ottoman forces.

[4] Aşıkpaşazade, *Altosmanische Chronik*, bab 46, p. 50.

indication of the introduction of tax farming some time towards the end of the fourteenth century.[5]

Western merchants are known to have been acting as tax farmers for the Ottoman state in the fifteenth century.[6] Francesco de Draperiis held the *appalto* of the alum mines of Turchia and Grecia from Murad II[7] and in 1452 Paris Giustiniano, Paolo Bocardo and Benedetto Salvaigo promised to pay Francesco if he obtained or renewed this *appalto*[8]. At the beginning of 1476 the customs of Istanbul on wheat, barley, oats, millet and flour were sold for three years to Kesaridoğlu Kaysara, Galatalu Petr Uri (or Petrauri) (پتر اورى) and to 'Amiloğlu Menteşe, for 1 million *akçe* and 12,000 *akçe* for *resm-i berat* (berat tax).[9] The name Petr Uri or Petrauri is clearly not Turkish but could well be Italian, Petro Auri or Petro Doria perhaps, and, being an inhabitant of Galata, it is possible that the person concerned was Genoese. Kesaridoğlu Kaysara was, judging from the name, probably Greek.

Greeks bought tax farms from the Ottoman sultans after the conquest of Constantinople. In 1476, for example, Palaloğoz Kandroz, Lefteri bin Galbanoz, Andiri bin Halkokandil, Manul Palaloğoz, and Ya'kub bought the farm of customs in ports including Istanbul, Galata, Gelibolu and Mudanya and the brokerage for cloth in Istanbul and Galata.[10] Several years later, in 1482, the farm of the customs of Samsun and Sinop was sold to Tebrizoğlu Ermeni Ya'kub and Kostandin 'nam zimmi'.[11] In 1476 the farm of the Istanbul customs was sold for three years to a four-man consortium of Muslims for 13 million *akçe*. To win the tax farm the consortium outbid a five-man consortium of Greeks who had offered 11 million *akçe* (*c*.245,000 *ducats*).[12] In 1480 Anton oğli Skroz(?) from Galata held the tax farm of the soap factories in Ankara.[13] At a much later date, at the end of the sixteenth century, *mültezim*s of mastic in Chios were often

---

[5] Colin Imber, 'The legend of Osman Gazi', in Elizabeth Zachariadou (ed.), *The Ottoman Emirate (1300–1389)* (Rethymnon, 1993), p. 72: 'As historical records, the early Ottoman chronicles are without value.'

[6] There are many examples from the second half of the fifteenth century of Christians buying tax farms from the Ottoman sultan Beldiceanu, *Actes*, vol. II, pp. 142–3.

[7] 1449.iv.1 = ASG, Notai, Tommaso de Recco, Sc. 77, filza 1, fo. LI.

[8] 1452.x(?).28 = ASG, Not. Bernardo de Ferrari, in Argenti, *Chios*, vol. III, no. 222, p. 659.

[9] 1476.i.14 = Anhegger and İnalcık, *Kanunname*, no. 33, p. 44; Beldiceanu, *Actes*, vol. I, no. 33, pp. 108–9. The same names appear also in Anhegger and İnalcık, *Kanunname*, no. 34, p. 46, and Beldiceanu, *Actes*, vol. I, no. 35, p. 111. See also facsimile 76a and 80a in Anhegger and İnalcık, *Kanunname*.

[10] 1476.i.28/ii.6 = Anhegger and İnalcık, *Kanunname*, no. 53, pp. 73–4; Beldiceanu, *Actes*, vol. I, no. 54, p. 146. The name 'Galbanoz' is given as 'Galyanoz' in Beldiceanu *Actes*.

[11] 1482.i.20 = Anhegger and İnalcık, *Kanunname*, no. 56, p. 80; Beldiceanu, *Actes*, vol. I, no. 57, p. 108.

[12] H. İnalcık, 'Capital formation in the Ottoman empire', *Journal of European History* 19 (1969), 124.

[13] 884.Zilka'.8/ 1480.1.21 = İnalcık, 'Ticaret tarihine dair vesikalar', no. 25, p. 82: 'Mahruse-i Ankara sabun hanelerin mukata'aya dutan Anton oğlı Skroz [?] 'an Galata.'

Jewish and the *emin* (the sultan's agent), was, according to a *mukataa defteri*, required to be a non-Muslim.[14] This is a striking example of the continuation of a system operating before Ottoman conquest which the Porte simply incorporated into its own administration. Before the Ottoman conquest, the Maona of Chios had often relied on Jewish money, in consequence of which Jews came to share in the mastic produced. When the Ottomans took over the island, the mastic crop became a *hass* of the *Valide Sultan*, and Jewish involvement continued.

It is clear therefore that the Ottomans did use tax farmers at an early date and that, certainly in the later fifteenth century, these tax farmers could be Latins. Latin merchants were active as tax farmers in Muslim lands in the thirteenth century. Catalans administered the *gabella* in Tunis where, in 1285, under the peace of Panissar, the sultan of Tunis agreed to grant the *gabella* of Tunis to a Catalan in preference to anyone else. According to Dufourcq, this seems to have meant that a Catalan became a sort of 'fermier général' of the customs taxes of Tunis.[15] In the same year the king of Aragon's instructions to his new ambassador to Tunis, Betran de Mesurata, were to ensure that the new consul was to take on as soon as possible the farm of the *gabella* of Tunis ('à ferme la gabelle de Tunis').[16] Two years later Alfonso III sent Conrad Lancia as ambassador to Tunis. Lancia was to make sure that the farming of the *gabella* was reserved for subjects of Aragon.[17] Similar instructions were given, again by Alfonso III, to the ambassador Bernat de Belvis in 1290. Catalans were to be given preference in the farming of the *gabella* over Genoese and Pisans while those who took the *gabella* were to be allowed to settle by monthly payments rather than one single one.[18] In 1291 the *gabella* of wine there was granted to Cervia de Riera.[19] In the same period, Marco Caroso bought the *gabella* of wine from the sultan of Tunis for 34,000 *bessants*. The Sultan later withdrew the *gabella* from him, selling it instead to a Pisan, thereby causing a Venetian complaint about Caroso's treatment.[20] The sultan behaved similarly to a Pisan, Raynerio Martello, to whom he at first sold the *gabella* on wine and from whom he later withdrew it.[21] In 1305 a Genoese held the *gabella* of Algiers.[22]

Taking the fact that the Ottomans did use tax farmers, that there were

---

[14] Suraiya Faroqhi, 'Rural society in Anatolia and the Balkans during the sixteenth century I' in *Turcica* 9, 1 (1977), 181.

[15] C. E. Dufourcq, *L'Espagne catalane et le Maghrib aux XIIIe et XIVe siècles* (Paris, 1966), p. 273, and nn. 5 and 6.

[16] Dufourcq, *L'Espagne catalane*, p. 274.

[17] Dufourcq, *L'Espagne catalane*, p. 282.

[18] Dufourcq, *L'Espagne catalane*, p. 292.

[19] Dufourcq, *L'Espagne catalane*, pp. 298, 523, 549.

[20] Tafel and Thomas, *Urkunden*, vol. III, no. 391, pp. 392–3.

[21] Tafel and Thomas, *Urkunden*, vol. III, no. 391, pp. 395–6.

[22] Dufourcq, *L'Espagne catalane*, pp. 368 n. 3, p. 452.

Latin tax farmers operating in Ottoman lands in the fifteenth century and that Latin tax farmers were active in Muslim lands in the thirteenth century, it seems feasible to argue that the Franks in the document of 1390 were tax farmers acting for the Ottoman ruler.

The next question that arises is who these Franks were. Clearly they were not Venetian, for the Franks whose hands the Venetian merchants had to go through did not always treat them well. This could indicate that they were Genoese, for relations between the two were often strained while Genoese relations with the Turks were, in contract, usually good. It is perhaps significant in this context that the tax farmer at Gelibolu referred to by Aşıkpaşazade early on in the reign of Murad II was instrumental in organising Genoese transport for Murad and his forces over the straits in their pursuit of Düzme Mustafa. Aşıkpaşazade describes him as having good contacts with the Genoese.[23]

While the Latin agents in the 1390 document were thus probably Genoese, it seems from this document either that Venetians could also act in this capacity or that the Venetian senate wished to bring this situation about. The fact that the senate instructed Quirino that, when it was necessary to deal with agents, it would be better if they were Venetian, indicates that there was some possibility that the Venetians too could farm taxes. Possibly the Venetians were here attempting to establish a new arrangement under the new Ottoman ruler, an alteration of the position that had existed under his predecessor, and one in which Venetians could operate as tax farmers. This perhaps could be taken as indicating that Venetians had not farmed taxes under Murad I.

Taking it therefore that these Franks, probably Genoese, were tax farmers, one needs next to ask what they were farming. As they were operating in the ports, it seem reasonable to assume that they were tax farmers of customs duties. As the above examples of foreign tax farmers operating for the Ottoman state in the later fifteenth century show, Latins were farming customs tax collection. Further, as Latin merchants were trading internationally, they would have been concentrated in the ports in the first place, and naturally interested in collection of customs dues.

The presence of western merchants in such a capacity needs some explanation. With tax farms there is one obvious point: those that bought them had to have money, something the large trading families from western city states would have had. They would also have had expertise. It would seem that the Ottomans were able to put this foreign wealth and expertise to

[23] Aşıkpaşazade, *Altosmanische Chronik*, bab 87, p. 88. Aşıkpaşazade does not actually name the Genoese. However, Dukas gives a full account of the contacts between Murad and Giovanni Adorno, the Genoese *podestà* of Phokaea (modern Foça), contacts of which he was well informed as he composed the correspondence between them (Dukas, *Historia Byzantina*, pp. 163–5, 178–9; Dukas, *Historia Turcobyzantina*, pp. 209–11, 225–7; Dukas, *Decline and Fall*, pp. 150–1, 158–60

use in the administration of their own empire, not merely in the initial stages of its development, but well after the conquest of Constantinople and the firm establishment of a large and flourishing state.

A tax farm had distinct advantages for the state which thereby gained an assured income without the attendant risks. The risk factor presumably explains in part why Turkish governments were interested in selling tax farms, for they were thereby guaranteed a fixed sum, were spared any problems involved in collection, and ran no risk of reduced profits on a fluctuating market. At the same time, of course, they could lose out if the market at any particular time entered a boom, in which case profits would naturally accrue to the tax farmers. In the second half of the fifteenth century the sultan apparently preferred to farm out mines, thereby assuring a secure source of income without any capital investment in what was after all a high-risk enterprise.[24] It seems that in the later period when in a difficult financial position, the Ottoman government chose to increase the use of tax farming as a way of avoiding risk, which fell instead on the tax farmers.[25] In the sixteenth century the Ottoman state, squeezed financially by an increasing population and rising prices induced by the European price inflation, sought to increase its revenue. One of the measures it adopted was to expand the sale of tax farms.[26] In the eighteenth century the Ottoman government expanded the use of tax farming as a method of resolving financial problems.[27]

The imposition of a tax farm could also have been a positive stimulant to trade, though it is a system always open to abuse, particularly when the central authority is weakened.[28] If someone bought a tax farm of, for example, customs taxes on certain commodities, it would then be very much in his own interests to encourage the import or export of those commodities as much as possible. In Tunis at the end of the thirteenth century, the sultan, on discovering how much wine the Venetian tax farmer Marco Caroso was handling, took the *gabella* on wine away from him, selling it instead for 10,000 *bessants* more, to a Pisan merchant.[29]

As the experience of Marco Caroso shows, a tax farm could have its

---

[24] Beldiceanu, *Actes*, vol. II, p. 141.

[25] Murat Cızakça, 'Ottoman economy and society as reflected by tax-farming records (16th–18th centuries)', paper presented at the International Symposium on The State, Decentralisation and Tax-Farming, 1500–1850: The Ottoman Empire, Iran and India held at Munich, 2–5 May 1990, referred to by Halil Berktay, 'Three Empires and the Societies they Governed: Iran, India and the Ottoman Empire', in Berktay and Faroqhi, *State and Peasant*, pp. 252–3.

[26] İslamoğlu-İnan and Keyder, 'Agenda', p. 56; Immanuel Wallerstein, Hale Decdeli and Reşat Kasaba, 'The Incorporation of the Ottoman Empire into the World-Economy', in İslamoğlu-İnan (ed.), *World Economy*, p. 90.

[27] Ariel Saltzmann, 'An Ancien Regime revisited: "privatization" and political economy in the 18th-century Ottoman empire', *Politics and Society* 21 (1993), 393–423.

[28] For the adverse effect of tax farming on trade in the nineteenth century see Elena Frangakis-Syrett, 'Implementation of the 1838 Anglo-Turkish convention on İzmir's trade: European and minority merchants', *New Perspectives on Turkey* 7 (Spring 1992), 91–102.

[29] Pre-1300 = Tafel and Thomas, *Urkunden*, vol. III, no. 391, p. 393.

disadvantages for those who bought it. In 1443 farmers of the tax on wine in Crete were compensated for the losses they had suffered in the preceding year because of the ban imposed on Venetian shipping to the island.[30] In 1388 Checho Bertoldo, who had bought various taxes at auction in Coron, complained that, due to the loss of ships and to the Turkish presence which deterred ships from sailing to Coron, he had lost much income and was thus unable to settle the remaining 200 *ducats* he owed for the tax farm. He was therefore allowed to pay in instalments of 40 *ducats* per annum.[31] Under Mehmed II, however, no leniency was shown to defaulting tax farmers. Various *'âmiller* who did not settle the amounts they had undertaken to pay were put to death.[32] Tax farmers were also on occasion attacked. Three Ragusan merchants who had bought the customs of Srebreniča from the Serbian despot were attacked, driven out and the customs money and accounts taken.[33]

It seems, therefore, that in reign of Murad I, and probably before, the Ottomans were using Latin, probably Genoese, tax farmers in their ports presumably to collect customs dues. The Ottomans thus availed themselves of the capital and expertise of such merchants, ensuring a fixed income for the state without attendant risks while at the same time creating a climate in which individuals were encouraged to greater activity, so stimulating trade.

This Ottoman ability to utilise the skills and money of outside traders may in some way have played a part in the successful early development of the state, for, while it is true that without military success there could not have been an empire, it is also true that military strength alone cannot be the sole explanation for the continuing Ottoman success. Another factor in the successful creation of a lasting state may well have been Ottoman ability to absorb from those they conquered systems that were in place and which worked, and to use the capital and know-how of foreign merchants.

The Ottomans do appear to have had a more dynamic economic policy than other Turkish rulers in the area. In contrast to Menteşe and Aydın, which appear to have been fairly acquiescent in their relations with western merchants, prepared to accept, for example, the situation Venice wanted, the Ottomans seem by and large to have been more prepared to dictate terms. They were apparently more aware of their economic strength and of the importance of the Turkish market to western trading nations, and did seek to use their economic assets to strengthen their political position. Bayezid I, for example, banned the export of grain and seems to have imposed restrictions over port access. Ottoman merchants may also have traded outside their own territories, for Bayezid, in his negotiations for a

---

[30] 1443.v.27 = Noiret, *Documents*, p. 404.
[31] 1388 = Chrysostomides, *Monumenta Peloponnesiaca*, no. 36, p. 85.
[32] M. Yayyib Gökbilgin, *XV–XVI Asırlarda Edirne ve Paşa Livası, Vakıflar–Mülker–Muktaalar* (Istanbul, 1952), no. 3, p. 135, no. 22, p. 152.
[33] 1444.ii.5 : Krekić, *Dubrovnik*, no. 1034, p. 336.

peace with the Hospitallers in 1393, required that he should be able to sell slaves in Rhodes without any restrictions,[34] a stipulation which implies that Ottoman traders were active in the markets on the Aegean islands. Ottoman merchants may well also have traded in Cairo, for Muslim slave merchants buying in the Turkish markets for the Mamluk sultanate travelled with their merchandise to Egypt.[35]

The importance of the Genoese contribution to the early economic development of this state seems, from the available sources, to have been of significance. To the early economic structure of this state the Genoese brought their wealth and their know-how. The early Ottoman state was therefore a field in which Ottoman economic acumen met Genoese capital, expertise and self-interest. Far from being a history shrouded in darkness, pierced only by battles and the clouds of an army on the march, the early Ottoman state needs to be seen not as something distinctly eastern as opposed to western, or viewed in the light of a western Christendom–Muslim Turkish conflict, but to be understood as an integral part of the Mediterranean economy. While it is undoubtedly true that the Turk was, for much of western Christendom, an infidel enemy, he was also the ruler of a huge trading bloc, and one to which merchants such as the Genoese flocked. Money largely formed the basis of the relationship between the Genoese and the Turks and this, rather than any religious scruple, dictated relations.

[34] Luttrell, 'Hospitallers', pp. 96–7, citing a document from the Malta archives.
[35] Piloti, L'Egypte, p. 15.

Exchange rates

Table A1.1. Ratio of Turkish *akçe* to *hyperpyron*

Date	*Akçe*	*Hyperpyron*	Source
1436.iv.8	11 *aspers* 2 *tornexi*	1	Badoer, *Libro*, col. 48 p. 96, col. 29 p. 59
1436.iv.10	11 *aspers* 2 *tornexi*	1	*ibid.*, col. 48 p. 96, col. 3 p. 7
1436.iv.30	11 *aspers* 2 *tornexi*	1	*ibid.*, col. 56 p. 112, col. 3 p. 7
1436.ix.7	11 *aspers* 6 *tornexi*	1	*ibid.*, col. 3 p. 6, col. 7 p. 15
1436.xi.8	11 *aspers* 4 *tornexi*	1	*ibid.*, col. 33 p. 66, col. 16 p. 33
1436.xi.8	11 *aspers* 4 *tornexi*	1	*ibid.*, col. 33 p. 66, col. 18 p. 37
1436.xi.8	11 *aspers* 4 *tornexi*	1	*ibid.*, col. 33 p. 66, col. 33 p. 67
1436.xii.5	11 *aspers* 4 *tornexi*	1	*ibid.*, col. 16 p. 32, col. 29 p. 59
1436.xii.7	11 *aspers* 4 *tornexi*	1	*ibid.*, col. 33 p. 66, col. 16 p. 33
1437.ii.17	11 *aspers*	1	*ibid.*, col. 175 p. 352, col. 125 p. 253 (the cross-reference is to col. 134 but should be to col. 125)
1437.iii.11	11 *aspers* 2 *tornexi*	1	*ibid.*, col. 36 p. 72, col. 55 p. 111
1437.iii.13	100 *aspers*	9	*ibid.*, col. 63 p. 126, col. 55 p. 111
1437.iii.16	11 *aspers* 9 *tornexi*	1	*ibid.*, col. 61 p. 122, col. 57 p. 115
1437.iii.31	11 *aspers* mancho *tornexi* 5	1	*ibid.*, col. 125 p. 252, col. 186 p. 375
1437.iii.31	11 *aspers*	1	*ibid.*, col. 125 p. 252, col. 204 p. 411
1437.iii.31	11 *aspers*	1	*ibid.*, col. 125 p. 252, col. 204 p. 411

Table A1.1. (*contd*)

Date	*Akçe*	*Hyperpyron*	Source
1437.iv.13	11 *aspers* 1.5 *tornexi*	1	*ibid.*, col. 55 p. 110 (cross-references to col. 48, but there is no corresponding entry there)
1437,iv.30	100 *aspers*	9	*ibid.*, col. 57 p. 114, col. 43 p. 87
1437.iv.30	11 *aspers* 1.5 *tornexi*	1	*ibid.*, col. 55 p. 110, col. 36 p. 73
1437.iv.30	11 *aspers* 1.5 *tornexi*	1	*ibid.*, col. 56 p. 112, col. 36 p. 73
1437.iv.30	100 *aspers*	9	*ibid.*, col. 56 p. 112, col. 57 p. 115
1437.vii.9	100 *aspers*	9	*ibid.*, col. 61 p. 122 (cross-references to col. 57 but there is no corresponding entry there)
1437.vii.9	100 *aspers*	9	*ibid.*, col. 61 p. 122 (cross-references to col. 57 but there is no corresponding entry there)
1437.vii.18	11 *aspers* mancho *tornexi* 5.5	1	*ibid.*, col. 125 p. 252, col. 183 p. 369
1437.vii.18	11 *aspers*	1	*ibid.*, col. 48 p. 96, col. 57 p. 115
1437.vii.18	11 *aspers*	1	*ibid.*, col. 48 p. 96, col. 57 p. 115
1437.vii.20	11 *aspers*	1	*ibid.*, col. 48 p. 96, col. 75 p. 153
1437.vii.23	11 *aspers* 4 *tornexi*	1	*ibid.*, col. 61 p. 122, col. 33 p. 67
1437.vii.23	11 *aspers*	1	*ibid.*, col. 48 p. 96, col. 75 p. 153
1437.vii.24	11 *aspers*	1	*ibid.*, col. 92 p. 186, col. 88 p. 179
1437.viii.5	11 *aspers*	1	*ibid.*, col. 175 p. 352, col. 125 p. 253
1437.viii.5	11 *aspers*	1	*ibid.*, col. 175 p. 352, col. 125 p. 253
1437.viii.5	11 *aspers*	1	*ibid.*, col. 175 p. 352, col. 125 p. 253
1437.viii.5	11 *aspers*	1	*ibid.*, col. 175 p. 352, col. 125 p. 253
1437.viii.21	11 *aspers*	1	*ibid.*, col. 93 p. 188, col. 92 p. 187
1437.ix.2	11 *aspers* mancho *tornexi* 5.5	1	*ibid.*, col. 125 p. 252, col. 231 p. 465 (c.231 = 1 *hyperpyron* = 11 *aspers mancho* 5 *tornexi*)
1437,ix.18	11 *aspers*	1	*ibid.*, col. 82 p. 166, col. 175 p. 353

Table A1.1. *(contd)*

Date	*Akçe*	*Hyperpyron*	Source
1437.ix.20	100 *aspers*	9	*ibid.*, col. 57 p. 114, col. 60 p. 121
1437.ix.20	100 *aspers*	9	*ibid.*, col. 57 p. 114, col. 43 p. 87
1437.ix.20	100 *aspers*	9	*ibid.*, col. 57 p. 114, col. 60 p. 121
1437.ix.20	100 *aspers*	9	*ibid.*, col. 116 p. 234, col. 57 p. 115
1437.x.9	11 *aspers*	1	*ibid.*, col. 92 p. 186, col. 47 p. 93
1437.xi.28	11 *aspers*	1	*ibid.*, col. 131 p. 264, col. 46 p. 93
1437.xi.28	11 *aspers*	1	*ibid.*, col. 131 p. 264, col. 46 p. 93
1437.xii.23	11 *aspers mancho* 1 *tornexe*	1	*ibid.*, col. 167 p. 336, col. 131 p. 265
1437.xii.24	11 *aspers* mancho 1 *tornexe*	1	*ibid.*, col. 167 p. 336, col. 131 p. 265
1438.iii.20	11 *aspers* mancho *tornexi* 5	1	*ibid.*, col. 197 p. 396, col. 186 p. 375
1438.iii.20	10.6 *aspers*	1	*ibid.*, col. 197 p. 396, col. 186 p. 375
1438.vi.1	11 *aspers* mancho *tornexi* 5.5	1	*ibid.*, col. 186 p. 374, col. 201 p. 405
1438.vi.7	11 *aspers* mancho *tornexi* 6	1	*ibid.*, col. 194 p. 390, col. 186 p. 375
1438.iv.16	10.5 *aspers* 3 *tornexi*	1	*ibid.*, col. 316 p. 634, col. 155 p. 313
1438.viii.5	11 *aspers*	1	*ibid.*, col. 191 p. 384, col. 175 p. 353
1438.viii.18	10.5 *aspers*	1	*ibid.*, col. 227 p. 456, col. 61 p. 123
1438.viii.18	10.5 *aspers*	1	*ibid.*, col. 230 p. 462, col. 89 p. 181
1438.ix.18	10.5 *aspers*	1	*ibid.*, col. 247 p. 496, col. 175 p. 353
1438.ix.18	10.5 *aspers*	1	*ibid.*, col. 247 p. 496, col. 175 p. 353
1438.xii.13	10.5 *aspers* 2 *tornexi*	1	*ibid.*, col. 227 p. 456, col. 209 p. 421
1438.xii.28	10.5 *aspers*	1	*ibid.*, col. 134 p. 270, col. 227 p. 457

Table A1.2. Ratio of *akçe* of Samsun to 1 *hyperpyron*

Date	*Akçe*	Source
1437.xi.28	19	Badoer, *Libro*, col. 102 p. 206, col. 152 p. 307. col. 102 has 17 *aspers* per *hyperpyron*. col. 152 has 19, the correct figure as shown by the calculation of the figures given in the entry
1437.xii.18	19	*ibid.*, col. 44 p. 188, col. 152 p. 307
1437.xii.18	19	*ibid.*, col. 44 p. 188, col. 152 p. 307
1437.xii.18	19	*ibid.*, col. 152 p. 306, col. 44 p. 89
1437.xii.18	19	*ibid.*, col. 152 p. 306, col. 152 p. 307

Table A1.3. Ratio of *akçe* of Trabzon to 1 *hyperpyron*

Date	*Akçe*	Source
1436.xi.5	33.3	Badoer, *Libro*, col. 21 p. 42, col. 7 p. 15
1436.xi.10	33.3	*ibid.*, col. 7 p. 14, col. 7 p. 15
1437.i.2	36	*ibid.*, col. 173 p. 348, col. 166 p. 335
1437.i.22	36	*ibid.*, col. 166 p. 334, col. 166 p. 335
1437.i.24	40	*ibid.*, col. 173 p. 348, col. 51 p. 103
1437.i.24	36	*ibid.*, col. 153 p. 308, col. 173 p. 349
1437.xii.5	36	*ibid.*, col. 153 p. 308, col. 51 p. 103
1437.xii.5	36	*ibid.*, col. 153 p. 308, col. 51 p. 103
1437.xii.5	36	*ibid.*, col. 153 p. 308, col. 51 p. 103
1437.xii.5	36	*ibid.*, col. 90 p. 182, col. 153 p. 309
1437.xii.18	40	*ibid.*, col. 51 p. 102, col. 166 p. 335
1437.xii.18	40	*ibid.*, col. 166 p. 334, col. 44 p. 89
1437.xii.18	40	*ibid.*, col. 166 p. 334, col. 152 p. 307
1438.iv.19	36	*ibid.*, col. 153 p. 308, col. 173 p. 349
1438.iv.19	36	*ibid.*, col. 153 p. 308, col. 153 p. 309
1438.iv.19	36	*ibid.*, col. 153 p. 308, col. 153 p. 309
1438.iv.19	36	*ibid.*, col. 185 p. 372, col. 153 p. 309
1438.iv.19	36	*ibid.*, col. 185 p. 372, col. 153 p. 309
1438.xii.8	36	*ibid.*, col. 278 p. 558, col. 185 p. 373
1438.xii.18	36	*ibid.*, col. 288 p. 578, col. 185 p. 373

Table A1.4. Ratio of *hyperpyron* to 1 Turkish *ducat*

Date	*Hyperpyra*	Source
1436.i.13	2 *hyperpyra* 1.5 *karati*	Badoer, *Libro*, col. 3 p. 7. The cross-reference is to col. 16 but there is no corresponding entry on that page. This and the next two entries are all part of the same transaction but with varying exchange rates
1436.i.13	2 *hyperpyra* 1 *karati* 2 *tornexi*	*ibid.*
1436.i.13	2 *hyperpyra* 2 *karati* 10 *tornexi*	*ibid.*
1436.ii.13	2 *hyperpyra* 10 *tornexi*	*ibid.*, col. 48 p. 96, col. 29 p. 59
1436.ii.20	2 *hyperpyra* 1.5 *karati*	*ibid.*, col. 3 p. 6, col. 48 p. 97
1436.ii.20	2 *hyperpyra* 1.5 *karati*	*ibid.*, col. 40 p. 80, col. 48 p. 97
1437.iii.8	2 *hyperpyra* 1.5 *karati*	*ibid.*, col. 51 p. 102, col. 48 p. 97 This and the next entry are the same transaction but with two different exchange rates
1437.iii.8	2 *hyperpyra* 2.5 *karati*	*ibid.*, col. 51 p. 102, col. 48 p. 97
1437.xi.2	2 *hyperpyra* 1.5 *karati*	*ibid.*, col. 40 p. 80, col. 48 p. 97
1438.iii.23	2 *hyperpyra*	*ibid.*, col. 180 p. 362, col. 186 p. 375

The price of slaves in Constantinople in the late 1430s

Table A2.1. *Price of slaves in Constantinople in the late 1430s*

Date	Description	Price	Source
1436.i.15	one female Russian ('sciava rossa'), *c.*16 years, called Maria, in sound health	114 *hyperpyra*	Badoer, *Libro*, col. 45 p. 90, col. 16 p. 33
1436.viii.7	eight slaves ('teste'), female Circassians and ? ('zirchase e avogaze'), five of whom were good and beautiful females, *c.*20–25 years, one other female was *c.*28 years, the other two were young boys ('garzone'), *c.*14 years, of clean and sound condition	91 *hyperpyra* each	*ibid.*, col. 45 p. 90, col. 50 p. 101 (they were sent to Venice)
1436.xi.23	one male slave ('sciavo avogaxo'), *c.*18 years, kept for work in the house, sold in sound condition	95 *hyperpyra*	*ibid.*, col. 45 p. 90, col. 141 p. 285
1437.i.24	two slaves ('teste') kept for service in the house, one of whom was a female Russian called Maria, *c.*16 years, and one male ? ('un sciavo avogaxo'), *c.*18 years	210 *hyperpyra*	*ibid.*, col. 172 p. 346, col. 45 p. 91
1437.ii.1	one female ('sciava'), *c.*20 years, Circassian, with some warts on her left hand	108 *hyperpyra*	*ibid.*, col. 178 p. 358, col. 169 p. 341
1437.iii.24	two Tatar slaves ('teste tartare'), one male, *c.*15 years, baptised and given the name Terzo, the other female, c.20 years, called Madalena, both in sound health	180 *hyperpyra* for the two	*ibid.*, col. 45 p. 90, col. 64 p. 129 (they were bartered for cloth)

Table A2.1. (*contd*)

Date	Description	Price	Source
1437.xi.12	one female Russian ('testa'), *c.*18 years, short stature, called Chatarina	110 *hyperpyra*	*ibid.*, col. 135 p. 272
1437.xi.12	one female Tatar ('testa'), *c.*18 years, tall, called Oraxi in her own language	135 *hyperpyra*	*ibid.*, col. 135 p. 272, col. 143 p. 289
1437.xi.21	one Russian male ('balaban'), *c.*20 years, ('desgreziado') castrated?	100 *hyperpyra*	*ibid.*, col. 135 p. 272, col. 143 p. 289
1437.xi.21	one male Tatar ('balaban'), *c.*26 years, of average height	100 *hyperpyra*	*ibid.*, col. 135 p. 272, col. 143 p. 289
1437.xii.10	one female Tatar ('sciava')	135 *hyperpyra*	*ibid.*, col. 143 p. 288, col. 148 p. 299
1437.xii.17	one male ('balaban')	100 *hyperpyra*	*ibid.*, col. 143 p. 288, col. 49 p. 99
1438.iii.17	one female Tatar, *c.*22 years	90 *hyperpyra*	*ibid.*, col. 172 p. 346, col. 169 p. 341
1438.vii.8	five slaves ('balabani'): two *c.*20 years, one *c.*25 years, two *c.*30 years	70 *hyperpyra* each	*ibid.*, col. 172 p. 346, col. 220 p. 443
1438.vii.16	seven slaves ('balabani') all aged between 20 and 25	80 *hyperpyra*	*ibid.*, col. 172 p. 346, col. 222 p. 447
1438.vii.26	slaves ('teste e balaban')	107.5 *hyperpyra* each	*ibid.*, col. 220 p. 442, col. 224 p. 451[a]
1438.vii.22	one male Tatar slave ('balaban tartaro')	74 *hyperpyra*	*ibid.*, col. 172 p. 346, col. 222 p. 447 (the slave was sent to Catalonia)
1438.x.2	thirteen slaves ('balabani')	11 at 74 *hyperpyra* 1 at 50 *hyperpyra* 1 at 30 *hyperpyra*	*ibid.*, col. 247 p. 496, col. 231 p. 465
1438.x.3	one slave ('balaban')	74 *hyperpyra*	*ibid.*, col. 247 p. 496, col. 231 p. 465
1438.x.3	one slave ('balaban')	73 *hyperpyra*	*ibid.*, col. 247 p. 496, col. 239 p. 465

[a] The entry concerns a partnership of merchants formed for a voyage to Majorca. Large numbers of slaves were involved, one merchant trading 150 slaves, worth 16,125 *hyperpyra*, another 19, worth 2,042.5 *hyperpyra*, another 13, worth 1,397.5 *hyperpyra*. At least some of these slaves were Tatars as one of the references is to a 'balaban tartaro'.

Table A2.1. (*contd*)

Date	Description	Price	Source
1438.x.11	del balaban da la quistion	74 *hyperpyra*	*ibid.*, col. 258 p. 518, col. 231 p. 465
1438.xi.22	one male Russian slave ('sciavo'), *c.*15 years	27 Venetian gold *ducat*s = 88 *hyperpyra* 14 *karati*	*ibid.*, col. 288 p. 578, col. 249 p. 501
1438.xii.8	one female Tatar ('tartara'), 20 years, with a scar on her forehead ('la qual à una bota sul fronte')	120 *hyperpyra*	*ibid.*, col. 293 p. 588, col. 258 p. 519
1438.xii.10	one tall female Russian ('sciava rosa atartarada, grande de persona'), *c.*18–20 years	110 *hyperpyra*	*ibid.*, col. 293 p. 588, col. 294 p. 591
1439.iii.2	one female ('testa')	110 *hyperpyra*	*ibid.*, col. 294 p. 590, col. 319 p. 641
1439.iii.9	two female Russian ('rose') slaves ('teste'), one aged 18–20, one aged 13–14 years	190 *hyperpyra* for the two	*ibid.*, col. 172 p. 346, col. 211 p. 425
1439.vi.7	two females ('teste')	204 *hyperpyra*	*ibid.*, col. 327 p. 656, col. 172 p. 347
1439.vii.18	two Russian females ('femene')	90 *hyperpyra* each	*ibid.*, col. 224 p. 450, col. 331 p. 665
1439.xi.22	one female ('teste')	107 *hyperpyra*	*ibid.*, col. 373 p. 748, col. 260 p. 523
1439.xi.28	one male ('avogaxo'), *c.*20 years, called Zorzi	95 *hyperpyra*	*ibid.*, col. 357 p. 716, col. 172 p. 347

Alum prices

Table A3.1. *Alum prices*

Date	Place	Type	Price in source	Price in *ducats*	Source
1323	Pisa	rock	1 *soldo* per *centinaio*	1 *ducat* = 16.5 *kantars*	Pegolotti, *Pratica*, p. 208
1336	Crete		8 *hyperpyra* per 1 *migliaio grosso*	1 *ducat* = 5.5 *kantars*	1336.x.20 = Zucchello, *Lettere*, no. 1, p. 8
1384			4 *hyperpyra* per 1 *kantar*	1 *ducat* = 0.5 *kantars*	Thomas, *Diplomatarium*, vol. II, p. 194
1394	Phokaea		40 gold *ducats* = 100 *kantars*	4 *ducats* = 1 *kantar*	1394.ii.18 = ASG, Notaio, Donato de Clavaro, Sc. 39, filza 1, doc. 97/240
1394	Phokaea	rock	400 *ducats* = 350 *kantars*	1.14 *ducats* = 1 *kantar*	1394.ii.18 = ASG, Notaio, Donato de Clavaro, Sc. 39, filza 1, doc. 97/240
1405	Chios/ Phokaea/ Mytilene	grain	3,000 gold *ducats* = 4,000 *kantars*	0.75 *ducat* = 1 *kantar*	1405.iv.4 = Doehaerd and Kerremans, *Relations commerciales*, no. 11, p. 12. The alum involved was 3,000 *kantars* of grain alum of Phokaea and 1,000 *kantars* of grain alum of Mitylene, the *kantars* being those of Chios

Table A3.1. (*contd*)

Date	Place	Type	Price in source	Price in *ducats*	Source
1408	Pera/ Scorpiata	rock	2 *hyperpyra* 12 *karati* = 1 Genoese *kantar*	c.0.66 *ducat* = 1 *kantar*	1408.viii.14 = ASG, Notaio Giovanni Balbi, Sc. 46, filza 1, doc. 384.
1408	Pera/ Scorpiata	grain	1 *hyperpyra* 9 *karati* = 1 Genoese *kantar*	c.033 *ducat* = 1 *kantar*	*ibid.*
1412				0.7 *ducat* = 1 *kantar*	1414.v.29 = Heers, 'Commerce de l'alun', 39
1438	Constan- tinople	*lume de sorta*	4 *hyperpyra* = 1 *kantar*	1.3 *ducats* = 1 *kantar*	1438.i.22 = Badoer, *Libro*, col. 261, p. 524 *(going to Maiorca)*
1438	"	rock	7 *hyperpyra* = 1 *kantar*	2.3 *ducats* = 1 *kantar*	*ibid.*
1438	"		22 *hyperpyra* 12 *karati* = 6 *kantars*	1.25 *ducats* = 1 *kantars*	1438.ii.26 = *ibid.*, col. 410 p. 822, col. 320 p. 643 (going to Venice)
1438	"	*lume neta*	4.5 *hyperpyra* = 1 *kantar*	1.5 *ducats* = 1 *kantar*	1438.iii.5 = *ibid.*, col. 194 p. 390, col. 186 p. 375
1438	"		3 *hyperpyra* = 1 *kantar*	1 *ducat* = 1 *kantar*	1438.iv.13 = *ibid.*, col. 320 p. 642, col. 316 p. 635 (going to Candia)
1438	"	rock	7 *hyperpyra* = 1 *kantar*	2.3 *ducats* = 1 *kantar*	1438.vii.26 = *ibid.*, col. 220 p. 442
1439	"		22 *hyperpyra* 12 *karati* = 6 *kantars*	1.25 *ducats* = 1 *kantar*	1439.ii.26 = *ibid.*, col. 410 p. 822, col. 320 p. 641 (going to Venice)
1439	"	*lume neta (?lume de sorta)*	3 *hyperpyra* 21 *karati* = 6 *kantars*	1.25 ducats = 1 *kantar*	1439.iii.30 = *ibid.*, col. 322 p. 646, col. 319 p. 641
1439	"	*lume de sorta*	4 *hyperpyra* = 1 *kantar*	1.33 *ducats* = 1 *kantar*	1439.vii.9 = *ibid.*, col. 322 p. 646, col. 341 p. 685
1439	"		5 *hyperpyra* = 1 *kantar*	1.7 *ducats* = 1 *kantar*	1439.xi.2 = *ibid.*, col. 322 p. 646, col. 371 p. 747

Table A3.1. (*contd*)

Date	Place	Type	Price in source	Price in *ducats*	Source
1439	Constan-tinople	*lume de sorta*	4 *hyperpyra* 18 *karati* = 1 *kantar*	1.6 *ducats* = 1 *kantar*	1439.ix.28 = *ibid.*, col. 322 p. 646, col. 284 p. 571
1439	"	"	4 *hyperpyra* 6 *karati* = 1 *kantar*	1.4 *ducats* = 1 *kantar*	1439.ix.28 = *ibid.*, col. 322 p. 646, col. 127
1448	"	"	"	0.375 *ducat* = 1 *kantar*	1449.i.21 = Heers, 'Commerce de l'alun', 39
1449	"	"	"	more than 0.5 *ducat* = 1 *kantar*	1449.iv.28 = *ibid.*
1450	"	"	"	more than 0.5 *ducat* = 1 *kantar*	1450.ii.18 = *ibid.*, no. 174
1450	"	"	"	45 *ducats*	1451.xii.28 = *ibid.*

Imported cloth prices

Table A4.1. *Imported cloth prices*

Date	Cloth	Place	Price	Source
1290	155 pieces of cloth of Champagne	Caffa	£G638 16s 6d	1290.v.23 = Bratianu, *Actes*, no. 330, p. 297
1297	cotton	Cyprus	4 *besanti saracinali* = 1 *kantar*	1297.iii.11 = Lamberto di Sambuceto (Balard) no. 34, pp. 45–7
1299	cotton from of Aleppo	Cyprus	60 *besanti saracinali* = 1 *kantar*	1299.v.22 = *ibid.* no. 147, p. 172
1300	Lombardy and French cloth	Cyprus	3,948 *bessant*s = 33 pieces of Lombardy cloth and 27 of French cloth	1300.ii.2 = Lamberto di Sambuceto (Desimoni), no. 42, pp. 25–28
1300	cloth of Avignon	Cyprus	968.5 *soldi* 8 *denari* = 4 bales	1300.ix.30 = Lamberto di Sambuceto (Polonio) no. 19, pp. 20–1
1300	cloth of Lombardy and cloth 'de Taolonis'	Cyprus	1,200 *soldi* = 3 bales of Lombardy and 1 bale of 'taolonis'	1300.ix.30 = *ibid.*
1307	cotton of Syria	Cyprus	28 silver *bessant*s = 1 *kantar*	1307.iv.5 = (Balard) no. 133, p. 20
1309	cloth of Chalons	?	252 *libri* 1 *solidus* = 2 bales (= 13 pieces)	1309.xi.5 = Giovanni de Rocha (Balard) no. 23, pp. 309–10
1310–40	buckram of Erzincan	Pisa	3 *denari* per piece	Pegolotti, *Pratica*, p. 208
1310–40	cloth of Narbonne	Theologos	14 gold *florin*s per cloth = 18 *ancone* of Theologos	*ibid.*, p. 55
1310–40	dyed woollens of Florence	Theologos	2–2.25 gold *florin*s = 1 *canna*	*ibid.*, p. 55

Table A4.1. (*contd*)

Date	Cloth	Place	Price	Source
1310–40	? dyed woollens of Florence	Theologos	32–6 gold *florin*s = 1 piece (= 12 *canne* and 2 *braccia* of Florence)	*ibid.*, p. 55
1310–40	cloth of Chalons	Antalya	8–10 *bessant*s of Cyrpus = 1 *canna*	*ibid.*, p. 58
1310–40	Narbonne	Antalya	9–12 gold *florin*s = 1 piece	*ibid.*, p. 58
1310–40	Perpignan	Antalya	9–12 gold *florin*s = 1 piece	*ibid.*
1310–40	Lombardy cloth	Antalya	8–9 gold *florin*s = 1 piece	*ibid.*
1310–40	Turkish silk	Pisa	6 *soldi* per *centinaio di libbre*	*ibid.*, pp. 208–9
1310–40	cloth of Chalon	Antalya	8–10 *bessant*s of Cyprus = 1 *canna*	*ibid.*, p. 58
1361	*saia Irlanda*	Chios	570 silver *bessant*s of Cyprus = 38 pieces	1361.xi.1 = Nicola de Boateriis, *Notaio*, no. 114, p. 116
1391	Florentine cloth	?Pera	19 *hyperpyra* 6 *karati* = 7 pieces	1391.xii.19 = ASG, Antico Comune, 22, fos. 70, 92
1392	*panni rosee*	"	21 *hyperpyra* = 7 pieces	*ibid.*, fos. 74, 193
1392	Florentine cloth	"	21 *hyperpyra* = 7 pieces	*ibid.*, fos. 76, 193
1392	Florentine cloth	"	21 *hyperpyra* = 7 pieces	*ibid.*, fos. 78, 196
1392	cloth	"	17 *hyperpyra* 12 *karati* = 7 pieces	*ibid.*, fos. 88, 175
1392	*panni rosee de grana*	"	32 *hyperpyra* 12 *karati* = 6 pieces	*ibid.*, fos. 84, 197
1392	*panni rosee*	"	16 *hyperpyra* 9 *karati* = 6 pieces	*ibid.*, fos. 84, 92
1392	*panni rose*	"	18 *hyperpyra* 10 *karati* = 6 pieces	*ibid.*, fo. 128
1392	*panni virmili Florentie*	"	36 *hyperpyra* 3 *karati* = 13 pieces	*ibid.*, fo. 174
1408	Florentine cloth	?	65 *hyperpyra* = 1 piece	1408.viii.14 = ASG, Notaio, Giovanni Balbi, Sc. 46, filza 1, doc. 384
1436	*pani loesti*	Constantinople	47.5 *hyperpyra* = 1 *peza*	1436.ii.12 = Badoer, *Libro*, col. 44 p. 88, col. 13 p. 27

Table A4.1. (*contd*)

Date	Cloth	Place	Price	Source
1437	Florentine cloth	Constantinople	150 *hyperpyra*= 1 *peza*	1437.iii.16 = *ibid.*, col. 14 p. 29
1437	*pani loesti*	Samsun	7,355 *asper*s (700 *hyperpyra*) = 12 *casete*	1437.xii.18 = *ibid.*, col. 44 p. 89
1437	taffeta	Samsun	172 *asper*s (9 *hyperpyra*) = 20 *palmi*	1437.xii.18 = *ibid.*, col. 52 p. 306
1437	*zanbeloti*	Samsun	126 *asper*s (6.6 *hyperpyra*) = 2 *peze*	1437.xii.18 = *ibid.*, col. 152 p. 306
1437	*bocasini*	Samsun	1,184 *asper*s (62 *hyperpyra*) = 60 *peze*	1437.xii.18 = *ibid.*, col. 152 p. 306
1437	*bocasini*	Trabzon	2,773 *asper*s (69 *hyperpyra*) = 60 *peze*	1437.xii.18 = *ibid.*, col. 152 p. 307
1438	*pani negri*	Constantinople	100 *hyperpyra* = 1 *peza*	1438.iv.30 = *ibid.*, col. 196, p. 394; 1438.iii.21 = *ibid.*
1438	muslin	Bursa	7,355 *asper*s (700 *hyperpyra*) = 12 *casete*	1438.viii.8 = *ibid.*, col. 227 p. 456, col. 61 p. 123
1438	*damascin biancho brochà d'oro e de seda*	Constantinople	10.5 *hyperpyra* = 1 *picho*	1438.ix.16 = *ibid.*, col. 244 p. 490
1438	*damascin verde scieto*	"	6 *hyperpyra* = 1 *picho*	1438.ix.16 = *ibid.*, col. 244 p. 490
1439	*pano bastardo (verde)*	"	65 *hyperpyra* = 1 *peza*	1439.ii.26 = *ibid.*, col. 329 p. 660
1439	*pani bastardi*	"	95 *hyperpyra* = 1 *peza*	1439.ii.26 = *ibid.*, col. 329 p. 660
1439	*pani da Parma (pano zalo)*	"	90 *hyperpyra* = 1 *peza*	1439.ii.26 = *ibid.*, col. 329 p. 660
1439	*pano scarlattini bastardo*	"	89 *hyperpyra* = 1 *peza*	1439.iv.18 = *ibid.*, col. 329 p. 660
1439	*pani Fiorenza de garbo*	"	80 *hyperpyra* = 1 *peza*	1439.iv.20 = *ibid.*, col. 329 p. 660
1439	*chanevaze*	"	14 *hyperpyra* = 100 *pichi*	1439.xi.16 = *ibid.*, col. 343 p. 689
1452	Genoese cloth	?	*c*.500 gold *duca*ts of Chios = 400 pieces	1452.x.28 = Argenti, *Chios*, vol. III, pp. 658–9

Documents

1 1364.x.8 = ASG, Notai Ignoti, XVIII.14, ist. doc.

Summary

The appointment by Giovanni Giustiniani and Francesco Giustiniani of two agents, Bartolomeo Longo and Raffaele Sasiano, with power to make treaties in accordance with the stipulations set down in the treaty made by Giovanni Giustiniani and Francesco Giustiniani with Sarchano (Saruhan) Turchus and Calozeto (Kalothetos), lord of Old Phokaea.

Text

In nomine domini amen. Discreti et sapientes viri domini Johannes Justinianus et Franciscus Justinianus quondam Domenici gubernatores generales et participes, condutores et emptores insulle Siy et Follie Nove et aliorum loquorum dependencium ab <e>andem insullam Siy pro duodecimis partibus et eciam procuratores et procuratoris nominibus aliorum dominorum dicte Maone, participum, emptorum et condutorum dicte insulle et dependencium ab eandem qu[ili] pro duodecim parte ut de predictis videlicet de procura dicti domini Johannis plene patet publico instrumento procuratore actorie scripto Janue manu Guidoris de Braccelis notarii MCCCLXIII, die XVIIII Julli et de procur<a>[1] et de bayllia dicti domini Francisci patet acto publico instrumento scripto manu dicti Guidoris notarii hoc anno die habentis ad infra scripta et allia plenum et sufficens mandatum vigore dictorum instrumentorum suis propris nominibus et procuratoris ante dictis fecerunt, sustituerunt et locho sui dictis nominibus posuerunt procuratores, actores et factores et negociorum gestores dicte Maone providos viros dominos Bartholomeum Longum et Raffaelem Sasianum absentes quam presentes[2] videlicet ad paciscendum, componendum et conpromitendum et composiciones et pacta faciendum et pacem et composicionem faciendam[3] atque triguam et ligam faciendum et ipsam pacem, triquam et conposicionem iurandum et[4] iuramentum faciendum et iuram entum

---

[1] End of the word obliterated by a hole in the manuscript.
[2] 'providos viros dominos Bartholomeum Longum et Raffaelem Sasianum absentes quam presentes' inserted above line and along right-hand margin.
[3] 'ad' and another word crossed out.
[4] Beginning of the second column.

proinde et pro ut in quodam decreto seu tratatu dominis procuratoribus dato et tradito per dictos dominos Johannem et Franciscum gubernatores et procuratores ante dictos continentur con dominis Sarchano Turcho[5] et Calozeto, domino Follis Veteris.

Dantes et concedentes dictis eorum procuratoribus in predictis et circha predicto plenam largam liberam bayliam et generalem administracionem con pleno largo libero et generali mandato.

Promitentes dicti domini Johannes et Franciscus suis propriis nominibus et nominibus ante dictis omnia et singula suprascripta mihi notario infrascripto tamquam publice persone[6] stipulanti et recipienti officio publico nomine et vice omnium et singulorum quorum interest, intererit vel inter esse poterit se ipsos perpetuo firmum et ratum habituros omne, id et totum quod, quid et quantum per dictos terorum procuratores actum, gestum, factum seu procuratum fuerit in predictis et quolibet predictorum factum,[7] gratum et firmum habere, tenere et in nulo contrafacere vel venire[8] <sub>[9]potecha et obligatione <omn>[10]ium bonorum suorum dictis nominibus et suis propris nominibus pro partibus eisdem spectantibus et cuiuslibet eorum habitorum et habendorum volerit quamdum et quolibet eorum. Relevantes dictos eorum procuratores et cuiuslibet eorum ab omne honere satisdandi promisera<unt> mihi iam dicto notario stipulanti et recipienti ut supra quod iudicio sisterint et iudicatum solverint dollo non comitentes nihi fuerint provocati de predictis versus me iam dicto notario stipulenti ut supra pro dictis eorum procuratoribus in [triceseru<   >] et fide iuserunt suma potecha et obligatione.

Renuncians iuri de[11] princip<io> et omni allii juri.

Actum in civitate insulle Syi in camera habitacionis dicti domini Johannis, anno dominice nativitatis MCCCLXIIII, indicione[12] secunda secundum cursum Ianue, die VIII Octubris paullo post nonam. Testes, Acelinus Sotus, Johannes de Podio filius Domenici et Anthonius de Sexania quondam Paganini.

2 1389.x.26 = ASG, Notario, Cartulare, C. 476, Donato de Clavaro, doc. 10[13]

Summary

The Podestà of Pera, Antonio Leardo, and others of the Comune, knowing that their ambassador, Jane de Draperiis, has made a treaty with Bayezid I, which the Sultan wished to have ratified, swore in the presence of Bayezid's ambassador, Hasan Bey, to abide by the treaties made with Orhan and Murad.

---

[5] 'Turcho' inserted above the line.   [6] 'off' crossed out.
[7] 'contractum' inserted above the line.
[8] Beginning of a new column.
[9] Top of the manuscript damaged by water.
[10] Top of the manuscript damaged by water.
[11] A word crossed out.   [12] 'prima' crossed out.
[13] A summary of this document has been published by Balard, Laiou and Otten-Froux, *Les Italiens à Byzance*, no. 66, p. 33.

Text

In nomine domini amen. Egregius et circumspectus vir dominus Antonius Leardus, podestas Peyre et Januensium in toto Imperio Romanie, circumspectus vir dominus Raffael Carpenetus, unius ex ambaxiatoribus, provissoribus et gubernatoribus pro comuni Janue in partibus orientalibus, absente domino Gentille de Grimaldis, altero ambaxitore provisore et gubernatore, et consilium octo Ancianorum dicti domini potestatis quorum nomina sunt: domini Petrus Ultramarinus, Percival de Porta, Brancaleo Grillus, Batista de Zoalio, Gandulfus de Turrilia, Thomas de Castellor, Raffael de Laurentiis, Johannes Demerode, habentes noticiam et certam scientiam de pace nuper firmata per Jane de Draperiis, burgensem Peyre, <a[14]>mbaxiatorem prefactorum dominorum potestatis provisoris et consilii, nomine comunis Janue et Peyre cum serenissimo principe et domino domino Basita bey Jhalabi, magno amirato amiratorum Turchie, et iuramento per eum facto presentato in scriptis in litera greca cum signo suo dicto domino potestati per dictum Jane, et volentem erga dictum dominum Basitam bey facere et iurare pro ut debent idcirco prefacti domini potestas, provissor et consilium constituti in presentia domini Casam[15] bey, ambaxiatoris prefacti domini Basite bey, destinati pro dicto iuramento videndo et recipiendo, iuraverunt ad sancta dei evangellia corporaliter tactis scripturis in manibus[16] fratris Petri de Taurixio[17] ordinis fratrum minorum in manu comunis Janue et Peyre et omnium Januensium, paces hinc retro factas cum dominis[18] Orcani bey et Morati bey et omnia et singulla in eis contenta actendere, complere et observare et actendi, compleri et observari facere per subdictos dicti comunis et contra ea in alliquo non facere vel venire aliqua racione occasione vel causa contradici vel excogitari possit [?] per prefactum dominum Basitam Bey et suos subdictos in omnibus observentur dicte paces ut supra.

Actum Peyra in camera consiliorum[19] palacii dicti domini potestatis, anno dominice nativitatis MCC<C[20]>LXXXVIIII, indicione XII secundum cursum Janue, die XXVI Octobris circa meridiem. Presentibus testibus, Johanne de Draperiis, burgense Peyre, Antonio de Grimaldis, filio Gentilis, et Bartholomeo Villanucio notario, vocatis et rogatis.

3 1390.i.11 = ASG, Notario, Cartulare, C. 476, Donato de Clavaro, doc. 26[21]

Summary

Constantino de Groto brought a case against Dagnano Spinulla and Petro de Groto, guarantors for Raffaele Capello, with whom he had formed a partnership to buy copper from Solimambasa (i.e. Süleyman Paşa, the İsfendiyaroğulları ruler of Kastamonu). Constantino had bought 16,000 Kastamonu pounds of copper, equivalent to col. 4,000 *kantar*s of Pera, for 476,000 silver Kastamonu *asper*s. Raffaele had not, however, paid Constantino the money as agreed.

---

[14] Letter obscured by hole in manuscript.   [15] Hasan.
[16] Beginning of second column.   [17] Treviso.
[18] 'dominis' inserted above line.   [19] 'pla' crossed out.
[20] The third 'C' obliterated by hole in manuscript.
[21] A summary of this document has been published in Balard, Laiou and Otten-Froux, *Documents*, no. 82, p. 37.

Text

In nomine domini amen. Constantinus de Groto, burgensis Peyre, in jure constitutus et in presentia Egregii et circumspecti viri domini Antonii Leardi honorabilis potestatis Peyre et Januensium in toto Imperio Romanium, pro tribunali sedentis ad solitum suum bancum juris, dicit, denunciat et proptestatur versus Dagnanum Spinullam et Petrum de Groto, burgenses Peyre, presentes[22] fideiussores et fideiussorio nomine Raffaelis Capelli, burgensis Peyre, de et super inferius denominatis et de scriptis, quod inter ipsum Constantinum ex una parte et dictum Raffaelem Capellum ex altera, fuit et extitit facta contracta celebrata et inita quedam conpositio sive societas de et super libris sexdecim milibus rami, ad pondus egregii et potentis domini Solimambasa Turchi, domini Castamene, que capiunt et astendunt ad pondus Peyre sommam cantariorum quatuormillium vel circa, quod ramum extitit emptum per dictum Constantinum a dicto domino Solimambassa pro pretio et nomine pretii asperorum mille millium quadringentorum septuaginta sex millium argenti de Castamena. In qua conpositione sive societate inita et contracta, dictus Raffael Capellus pacto convenit et solempni stipulacione et promisione convenit et promisit dicto Constantino, ibidem presenti et recipienti, dare, solvere, numerare et amaonare dicto Constantino dictos asperos sive dictam[23] quantitatem asperorum mille millium quadringentorum septuaginta sex millium argenti de Castamena nomine et ex causa dicte emptionis dicti rami, dandam et solvendam per ipsum Constantinum dicto domino Castamene, ut de predictis omnibus seriorius et lacius apparet quadam apodixia sive scriptura scripta manu dicti Raffaelis MCCCLXXXVIII, die XX, mensis Januarii. Item per formam duorum publicorum instrumentorum, compositorum et scriptorum manu Bernabonis de Groto, notarii publici, MCCCLXXXVIIII, die XVI Septembris, initorum et factorum inter dictum Constantinum ex una et pro una parte, et Georgium de Cornilia, notarium, civem Janue, procuratorem et procuratorio nomine dicti Raffaelis Capelli, ex altera parte cum plena, larga, ampla, libera bailia et administracione ut de ipsius constitucione et mandato patet publico instrumento scripto manu Lodisii Carpeneti, notarii publici, MCCCLXXXVIII, die VII Decembris, ad quorum instrumentorum et apodixie ratificacionem, convalidacionem, caupcionem et observacionem efficaciorem efficacius observandam et adimplendam et ut securum et cauptum esset dictis partibus in observacione et satisfacione plenaria contentorum in dictis apodixia sive scriptura et instrumentis et ne dicte partes seu altera[24] earum et super contentis in eisdem apodixia sive scriptura et instrumentis valleant seu valleat et possit apromisis et concordentes a se se et vicisim resillere et in aliquo contrafacere vel venire[25] precibus mandato dicti Georgii dicto nomine inter cesserunt et fideiusserunt dicti Dagnanus Spinulla et Petrus de Groto et pro dicto Constantino dictus Petrus de Groto cumque dictus Raffael principalis nec non dicti Dagnanus et Petrus fideiussores ipsius Raffaelis sepe et sepius interpelati et requisiti per dictum Constantinum non solverit, numerarverit, tradiderit, preparaverit,[26] amaonaverit nec solverint, numeraverint, tradiderint, preparaverint[27] et amaonaverint dicto Constantino emptori dicte quantitatis rami ut promititur dictam quantitatem asperorum mille millium

---

[22] 'presentes' inserted above line.   [23] Beginning of second column.
[24] 'm' crossed off at end of 'altera'.   [25] Beginning of third column.
[26] Abbreviation for 'er' crossed out and replaced by abbreviation for 'pre'.
[27] Abbreviation for 'er' crossed out and replaced by abbreviation for 'pre'.

quadringentorum septuaginta sexmillium argenti de Castameni debitam ex causa dicte empcionis dicto domino Castamene iuxta convencionem et promisionem[28] dicti Raffaelis nec non dicti Georgii procuratorio nomine ipsius et tenorum dicte apodisie scripture et instrumentorum et in ipsorum observacione prout tenebatur et tenetur dictus Raffael principalis et Dagnanus et Petrus fideiussores contra et preter tamen formam dicte apodixie et instrumentorum.

Et ex eo vel ob hec dictus Constantinus[29] substinuerit, substineat et substinet grande dampnum detrimentum et interesse et in posterum putat seu dubitat plus sua interesse maiusque dampnum seu detrimentum substinere et sibi adventurum[30] ex eo quod dictus Raffael principalis seu dicti Dagnanus et Petrus fideiussores non solvunt, numarant,[31] tradunt,[32] preparant et amaonant dicti principalis seu fideiussores dictam quantitatem asperorum mille millium quadringentorum septuaginta sex millium argenti de Castamena nomine et ex causa predicta.

Idcirco dictus Constantinus, constitus in jure et in presentia dicti domini potestatis Peyre, volens consultum sibi fore et sibi prospicere super jure suo et sibi competenti et compecdituro et consulte dampna interesse et expensas evitare et jus suum salvum fore et illesa ac intacta jura habere contra dictos Raffaelem et fideiussores infuturum ad cautellam ne dicti fideiussores valleant pretendere ignorantiam infuturum super premissis seu altero eorum et ut de jure sibi competenti et compectituro valleat et possit idem Constantinus experiri et jus suum consequi et habere tam contra dictum Raffaelem quam contra dictos Dagnanum et Petrum fideiussores et fideiussorio nomine ipsius suo loco et tempore et bona eorum et cuiuslibet ipsorum denunciat proptestatur[33] ac denunciant et proptestatur fuit contra et adversus dictos Dagnanum Spinullam et Petrum de Groto fideiussores et fideiussorio nomine dicti Raffaelis de omni dampno interesse quod substinuerit, substineat et substiniet dictus Constantinus ex eo quia dictus Raffael sive fideiussores sui non solvit, numaravit, tradidit, preparavit, amaonavit dicto Constantino dictam quantitatem asperorum mille millium quadringentorum septuaginta sexmillium argenti seu non solverunt, numaraverunt, tradiderunt, preparaverunt,[34] amaonaverunt iuxta contentorum in dictis apodixia et instrumentis et de omni dampno, interesse et expensis quod et quas dictus Constantinus infuturum substinuerit, subierit et passus fuerit ac subtubuerit nomine et ex causa promissorum et cuiuslibet eorum non actenditorum, observatorum et adimpletorum tam in toto quam in parte et qualibet parte quantecumque quantitatis fuerit offerens seperatum recipere residuum dicte quantitatis asperorum

[28] 'com' crossed out at the beginning of 'promisionem'.
[29] There is a sign here indicating that something should be inserted but there is nothing obvious to insert. The sign is similar to one on the first column of the manuscript but there is no apparent way of connecting them.
[30] Beginning of fourth column.   [31] Thus in text for 'numerant'.
[32] Abbreviation for 'per' crossed out and replaced by abbreviation for 'pre'.
[33] 'Actum Peyre ad staciam ubi jus reditur per dictum dominum potestatem Peyre, anno dominice nativitate MCCCLXXXX, indicione XII secundum cursum Janue, die XI Januarii in vesperis. Presentibus testibus, Bartolomeo Villanucio notario, Paullo de Valegia de Rapallo et Lodisio Carpeneto notario civitatis Peyre, vocatis et rogatis' is crossed out here. It is almost word for word the same as the paragraph at the end of the document. Beginning of fifth column.
[34] Abbreviation for 'per' crossed out and replaced by abbreviation for 'pre'.

sub proptestacione tamen promissa a dictis Dagnano et Petro fideiussoribus et fideiussorio nomine dicti Raffaelis seu ab alio seu alliis nomine eorum seu dicti Raffaelis proptestans per eum non stare contra dictos fideiussores et dicto nomine quominus predicta fiant proptestans eciam idem Constantinus contra dictos fideiussores in dicto nomine quod est recessurus de Peyra causa eundi[35] et dirigendi gressus suos versus dictum locum Castamene et dictum dominum Solemam Bassa infra terciam diem proxime venturam de quibus omnibus et singulis ex nunc pro ut ex tunc et ex tunc pro ut ex nunc solempniter proptestatur et de quolibet jure suo contra dictum Raffaelem principalem et dictos Dagnanum et Petrum fideiussores et fideiussorio nomine ipsius Raffaelis.

Et de predictis dictus Constantinus rogavit me notarium infrascriptum, ut inde conficere debeam presens publicum instrumentum in testimonium premissorum.[36]

Actum Peyre ad staciam ubi jus reditur per dictum dominum potestatem Peyre, anno dominice nativitate MCCCLXXXX, indicione XII secundum cursum Janue, die XI Januarii in vesperis. Presentibus testibus, Bartolomeo Villanucio, notario, Paullo de Vallegia de Rapallo, milite prefacti domini Potestatis et Lodisio Carpeneto, notario, vocatis et rogatis.

⌈Ea die in continenti⌉

dicti Dagnanus et Petrus fideiussores utsupra et dicto fideiussorio nomine dicti Raffaelis audictis predictis ipsi protestacioni et contentis in ea non consentiunt nisi si et in quamtum faciat pro eis dicto fideiussorio nomine et non aliter nec alio modo.

Summary

The following four documents form a series dealing with relations between the *capitaneus* and the *subaşı* of İzmir involving Chios and the Hospitallers. Antonio Leardo was sent by the *podestà* of Chios to İzmir to organise the release of two sons of the *subaşı*, captured by the *capitaneus*, and to negotiate a peace between the *capitaneus* and the *subaşı*. A seven-year peace was arranged and signed. As a guarantee of abiding by the treaty, the *subaşı* paid 10,000 gold *ducat*s which he handed over to Antonio for depositing with the government in Chios. The deposit, in the form of gold money, pearls, jewels and other goods, was loaded onto the galley of the Hospitaller Domenico de Alamania, for shipment to Chios. Antonio acted as guarantor for the *subaşı*, pledging himself as surety for him to Domenico for 2,000 gold *ducat*s. If the *subaşı* or any other Turk contravened the agreement, the *capitaneus* had redress against Antonio, and the lord of Mytilene. If the *subaşı* broke the treaty, Antonio was to pay 2,000 *ducat*s to Domenico, and send a galley from Chios to the *capitaneus*'s aid. If the *capitaneus* did not observe the agreement, then Antonio and the lord of Mytilene had redress against Domenico. Antonio set off for Chios on the galley of Domenico together with the *subaşı*'s deposit. But at Old

---

[35] Beginning of sixth column.

[36] 'Qua Dagnanus et Petrus fidemissores utsupra et dicto fideiussorio nomine dicti Raffaelis audictis predictis ipsi protestacioni et contentis in ea non consentiunt nisi si et in quamtum faciat pro eis dicto fideiussorio nomine et non aliter nec alio modo' is crossed out. The paragraph is rewritten at the end of the document.

Phokaea he received letters from the *podestà* telling him that they would not accept the deposit in Chios. Antonio opposed this decision, saying that it would damage Chios in the future, but without success. The deposit, on the authority of the *subaşı*, was handed back by Antonio to Domenico to be returned. Domenico acknowledged receipt of the deposit in the condition in which Antonio had received it from the *subaşı* and promised to hand it over to Antonio or the *subaşı* or any legitimate person on request.

4 1394.ix.1 = ASG, Notaio, Donato di Clavaro, Sc. 39, filza 1, doc. 169 (170)

In nomine domini amen. Dominus Antonius Justinianus de Roca, sciens et cognoscens se destinatum fuisse per dominum potestatem, gubernatores et consilium ad dominum capitaneum Smirarum[37] pro relaxacione duorum filiorum domini subasi Smirarum, captorum et arestatorum per ipsum dominum capitaneum Smirarum, et similiter pro pace tractanda inter prefactos dominos capitaneum et subassi Smirarum ac dictam pacem et concordium inter eos firmasse in qua continetur quod dominus subasi Smirarum pro observatione dicte pacis duratura annos septem proxime venturos tenetur deponere ducatos decem millia[38] auri sive valumentum eorum, et similiter dictum dominum subasi requivisse ipso domino Antonio depositum predictum fieri et esse debere penes dominacionem Syi pro ut idem dominus subassi per suas literas scribit dictis domino potestati gubernatoribus et et[39] consilio similiter sciens[40] valorem dictorum ducatorum decem millium deponendorum ut supra per dictum dominum subassi depositum fuisse penes dictum dominum Antonium pro ipsis consignandis dominacioni Syi ut supra, et dictum depositum oneratum fuisse in galea Reverendi in Christo Patris domini fratris Domenici de Alamania et conductum in Syo pro ipso deponendo penes dominacionem Syi ut supra. Et sciens similiter literas prefactorum domini potestatis, gubernatorum et consilii post recessum ipsius galee factum de Smiris cum dicto deposito super qua erat dictus dominus Antonius veniendo in Syo recepisse in[41] Folia Veteri in quibus continebatur ipsos deliberasse dictum depositum in Syo fieri non debere et actento propter deliberacionem predictam dampnum, interesse et expensas sequi posse ipsi domino Antonio et dominacioni Syi cum per ipsos dominum potestatem, gubernatores et consilium transmissus fuerit[42] pro predictis peragendis ut supra.

Idcirco constitutus in presentia mei notarii et testium infrascriptorum ad hoc specialiter vocatorum et rogatorum, proptestatus fuit et protestatur prefactis domino potestati dominis Lodisio et Bartholomeo Justinianis, gubernatoribus Danielli Justiniano, Domenico Justiniano de Garibaldo, Batiste Justiniano de Roca et Antonio Rondame Castellano, quatuor ex consiliariis prefacti domini potestatis, presentibus, audientibus et inteligentibus de omni suo dampno, interesse et expensis que et quas dictus dominus Antonius[43] pateretur seu substinent eo quia prefacti dominus potestas, gubernatores et consilium dictum depositum acceptare noluerunt sed ipsum dimiserunt ire in galea predicta. Protestans similiter quod ipse dominus Antonius non consensit dicte deliberationi nec consentit cum sibi vidiatur hoc preiudicare debere in posterum presenti insulle.

---

[37] 'et ad dnm' crossed out.   [38] 'sive' crossed out.
[39] 'sic' in manuscript.   [40] 'dicto depo' crossed out.
[41] Beginning of second column.   [42] 'ad' crossed out.   [43] 'passis' crossed out.

Et de predictis prefactus dominus Antonius rogavit me notarium infrascriptum ut inde confacere debeam presens publicum instrumentum in testimonium premissorum.

Et dictus dominus Bartholomeus, gubernator,[44] audiens predicta et volens respondere[45] predictis, dicit quod[46] per ipsos dominum potestatem, gubernatores et consilium non fuit deliberatum ipsum dominum Antonium transmitti debere ut supra sed ipse dominus Antonius sua voluntate propria accedit ergo ad predictam in aliquo non tenentur.

Et dictus dominus Lodisius gubernator respondit quod de ellectione ipsius domini Antonii nichil scit cum non erat presens ipsi ellectioni tamen ipsum dominum Antonium scripsisse per suas literas prefactis domino potestati, gubernatoribus et consilio de dicta depositione dicti deposito et quod ipse dominus Antonius expectare debebat responsionem eorum in Smiris quam non fecit quare in nichilo tenentur ad predicta.

Actum in Syo in a<u>lla palacii domini potestatis Syi, anno dominice nativitatis MCCCLXXXXIIII, indicione prima secundum cursum Janue, die prima Septembris in vesperis, presentibus testibus Francisco Goardino et Silvestro de Bracelli, vocatis et rogatis.

5 1394.ix.1 = ASG, Notaio, Donato di Clavaro, Sc. 39, filza 1, doc. 170 (172)

In nomine domini amen. Reverendus in Christo[47] Pater Dominus Frater Domenicus de Alamania, Preceptor Neapolis et Avinonensis, sciens et cognoscens nobilem virum dominum Antonium Justinianum de Roca eidem obligatum esse[48] pro ducatis duobus milibus auri pro securitate et tanquam fidemissore[49] domini subassi Smirarum vigore et ex forma presenti instrumenti, paullo ante per me, notarium infrascriptum, confecti et nolens ipsum dominum Antonium pro predictis nec pro aliquibus contentis in dicto instrumento aliquod dampnum et incurrere posse preiudicium seu[50] gravamen dummodo[51] ipse dominus Antonius toto suo posse faciat si casus ad esset in recuperatione et exactione dictorum ducatorum duorum millium auri petendorum, exigendorum et recuperandorum a dicto domino subassi Smirarum[52] quitavit, liberavit et absoluit dictum dominum Antonium a dicta fidemissione sive debito dictorum ducatorum duorum millium contentorum in dicto instrumento per aceptillationem et acquilianam stipulato[53] solempniter introductis faciens eidem domino Antonio, presenti et stipulanti,[54] de predictis finem quitacionem, liberacionem et omni modam remissionem ac pactum de ulterius non petendo et promitte<n>s eidem domino Antonio, presenti et stipulanti, quod per ipsum Reverendum dominum fratrem Domenicum, heredes suos seu habentes vel habituros[55] tamen ab eo dicto domino Antonio vel[56] heredibus suis aut in bonis suis nulla decetero de predictis seu aliqua parte predictorum non fiet nec movebitur lex

---

[44] 'pred' crossed out.   [45] Beginning of third column.
[46] 'ipse dominus Antonius non fuit' crossed out.   [47] 'pre' crossed out.
[48] 'vigor' crossed out.   [49] 'ip<sius>' crossed out.
[50] 'et' crossed out and 'seu' added above the line.   [51] 'per eum' crossed out.
[52] 'pro ut est in dicto instumento cont<inent>ur' crossed out.
[53] 'stipulato' inserted above the line.   [54] 'f<   >' crossed out.
[55] Beginning of the next column.   [56] 'vel' inserted above the line.

quod actio, peticio,[57] requisicio seu conversia in judice et extra de jure seu de facto. Renuncians exceptioni presentis confesionis, promisionis[58] jure remisionis, quitacionis et liberacionis non factarum rei sic ut supra et infra non esse vel sic non se habentis doli, mali, metus infactum actioni condicioni, secundum casua et omni jure.

Que omnia et singula supradicta prefactus Reverendus dominus frater Domenicus juravit ad sancta dei evangelia[59] corporaliter tactis scripturis et promisit et convenit dicto domino Antonio, presenti et stipulanti ut supra, proprio habere et tenere firma et rata et actendere, complere et observare et in nullo contrafacere vel venire aliqua ratione, occasione vel causa que diti vel excogitari possit de jure seu de facto, sub pene dupli to<tiu>s[60] eius de quo et quanto contrafient vel ut supra non observaretur tamen restitutis[61] etiam omnium alliorum dampnorum, interesse et expensarum que propterea fierunt literis et ex ratis manentibus supradictis et sub ypotheca et obligatione omnium bonorum prefacti reverendi domini fratris Domenici habitorum et habendorum.

Et voluit et mandavit prefactus reverendus dominus frater Domenicus instrumentum predicte obligacionis[62] sive fideiussionis dictorum ducatorum duorum millium ut supra esse cassum, irritum et nullius valoris quantum pro facto dicit domini Antonii ut supra.

Actum in Syo sub logia ponderis Syi, anno dominice nativitatis MCCCLXXXXIIII, indicione prima secundum cursum Janue, die prima Setembris, post vesperas et ante completorium. Presentibus testibus, Raffaele de Ceronate, Pasqualino de Pontremillo, burgensibus Syi, et Nicolao Marcia de Diano, Cancellario dicti domini fratris Domenici, vocatis et rogatis.

6 1394.ix.1 = ASG, Notaio, Donato de Clavaro, Sc. 39, filza 1, doc. 171

In nomine domini amen. Nobilis vir dominus Anthonius Justinianus olim de Rocha sciens et cognoscens se destinatum fuisse ad dominum capitaneum Smirrarum et ad dominum subasi Smirrarum per egregium et nobiles viros, dominum podestatem Syi, gubernatores et consilium eiusdem, super relasacione duorum filiorum dicti domini subasi Smirrarum, captorum et arestatorum per dictum dominum capitaneum Smirrarum, et pro pace inde inter eos tractanda[63] et observanda et actento quod inter dictos dominos capitaneum Smirarum et subasi Smirrarum dicta pax de novo[64] fuerit confirmata[65] pro qua actendenda, complenda et observanda per annos septem pro<xime>[66] venturos ipse dominus Antonius suprascriptis[67] reverendum in Christo Patrem <dominum> Fratrem Domenicum de Alamania preceptorem

---

[57] 'seu' crossed out.   [58] 'promisionis' inserted above the line.
[59] 'et que' crossed out.
[60] The middle of the word is obliterated by a hole in the paper.
[61] 'omnium all' crossed out.   [62] 'di' crossed out.
[63] 'tractanda' inserted above line.
[64] 'dicta pax de novo' written down right-hand margin.
[65] 'de novo' crossed out and 'di' written above line.
[66] Manuscript damaged here, obliterating part of the word.
[67] 'dicto domino capitaneo Smirarum' crossed out.

Neapolis et Avignonensis[68] proprium se obligaverit pro[69] ducatis duobus millibus auri[70] pro quibus fuit fideiussor prout est pro dicto domino[71] subasi Smirrarum suprascripto dictum dominum fratrem Domenicum proprium[72] tali videlicet quando quod[73] semper et quandocumque per dominum subasi Smirrarum vel per aliquem turchum turchum vel dominum in aliquo foret contrafactum sacramentis, promisionibus, pactis et conventionibus initis inter dictas partes quod tunc dominus capitaneus Smirrarum reversum habere debeat ad dominum subasi Smirrarum de contrafactis et si dictus dominus subasi Smirrarum[74] aptaverit et remediabitur in eis benequidam quod si contrarium fecerit teneatur dictus dominus capitaneus Smirrarum habere reversum ad magnificum dominum dominum Mitelini et dictum dominum Antonium qui teneantur et debeant super lamentacionibus et contra factionibus pro videre et taliter operare quod dictus dominus subasi Smirrarum faciet et observet que debit et tenetur vigore dictorum sacramentorum et composicionium ut supra quod si tunc dictus dominus subasi Smirrarum non fecerit dictus dominus Antonius dabit et soluit dicto domino fratri Domenico proprio[75] dictos ducatos duomilia auri et tunc operabitur quod galeam Syi parata[76] in subsidium dicti domini capitanei Smirrarum trasmittit[77] et voluit ipse dominus Antonius[78] actendus que ut supra <p   >[79] promisit et convenit prefacto[80] reverendo[81] domino fratri Domenico de Alamania proprio,[82] presenti stipulanti et recipienti,[83] sicut eidem domino fratri Domenico proprio[84] dare et solvere debere dictos ducatos duomillia auri ut supra ad liberam et nudam requisitionem ipsius dicti fratris Domenici proprii.

Renuncians exceptioni presentis confesionis et promisionis non facte rei sic ut supra et infra non esse vel sit non se habentis doli, mali metus infactum actioni condicioni secundum causa et omni jure.

Qua omnia et singula supradicta prefactus dominus Antonius juravit ad sancta dei evangelia corporaliter tactis scriptoris et promisit et convenit prefacto reverendo

---

[68] 'reverendum in Christo Patrem <dominum> Fratrem Domenicum de Alamania preceptorem Neapolis et Avignonensis proprium' written above the line and down the right-hand margin.

[69] 'flor' crossed out.   [70] 'prout in . . .' crossed out.

[71] 'capitaneo' crossed out.

[72] 'capitaneo Smirarum' crossed out and 'fratrem Domenicum proprium' written above.

[73] 'dicti domini Antonii promissit et convenit' crossed out.

[74] Beginning of next column.

[75] 'capitaneo Smirrarum vel religioni hospitalis sancte Johanis Jherusalemitani Roddi' crossed out and 'fratri Domenico proprio' written above.

[76] Abbreviation for 'paratam' crossed out.

[77] 'tunc operabitur quod galeam Syi parata in subsidium dicti domini capitanei Smirrarum trasmittit' inserted between two lines of the text and down the right-hand margin.

[78] Word crossed out.

[79] Part of word obliterated by a hole in the manuscript.

[80] 'prefacto' inserted above the line.

[81] '<   > in christo patri' crossed out.

[82] 'preceptori Neapoli et Avinionensis' crossed out.

[83] 'nomine et vice <dicti> domini capitanei Smirrarum' crossed out.

[84] 'proprio' inserted above the line.

domino fratri[85] Domenico proprio,[86] presenti et stipulanti, actendere, complere et observare et contra in aliquo non facere vel venire aliqua ratione, occasione vel causa que dici vel excogitari possit de jure seu de facto, sub pena dupli totius eius de quo et quanto contrafieret vel ut supra non observarentur solempni stipulacione promissa cum restitucione etiam omnium aliorum dampnorum, interesse et expensarum que propterea fierent lictis etc. Rattis manentibus supradictis et sub ypotheca et obligatione omnium bonorum dicti domini Antonii habitorum et habendorum.

Acto quod pro predictis omnibus et singullis prefactis dominus Antonius realiter et personaliter conveniri possit capi et detineri hic Janue, partes Nicie, Neapole, Rodo, Peyre, Caffa, Famagoste et ubique alibi locorum et terrarum et sub quocumque iudice, officio et magistratis, ecclesiastico et civili, et ubi inventis, conventis seu requisitis fuerit ibi per pactum de predictis eidem reverendo domino fratri Domenico proprio[87] iure, stare, respondere, solvere[88] et satisfacionem facere, teneatur et promisit eidem ac si per inde presens contrattus ibidem fuisset celebratis abrogans in predictis fori privilegio non sui et non conpetentis inde legi si convenerit capitulo conventioni et omni alli juri.

Actum in Syo sub logia ponderis Syi, anno dominice nativitatis MCCCLXXXXIIII, indicione prima secundum cursum Janue, die prima Septembris, post vesperas et ante completorium. Presentibus testibus, Symone Perollo de Vultero, Raffaele de Coronato, Pasqualino de Pontremullo, burgensibus Syi, fratre Angello de Perusio, priore Romano, fratre Antoniode Perusio, fratre Gonzallo de Eredia, fratre Artaldo de Valseris et Nicolo Macia de Diano, cancellario dicti domini fratri Domenici, vocatis et rogatis.

7 1394.ix.1 = ASG, Notaio, Donato de Clavaro, Sc. 39, filza 1, doc. 172 (173)

In nomine domini amen. Cum inter dominum capitaneum Smirrarum ex una parte et dominum subasi Smirrarum ex altera confirmata fuerint sacramenta composiciones et pacta aliarum inter ipothetica[?] jurita et facta pro quibus observandis dictus dominus subasi Smirrarum deposuerit penes nobilem virum dominum Antonium Justinianum[89] ducatos decem milia auri sive valorem ipsorum videlicet in peccunia auri, perlis, jochalibus et alliis rebus pro ipsis deponendis penes dominacionem Syi sub cortis pactis videlicet ex tali modo contentis videlicet quod semper et quandocumque per unam ex dictis partibus fuerit contrafactum sacramentis pactis et conventionibus predictis quod altera pars reversum habere debeat ad dictam pronotam[?] contrafacionem etc quod si tunc aptaverit per eam[90] et remediabitur in eis benequidam, et si[91] non adimpleverit tunc[92] teneatur habere reversum ad magnificum dominum Metelini et dictum dominum Antonium qui teneantur et debeant super lamentacionibus et contrafactionibus[93] providere et taliter operare quod per dictam partem contrafacientem observetur que debet et tenetur vigore

---

[85] 'alioquam penam dupli' crossed out.   [86] 'proprio' inserted above the line.
[87] 'proprio' inserted above the line.   [88] 'ubique' in margin.
[89] 'flor' crossed out.   [90] 'per eam' inserted above the line.
[91] 'g' crossed out.   [92] 'tunc' inserted above the line.
[93] 'pro <dictis>' written above the line and crossed out.

dictorum sacramentorum et composicionum ut supra quod si tunc non fecerit[94] dicta pignora dari et tradi debeant parte observante si vero per dominum capitaneum Smirrarum non observerentur que in dictis sacramentalibus continentur[95] quod tunc prefactus dominus Metelini et dictus dominus Antonius vel al<ius>[96] ipsorum reversum habere debeant ad reverendum in Christo patrem[97] dominum fratrem Domenicum Alamania preceptorem Neapolis et Avenionensis[98] qui tunc teneatur facere observari per dominum capitaneum Smirrarum[99] ea in quibus ipse delinquit quod tunc et eo casu dictus dominus frater Domenicus teneatur restituere d<i>cta[100] pignora peccuniam etc et merces sive depositum ad manus dicte domini Antonii vel domini[101] subasi Smirrarum[102] et sciens ipse dominus Antonius dictam depositionem peccunie et rerum ut supra captam non fuisse[103] per dominacionem Syi[104] nec ipsam dominacionem ipsum dictum depositum aceptasse sciens, quod eo casu se habere bayliam a dicto domino subasi Smirrarum[105] dictum depositum dandi et consignandi[106] dicto[107] reverendo in Christo patri domino fatri Domenico de Alamania[108] in proprio vigore lisani dicti domini subasi[109] et cognito quod dictum depositum sive peccunia etc et merces predicte delicte fuerint in sindicis in Syo super galeam ipsius domini fratris Domenici.

Et volens in observatione predictorum dictas ut supra peccuniam, jochalia et merces ut supra dare et tradere et consignare dicto domino fratri Domenico proprio[110] in observatione predictorum. Id circo prefactus dominus frater Domenicus

---

[94] Abbreviation for 'fecerint' crossed out.

[95] 'quod d<   > et cognita per supradictos dominum Metilini et dominum Antonium' crossed out and 'que in dictis sacramentalibus continentur' written above.

[96] Part of the word is obliterated by the fold in the paper.

[97] 'prefactum' crossed out and 'reverendum in Christo patrem' written above.

[98] 'Alamania preceptorem Neapolis et Avenionensis' is written at the bottom of the right-hand column of the manuscript. It is not clear where it should be inserted, but here seems the most likely place.

[99] 'q<   > declarata et cognata fuerit per predictos' crossed out. Most of the first word is obliterated by a fold in the paper.

[100] Word partly obscured by fold in the paper.

[101] 'domini' inserted above the line.

[102] 'si vero per dominum capitaneum Smirrarum non observerentur que in dictis sacramentalibus continentur quod tunc prefactus dominus Metelini et dictus dominus Antonius vel al<ius> ipsorum reversum habere debeant ad reverendum in Christo patrem dominum fratrem Domenicum Alamania preceptorem Neapolis et Avenionensis qui tunc teneatur facere observari per dominum capitaneum Smirrarum ea in quibus ipse delinquit quod tunc et eo casu dictus dominus frater Domenicus teneatur restituere d<i>cta pignora peccuniam etc et merces sive depositum ad manum dicte domini Antonii vel domini subasi Smirrarum' is written at the bottom of the page with a mark for insertion into the text.

[103] Word crossed out.

[104] 'aceptatam' is inserted above the line and crossed out. The accompanying insertion mark is also deleted.

[105] Word crossed out.

[106] 'et consignandi' is added at the end of the line.

[107] 'dicto' added at the beginning of the line and 'domino' crossed out.

[108] 'preceptori Neapoli' crossed out. Beginning of new column. 'et Avenionensis' crossed out at beginning of new column.

[109] 'vigore lisani dicti domini subasi' inserted above the line. 'Lisani' is the *nişan*: see Zachariadou, *Trade and Crusade*, p. 241.

[110] 'proprio' inserted above the line.

proprius[111] confesse fuit et in veritate recognovit prefacto domino Antonio Justiniano presenti, stipulanti et recipienti, se ab ipso habuisse et recepisse dictum depositum sive dictam peccuniam, jochalia etc et merces preciatas pro ipso deposito dictorum ducatorum decem millium ut supra eo modo et forma quibus dictus dominus Antonius cepit a dicto domino subasi Smirarum.

Renuncians exceptioni presentis confesionis et recognicionis non facte[112] peccunie, jocalium, rerum et mercium ut supra ext<unc>[113] pro dicto deposito non habitis, non receptis et non[114] numerate[?] rei sic ut supra et infra non esse vel sic non se habentis doli, mali, metus infactum actioni condicioni secundum causa omni jure.

Quas quantitates peccunie, rerum, jocalium et mercium pro dicto deposito ut[115] ut supra dictus dominus frater Domenicus proprius promitit et convenit dicto domino Antonio, presenti et stipulanti,[116] restituere et restitui facere ipsi domino Antonio sive prefacto domino subasi Smirrarum vel legiptime persone pro eis finitis annis quinque proxime pre venturis dummodo per dictas partes sibi ad invicem et vicisim fuerint observata sacramenta pacta et conventiones supradicta.[117]

Que omnia et singula supradicta[118] prefactus reverendus dominus frater Domenicus juravit ad sancta dei evangelia corporaliter tactis scripturis et promisit et convenit dicto domino Antonio, presenti et stipulanti, actendere, complere et observare et in nullo contrafacere vel venire aliqua racione, occasione vel causa que dicti vel excogitari possit de jure seu de facto, sub pena dupli totius eius de quo et quanto contrafieret vel utsupra non observaretur cum restitucione etiam omnium aliorum dampnorum, interesse et expensarum que proterea fierent lictis et extra. Rattis manentibus supradictis, et sub ypotheca et obligatione omnium bonorum prefacti reverendi domini fratris Domenici habitorum et habendorum.

Acto in presenti instrumento solempniter et convento quod pro predictis omnibus et singulis prefactus reverendus dominus frater Domenicus realiter et personaliter conveniri possit capi et detineri hic Janue, Pise, Nicie, Neapoli, Rodo, Peyre, Caffa, Famagoste et ubique alibi locorum et ubique[119] et terrarum et sub quocumque iudice, officio et magistratu ecclesiastico et civili et ubi inventis, conventis seu requisitis fuerit ibi per pactum de predictis eidem domino Antonio sive procuratori suo juri stare, respondere solutionem et satisfactionem ac restitutionem de predictis[120] facere teneatur et promisit eidem ac si per inde pars[121] contractus ibidem fuisset celebratis abrenuncians in predictis fo [?] previlegio non sui et non conpetentis judicis legi si convenit capitulo convencioni et omni alii juri.

---

[111] 'proprius' inserted above the line.
[112] 'depositi predicti ut supra non habiti et [?] recepti sive' crossed out.
[113] Word partly obliterated by a hole in the paper.
[114] 'non' inserted above the line.
[115] 'pro dicto deposito ut' inserted above the line.
[116] Several words crossed out.   [117] Beginning of a new column.
[118] 'supradicta' inserted above the line. 'dicte partes sibi ad invicem et vicisim iuraverunt ad sancta dei evangelia corporaliter tactis scripturis et promisserunt et con' crossed out.
[119] 'ubique' added at the left hand of the line.
[120] 'ac restitutionem de predictis' inserted above the line.
[121] Beginning of a new column.

Actum in Syo sub logia ponderis Syi, anno dominice nativitatis MCCCLXXXXIIII, indicione prima secundum cursum Ja<nue>, <d>ie[122] prima Septembris post vesperas et ante completorium. Presentibus testibus, Symone Perello de Vultero, Raffaele de Coronato, Pasqualino de Pontremullo, burgensibus Syi, fratre Angello de Perusio, priore Rome, fratre Antonio de Perusio, fratre Gonzallo de Eredia, fratre Altaldo de Varseris et Nicolao Macia de Diano, cancellario dicti domini fratris Domenici, vocatis et rogatis.

8 1413.i. = ASG, Notaio, Giovanni Balbi, Sc. 46, filza 1, f.104[123]

Summary

Georgio, ambassador from Rhodes, makes an offer to the *podestà* and others of Chios to intercede on their behalf with Paşa Turchus over their current war with Cüneyd, ruler of Aydın.

Text

MCCCCXIII <   >[124] Januarii

Spectabilis dominus Potestas, domini Bernardus Paterius, Otobonus Justinianus, Baptistus de Rocha, Quilicus Justinianus, Franciscus et Johannes Justinianus de Campis considerantes et ad[vertentes] dominum Georgium ambaxiatorem de Roddo rogamento ipsorum se velle interponere con domino Bassa Turcho de querra vigenti inter dominum Jonoiti Turchum et ipsos dominos et ob ad fore dignum sibi domino Georgio quod videri de expensis digno premio ac in reditum ipsius de passagio con quo habiliter R<oddum>[125] se transfer[e] possit nec minus advertentes pro predictis ad dictum dominum Georgium transmissise[126] nobiles viros dominos Otobonum et Franciscum Justinianos qui parte ipsorum spectabilium dominorum potestatis et consiliariorum sibi promiserunt dum intendat de ipsa pace se ministeri et ad dictum Bassa se tran[sferre][127] subvenire de expensis <dicto>[128] premio et[129] passagio predictis, scientis et de foris factum, de sciencia et voluntate ipsorum promiserunt[130] et decreverunt autoritate[131] presentium predicta attendere[132] et adimplere ipsi nobili viro domino Georgio adveniento casu predicto.

---

[122] Some letters obliterated by a hole in the paper.
[123] It seem probable that this document was enacted in Chios as it is found together with others enacted there.
[124] The word or words here are obscured by a splodge of ink.
[125] The word here is obscured by a splodge of ink.
[126] 'dictum' crossed out in manuscript.
[127] This word is somewhat obscured by a hole in the manuscript.
[128] This word is somewhat obscured by a hole in the manuscript.
[129] 'ac' crossed out in manuscript.
[130] The end of this word is obscured by an ink splodge.
[131] 'partium' crossed out in manuscript.
[132] The word in the manuscript is 'adttendere' with the 'd' crossed out.

9 1413.viii.28 = ASG, Notaio, Giovanni Balbi, Sc. 46, filza 1, doc. 255

Summary

Cagi (Kadı/Hacı) Sati ogli (Satıoğlu?) Turchus, ambassador of Cüneyd, the ruler of Aydın, appeared before the *podestà* of Chios with letters to the *podestà* translated from Greek into Latin protesting over a court case involving Cagi (Kadı/Hacı) Sorti of Theologos, a subject of Cüneyd. Cagi Sorti had a financial claim against the *fideicommissors* of the late Sorleone Salvaigo. He had, however, been unable to appear in Chios for the case, and an adjournment for one year had been granted. Now, the year having elapsed, Cagi was still unable to attend and had heard that the Genoese authorities wanted the case heard not in Chios but in Genoa. This, the letter said, would be unjust/unlawful.

Text

In nomine domini amen. Anno domini MCCCCXIII die vigesima octava Augusti.

Vir prudens Cagi Sati[133] ogli Turchus lugatus[134] et ambaxiator magnifici domini Joanit Turchi smirrarum domini etc. comparuit coram spectabili domino[135] Paulo de Montaldo, honorabili potestate et gubernatore civitatis et insulle Chii, literas tenoris infrascriptis [credencie] representans in literis grecis redatas in literis latinis[136] per me notarium infrascriptum retradente.[137]

Eidem egregio domino potestati et consillio eius quorum nomina sunt hec.[138]

Exponens pro parte prelibati domini domini Jonait quod skillicet quidam Cagi Sorti de Theologo subditus domini domini Jonait iam mensibus XVII incirca quandam causam habuit in curia Chii con fideicommisariis contra Sorleonis Salvaigi pro ducatis III in circa secundum quod patet in actis curie predicte, et quod huc usque dictus eius subditus non potuit expedicionem in dicta curia consequi < >[139] ymo dictis fideicommisariis data fuit per ollim dominum vicarium ollim dominum potestatis dillacio contra dictum Cagi ad probandum anni unius qui terminus elapsus est, et nichilominus non potest dictus Cagi suum jus consequi contra dictos fideicomisarios, nec expedicionem dicte cause haberi, ymo quod plus est sentit quod de civitate Janue emanavit quandam literam pro parte ilustris domini Marchionis Montisferati capitanei Januensium etc. domino potestati predicto per quam jubet ipsi domino potestati ut jus administrare dicto Cagi non vellit nec cum in dicta causa audire, sed ymo ipsum transmitere ad audienciam magistratus civitatis Janue quod quedem iniuriose et cavilose.

---

133 The manuscript has 'satiogli' with 'ogli' crossed out and written separately.
134 Thus in the manuscript, presumably for 'legatus'.
135 Followed in manuscript by 'potestate et gubernatore' crossed out.
136 'inter' crossed out.
137 This is followed by a blank page, presumably for filling in later.
138 This is followed by a blank page, presumably for filling in later.
139 The word is obscured by a hole in the manuscript.

10 1414.iii.18 = ASG, Notaio, Giovanni Balbi, Sc. 46, filza, 1, doc. 288

Summary

Moyses de Meir was granted exemption by the Chian authorities for payment of taxes on grain and also on money either handed to or received from Cüneyd.

Text

In nomine domini amen. Spectabilis dominus Paulus de Montaldo honorabilis potestas et gubernator civitatis et insule Chii. In presentia, auctoritate et consenssu prudentium virorum dominorum Bernardi Paterii, Baptisti Justiniani de Campis, Johannis Justiniani de Garibaldo, Octoboni Justiniani, Gabrieli Justiniani olim Recaneli, Ambrosii Justiniani de Banca,[140] Quilici Justiniani olim de Furneto, Francischi Justiniani[141] olim de Furneto et Johannis Justiniani olim de Campis. Et ipsi prudentes domini consiliarii in presentia, auctoritate, voluntate et consenssu prefacti spectabillis domini potestatis, existentes in sala palacii residencie ipsius prefacti[142] spectabilis domini potestatis, ubi consilia solita sunt et librari. Advertentes et certam scientiam habentes iam per dictum Anthonium Marruffum olim potestatum Chii et eiusdem consilium magistrem Moysem[143] de Meir, Judeum, fixicum, civem et habitatorem Chii, fuisse pluribus condignis racionibus et respectibus franchitum et liberatum a quibuscumque honeribus, gr<av>aminibus,[144] imposicionibus et angariis.[145] Advertentes nec minus de presenti ortam esse controversiam super dicta franchixia qua vertitur in dubium utrum ipse magister Moyses teneatur et obligatus sit prestancionibus peccuniarum porectarum Jonayt bey Turcho et pro grano distributo per dominos officiales provissionis presentis civitatis Chii. Scientes et advertentes nec minus esse intencionis ipsorum prefactorum spectabilis domini potestatis et dominorum consiliariorum quod idem magister Moyses penitus a dictis prestacionibus et aliis quibuscumque gravaminibus[146] de cetero imponendis totaliter liberetur et pro[147] excepto habeatur.[148] Id circo auctoritate presentis publici decreti proprio valituri dictum magistrem Moysem presentem et humiliter requirentem justis precedentibus causis, franchiverunt, liberaverunt et penitus a quibuscumque angariis, prestacionibus, mutuis, avariis realibus et personalibus acepcione grani predicti seu alio quo[vis] modo sibi imponendis et a contrabucione peccuniarum aliquarum sibi quoquo modo de cetero imponendarum et sive ipse peccunie traderentur alicui domino Turcho sive de ipsis aliqualiter disponerentur absolverunt.[149] Decernentes auctoritate presenti franchixie et immunitatis fuisse et esse derogatum quibuscumque legibus, statutis previlegiis et decretis quibus contra predictam quis opponere velet seu intenderet ac omni alii juri quo

---

[140] word crossed out in manuscript after 'Banca'.
[141] 'Justi' crossed out in the manuscript.
[142] 'spest' crossed out in manuscript.   [143] 'Moyses', thus in manuscript.
[144] A hole in the manuscript here obliterates some letters.
[145] 'quibuscumque' crossed out.
[146] 'gravaminibus' is written above the line.
[147] A few letters are crossed out here.
[148] 'totaliter' to 'habeatur' is written down the margin and it is not clear where it fits in. I think it should go in here.
[149] Several lines crossed out here.

caveretur[150] quod contra predictam responciari non potuisset seu posset. Mandantes quibuscumque officialibus, provissionibus, partitoribus seu distributoribus sive grani sive peccuniarum sive aliorum onerum. Quatenus predictum magistrem Moysem de cetero[151] occassionibus predictis non molestent nec in hiis cum aliqualiter nominent ymo totaliter exclusum habeant et teneant sub pena solvendi de eorum proprio illas prestaciones, dacitas, soluciones et acepciones grani et peccuniarum[152] quas eidem imponeretur mandantes de predictis per me notarium et cancilarium infrascriptum ipsorum[153] prefactorum spectabilis domini potestatis et dominorum consiliariorum confit debere presentem publicum decretum[154] commpressione sigilli ipsorum assueti ad robur premissorum.[155]

11 1414.iv.2 = ASG, Notaio, Giovanni Balbi, Sc. 46, filza 1, doc. 286

Summary

Case of arbitration over the sale of cotton involving Katib Paşa Turchus of Bergama.

Text

In nomine domini amen. Raffaelis Centurionus domini Johannis, civis Janue et Johannes Paterius civis Chii[156] tamquam factor Alamani[157] Sofiano de Foliis Veteribus necnon nomine et vice Catip Bassa Turchi de Bergamo pro quibus de rato habitus ad cautelam promixerunt subditis[158]

De et super omnibus littibus, questionibus, differenciis et[159] controverssiis vertentibus et verti sperantibus occassione[160] emptionis certorum cotonorum factis hoc anno per dictum Raffaelem a predictis Alamano et Chitipi.[161]

Sese compromisserunt plenum, largum, liberum et generalem compromissum facerunt in duos Enricum[162] Justinianum et Ugolinum de Vinaldis tamquam in eorum arbitros arbitratores et amicabiles compositores et caros amicos[163]

---

[150] 'presentas predictas' crossed out.   [151] 'occ' crossed out.
[152] 'et peccuniarum' written above the line.   [153] 'specta' crossed out.
[154] 'Actum ut supra anno dominice nativitate millessimo quadringentessimo quarto indicione sexta secundum cursum Janue die decimo otavo Marcii.
        Actum in civitate Chii videlicet in sala palacii residencie prefactorum spectabilis domini potestatis et dominorum consiliariorum ubi consilia solita sunt ac librari, anno dominice nativitatis millesimo quadringentessimo decimo quarto, indicione sexta secundum curssum Janue, die decima octava Marcii in terciis' crossed out. 'Sala' is written 'salalla' in the MS with 'lla' crossed out. 'dominorum' is crossed out after 'prefactorum'.
[155] 'commpressione sigilli ipsorum assueti ad robur premissorum' is inserted after 'publicum decretum'.
[156] 'de et super omnibus littibus questionibus differenciis' crossed out in manuscript.
[157] 'so' crossed out in manuscript.
[158] There follows a large empty space in the manuscript.
[159] 'contro' crossed out in manuscript.
[160] Word crossed out here in manuscript.
[161] There follows an empty space in the manuscript.
[162] 'Enricum' is written in full and the abbreviation sign above 'um' is crossed out.
[163] This is followed by a gap in the manuscript.

Dantes etc.[164]

Promitentes etc.[165]

Sub pena ducatorum viginti quinque auri duratarum[166] hinc ad festum pasce proxime venturum[167]

Sub etc.[168]

Actum in civitate Chii videlicet ad bancham civem portum in barbachana murorum dicte civitate, anno dominice nativitatis M CCCCXIIII, indicione sexta secundum cursum Janue, die secondo Aprilis. Presentibus Johane de Serra, notor,[169] Benedeto de Plano, civibus Janue.

12 1414.vii.16 = ASG, Notaio, Giovanni Balbi, Sc. 46, filza 1, doc. 311

Summary

Sipahi Bayezid, son the the late Jhacsi, a Turk from cazali isich obasi (the small settlement of ?Ece Ovası), acknowledged to Giovanni Balbi, acting for Domenico Giustiniano, receipt of payment for grain, money and other goods which Bayezid had on any occasion sold to Domenico.

Text

In nomine domini amen. Sapihi[170] Bayazit[171] quondam Jhacsi, Turchus de Cazali isich obasi sponte et ex certa scientia et nulo juris vel facti ducto errore[172] fuit confessus et in veritate publice recognovit mihi notario infrascripto tamquam publice persone officio publico[173] stipulanti et recipienti nomine et vice domini Domenichi Justiniani quondam Andrioli et habentum ab eo causam et per me eidem domino Domenicho licet absenti[174] se a dicto domino Domenicho habuisse et recepisse integram solucionem,[175] racionem et veram satisfacionem de omni eo et toto quidquid et quamto[176] ullo umquam tempore de bonis peccuniis grano specialiter et rebus ipsius Sapihi Bayaxit pervenerit ad manus gubernacionem seu vertutem ipsius domini Domenichi.

---

[164] These two words are written under each other in the left-hand side of the page and followed by an empty space in the manuscript.

[165] These two words are written under each other in the left-hand side of the page and followed by an empty space in the manuscript.

[166] 'du[?]bus tribus' is crossed out here in the manuscript.

[167] This is written partly down the left-hand side of the second page of this document and followed by an empty space in the manuscript.

[168] These two words are written under each other in the left-hand side of the second page of this document and followed by an empty space in the manuscript.

[169] 'Jo' crossed out in manuscript.   [170] Sipahi.

[171] 'Bayz' crossed out before this word.

[172] 'sponte et ex certa scientia et nulo juris vel facti ducto errore' written above the line and down the right-hand side of the margin.

[173] 'publico' inserted above the line.   [174] 'se' crossed out.

[175] 'solucionem' inserted above the line.

[176] 'dictus dominus dominus Domenicus et dictus Sapihi Bayaxit <   >' crossed out.

Renuncians exceptis presentis confessionis non fa<ctis>[177] rei sic ut supra non esse, non fuisse et sic vel aliter non se habente dolli, mali, metus infactum actioni condicioni cum causa vel sine et omni alii juri. Quas volens facere que juris sunt et ipsum dominum Domenichum licet absentem agnoscere bonam fidem eumdem dictum Domenichum verssus me notarium jam dictum ut supra stipulantem et recipientem nomine ipsius[178] quitavit, liberavit et absolvit de omni eo et toto quitquid et quanto ipse Sapihi Bayaxit a dicto domino Domenicho vel in bonis ipsius pettere vel requirere posset quavis raccione, occassione vel cause quo modo[179] aliquo vel ingenio diti seu excogitari possit.[180] Promittens mihi, notario infrascripto tamquam publice persone officio publico ut supra stipulanti et recipienti nomine et vice dicti domini Domenichi, per dicta omnia et singula attendere, complere et observare et in nichillo contrafacere vel venire aliqua racione, occassione vel cause que modo aliquo vel ingenio diti seu excogitari possit de jure seu de facto.

Sub pena dupli totius eiusdem quo et quamto contrafieret vel ut supra non obervaretur solempni stipulat[a], valata et in tanta quantitatis taxata[181] et conventa de comuni acordio et voluntate[182] ipsarum partium pro vero dampno et interesse et qua pena soluta vel non soluta nichilominus[183] raticare remaneant omnia et singula supra et infrascripta. Et pro inde et ad sic observandum pignori obligavit omnia bona sua presencia et futura.

Acto quod predictis dictus[184] Sapihi Bayazit posit ubique locorum et terrarum conveniri[185] reali<ter> et specialiter proinde ac si presens contractus ibidem esset celebratus.

Actum in civitate Chii videlicet ad bancum civem ubi jura redduntur per spectabilem <dominum>[186] potestatum Chii, situm in barbacana murorum dicti civitatis, anno dominice nativitatis millessimo quadringentessimo decimo quarto, indicione sexta secundum cursum Janue, die[187] sexta decima Jullii in vesperis. Presentibus testibus, Galvaro de Levento, Bartholomeo de Portufino notario, Lanfranco Paterio, Micalli Verioti de Foliis veteribus Grecho, Bayrambey[188] Turcho de Smirris quondam Ezedim,[189] Elies[190] Turcho de Smirris quondam Tagdira et Cristoforo Picenino interpetre civem Chii lingue turche ex parto interpretante ad instanciam dicti Sapihi Bayazit[191] de linqua turcha in latina, vocatis specialiter et rogatis
Johannes Balus, notarius

---

[177] Part of the word obliterated by a hole in the paper.
[178] 'nomine ipsius' inserted above the line.   [179] 'mo' crossed out.
[180] Beginning of a new column.   [181] 'et quod' crossed out.
[182] 'voluntatat' in manuscript with the second 'ta' crossed out.
[183] 'Et proinde etc' crossed out.   [184] 'dictus' inserted above the line.
[185] 'possit' crossed out.   [186] Word obliterated by a hole in the paper.
[187] 'qua' crossed out.   [188] Bayram Bey.   [189] İzeddin.   [190] İlyas.
[191] 'ad instanciam dicti Sapihi Bayazit' inserted above the line.

Glossary

accono – a cloth measurement of an arm's length used in Theologos

akçe – Greek *aspron*, Latin *asper*, silver coin used by the Turkish rulers

amalim, amalium – seems to be the Latin equivalent of the Arabic *'amal*, a tax farm

anaris – a general term for tax

ancona – see *accono*

apaltator, appaltator – tax farmer

Apalto, appalto – tax farm; see also *gabella*

aurepelium – Dutch gold, imitation gold leaf, very malleable alloy of two parts zinc and eleven parts copper, beaten into thin leaves

bac – tax, toll, market dues

barcha – a small boat

batman – also *battimano* or *patumani*, measurement of weight used in Theologos and Balat, and also in North Africa and the Black Sea region; its weight varied according to place: 1 *batman* of Theologos was 9.993 kg, that of Balat was 15.741 kg (see Schilbach, *Metrologie*, p. 284, but see also Zachariadou, *Trade and Crusade*, pp. 151–2, where she argues that in fact the measurement may have been the same in both beyliks)

bessant – term used by Latins for the gold *dinar*, and for other units of account derived from the *dinar*; very widespread as unit of account used by Europeans in the Maghreb and the Levant

beylerbeyi – top Ottoman official in provincial government, head of a *beylerbeylik*; there were originally two *beylerbeyi*s, one as governor of Anatolia, one of Rumeli

bocasini – a cloth of very fine linen

botte – a wine measurement varying from place to place

braccia – a cloth measurement, an arm's length, exact length varied from place to place

buckram – a fine material

burgensis – inhabitant of a town

buta, buta de mena – a wine measurement

calbano – steelyard balance; see also *stadera*

camelot, camlet – a type of cloth made, possibly, from camel's fur, and from mohair

canna – a cloth measurement: 3–4 *braccia* = 1 *canna*

capsa – see *cassa*

caricum – a load

cassa – or *capsa*, a container for soap.

chanela – a measurement of approximately ten to twelve palms

cizye – a poll tax paid by non-Muslims

cocha – Turkish *köke*, a round sail-powered ship, three or four decks

comerchium, commerchium – customs tax

comerclum – see *comerchium*

concilius – a member of a council

çiliatos – see *gigliato*

datium – a general term for tax

dellal – broker who collected the *dellaliyye*, an important official in Ottoman markets

dellaliyye – brokerage tax

denaro – a general term for silver *penny* coinages. In the thirteenth century, larger silver coins, *grossi*, were struck in northern Italian cities. In contrast to these new coins, *denari* began to be called *piccoli*

deniers – silver *penny* coinage in France; see *denaro*

dexena – an amount of ten

dinar – Arab coin, called *besant* by Latins. Divided into 24 *karati*

dirhem – Arab silver coin, called *migliorese* or *millarenses* by Latins

ducat – a Venetian gold coin; struck first in 1284, it became the 'dollar' currency of the eastern Mediterranean in the fifteenth century

fardello – a bundle, particularly used for silk

fideicommissor – one who receives an inheritance through a *fideicommissum*, a bequest given for the benefit of a third person

fil de fero – iron wire

florin – a gold coin struck first in Florence in 1252. It replaced the *hyperpyron* as the 'dollar' currency of the eastern Mediterranean in the fourteenth century and was in turn superseded by the *ducat*

gabella – a tax farm

galley – Turkish *kadırga*, large warship with a single bank of oars, usually twelve on each side, also used for cargo transport

gaza – a raid for plunder, which later came to mean holy war fought for Islam

gazi – a fighter in *gaza*

genovino – a Genoese gold coin, struck first in 1252. Although of great importance in general in the Mediterranean, it never became a dominant coinage in the Levant

gigliato – or *carlino*, a silver coin struck by Charles II of Anjou in Naples at the beginning of the fourteenth century which became a common currency in the eastern Mediterranean. It was imitated by the rulers of Aydın and Menteşe

gripa – Turkish *iğribar*, a small ship used for trading

hass – lands belonging to the sultan, to royal princes, to the *beylerbeyi* or to the *sancakbeyi*

hyperpyron – a Byzantine gold coin, divided into 24 *karati*. Initially the dominant currency in the eastern Mediterranean, it declined in significance during the fourteenth century, becoming a money of account. After the middle of the fourteenth century the *hyperpyron* in circulation was silver

introytus – import tax or revenues

kadı – judge of Islamic *şeriat* law and the chief administrator of a judicial district

kamkha – Camaca, a fine material, probably silk

kantar – a measurement of weight, varying according to location: a Genoese *kantar* = *c*.47 kg *kanun* – law, code of laws

kapan – a balance used for heavy goods such as foodstuffs

karati – division of a *hyperpyron*: there were 24 *karati* to 1 *hyperpyron*

kethüda – Ottoman government official, agent

lala – the person who had been tutor to the reigning sultan as a child

lepton – a silver coin, also called *aspron* or *argyron*

ligno – a small boat

mazo – a bundle

migliaro – a measurement: a Genoese *migliaro* was equal to 1483,53 metres

mine – common weight and dry measure: in Genoa 1 *mine* of grain = on average *c*.82 kg

mizan – a balance used for cloth and other commodities which were not very weighty

modio – a dry measure, varying widely according to location: 1 *modio* of Romania = *c*.317 litres

montonine – sheepskin

mudd – a dry measure, varying according to location, used for grain

mukataa – tax farm

pani – cloth

pani bastardi – very fine textiles, popular in the eastern Levant; originally made in England, but then imitated in Padua and probably elsewhere

pani loesti – coarse cloth; the name possibly derives from Lowestoft, or from the word 'lowest'. It was made originally in England

pele de chastron – goatskin

peşkeş – present or offering given by an inferior to a superior

podestà – the top government official in Genoese colonies

ribebe – a measurement of grain used in Alexandria, the exact weight of which is not established, but perhaps somewhere in the region of 150–60 litres (see Zachariadou, *Trade and Crusade*, p. 147)

rotol – a division of weight: 100 *rotol*s = 1 Genoese *kantar*

sancakbeyi – Ottoman governor of a *sancak*, an administrative division of an Ottoman province

saye – a type of cloth, a woollen or linen serge

scarlattini – fine woollen cloth, usually, though not always, scarlet coloured

senseraggio – brokerage

seruch – seems to have been a grain measurement, possibly, according to Professor Zachariadou, equivalent to the capacity measure, the *çeyrek*, equal to between 60 and 62 litres (see Zachariadou, *Trade and Crusade*, p. 149)

simsar – the head of the brokers in the market

società – business partnership.

soldo – a shilling, made up of 12 *denari*

sommo – silver coin used in Black Sea region, made up of 45 *saggi*

sous – a shilling; see *soldo*

stadera – a steelyard balance with one arm

straperronos – a cloth measurement

subaşı – an Ottoman official, holder of a military grant and in charge of an administrative district, or an agent acting for a provincial governor

yasak kulu – an Ottoman official dispatched specifically from the central administration to ensure the application of law and to deal with infringements

yük – a load, a weight measurement varying widely according to merchandise and location

zanbeloti – camlet

Place names

Modern name	Other names
Alanya	Alaiye, Caloronos, Candelor, Candelore, Korakesion
Alaşehir	Philadelphia
Amasra	Amastris, Samachi, Samastri, Samastro
Amasya	Amaseia
Antalya	Adalia, Attaleia, Attalia, Satarea, Setalia
Asınkalesi	Iasis, Lasso
Balat	Milet, Miletus, Palatia
Bayburt	Paypert
Bergama	Pergamon
Bilecik	Bekloma
Birgi	Pyrgion
Bodrum	Petronion
Bozcaada	Tenedos
Bursa	Brusa, Prousa, Prusa
Büyükçekmece	Gulf of Atira
Çeşme	Aerythrea
Chios	Sakız
Crete	Candia, Girid
Denizli	Ladhik, Laodikeai, Thingozlou
Didimotiho	Didymoteichon, Dimetoka
Dubrovnik	Ragusa
Edirne	Adrianople
Edremit	Adramyttion
Eğriboz	Ağriboz, Chalcis, Egripos, Euboea, Negroponte
Enez	Ainos, Enos
Ereğli	Benderereğli, Heraclea Pontica
Erzıncan	Arsinga, Arzinga, Arzingaal
Eski Liman	Diaschilo
Eskişehir	Dorylaeum
Fethiye	Makre, Makri, Meğri
Finike	Finica, Finika, Fine
Foça	Fogis, Phokaea
Gelibolu	Gallipoli, Kallipolis

179

Giresun	Cerasonte, Chisenda, Jursona, Kerasus
Gümüşhane	Argiron, Argyropolis
İncir Liman	Liminia, Limnia, Paralime, Paralimine
İzmir	Smyrna
İzmit	Nicomedia
Iznik	Nicaea
Kadı Kalesi	Anaea, Ania
Kapıdağ	Aydıncık, Cassico, Chisico, Cyzicus
Karpathos	Kerpe, Scarpanto
Kayseri	Caesarea, Kayseriye
Kırklareli	Kırkkilise, Kirk Kilise
Kos	İstanköy
Küçükçekmece	Rhegion
Kütahya	Coltai, Cottai, Kotaion
Lapseki	Lampsacus
Lemnos	Limni
Lesbos	Midilli, Mytilene, Mitylini
Manisa	Magnesia
Meriç	Ebros, Maritsa
Milas	Mylassa
Niğbolu	Nikopolis
Plovdiv	Filibe, Philippopolis
Rhodes	Rodos
Sakarya	Sangarios
Samos	Sisam
Samsun	Amisos, Simisso
Şebinkarahisar	Colonna, Karahisar, Koloneia
Selçuk	Altoluogo, Ayasoluk, Ephesus, Theologos
Setia	Sithe
Silivri	Selembria
Sinop	Sinopoli, Sozopolis
Sivas	Salvastro, Savasco, Sebasteia
Sultanhisar	Nyssa
Tekirdağ	Rodosçuk, Rodosto
Thessaloniki	Salonica, Selanik, Solun
Trabzon	Trebizond
Ulubat	Lopadion, Lupai, Lupaio, Ulek Abad
Üsküdar	Scutari
Yalova	Helenopolis, Yaylakabad

Select bibliography

Unpublished primary sources

Archivio di Stato di Genova

Notario, cartulare
Giovanni Veggio, C. 20/I; Guilielmus de Cendata, C. 101; Vivaldus de Sarzana, Antonius de Quarto, C. 105; Simonis de Albario, C. 120/I; Antonius Feloni, C. 174; Antonius Feloni, C. 175; Tommaso de Casanova, C. 229; Tommaso de Casanova, C. 235; Domenico Ottone, C. 271; Georgius de Ponte de Framura, C. 296/I; Georgius de Ponte de Framura, C. 296/II; Pellegrini Bracelli, C. 317; Giovanni Ognibono *et altri*, C. 318; Giovanni Bardi, C. 381; Rafaele Cazanova, C. 385; Antonio de Credentia, C. 411; Giovanni Nole et Michele Bonaventura, C. 412; Antonio Foglietta, C. 468/I; Antonio Foglietta, C. 468/II; Johannis de Alegro, C. 472; Oberto Grassi di Voltri, C. 473; Donato de Clavaro, C. 476; Julianus Cannella, C. 478; Antonio Senior Fazio, C. 586 (Sc. 44, filza 12); Giovanni de Recco, C. 596 (Sc. 46, filza 1); Bernardo de Ferrari, C. 765

Notai Filze
Gregorio Panissario, Sc. 37, filza 1; Donato de Clavaro, Sc. 39, filza 1; Giovanni Labaino, Sc. 40, filza 1; Giovanni Balbi, Sc. 46, filza 1; Antonio Foglietta, Sc. 77, filza 1; Tommaso de Recco, Sc. 77, filza 1

Notai Ignoti
Notai Ignoti A; Notai Ignoti B; Notai Ignoti E; Notai Ignoti E *bis*; Notai Ignoti O; Notai Ignoti VI; Notai Ignoti XIV; Notai Ignoti XV; Notai Ignoti XVIII; Notai Ignoti XXI; Notai Ignoti 15

Archivio di San Giorgio
Caffa Massaria 1221 *bis*; Sala 34 590/1268 (Famagusta Massaria); Sala 34 590/1304 (Peira Massaria); Sala 34 590/1305 (Peira Massaria); Sala 34 590/1306 (Peira Massaria); Sala 34 590/1307 (Peira Massaria); Sala 34 607/2232 (registri); Sala 34 607/2233 (registri); Sala 35, Cancellieri Gerolamo Spinula 223/35; Sala 35, Cancellieri Gerolamo Spinula 228; Sala 39, Primi Cancellieri, busta 88; Manoscritti Membranacei IV; Manoscritti Membranacei V; Manoscritti Membranacei VI

Archivio Segreto, diversorum Communis Janue
3021, filza 1

Archivio Segreto, diversorum
496; 497; 498; 499; 512; 513; 514; 526; 547; 548; 549; 550; 551; 552; 553; 554; 555

Archivio Segreto, istruzioni e relazioni
2707 A; 2707 G

Archivio Segreto, politicorum
1647, mazzo 1; 1648, mazzo 2

Archivio Segreto, materie politiche
2726; 2727; 2729; 2730; 2731; 2737 A; 2737 B; 2737 C; 2774 A; 2774 B; 2774 C;
    2774 D

Antico Comune
83 (Magistrorum rationalium, 1388); Communis Ianuae Massaria 16; Communis
    Ianuae Massaria 17; Communis Ianuae Massaria 18; Communis Ianuae Mas-
    saria 19; Communis Ianuae Massaria 20; Communis Ianuae Massaria 22

Archivio di Stato di Torino
Il Viaggi di Levante, mazzo 1 d'addizione, docs. 1–8, 13, 15; Il Viaggi di Levante,
    mazzo 1, doc. 2 (this document consists of the accounts of Antonio Barberis,
    treasurer of Count Amadeo VI of Savoy, for 1366–8)[a]

Corpus Christi College, Cambridge
MS 66A, fos. 67r–110r (William of Rubruck); MS 181, fos. 321–98 (William of
    Rubruck)

Published primary sources
Abu'l Fida, *Géographie d'Aboulféda*, ed. M. Rainaud and M. Le Bon Mac Guckin
    de Slane (Paris, 1840)
Acta Urbani V (1362–1370) e Regestis Vaticanis Aliique Fontibus Collegit, ed.
    Aloysius L. Täutu, Fontes Series 3, Typis Pontificiae Universitatis Gregorianae
    (Rome, 1964), vol. XI
Aflaki, *Les saints des derviches tourneurs (Manaqib ul-'arafin)*, trans. Clément Huart
    (Paris, 1918), vols. 1–II
Andraea Naugerii, 'Historia Veneta', in *RIS*, vol. XXIII

---

[a] In the handwritten summary of this document reference was made to Murad I. I was,
however, unable to find any such reference in the manuscript, and it may therefore be that the
reference to Murad I was in one of the folios (fos. 1, 2, 51, 53, 108, 109) which were sent to
Naples for an exhibition and destroyed there during the Second World War. The sources
from the archives in Turin do not appear to contain information relevant to trade from the
western city states into Turchia.

Anhegger, Robert and Halil İnalcık, *Kanunname-i Sultani ber Muceb-i 'Örf-i 'Osmani II Mehmed ve II Bayezid devirlerine ait yasakname ve kanunnameler*, Türk Tarih Kurumu Yayınlarından, eleventh series 5 (Ankara, 1956)

Argenti, Philip R., *The Occupation of Chios by the Genoese and their Administration of the Island 1346–1566* (Cambridge, 1958), vols. 1–III

Aşıkpaşazade, *Die altosmanische Chronik des Ašıkpašazade*, ed. Fredrich Giese (Leipzig, 1929; repr. Osnabrück, 1972)

Tevarih-i al-i 'Osman, ed. Ali (Istanbul, 1332)

Badoer, Giacomo, *Il libro dei Conti Giacomo Badoer (Costantinopoli 1436–1440)*, ed. Umberto Dorini and Tommaso Bertelè, Il Nuovo Ramusio 3, Istituto Poligrafico dello Stato, Libreria dello Stato (1956)

Balbi, Giovanni, *L'Epistolario di Iacopo Bracelli*, CSFS 2 (Genoa, 1969)

Barker, J., 'Miscellaneous Genoese documents on the Levantine world of the late fourteenth and early fifteenth centuries', *Byzantine Studies/Etudes byzantines* 37 (1979), 49–82

Balard, Michel, *Notai Genovesi in Oltremare. Atti Rogati a Cipro da Lamberto di Sambuceto (11 ottobre 1296–23 giugno 1299)*, CSFS 39 (Genoa, 1983)

Balard, Michel, *Notai Genovesi in Oltremare. Atti Rogati a Cipro da Lamberto di Sambuceto (31 marzo–19 iuglio 1305, 4 gennaio–12 Iuglio 1307), Giovanni de Rocha (3 agosto 1308–14 marzo 1310)*, CSFS 43 (Genoa, 1984)

Balard, M., Angeliki E. Laiou and C. Otten-Froux, *Les Italiens à Byzance et présentation de documents*, Série Byzantina Sorbinensia 6, Centre de Recherches d'Histoire et de Civilisation Byzantine (Paris, 1987)

Barbaro, Nicolò, *Nicolò Barbaro. The Diary of the Siege of Constantinople 1453*, trans. J. R. Jones (New York, 1969)

Bassano, *Costumi et i modi particolari della vita de' Turchi: ristampa fotomecanica dell'edizione originale – Roma, 1545*, ed. F. Babinger (Monaco di Baviera, 1963)

Basso, Enrico, *Notai Genovesi in Oltremare. Atti Rogati a Chio da Giuliano de Canella (2 Novembre 1380–31 Marzo 1381)*, Accademia Ligure di Scienze e Lettere 1 (Athens, 1993)

Ibn Battuta, *Voyages d'ibn Batoutah*, ed. and trans. C. Defremery and B. R. Sanguinetti (Paris, 1854), vol. II

Beldiceanu, Nicoră, *Les actes des premiers sultans conservés dans les manuscrits turcs de la Bibliothèque Nationale à Paris I*, Ecoles Pratique des Hautes Etudes, section 6 (Paris and The Hague, 1960–4), vols. I–II

Belgrano, L. T., 'Cinque documenti Genovesi–Orientali', *ASLSP* 17 (1885–6), 221–51 'Documenti riguardanti la colonia Genovese di Pera', *ASLSP* 13 (1877–84), 146–317

'Seconda serie di documenti riguardanti la colonia di Pera', *ASLSP* 13 (1877–84), 931–1004

Benvenuto de Brixano, *Benvenuto de Brixano, notaio in Candia (1301–1302)*, ed. T. Morozzo della Rocca, Fonti Relative alla Storia di Venezia, Archivi Notarili (Venice, 1950)

Borlandi, Antonia, *Il manuale di mercatura di Saminiato de'Ricci*, Università di Genova, Fonti e Studi 4 (Genoa, 1963)

Borlandi, Franco, *El libro di mercantantie et usanze de'paesi* (Torino, 1936)

Bratianu, G. I., *Actes des notaires génois de Péra et de Caffa de la fin du treizième siècle (1281–1290)*, Académie Roumaine, Etudes et Recherches 2 (Bucharest, 1927)

Broquière, Bertrandon de la, *Le voyage d'Outremer de Bertrandon de la Broquière*, ed. C. Schefer (Paris, 1892)

Carducci, G. and V. Fiorini (eds.), 'Marcha di Marco Battagli da Rimini (1212–1354)', in *RIS*, vol. XVI/3 (Città di Castello, 1912)

Casula, Francesco C., *Carte reali diplomatiche di Alfonso III il Benigno, re d'Aragon riguardanti l'Italia* (Padua, 1970)

Chalcocondyles, *Historiarum Demonstrationes*, ed. E. Darkó (Budapest, 1922–7), vol. I

  Historiarum Libri Decem, ed. I. Bekker (Bonn, 1843)

Chrysostomides, J., *Manuel II Palaeologos Funeral Oration on his Brother Theodore*, CFHB 26, Association for Byzantine Research (Thessaloniki, 1985)

  'Studies on the chronicle of Caroldo, with special reference to the history of Byzantium from 1370 to 1377', *Orientalia Christiana Periodica* 35 (1969), 123–82

  'Venetian commercial privileges under the Palaeologi', *Studi Veneziani* 12 (1970), 267–356

  (ed.), *Monumenta Peloponnesiaca. Documents for the History of the Peloponnese in the 14th and 15th Centuries* (Camberley, 1995)

Day, John, *Les douanes de Gênes 1376–1377* (Paris, 1963), vols. I–II

Dei, Benedetto, *Benedetto Dei, La Cronica dell'anno 1400 all'anno 1500*, ed. Roberto Barducci, with preface by Anthony Molho (1990)

Dennis, G. T., 'The Byzantine–Turkish treaty of 1403', *Orientalia Christiana Periodica* 33 (1967), 72–88

  'Three reports from Crete on the situation in Romania', *Studi Veneziani* 12 (1970), 243–65

Desimoni, C., 'Trattato dei genovesi col Khan dei Tatari nel 1380–1381, scritto in lingua volgare', *Archivio Storico Italiano* 20 (1887), 161–5

Doehaerd, Renée, *Les relations commerciales entre Gênes, la Belgique et l'Outremont d'après les archives notariales génoises aux XIIIe et XIVe siècles*, Institut Historique Belge de Rome, Etudes d'Histoire Economique et Sociale 2 (Brussels and Rome, 1941), vol. III

Doehaerd, Renée and C. Kerremans, *Les relations commerciales entres Gênes, la Belgique et l'Outremont d'après les archives notariales génoises, 1400–1440* (Brussels and Rome, 1952)

Dukas, *Decline and Fall of Byzantium to the Ottoman Turks*, ed. and trans. H. J. Magoulias (Detroit, 1975)

Dukas, *Historia Byzantina*, ed. I. Bekker, CSHB (Bonn, 1843)

Dukas, *Ducae Historia Turcobyzantina (1341–1462)*, ed. B. Grecu (Bucharest, 1958)

Elezović, Gliša, *Turski Spomenici* (Belgrade, 1952), vol. I, book 2

Enveri, *Le destan d'Umur Pacha (Dusturname-i Enveri). Text, translation et notes*, ed. I. Melikoff-Sayar (Paris, 1954)

  Dusturnamei Enveri, ed. M. Halil, Turk Tarih Encumeni Kulliyatı 15 (Istanbul, 1928)

  Dusturnamei Enveri Medhal, ed. M. Halil, Turk Tarih Encumeni Kulliyatı 15 (Istanbul, 1930)

Fleet, Kate, 'The treaty of 1387 between Murad I and the Genoese', *BSOAS* 56 (1993), 13–33

Frescobaldi, *Visit to the Holy Places of Egypt, Sinai, Palestine and Syria in 1384 by Frescobaldi, Gucci and Sigoli*, trans. Fr Theophilus Bellorini OFM and Fr

Eugene Hoade OFM, with a preface and notes by Fr Bellarmino Bagatti OFM (Jerusalem, 1948)

Gioffrè, Domenico, 'Atti rogati in Chio nella seconda metà del XIV secolo', *Bulletin de l'Institut Historique Belge de Rome* 34 (1962), 319–404

Lettere di Giovanni da Pontremoli, mercante genovese 1453–1459, CSFS 33 (Genoa, 1982)

Gökbilgin, M. Yayyib, *XV–XVI Asırlarda Edirne ve Paşa Livası, Vakıflar–Mülkler–Muktaalar* (Istanbul, 1952)

Gregoras, *Byzantina Historia*, ed. L. Schopen and I. Bekker, CSHB (Bonn, 1828–55)

Hayez, Michel, *Urbain V (1362–1370), lettres communes*, Bibliothèque des Ecoles Françaises d'Athènes et de Rome (Paris, 1964–72), vol. II, fascs. I–IV

Heers, J., *Le livre de comptes de G. Picamiglio, homme d'affaires génois, 1456–9*, Ecole Pratique des Hautes Etudes, section 6, Centre de Recherches Historique – Affaires et Gens d'Affaires 13 (Paris, 1959)

Iacopo de Promontorio, *Die Aufzeichungen des Genuesen Iacopo de Promontorio-de Campis über den Osmanenstaat um 1475*, ed. Franz Babinger, Bayerische Akademie der Wissenschaften, Philosophisch–Historische Klasse Sitzungsberichte, Jahrgang 1956 (Munich, 1957), vol. VIII

İnalcık, Halil, 'Bursa I:xv asır sanayi ve ticaret tarihine dair vesikalar', *Belleten* 24, 93 (1960), 45–102

'Bursa Şer'iye Sicillerinde Fatih Sultan Mehmed'in Fermanları', *Belleten* 2, 44 (1947), 693–708

Iorga, N., 'Notes et extraits pour servir à l'histoire de croisades au XVe siècle: comptes des colonies génoise de Caffa, Pera et de Famagusta', in *ROL*, vol. IV, pp. 25 fos.

Kantakuzenos, *Ioannes Kantakuzenos, Historiarum libri IV*, ed. L. Schopen, CSHB (Bonn, 1828–32)

Kourouses, S. I., Μανουὴλ Γαβαλᾶς ἔιτα Ματθαῖος μητροπολίτης Ἐρέσου (1271/2–1355/60) (Athens, 1972)

Krekić, B., *Dubrovnik (Raguse) et le Levant au Moyen-Age* (Paris and The Hague, 1961)

Kritovoulos, *History of Mehmed the Conqueror. By Kritovoulos*, trans. C. T. Riggs (Westport, Conn., 1954)

De Rebus per Annos 1451–1467 a Mechemet II Gestis, ed. V. Grecu (Bucharest, 1963)

Kydones, Demetrius, *Oratio pro subsidio Latinorum*, ed. J. P. Migne, *Patrologica Graeca*, vol. CLIV, cols. 961–1008

Lamberto di Sambuceto, in C. Desimoni, 'Actes passés à Famagouste de 1299 à 1301 par devant le notaire génois Lamberto di Sambuceto', Archives de l'Orient Latin 2 (Brussels, 1964)

in Romeo Pavoni, *Notai Genovesi in Oltremare. Atti Rogati a Cipro da Lamberto di Sambuceto (Gennaio–Agosto 1302)*, CSFS (Genoa, 1957)

Lefebvre, Marie Magdeleine, 'Quinze firmans du Sultan Mehmed le Conquérant', *Revue des Etudes Islamiques* 39, 9 (1971), 147–73

Liagre-de Sturler, Léone, *Les relations commerciales entre Gênes, la Belgique et l'Outremont d'après les archives notariales génoises (1320–1400)* (Brussels and Rome, 1969), vols. I–II

Liber Jurium Reipublicae Genuensis, ed. Ercole Ricotti, Monumenta Historiae Patriae 9 (Turin, 1857), vol. II

Ludolfus de Sudheim, *De Itinere Terre Sancte*, ed. G. A. Neumann, Archives de l'Orient Latin 2 (Paris, 1884), pp. 305–77

Ludolphi Rectoris Ecclesiae Parochialis in Suchem, de Itinere Terrae Sanctae Liber, ed. F. Deycks, Bibliothek des Litterarischen Vereins 25 (Stuttgart, 1851)

Marco Polo, *Le livre de Marco Polo citoyen de Venise conseiller privé et commissaire impérial de Khoublaï-Kaàn rédigé en français sous sa dictée en 1298 par Rusticien de Pise*, ed. M. G. Pauthier (Paris, 1865), vol. II

The Travels of Marco Polo, trans. Aldo Ricci, with introduction and index by Sir E. Dennison Ross (London, 1931)

Martin da Canal, 'La cronique des Veniciens', in *Archivio Storico Italiano* (Florence, 1845), vol. VIII, pp. 268–707

Mas Latrie, L. de, 'Privilège accordé par Héthoum ler, roi d'Arménie aux Vénetiens, en 1261', Bibliothèque de l'Ecole des Chartes 31 (1870) (Paris, 1871), pp. 407–11

'Privilège commercial accordé en 1320 à la République de Venise par un roi de Perse faussement attribué à un roi de Tunis', Bibliothèque de l'Ecole des Chartes 31 (1870) (Paris, 1871), pp. 73–102

Massa, Paola, 'Alcune lettere mercantili toscane da colonie genovesi alla fine del trecento', *ASLSP*, n.s. 11, fasc. 11 (1971), 345–59

Melis, Frederigo, *Documenti per la storia economica dei secoli XIII–XVI* (Florence, 1972)

Miklosich, F. and J. Müller, *Acta et Diplomata Graeca Medii Aevi* (Vienna, 1870), vol. III

Mollat, G., *Lettres secrètes et curiales du Pape Grégoire XI (1370–1378)*, Bibliothèque des Ecoles Françaises d'Athènes et de Rome 3 (Paris, 1962–5), 3 fascicles

Morozzo della Rocca, R., 'Notizie da Caffa', in *Studi in onore di A. Fanfani* (Milan, 1962), vol. III, pp. 267–95

Muller, G., *Documenti sulle relazioni delle città toscane coll'Oriente cristiano e coi Turchi fino all'anno 1531* (Florence, 1879)

Muntaner, R., *L'expedició dels Catalans a Orient*, ed. Lluis Nicolau d'Olwer, Els Nostres Clássics 7 (Barcelona, 1926)

Musso, G. G., *Navigazione e commercio genovese con il Levante nei documenti dell'Archivio di Stato di Genova (secc. XIV–XV) con appendice documentaria a cura di Maria Silvia Jacopino* (Rome, 1975)

Neşri, *Ğihannüma di altosmanische Chronik des Mevlana Mehemmed Neschri*, ed. Franz Taeschner, vol. I: *Einleitung und Text des Cod. Menzel* (Leipzig, 1951)

Ğihannüma di altosmanische Chronik des Mevlana Mehemmed Neschri, ed. Franz Taeschner, vol. II: *Text des Cod. Manisa 1373* (Leipzig, 1955)

Kitabi-i Cihan-nüma, ed. Faik Reşit Unat and Dr Mehmed A. Köymen (Ankara, 1949, 1957), vols. I–II

Nicola de Boateriis, *Nicola de Boateriis, Notaio in Famagosta e Venezia (1355–1365)*, ed. Antonio Lombardo, Fonti per la Storia di Venezia 3, Archivi Notarili (Venice, 1973)

Noiret, H. *Documents inédits pour servir à l'histoire de la domination vénitienne en Crète de 1380 à 1485* (Paris, 1892)

Pachymeres, George, *George Pachymeres, De Michaele et Andronico Palaeologis libri XIII*, ed. I. Bekker, CSHB (Bonn, 1835), vols. I–II

Panaretos, *Eustathii Metropolita Thessalonicensis Opuscula accedunt Trapezuntinae Historiae Scriptores Panaretus et Evgenicus*, ed. T. F. Tafel (Frankfurt am Main, 1832)

Pavoni, Romeo, *Notai Genovesi in Oltremare. Atti Rogati a Cipro da Lamberto di Sambuceto (6 Iuglio–27 Ottobre 1301)*, CSFS 32 (Genoa, 1982)

Pegolotti, *Fr Balducci Pegolotti, La pratica della mercatura*, ed. A. Evans, Medieval Academy of America 24 (Cambridge, Mass., 1936)

Pertusi, Agostino, *La caduta di Costantinopoli* (Milan, 1976), vol. I: *Le testimonianze dei contemporanei*

La caduta di Costantinopoli (Milan, 1976), vol. II: *L'eco nel mondo*

'Primi studi in occidente sull'origine e la potenza dei Turchi', *Studi Veneziani* 12 (1970), 465–552

Testi inediti e poco noti sulla caduta di Costantinopoli: Edizione postuma a cura di Antonio Carile, Il Mondo Medievale; Sezione di Storia Bizantina e Slava (Bologna, 1983)

Piloti, *L'Egypte au commencement du quinzième siècle d'après le traité d'Emmanuel Piloti de Crète (incipit 1420) avec une introduction et des notes par P-H Dopp* (Cairo, 1950)

Pizolo, Pietro, *Pietro Pizolo, notaio in Candia*, ed. S. Carbone, Fonti per la Storia di Venezia, Archivi Notarili (Venice, 1978), vol. I (1300)

Planoudes, *Mamimi monachi Planudis epistolae*, ed. M. Treu (Breslau, 1890)

Pliny the Elder, *Natural History*, Loeb Classical Library (Cambridge, Mass., 1942)

Polonio, Valeria, *Notai Genovesi in Oltremare. Atti Rogati a Cipro da Lamberto di Sambuceto (3 Iuglio 1300–3 Agosto 1301)*, CSFS 31 (Genoa, 1982)

Ratti Vidulich, Paola, *Duca di Candia Bandi (1313–1329)* (Venice, 1965)

Duca di Candia, Quatenus (1340–1350) (Venice, 1976)

Rocca, *Pesi e misure antiche di Genova e del Genovesato* (Genoa, 1871)

Roccatagliata, Ausilia, *Notai Genovesi in Oltremare. Atti Rogati a Chio (1453–1454, 1470–1471)*, CSFS 35 (Genoa, 1982)

Notai Genovesi in Oltremare. Atti Rogati a Pera e Mitilene (Genoa, 1982), vol. I: *Pera (1408–1490)*

Notai Genovesi in Oltremare. Atti Rogati a Pera e Mitilene (Genoa, 1982), vol. II: *Mitilene (1454–1460)*

'Nuovi Documenti su Pera Genovese', in *Atti del Convegno di Studi sui Ceti dirigenti nelle istituzioni della Repubblica di Genova, Genova 29–30–31 maggio–1 giugno 1990*, vol. XI, pp. 127–43

Saminiato de'Ricci, *Il manuale di mercatura di Saminiato de'Ricci*, ed. Antonia Borlandi, Università di Genova, Istituto di Storia Medievale e Moderna, Fonti e Studi 4 (Genoa, 1963)

Santschi, Elisabeth, *Régestes des arrêts civils et des Mémoriaux (1363–1399) des Archives de duc de Crète*, Bibliothèque de l'Institut Hellénique d'Etudes Byzantines et Post-Byzantines de Venise 9 (Venice, 1976)

Sanudo, Marino, *J. Bongars, Gesta Dei per Francos, Marino Sanudo Torsello, Secreta Fidelium Crucis* (Hanover, 1611), vol. II

Studien über Marino Sanudo den Aelteren, Abhandlungen der historischen Classe

der königlich bayerischen Akademie der Wissenschaft, ed. Fr Kuntsmann (Munich, 1855), vol. VII, pp. 617–819

Sathias, C. N., *Documents inédits à l'histoire de la Grèce au Moyen Age* (Paris, 1881), vol. II

Schiltberger, Johann, *The Bondage and Travels of Johann Schiltberger, a Native of Bavaria, in Europe, Asia and Africa 1396–1427*, ed. and trans. Commander J. Buchan Telfer (London, 1879)

Schreiner, P., *Die byzantinischen Kleinchroniken* (Vienna, 1975–9), vols. I–III

Tafel, Fr G. L. and G. M. Thomas, *Urkunden zur älteren Handels- und Staatsgeschichte der Republik Venedik mit besonderer Beziehung auf Byzanz und die Levante. vom neunten bis zum Ausgang des fünfzehnten Jahrhunderts*, Fontes Rerum Austriacarum. Diplomataria et Acta 14 (Vienna, 1857), vols. I–III

Theotokes, S., *Ἱστορικὰ Κρητικὰ Ἔγγραφα ἐκδιδόμενα ἐκ τοῦ Ἀρχείου τῆς Βενετίας Μνημεία τῆς Ἑλληνικῆς Ἱστοίας*, Academy of Athens (Athens, 1933–7), vols. I/2, II.1–2

Thiriet, F., *Déliberations des Assemblées Vénitiennes concernant la Romanie* (Paris and The Hague, 1964), vols. I–II

Régestes des délibérations du sénat de Venise concernant la Romanie (Paris, 1958–61), vols. I–III

Thomas, G. (ed.), *Diplomatarium Veneto-Levantinum* (Venice, 1890–9), vols. I–II

Toniolo, Paola Piana, *Notai Genovesi in Oltremare. Atti Rogati a Chio da Gregorio Panissario (1403–1405)*, Academia Ligure di Scienze e Lettere, Serie Fonti 2 (Genoa, 1995)

Tursun Bey, *The History of Mehmed the Conqueror by Tursun Beg*, ed. Halil İnalcık and Rhoads Murphey (Minneapolis and Chicago, 1978)

Tursun Bey Tarih-i Ebü'l-Feth, ed. Mertol Tulum (Istanbul, 1977)

al-'Umarī, 'Notice de l'ouvrage qui a pour titre Masalek alabsar fi memalek alamsar, voyages des yeux dans les royaumes des différentes contrées (ms. arabe 583)', trans. E. Quatremère, in *Notices et Extraits des mss. de la Bibliothèque du Roi* (Paris, 1838), vol. XIII, pp. 334–81

Uzunçarşili, I. H., *Kitabeler* (Istanbul, 1347/1929)

William of Rubruck, *The Mission of Friar William of Rubruck. His Journey to the Court of the Great Khan Mönke, 1253–1255*, trans. Peter Jackson, with intro., notes and appendices by Peter Jackson with David Morgan (London, 1990)

Zachariadou, Elizabeth A., *Trade and Crusade, Venetian Crete and the Emirates of Menteshe and Aydın*, Library of the Hellenic Institute of Byzantine and Post-Byzantine Studies 11 (Venice, 1983)

Zibaldone da Canal, *Zibaldone da Canal, manoscritto mercantile del sec. XIV, a cura di A. Stussi con studi di F. C. Lane, Th. E. Marston, O. Ore*, Fonti per la Storia di Venezia, Fondi Vari (Venice, 1967)

Zucchello, *Lettere di mercanti a Pignol Zucchello (1336–1350)*, ed. Raimondo Morozzo della Rocca, Comitato per la Pubblicazione delle Fonti Relative alla Storia di Venezia, Fonti per la Storia di Venezia 4, Archivi Privati (Venice, 1957)

Secondary works

Abu-Lughod, Janet L., *Before European Hegemony. The World System AD 1250–1350* (Oxford, 1989)

Ahrweiler, Hélène, 'L'Histoire et la géographie de la région de Smyrne entre les deux occupations turques (1081–1317) particulièrement au XIIIe siècle', *Travaux et Mémoires* 1, Centre de Recherche d'Histoire et Civilisation Byzantines (Paris, 1965), pp. 1–204

Àgoston, Gàbor, 'Ottoman artillery and European military technology in the fifteenth and seventeenth centuries', *Acta Academiae Scientiarum Hungaricae* 47 (1994), 15–48

Airaldi, Gabriella and Paolo Stringa (eds.), *Mediterranea Genovese. Storia e architettura*, Atti del Convegno Internazionale di Genova 29 ottobre 1992 organizzato dall'Istituto di Storia del Medioevo e dell'Espansione Europea e dell'Istituto di Urbanistica dell'Università di Genova, Edizioni Culturali Internazionali Genova (Genoa, 1995)

Akin, H., *Aydin ogulları Tarihi hakkinda bir Araştirma*, Ankara Üniversitesi Dil ve Tarih-Coğrafya Fakültesi Yayınları 60 (Ankara, 1968)

Alexandrescu-Dersca, M. M., *La campagne de Timur en Anatolie (1402)* (London, 1977)

Antoniadis-Bibicou, Hélène, *Recherches sur les douanes à Byzance. L''octava', le 'kommerkion' et les commerciares*, Cahiers des Annales 20 (Paris, 1963)

Arbel, Benjamin, Bernard Hamilton and David Jacoby (eds.), *Latins and Greeks in the Eastern Mediterranean after 1204* (London, 1989)

Artuk, İbrahim, 'Early Ottoman Coins of Orhan Ghazi as Confirmation of his Sovereignty', in Dickran K. Kouymijan (ed.), *Near Eastern Numismatics, Iconography, Epigraphy and History. Studies in Honor of George C. Miles* (Beirut, 1974), pp. 457–63

'Karesi-oğulları adına basılmış olan iki sikke', *İstanbul Üniversitesi Edebiyat Fakültesi Tarih Dergisi* 33 (1980/81) (Istanbul, 1982), 283–9

'Murad'ın sikkelerine genel bir bakış 761–792 (1359–1389)', *Belleten* 184 (1982), 787–93

Ashtor, E., 'L'artiglieria veneziana e il commercio di Levante', in *Armi e cultura nel Bresciano, 1420–1870* (Brescia, 1981)

'Il commercio italiano col Levante et il suo impatto sull'economia tardomedioevale', in *Aspetti della Vita Economica Medievale. Atti del Convegno di Studi nel X Anniversario della Morte di Frederigo Melis. Firenze–Pisa–Prato 10–14 Marzo 1984*, Università degli Studi di Firenze, Istituto di Storia Economica (Florence, 1985), pp. 15–63

East–West Trade in the Medieval Mediterranean (London, 1986)

'L'exportation des textiles occidentaux dans le Proche Orient musulman au bas Moyen Age (1370–1517)', in *Studi in Memoria di Frederigo Melis* (Naples, 1978), vol. II, pp. 303–77

Levant Trade in the Later Middle Ages (Princeton, 1983)

'Levantine weights and standard parcels: A contribution to the metrology of the later Middle Ages', *BSOAS* 445 (1982), 471–88

Les métaux précieux et la balance des payements du Proche-Orient à la Basse Epoque (Paris, 1971)

'Observations on Venetian trade in the Levant in the XIVth century', *JEEH* 5 (1976), 533–86

'Pagamento in contanti e baratto nel commercio italiano d'Otremare (secoli XIV–XVI)', in *Storia d'Italia Annali 6: Economia naturale, economia monetaria* (Turin, 1983), pp. 363–96

'La recherche des prix dans l'Orient médiéval. Sources, méthodes et problèmes', *Studia Islamica* 5, 21 (1964), 101–44

A Social and Economic History of the Near East in the Middle Ages (London, 1976)

'Underdevelopment in the pre-industrial era. The case of declining economies', *JEEH* 7 (1978), 285–310

'The volume of medieval spice trade', *JEEH* 9 (1980), 753–63

Atan, Turhan, *Türk Gümrük Tarihi. I Cilt. Başlangıçtan Osmanlı Devletine kadar*, Atatürk Kültur, Dil ve Tarih Yüksek Kurumu. Türk Tarih Kurumu Yayınları 7, Dizi-Sa. 109 (Ankara, 1990)

Babinger, Franz, *Mehmed the Conqueror and his Time*, trans. Ralph Manheim, ed. and with a preface by William C. Hickman, Bollingen Series 96 (Princeton, 1978)

'A proposito delle coniazioni d'oro ottomane nel XV secolo sotto Murad II e Maometto II', *Rivista Italiana di Numismatica e Scienze*, series 5, 5, 59 (1957), 90–4

Balard, Michel, 'La fiscalità di Caffa nel quattrocento', in Airaldi and Stringa (eds.), *Mediterranea Genovese*, pp. 39–45

'The Genoese in the Aegean (1204–1566), *Mediterranean Historical Review* 4 (June 1989), 158–74

'A propos de la bataille du Bosphore. L'expédition génoise de Paganino Doria à Constantinople', *Travaux et Mémoires* 4 (1970), 431–69

La Romanie génoise (XIIe–début du XVe siècle), ASLSP, n.s. 18 (92), fasc. I, Bibliothèque des Ecoles Françaises d'Athènes et de Rome 235 (Genoa and Paris, 1978)

Balard, Michel and Alain Ducellier (eds.), *Coloniser au Moyen Age* (Paris, 1995)

Basso, Enrico, *Genova: Un impero sul mare*, Consiglio Nazionale delle Ricerche, Istituto sui Rapporti Italo-iberici (Cagliari, 1994)

Beldiceanu, N. and Irène Beldiceanu-Steinherr, *Deux villes de l'Anatolie préottomane: Develi et Qarahisar d'après des documents inédits* (Paris, 1973)

Bendall, S. and C. Morrison, 'Un trésor de ducats d'imitation au nom d'Andrea Dandolo (1343–1354)', *Revue Numismatique*, series 6, 21 (1979), 176–93

Berktay, Halil and Suraiya Faroqhi (eds.), *New Approaches to State and Peasant in Ottoman History* (London, 1992)

Bertelé, T., 'L'iperpero bizantino dal 1261 al 1450', *Rivista Italiana di Numismatica e Scienze Affini*, series 5/59 (1957), 70–89

Blake, Robert P., 'The circulation of silver in the Moslem East down to the Mongol epoch', *Harvard Journal of Asiatic Studies* 2 (1937), 291–328

Bratianu, G. I., 'Nouvelles contributions à l'étude de l'approvisionnement de Constantinople sous les paléologues et les empereurs ottomans', *Byzantion* 6 (1931), 641–56

'La question de l'approvisionnement de Constantinople à l'époque byzantine et ottomane', *Byzantion* 5 (1929–30), 83–107

Braunstein, Philippe, 'Le commerce du fer à Venise au XVe siècle', *Studi Veneziani* 8 (1966), 267–302

Brummett, Palmira, *Ottoman Seapower and Levantine Diplomacy in the Age of Discovery*, SUNY Series in the Social and Economic History of the Middle East (Albany, 1993)

Bryer, Anthony, 'The treatment of Byzantine place names', *Byzantine and Modern Greek Studies* 9 (1984/5), 209–14

Bryer, Anthony and Heath Lowry (eds.), *Continuity and Change in Late Byzantine and Early Ottoman Society* (Birmingham and Washington, 1986)

Byrne, Eugene H., *Genoese Shipping in the Twelfth and Thirteenth Centuries*, Medieval Academy of America (Cambridge, Mass., 1930)

Cahen, Claude, 'Douanes et commerce dans les ports méditerranéens de l'Egypte médiévale d'après le Minhâdj d'al-Makhzūmī', *JESHO* 7 (1964), 217–314

Pre-Ottoman Turkey. A General Survey of the Material and Spiritual Culture and History c.1071–1330 (London, 1968)

Çizakça, Murat, 'Price History and the Bursa Silk Industry: A Study in Ottoman Industrial Decline, 1550–1650', in İslamoğlu-İnan (ed.), *World-Economy*, pp. 247–61

Cook, M. A. (ed.), *Studies in the Economic History of the Middle East from the Rise of Islam to the Present Day* (London, 1970)

Day, John, *The Medieval Market Economy* (Oxford, 1987)

Delilbasi, Melek, 'Ortaçağ'da Türk hükümdarları tarafından batılara ahidnamelerle verilen imtiyazlara genel bir bakış', *Belleten* 47, 185 (Ocak, 1983; Ankara, 1984), 95–103

Delumeau, Jean, *L'alun de Rome XVe–XIXe siècle*, Ecole Pratique des Hautes Etudes 6, Centre de Recherches Historiques, Ports–Routes–Trafics 13 (SEVPEN, 1962)

Dufourcq, C. E., *L'Espagne catalane et le Maghrib aux XIIIe et XIVe siècles* (Paris, 1966)

'Prix et niveau de vie dans les pays catalans et maghribins à la fin du XIIIe et au début du XIVe siècles', *Le Moyen Age*, 4th series, 20 (1965), 475–520

Edbury, Peter W., *The Kingdom of Cyprus and the Crusades 1191–1374* (Cambridge, 1991)

Ehrenkreutz, Andrew S., 'Monetary Aspects of Medieval Near Eastern Economic History', in Cook (ed.), *Economic History*, pp. 37–50

Epstein, Steven A., *Genoa and the Genoese 958–1528* (Chapel Hill and London, 1996)

Faroqhi, Suraiya, 'Alum production and alum trade in the Ottoman empire (about 1560–1830), *WZKM* 71 (1979), 153–75

'Notes on the production of cotton and cotton cloth in XVIth and XVIIth century Anatolia', *JEEH* 8, 2 (Fall 1979), 405–17

Peasants, Dervishes and Traders in the Ottoman Empire (London, 1986)

'Rural society in Anatolia and the Balkans during the sixteenth century, I', *Turcica* 9, 1 (1977), 161–95

Fleet, Kate, 'Ottoman grain exports from Western Anatolia at the end of the fourteenth century', *JESHO* 40, 3 (1997), 283–93

'Turkish–Latin relations at the end of the fourteenth century', *Acta Orientalia Academiae Scientiarum Hungaricae* 49, 1 (1996), 131–7

Foss, Clive, *Ephesus after Antiquity: A Late Antique, Byzantine and Turkish City* (Cambridge, 1979)

Frangakis-Syrett, Elena, 'Implementation of the 1838 Anglo-Turkish convention on Izmir's trade: European and minority merchants', *New Perspectives on Turkey* 7 (Spring 1992), 91–102

Gioffrè, Domenico, *Il mercato degli schiavi a Genova nel secolo XV*, CSFS 11 (Genoa, 1971)

Grendi, Edoardo, 'Genova alla metà del cinquecento: una politica del grano?' *Quaderni Storici* 13 (1970), 106–60

Heers, J., 'Il commercio nel Mediterraneo alla fine del sec. XIV e nei primi anni del XV', *Archivio Storico Italiano* 13 (1955), 157–209

Genova nel '400. Civiltà mediterranea, grande capitalismo e capitalismo popolare (Milan, 1991)

Heers, Marie-Louise, 'Les Génois et le commerce de l'alun à la fin du Moyen Age', *Revue d'Histoire Economique et Sociale* 32 (1954), 31–53

Heldman, Marilyn E., 'A chalice from Venice for Emperor Dawit of Ethiopia', *BSOAS* 53, 3 (1990), 422–5

Heyd, W., *Histoire du commerce du Levant au Moyen-Age* (Amsterdam, 1967), vols. I–II

Heywood, Colin, 'The activities of the state cannon foundry (tophane-i 'amire) at Istanbul in the early sixteenth century according to an unpublished Turkish source', *Orijentalni Institut u Sarajevu* 30 (1980), 209–17

'Notes on the Production of Fifteenth Century Ottoman Cannon', in *Proceedings of the International Symposium on Islam and Science (Islamabad)* (Islamabad, 1981)

Heywood, Colin and Colin Imber (eds.), *Studies in Ottoman History in Honour of Professor V. L. Ménage* (Istanbul, 1995)

Holt, P. M., *Early Mamluk Diplomacy (1260–1290). Treaties of Baybars and Qalawun with Christian Rulers* (Leiden, 1995)

Hoshino, Hidetoshi, 'Il commercio Fiorentino nell'impero Ottomano: costi e profitti negli anni 1484–1488', in *Aspetti della Vita Economica Medievale. Atti del Convegno di Studi nel X Anniversario della morte di Frederigo Meli. Firenze–Pisa–Prato, 10–14 Marzo 1984*, Università degli Studi di Firenze, Istituto di Storia Economica (Florence, 1985)

Imber, Colin, 'The Legend of Osman Gazi', in Zachariadou (ed.), *Ottoman Emirate*, pp. 67–75

'The Ottoman dynastic myth', *Turcica* 19 (1987), 7–27

The Ottoman Empire 1300–1481 (Istanbul, 1990)

'Paul Wittek's 'De la défaite d'Ankara à la prise de Constantinople'', *Osmanlı Araştırmaları* 5 (1986), 65–81

İnalcık, Halil, 'Bursa and the commerce of the Levant', *JESHO* 3, 2 (1960), 131–47

'Capital formation in the Ottoman empire', *Journal of European History* 19 (1960), 97–140

The Middle East and the Balkans under the Ottoman Empire. Essays on Economy and Society, Indiana University Turkish Studies and Turkish Ministry of Culture Joint Series 9 (Bloomington, 1993)

'Notes on a Study of the Turkish Economy during the Establishment and Rise of the Ottoman Empire', in İnalcık, *The Middle East and the Balkans*, pp. 205–63

'The Ottoman Economic Mind and Aspects of the Ottoman Economy', in Cook (ed.), *Economic History*, pp. 207–18

The Ottoman Empire. The Classical Age 1300–1600 (London, 1973)

'The Problem of the Relationship between Byzantine and Ottoman Taxation', in *Akten des XI internationalen Byzantinisten-Kongresses 1958* (Munich, 1960), pp. 237–42

'Sources for Fifteenth-century Turkish Economic and Social History', in İnalcık, *The Middle East and the Balkans*, pp. 177–93

'*Yük (Himl)* in the Ottoman Silk Trade, Mining and Agriculture', in İnalcık, *The Middle East and the Balkans*, pp. 432–960

İslamoğlu-İnan, Huri, 'State and Peasants in the Ottoman Empire: A Study of Peasant Economy in North-Central Anatolia during the Sixteenth Century', in İslamoğlu-İnan (ed.), *World-Economy*, pp. 101–59

İslamoğlu-İnan, Huri (ed.), *The Ottoman Empire and the World-Economy* (Cambridge, 1987)

İslamoğlu-İnan, Huri and Çağlar Keyder, 'Agenda for Ottoman History', in İslamoğlu-İnan (ed.), *World-Economy*, pp. 42–62

Jacoby, David, 'L'alun et la Crète vénitienne', *Byzantinische Forschungen* 12 (1987), 129–42

Kafadar, Cemal, *Between Two Worlds. The Construction of the Ottoman State* (Berkeley, 1995)

Karabacek, J., 'Gigliato des jonischen Turkomanenfürsten Omar-beg', *Numismatische Zeitschrift* 2 (1870), 525–38

'Gigliato des karischen Turkomanenfürsten Urchan-beg', *Numismatische Zeitschrift* 9 (1877), 200–15

Karpov, Sergej Pavlovič, *L'Impero di Trebisonda Venezia Genova e Roma 1204–1461. Rapporti politici, diplomatici e commerciali* (Rome, 1986)

Kedar, Benjamin Z., *Merchants in Crisis. Genoese and Venetian Men of Affairs in the Fourteenth-century Depression* (New Haven, 1967)

Kiepert, Heinrich, *Über Pegolotti's vorderasiatisches Itinerar*, Monatsberichte der K. preussischen Akademie der Wissenschaften zu Berlin (Berlin, 1881)

Komroff, Manuel, *Contemporaries of Marco Polo* (New York, 1928)

Köprülü, M. Fuad, *Alcune osservazioni intorno all'influenza delle istituzioni bizantine sulle istituzioni ottomane*, Pubblicazioni dell'Istituto per l'Oriente 50 (Rome, 1953)

Köymen, Mehmet Altay, 'Türkiye Selçukluları Devleti'nin Ekonomik Politikası', *Belleten* 50, 198 (December 1986), 613–20

Krekić, Bariša, *Dubrovnik in the 14th and 15th Centuries. A City between East and West* (Norman, 1972)

Laiou, Angeliki E., *Constantinople and the Latins. The Foreign Policy of Andronikos II 1282–1328* (Cambridge, Mass., 1972)

'The provisioning of Constantinople during winter 1306–1307', *Byzantion* 37 (1967), 91–113

Laiou-Thomadakis, A. E., 'The Byzantine economy in the Mediterranean trade system: 13th–15th centuries', *Dumbarton Oaks Papers* 34, 5 (1980/1), 177–222

Lambros, P. 'Monnaie inédite de Sarukhan émir d'Ionie, frappée à Ephèse (1299–1346), *Revue Numismatique*, n.s., 14 (1869–70), 335–43

Lemerle, P. *L'Emirat d'Aydin Byzance et l'Orient. Recherches sur 'La geste d'Umur Pacha'* (Paris, 1957)

Liagre, Léone, 'Le commerce de l'alun en Flandre au Moyen Age', *Le Moyen Age* 61 (1955), 177–206

Lokkegaard, Frede, *Islamic Taxation in the Classic Period with Special Reference to Circumstances in Iraq* (Copenhagen, 1950)

Lopez, Robert, Harry Miskimin and Abrahim Udovitch, 'England to Egypt, 1350–1500: Long-term Trends and Long-distance Trade', in Cook (ed.), *Economic History*, pp. 93–128

Luttrell, Anthony, 'The Hospitallers of Rhodes Confront the Turks: 1306–1421', in Philip F. Gallagher (ed.), *Christians, Jews and Other Worlds. Patterns of Conflict and Accommodation* (New York and London, 1988)

  'Intrigue, schism and violence among the Hospitallers of Rhodes: 1377–1384', *Speculum* 41 (1966), 30–48

  'The Latins and life on the smaller Aegean islands, 1204–1453', *Mediterranean Historical Review* 4 (June 1989), 146–57

  'Slavery at Rhodes: 1306–1440', *Bulletin de l'Institut Historique Belge de Rome* 46–7 (1976–7), 81–100

  'Venice and the Knights Hospitallers of Rhodes in the fourteenth century', *Papers of the British School at Rome* 26, n.s. 5 (1958), 195–212

Manz, Beatrice Forbes, *The Rise and Rule of Tamerlane* (Cambridge, 1989)

Mas Latrie, L. de, 'Commerce d'Ephèse et de Milet au Moyen Age (Traité Vénetien de 1403 avec l'émir de Palatcha)', Bibliothèque de l'Ecole des Chartes 5 (5th series) (Paris, 1864), 219–31

  'Des relations politiques et commerciales de l'Asie Mineure avec l'Ile de Chypre sous le règne des princes de la maison de Lusignan', Bibliothèque de l'Ecole des Chartes 2 (2nd series) (Paris, 1845–6), 120–42

Ménage, V. L., *Neshri's History of the Ottomans. The Sources and Development of the Text* (London, 1964)

Musso, G. G., 'Fonti documentarie per la storia di Chio dei genovesi', *La Berio* 8, 3 (1968), 5–30

  'Nuovi documenti dell'Archivio di Stato di Genova sui Genovesi e il Levante nel secondo quattrocento', *Rassegna degli Archivi di Stato* 27 (1967), 443–96

Olgiati, Giustina, 'I Genovesi in Oriente dopo la caduta di Costantinopoli', *Studi Balcanici – Quaderni di Chio* 8 (Rome, 1989), 45–59

Origo, I., 'The domestic enemy: Eastern slaves in Tuscany in the fourteenth and fifteenth centuries', *Speculum* 30 (1955), 321–65

  The Merchant of Prato, Francesco di Marco Datini (London, 1957)

Origone, Sandra, 'Chio nel tempo della caduta di Costantinopoli', in *Saggi e Documenti II*, Civico Istituto Colombiano, Studi e Testi, Serie Storica 3 (Genoa, 1982), vol. I, pp. 121–209

  'Genova e i genovesi tra la fine di Bisanzio e i Turchi', in *Atti dell'Academia Ligure di Scienze e Lettere, annata 1986* (Genoa, 1988), vol. XLIII, pp. 389–402

Pistarino, Geo, 'La Caduta di Costantinopoli: da Pera Genovese a Galata Turca', in *La Storia Genovese. Atti del Convegno di Studi sui Ceti dirigenti nelle istituzioni della Repubblica di Genova. Genova 12–13–14 Aprile 1984*, vol. V, pp. 7–47

  'Tra i Genovesi dell'Oriente Turco dal tramonto del medioevo al primo tempo dell'età moderna', *Atti dell'Academia Ligure di Scienze e Lettere, annata 1986* (Genoa, 1988), vol. XLIII, pp. 200–12

Ramsey, W. M., *The Cities and Bishoprics of Phrygia* (Oxford, 1895), vol. I: *The Lycos Valley and South-western Phrygia*

The Cities and Bishoprics of Phrygia (Oxford, 1895), vol. II: *West and West-Central Phrygia*

The Historical Geography of Asia Minor (London, 1890)

Romani, Ruggerio, 'A propos du commerce du blé dans la Mediterranée des XIVe et XVe siècles', in *Hommage à Lucien Febvre. Eventail de l'histoire vivante offert par l'amitié d'historiens, linguistes, géographes, économistes, sociologues, ethnologues* (Paris, 1953), pp. 149–61

Saltzmann, Ariel, 'An Ancien Regime Revisited: "Privatization" and Political Economy in the 18th Century Ottoman Empire', *Politics and Society* 21 (1993), 393–423

Schlumberger, G., *Numismatique de l'Orient Latin* (Paris, 1878)

Spufford, Peter, *Money and its Use in Medieval Europe* (Cambridge, 1988)

Thiriet, Freddy, *La Romanie vénitienne au Moyen Age. Le développement et l'exploitation du domaine colonial vénitien (XII–XV siècles)* (Paris, 1975)

Turan, Osman, 'Orta çağlarda Türkiye Kibris münasebetleri', *Belleten* 28, 109 (January 1964), 209–27

Turan, Şerafettin, *Türkiye–İtalya İlişkileri I Selçuklar'dan Bizans'ın sona erişine* (Istanbul, 1990)

Uluçay, C., *Saruhan Oğulları ve Eserlerine dair Vesikalar* (Istanbul, 1940–6), vols. I–II

Urbani, Rossana, 'Note d'archivio sui notai genovesi del '400: l'attività di Bartolomeo Canessa', *La Berio* 11, 1 (1979), 10–21

Uzunçarşili, I. H., *Anadolu Beylikleri ve Akkoyunlu Karakoyunlu Devletleri* (Ankara, 1988)

'Gazi Orhan Bey vakfiyesi 724 Rebiülevvel – 1324 Mart', *Belleten* 5 (July 1941), 277–88

'Ondört ve onbeşinci asırlarda Anadolu Beyliklerinde Toprak ve halk idaresi', *Belleten* 2 (1938), 99–106

'Osmanlı hükümdarı Çelebi Mehmed tarafından verilmiş bir temlikname ve Sasa Bey ailesi', *Belleten* 3 (October 1939), 389–99

'Osmanlılarda ilk vezirlere dair mutalea', *Belleten* 3 (January 1939), 99–106

Varlik, M. C., *Germiyan-oğulları Tarihi (1300–1429)* (Ankara, 1974)

Vatin, Nicolas, *L'Ordre de Saint-Jean-de-Jerusalem, l'empire ottoman et la Méditerranée orientale entre les deux sièges de Rhodes 1480–1522*, Collection Turcica 7 (Paris, 1994)

Verlinden, C., 'La Crète, débouché et plaque tournante de la traite des esclaves aux XIVe et XVe siècles', in *Studi in onore di A. Fanfani* (Milan, 1962), vol. III, pp. 593–669

'Le recrutement des esclaves à Venise aux XIVe et XVe siècle', *Bulletin de l'Institut Historique Belge de Rome* 39 (1968), 83–202

Vismara, Giulio, *Bisanzio e l'Islam. Per la storia delle potenze musulmane*, Studi Urbinati di Scienze Giuridiche ed Economiche, NSA 1–2 (1948–9; 1949–50) (Milan, 1950)

Vryonis, S., *The Decline of Medieval Hellenism* (Berkeley, 1971)

'Laonicus Chalcocondyles and the Ottoman budget', *International Journal of Middle Eastern Studies* 7 (1976), 423–32

'The question of Byzantine mines', *Speculum* 37 (1962), 1–17

Studies on Byzantium, Seljuks and Ottomans (Malibu, 1981)

Wallerstein, Immanuel, Hale Decdeli and Reşat Kasaba, 'The Incorporation of the Ottoman Empire into the World-Economy', in İslamoğlu-İnan (ed.), *World-Economy*, pp. 88–97

Wansborough, John, 'A Mamluk Commercial Treaty Concluded with the Republic of Florence', in S. M. Stern (ed.), *Documents from Islamic Chanceries* (Oxford, 1965), pp. 39–79

Watson, Andrew M., 'Back to gold – and silver', *Economic History Review*, second series, 20, 1 (1967), 1–24

Wittek, P., *Menteşe Beyliği* (Ankara, 1986)

Zachariadou, Elizabeth, 'Ertogrul Bey il sovrano di Teologo (Efeso)', *ASLSP* 79, n.s. 5 (Genoa, 1965), 155–61

'Holy war in the Aegean during the fourteenth century', *Mediterranean Historical Review* 4 (June 1989), 212–25

'Prix et marchés des céréales en Romanie (1343–1405), *Nuova Rivista Storica* 61 (Milan, 1977), 291–306

'S'enrichir en Asie Mineure au XIVe siècle', in V. Kravari, J. Lefort and C. Morrison (eds.), *Hommes et richesses dans l'empire byzantine*, vol. II: *VIIIe–XVe siècle* (Paris, 1992)

Zachariadou, Elizabeth (ed.), *The Ottoman Emirate (1300–1389)* (Rethymnon, 1993)

The Via Egnatia under Ottoman Rule 1380–1699 (Halcyon Days in Crete II. A Symposium Held in Rethymnon 9–11 January 1994), Foundation for Research and Technology – Hellas, Institute for Mediterranean Studies (Rethymnon, 1996)

Zhukov, K. A. Эгейске Эмираты BXIV–XV BB (Moscow, 1988)

Dictionaries and reference books

Calvini, Nilo, *Nuovo glossario medievale ligure*, Civico Istituto Colombiano, Studi e Testi 6 (Genoa, 1984)

Çetin, Atilla, *Başbakanlık Arşivi Kılavuzu* (Istanbul, 1979)

Du Cange, Charles du Fresne, *Glossarium Mediae et Infimae Latinitatis* (London, 1884)

Edler, Florence, *Glossary of Medieval Terms of Business. Italian Series 1200–1600*, Medieval Academy of America (Cambridge, Mass., 1934)

Lane, Edward William, *An Arabic–English Lexicon* (London and Edinburgh, 1863–85), book 1, parts 1–7

Latham, R. E., *Dictionary of Medieval Latin from British Sources* (London, 1975)

Lewis, Charlton T. and Charles Short, *A Latin Dictionary* (Oxford, 1907)

Liddell, H. G. and R. Scott, *Greek–English Lexicon* (Oxford, 1940)

Moravcsik, Gyula, *Byzantinoturcica*, vol. I: *Die byzantinischen Quellen der Geschichte dere Türkvölker* (Budapest, 1942)

Byzantinoturcica, vol. II: *Sprachreste der Türkvölker in den byzantinischen Quellen* (Budapest, 1943)

Niermeyer, J. F., *Mediae Latinitatis Lexicon Minus* (Leiden, 1976)

Orbis Latinus. Lexikon lateinischer geographischer Namen des Mittelalters und der Neuzeit, ed. Graesse, Benedicts and Pechl (Braunschweig, 1972), vols. I–III

Pakalin, Mehmet Zeki, *Osmanlı Tarih Deyimleri ve Terimleri Sözlüğü* (Istanbul, 1946–56), vols. I–III

Pitcher, Donald Edgar, *An Historical Geography of the Ottoman Empire* (Leiden, 1972)

Redhouse, Sir James W., *A Turkish and English Lexicon* (Istanbul [Constantinople], 1890)

Rossi, Girolamo, *Glossi medioevale ligure* (Turin, 1896–1909; repr. 1988)

Schilbach, Erich, *Byzantinische Metrologie* (Munich, 1970)

Souter, Alexander, *A Glossary of Later Latin to 600 AD* (Oxford, 1949)

Spufford, Peter, *Handbook of Medieval Exchange*, Offices of the Royal Historical Society (London, 1986)

Tarama Sözlüğü, Türk Dil Kurumu Yayınlari–Sayı, 212–212/7, Türk Tarih Kurumu Basımevi (Ankara, 1963–74), vols. I–VII

Tommasea e Bellini, *Dizionario della lingua Italiana* (Turin, 1929)

Türkiye'de halk Ağzından Derleme Sözlüğü, Türk Dil Kurumu Yayınları–Sayı, 211–211/12, Türk Tarih Kurumu Basımevi (Ankara, 1963–82), vols. I–XII

Index